THE POLITICOS GUIDE TO
THE 2015 GENERAL ELECTION

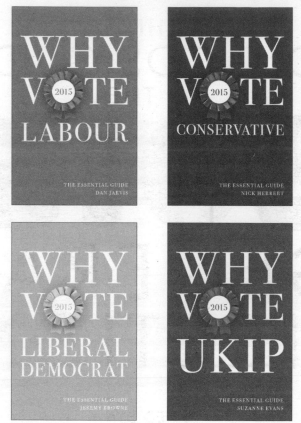

THE
POLITICOS GUIDE
TO THE
2015
GENERAL
ELECTION

EDITED BY
IAIN DALE, DANIEL HAMILTON,
ROBERT WALLER & GREG CALLUS

Biteback Publishing

First published in Great Britain in 2014 by
Biteback Publishing Ltd
Westminster Tower
3 Albert Embankment
London SE1 7SP

ISBN 978-1-84954-719-2

10 9 8 7 6 5 4 3 2 1

A CIP catalogue record for this book is available from the British Library.

Set in Minion Pro

Printed and bound in Great Britain by
CPI Group (UK) Ltd, Croydon CR0 4YY

Contents

**What will happen to the Liberal Democrat vote:
a seat-by-seat prediction**
Iain Dale

Regional & constituency profiles
Regional profiles by Robert Waller
Constituency profiles by Dan Hamilton
Election data tables by Greg Callus

Editors' introduction and acknowledgements

Iain Dale on behalf of Greg Callus, Daniel Hamilton and Robert Waller

Editing a book like this is, as you can imagine, a pleasure for political enthusiasts like the four of us. We have tried to cater for the political enthusiast as well as the casual observer of the political scene, and hopefully both will be satisfied.

We have tried to give a blend of material – ranging from lists and statistics, through to thematic essays, mixing detailed opinion polling and electoral law with insightful chapters on the media and the hidden party 'machines'. No book like this could cover every aspect of the next election, but hopefully this will prove a useful and thought-provoking tome to accompany what is promising to be an exciting year in British politics. And we've added a bit of fun too, with some political trivia.

Such a project requires the effort of many talented people who have been as patient with our requests as they have been generous with their time. All our contributors have given us interesting and well-written material for which we are very grateful, but some individuals merit a special mention.

We would also like to extend our sincere gratitude to Professors Colin Rallings and Michael Thrasher from the Elections Centre at the University of Plymouth. Many of the election statistics (especially in the constituency profiles section) which appear in this book are courtesy of their great work, and appear with their permission. Their *Media Guide to the New Parliamentary Constituencies* is rightly considered a psephological bible. Their book *British Electoral Facts 1832–2012* should be on the bookshelf of every self-respecting politico.

We are also grateful to the House of Commons Library for their original research for many of the tables listed, and to Anthony Wells of YouGov and the UK Polling Report for his marginal seat lists. We have also made use of data from the Office of National Statistics and British Social Attitudes Survey and we thank them for the work they do. We have also consulted the *Times Guide to the House of Commons 2010* (Times Books, 2010) and the latest of the Nuffield Series, *The British General Election of 2010* (ed. Cowley & Kavanagh, Macmillan, 2010). Thanks also to Dr Matthew Goodwin and Dr Robert Ford for allowing us to use their data on likely UKIP target seats. Their book *Revolt on the Right* (Routledge, 2013) is a must for anyone who wants to understand the rise of UKIP.

I'd like to thank all those who have contributed essay chapters to this book. Their insight is invaluable. They are Lord Ashcroft, Isabel Hardman, Joey Jones, Mark Wallace, Paul Richards, Caron Lindsay, Gareth Knight, Mike Smithson, David Torrance, Anthony Wells, Theo Usherwood, Jag Singh, Donal Blaney, Gawain Towler, Nel McDonald, Adam Smith and Stephanie Anderson.

Because we wanted this book to be out for the party conferences of 2014, David Torrance's chapter on Scotland had, necessarily, to be written without knowing the result of the referendum. We ask for your understanding! There are one or two other chapters which will need to be added to between publication and the election – the list of retiring MPs and Mike Smithson's chapter on by-elections to name but two. Many candidates have also not yet been selected, but the constituency profiles are all up to date as of August 2014.

Our gratitude is also due to Olivia Beattie and Phil Beresford at Biteback for their editing and design of this magnificent tome. They had to put up with a lot of last-minute faffing and dealt with it very calmly when they must have wanted to scream.

In a book of this scope there are bound to be a few errors, and some necessary omissions (parliamentary candidates yet to be chosen, black swans yet to be spotted etc.). We take full responsibility, of course, but hope that any such instances will be so few and marginal as not to detract from the book as a whole.

Foreword

Every single election since 1992 has been eminently predictable. Everyone knew Labour would win in 1997, 2001 and 2005. In 2010 it was pretty clear Gordon Brown would lose, although commentators were split on whether Cameron could actually win. The 2015 election is the most difficult to predict for twenty years, and therefore it should not only be incredibly exciting, but turnout should be high. But even that is difficult to predict at a time when people are more disillusioned with politics and politicians than at any point in my lifetime.

There are many things that make this election unpredictable. Here are just a few:

- We are for the first time experiencing four-party politics.
- No one knows what will happen to the UKIP vote. Will it hold up? Where is it coming from?
- No one knows where former Lib Dem voters will go, or if they may return to the Lib Dems.
- Can Labour win when the polls show they are behind on economic competence and on leadership quality?
- How big will the stay-at-home vote be?

For David Cameron this election is s*** or bust. If he doesn't win an outright majority his position as leader of the Conservative Party may well be untenable. It is almost inconceivable that his own MPs would rubberstamp a renewal of the coalition, even if it were the only way to form a majority government. Last time it was possible to argue for it to enable Britain to withstand the economic crisis. That argument is unlikely to be valid in 2015 barring unforeseeable circumstances. There is also a visceral dislike on the Tory benches for the Lib Dems, which wasn't so apparent last time. Tories are fed up with the way the Lib Dems have tried to claim credit for every coalition success, but blame any failures on the 'wicked Tories'. But how on earth can the Tories win an overall majority, when all the polls, including Lord Ashcroft's monthly poll of marginal seats, show that Labour is doing better in the marginal than elsewhere?

There is only one answer to that question and it is this. No one knows what will happen to the Lib Dem and UKIP votes, and how big the stay-at-home vote will be. In theory, most of the former Lib Dem vote should go to Labour, but that's not how it is working out in practice. Some of it goes to UKIP and some of it goes to the Tories – it is slightly dependent on where in the country you live.

Since the European elections, the UKIP vote has remained fairly constant. It is entirely reasonable to assume that it will remain at 14–18 per cent right up until the election. They may well win a few seats, and the devil in me hopes they do, as they would certainly liven up politics a bit in the House of Commons, but the more pertinent thing is that they could stop both the Conservatives and Labour winning seats. Just as UKIP may stop the Tories winning or retaining marginal seats in the south of England, I believe they will do the same to Labour in the north. The key to a Tory majority is how these two things balance each other out, if they do at all. If you look at some of Robert Waller's regional profiles, and Dan Hamilton's constituency profiles, it is extremely difficult to make any rational judgement as to what the UKIP effect will actually be.

In 2010 the Lib Dems lost five seats, winning fifty-seven all told. I must admit that I had tipped them to win seventy or eighty and I remember uttering these words, live on LBC's election night show when the BBC exit poll came in: 'If the Lib Dems win fifty-nine seats I'll run down Whitehall naked.' Danny Alexander, when he came on the show some time later, said he would join me if that turned out to be true. Neither of us has delivered on that pledge. My excuse is that they won fifty-seven, not fifty-nine, and I'm sticking to it! You can see my detailed predictions, seat by seat, for the Lib Dems later in this book, but this time I am predicting they could well lose at least half their seats, with the majority going to the Conservatives. The consolation for the Lib Dems is that my track record in predicting their results isn't exactly stellar.

At each of the last two elections we've been told that they would be the 'internet elections'. On both occasions the pundits were wrong. Jag Singh has a fascinating chapter later in the book on the likely impact of the internet in this election. Last time, blogging was in its heyday, but did it really have any effect on the result? Very little. Twitter was in its infancy, but even now, I don't think Twitter will have much impact beyond turning a drama into a crisis for any hapless candidate who commits a so-called gaffe. YouTube, together with *The Guardian* and the *Telegraph*, have bid to do an election debate with the party leaders, but I can't see what's in it for the politicians to do a debate which wouldn't get anywhere near the likely audience for a TV debate. David Cameron reckons the debates sucked the air out of the last campaign and he was right, but that's not a reason to scrap them. At the time of writing, Labour and the Lib Dems have signed up to repeat the debates in the same format as last time, whereas the Conservatives say they won't enter into talks until the autumn, following the party conferences. Their election strategist Lynton Crosby is said to want to pull Cameron from the debates as he sees no advantage in him taking part. You can see the logic, but politically it's impossible. If Cameron refused to take part I imagine there would be many people who wouldn't vote for him on principle. No one respects a politician they think of as 'frit'.

I'd like to see one debate take place in mid-March between the five main political leaders, a second one in early April between Clegg, Cameron and Miliband, and a final one in the last week of April between the only two men who could realistically be Prime Minister – Cameron and Miliband. In reality I suspect we'll get a repeat of the format from 2010.

Politics should really be about policy, but I suspect we're going to get three of the most non-committal manifestos in the history of elections. The Tories will make a big thing of their European referendum promise (such as it is), Labour will concentrate on their energy price freeze (such as it is) and the Liberal Democrats will, well, will anyone take any notice? Their failure to honour their student tuition fees promise has all but rendered any election promise they make this time valueless. Well, that's what their opponents will say with every opportunity that comes their way.

Even though the election is only eight months away at the time of writing, I would be hard pushed to write a list of ten likely manifesto promises for each party. When UKIP's policy platform is clearer than the other three parties, you know they have a problem.

This won't be an election about policy. It will be about slogans. I despair of the number of times politicians utter the phrases 'cost of living crisis', 'long-term economic plan' or 'hard-working families' on my radio show. In fact I despair so much I have banned them on my radio show. This will be the most 'on-message election' ever, and woe betide any candidate who strays from the party line.

Whatever happens though, it's going to be one hell of a ride.

Iain Dale
Drivetime presenter, LBC Radio

State of the leaders

Isabel Hardman

DAVID CAMERON

Given the rough-and-tumble he's had with his party over the past few years, David Cameron is heading into this election in surprisingly good shape. Troublesome backbenchers who had given him grief every step of the way through his premiership have faded into the background, for the time being at least. Some have cheered up because they've seen the improving economic situation, Labour's failure to move the polls and the Prime Minister's 2013 referendum pledge as a sign that Conservative victory of one sort or another is possible next year. The most dangerous figure, David Davis, is far less of a threat to Cameron than he once was, with former supporters melting away. One told me recently that 'You have got to have some sort of following to do something, but any following he might have had has evaporated because all his predictions of oblivion under Cameron haven't come true.' Davis's interventions after the European elections made far less of a dent than they might have done: many of his sympathisers are simply not interested in causing trouble for the leadership.

Other MPs have required a little more work to bring into line: Andrew Bridgen, for instance, who once hated the Prime Minister so much that he was happy to make public his letter to 1922 Committee

Chair Graham Brady calling for a leadership contest. Bridgen retracted that letter this spring after a concerted effort from No. 10 to listen to him and encourage him to back the Prime Minister. The work of this reconciliation team in Downing Street continues, and Cameron himself continues to try harder with his MPs. They accept that he will never really be a natural people person, particularly with people he finds a bit dull or unimportant. But they appreciate his effort, both in holding briefing meetings where Lynton Crosby reassures the party with PowerPoint presentations about strategy, and in inviting more MPs around to Downing Street. His PPS Gavin Williamson's extraordinary energy has come in handy on this front, too.

But Cameron must not mistake the improved mood in his party for loyalty. Many of those who were his harshest critics are pulling together only for the sake of the Conservatives, not the Prime Minister himself. They will still turn on him after the election if he tries to enter another coalition. It's not just the troublesome backbenchers: influential ministers have made it known to their colleagues that they would vote against another partnership with the Lib Dems if they were offered a secret ballot to approve a deal.

He also risks giving the impression of stalling on his plans for European reform. He has not appointed a full-time negotiator to work on his behalf and his deliberations over whom to appoint as European Commissioner seemed more focused on pragmatic considerations about by-elections and ministers at the end of their Westminster careers than the key role the new commissioner can play in a renegotiation. His view that he will be campaigning for Britain to stay in the EU because he knows for sure that he can get the reformed Europe and reformed relationship with Europe that he wants has not been scrutinised as fiercely as it might have been by backbenchers, because backbenchers are saving that sort of forceful behaviour for after the 2015 election. But the Prime Minister's confidence suggests either that he has such a modest vision of a renegotiated settlement that it really will be very easy to get what he wants, or that he is quite deluded: European leaders do recognise that the EU must change, but they are not quite keen for the changes that Cameron is suggesting.

Part of the problem for Cameron is that he's just not that ideological about Europe. Neither is he ideological about much else. This sounded quite nice in opposition: 'ideological' is often used as a synonym for 'dogmatic' and 'stubborn'. But it does mean that it's easy for this Prime Minister to U-turn, because his initial ideas never had an intellectual underpinning in the first place. Hence his shift from greenery in opposition to 'taking out the green crap' in government. Some of the ideas he adopted before entering government deserved to be shrugged off, but perhaps the Conservative leader could approach the 2015 election with greater conviction about what he wants to do with the next five years, and what's driving him to do it.

ED MILIBAND

No one could accuse Ed Miliband of lacking conviction. The Labour leader boasted that he had greater 'intellectual self-confidence' than David Cameron, and while it sounded a pompous thing for someone who graduated with an upper second to say to a first-class graduate, it's true. Ever since the Labour autumn conference in 2013, Miliband has shown the courage of his convictions by the bucketful. He spent the first few years of leading his party talking about his family background and producing long, confusing and off-putting arguments about producers and predators. Then he announced price controls in the energy sector, and suddenly began to look a whole lot more confident.

Miliband finds himself in a nice groove where he can announce appealing retail offer policies, and sit back and watch the government panic for a few weeks before announcing something to relieve the pressure he's put on ministers. He's certainly made politics more interesting by moving to the left. The problem is that the energy price freeze, plans to improve the private rented sector and an eye-watering pledge for all patients to see their GP within forty-eight hours have not translated into eye-watering poll leads. Perhaps this is because, as his election strategy chief Douglas Alexander claims, the era of four-party politics means Labour cannot expect runaway poll leads in the run-up to the general election. But perhaps it's because voters are worried about something bigger than the nice-sounding pledges that Miliband throws at them. Labour still needs to work out a way of talking about the cuts it would make after 2015 without resorting to fine language about long-termism. Cuts that are brutal and produce short-term savings are needed, yet naturally frontbenchers don't want to talk about them. But the public will struggle to believe in pledges about GP access if they can't trust Labour to manage the public finances properly.

The low poll leads have not translated into party panic, yet. But grumblings won't just be directed at the party leader. Ed Miliband has invested heavily in his MPs. Even those who didn't support him in 2010 are won over by his personal warmth and his desire to consult them. Indeed, his consultation exercises in the run-up to big changes of tack on issues such as immigration and welfare put Whitehall departments to shame when it comes to the amount of time the Labour leader and his team spend talking any backbencher who is vaguely interested in the policy through the details.

This means that not only can Miliband set his party on a course where it pledges to be tougher than the Tories on welfare and immigration, but that when the chips are down he can rely on his party colleagues not to stick their heads above the parapet immediately. He can't take that for granted forever, though: more people were rattled and became chatty by the European elections. He has been let down consistently by underperforming shadow Cabinet members, and this problem has not been solved by reshuffles. Some of the least proactive or most troublesome members of his team are the most difficult to move, such as Yvette Cooper and Ed Balls. So this leader is not in as strong a state as he could be, because of the team around him.

NICK CLEGG

Nick Clegg does have some similar personnel problems to Miliband – mostly in the form of the Business Secretary Vince Cable, but the Liberal Democrat leader is heading into the election having won many battles in the war for the soul of his party, albeit without any marked improvement in the polls. Cable is no longer such an authoritative figure after a bruising 2013 conference season in which he appeared to have a hissy fit and a sulk over the position the party was taking on the economy. His ally Lord Oakeshott, whose plots to remove whoever is the leader of the day and install his preferred candidate are almost as old as the party itself, has also gone. Oakeshott's departure from the Lib Dems in May means Clegg no longer has a powerful parliamentarian briefing against him at every turn. He will continue to face grumbles from the Social Liberal Forum, a left-leaning faction within the Lib Dems who have never supported Clegg's vision for the party or indeed his leadership. But there are insufficient numbers of MPs keen to remove their leader, and members don't seem hungry for a leadership contest either.

One question for Clegg as he prepares for 2015 is which party he'd instinctively rather do business with, in the event of a coalition with either Labour or the Conservatives being viable. Conventional wisdom is that it is easier for the Liberal Democrats to do a deal with Labour this time around, given the angst that sharing a pillow with the Tories has provoked among the grassroots. But the Lib Dem leader knows that it's not that simple. In coalition with the Tories, the Lib Dems have been able to portray themselves as the nice, sweet party who stop savage Tory cuts and rein in the worst free market instincts of their partners. But in coalition with Labour, they would be the party blocking new school building projects and other nice goodies that voters quite like but which the government may not be able to afford. The clue is in the line Clegg himself offered at his party's conference when describing how the Lib Dems could anchor either party: 'Labour would wreck the recovery. The Conservatives would give us the wrong kind of recovery. Only the Liberal Democrats can finish the job and finish it in a way that is fair.' Suddenly, the Lib Dems would be the nasty party.

More immediately, Clegg needs to decide how he can persuade voters that the Lib Dems aren't a 'nothing' party or a niche party. His 'party of IN' campaign for the 2014 European elections damaged his leadership because he had personally set so much store by this bold and proud Europhile stance. Privately, he admits that his big mistake was to appear an apologist for the EU rather than caveating his enthusiasm with ideas for proper reform of the bloc. But while he tries to cheer up his party with announcements on international development and other policy areas that excite Lib Dem activists, Clegg needs to be careful that he doesn't neglect exciting voters with the big Lib Dem achievements on the economy.

Clegg may be mocked by Labour for being a pushover when it comes to nasty Tory ideas, but he has wielded great power through the Quad and a seldom-mentioned committee that he chairs which examines all the government's domestic policies. The Home Affairs Committee is Clegg's opportunity to stop the ideas he doesn't like, or at least to slow them up considerably, and it is the stranglehold that he places on reform that has led some Tory ministers to think minority government would be preferable in 2015 to another five years of Chairman Clegg.

NIGEL FARAGE

Perhaps Clegg will be robbed of the opportunity to pick 2015's winner by Nigel Farage, who hopes that UKIP can 'hold the balance of power' in the House of Commons next year and possibly offer a confidence and supply agreement. This is a very bold ambition, to put it politely. But the UKIP leader is dead set on getting MPs in the House of Commons, and has made noises about resigning if he fails to do so.

He has failed to secure more than a single defection from the

Conservative party, even though these were eminently possible at one stage. One Conservative MP who was on the brink of defecting to UKIP told me that it was Farage himself who put him off. He said: 'When I looked Farage in the eyes, eyeball to eyeball, I felt this was a person I could not trust and do business with.'

Farage's own character has certainly come in for plenty of scrutiny over the past few months, and he hasn't always thrived under the spotlight. At times in the European elections campaign, he appeared to visibly wilt, either giving off-colour answers to questions in interviews, or becoming rattled. One of his challenges in 2015 is to keep his cool while both running for what could be the first UKIP seat in the House of Commons and managing his party's national campaign. The European election spotlight has considerably less candlepower than the one that will be beamed on Farage for the general election.

ALEX SALMOND

Nigel Farage and Alex Salmond are two insurgents who have shaken up British politics far more than any of the main party leaders could ever dream. Both are also leaders responsible for a large proportion of the profile that their parties enjoy, and this is a challenge for both: what are the SNP and UKIP without Salmond and Farage?

The former is less rattled by being caught out than the latter, but Salmond has still struggled when confronted with details – big details at that – such as the legal advice his government took on an independent Scotland's membership of the European Union. Nevertheless, he has benefitted from a confused and lacklustre 'no' campaign, which contrasts with his party's old-fashioned campaign style of meetings in village halls and an emotional case for independence.

Even if Salmond doesn't get the result he wants on 18 September 2014, he has prepared his case for devo-max sufficiently carefully that he can switch from his current campaign for independence-lite to campaigning for a huge handover of power from Westminster. So in some senses, the First Minister will win the referendum if he gets a 'yes' vote, or if he gets the close result that gives him the moral victory on which to keep going.

NATALIE BENNETT

The Greens aren't claiming a political 'earthquake' after 2014's local and European elections. But they're still tunnelling away, beating the Lib Dems in the European polls to come fourth with nearly 8 per cent of the vote nationally and three MEPs. The party also expanded its local base, gaining seventeen new councillors. Yet many of its activists complain that they're losing out to UKIP in media coverage. Party leader Natalie Bennett has made the same accusation. She thinks the Greens are now a 'national party'. That may be true, but the party is going through the sort of difficult adolescence that UKIP would like to avoid: it has not earned universal plaudits for the way it has run Brighton & Hove Council, and since Caroline Lucas relinquished the party leadership, it struggles to get the same kind of headlines as the other insurgent party that it despises – UKIP. Bennett is a useful second voice in the Green Party, but because she does not speak from the Chamber of the House of Commons, her interventions are easy to miss. The next step for the Greens is to work out how to bag national headlines that aren't just about local political rows.

Isabel Hardman is Assistant Editor of The Spectator.

The Conservative Party general election campaign

Mark Wallace

The next general election will be unlike any other in British political history.

Previously, the timing of every election has been uncertain. Will the Prime Minister go early? Might he or she call a snap election on the back of a sudden bit of good news?

This time round, though, we have known the date for years. The coalition's decision to introduce fixed-term parliaments didn't attract as much attention as the ill-fated attempt to introduce the Alternative Vote, but it has had a huge impact on our politics.

Removing the uncertainty gives the parties and leaders greater ability to plan everything down to the last detail, but it also provides the potential to bore the electorate silly.

The challenge is to take advantage of the opportunity for fundraising and recruiting your team, while avoiding the risk of getting bogged down and boring in the lengthy slog.

Combine that fixed-term factor with the reality that the Conservatives are incumbents in government, and the party faces a difficult job. Not only is the date of the election conducive to boredom, but incumbents have to fight to 'finish the job' and are denied the more exciting ground of demanding 'change'.

That's the bad news. The good news is two-fold.

First, governing as part of a coalition is not the same as being a single-party government. There is still room to pitch new, exciting ideas on the basis that they aren't possible while hobbled by the Liberal Democrats but would be delivered by a majority Conservative government.

Second, boring conservatives have recently proved electorally successful in other countries. Germany's Merkel, Australia's Abbott, Canada's Harper – all are examples of what Tim Montgomerie has called the 'BoreCons', and all have won elections in recent years.

Maybe being boring isn't all that bad. Throw in the fact that when Ed Miliband does manage to excite interest, people tend to find it worrying or just plain weird, and you have the genesis of an opportunity.

THE LESSON OF 2010

The 2010 general election is a bitter memory for the Conservative leadership. Up against Gordon Brown, who boasted a toxic combination of economic disaster and personal unpleasantness, the fresh, young Tory pitch was supposed to sweep the board.

'Let sunshine win the day' was David Cameron's call in opposition. But when polling day came around, voters drew the curtains.

Thankfully, for the nation's sake, a coalition was hammered together in order to avoid the harmful experience of any more Brownism. But that success also allowed the Conservative Party to avoid fully facing up to the grim fact that we failed to win outright in the most favourable circumstances for a quarter of a century.

Belatedly, and largely behind closed doors, that failure has eventually been analysed. What should have been a stark contrast between tired, bitter Labour and positive, modernised Conservatism was allowed to blur thanks to a confused and confusing pitch to voters.

The Big Society is the most famous example – it took loads of good ideas and naturally conservative principles and hid them in a mush of management speak and sloganeering. Indeed, it grabbed so much of the wrong sort of attention that it distracted from other policies which would have been more easily understood and offered concrete improvements in people's lives

SAFETY FIRST

So highfalutin language and airy messaging is out for 2015. Instead, Lynton Crosby has made a welcome return as the party's full-time election strategist, and with him comes a focus on real life and stark divides. Crucially, he also believes in research rather than instinct – he has little time for the commentariat, and prefers to find out scientifically what actual voters are thinking.

No longer are the Conservatives sketching castles in the sky, instead they are down on the ground implementing the now-famous OLTEP (Our Long Term Economic Plan).

Note the second and third words – 'long' and 'term'. OLTEP may have emerged in the language of government, but it is targeted at winning elections. By implication, this is a plan that takes longer than one five-year term in power – and it isn't a question of ill-defined philosophy, it's squarely about the economy, meaning the future of your job, your kids' jobs, your house and your town depend on it.

This is the language of safety, the greatest asset an incumbent party can possess. The plan revolves around tough decisions, cutting the deficit, making welfare more fair, improving education and returning to growth – if you've taken the pain of the first few years, do you really want to ditch it just when it starts to pay off?

Like all the best political questions, that only has one answer.

Effectively, the Conservatives will also seek to make Ed Miliband's theme – 'the choice' – answer itself. Your choice is between a long-term economic plan and … what? A return to the bad old days of tax and debt? Trade union-controlled loony Labour? Or, even worse, an ill-defined alternative that no one knows anything about other than the fact that its main proponent can't eat a sandwich competently?

Crosby is decisive and blunt – fortunately the Prime Minister has given him the necessary authority to do things his way, or else his job would be rather more difficult. He hosts weekly meetings in CCHQ with the top team to ensure that every element of the party is pointing in the right direction, that the left hand knows what the right hand is doing and, most of all, to ensure message discipline.

THE TOP TEAM

With that approach in mind, the team at the top of the Conservative Party should be seen primarily as a campaigning outfit.

Of course, the Prime Minister and the Chancellor still maintain the close alliance which so distinguished them from Blair and Brown's smouldering rivalry. Each knows that the other is a major reason why they have got this far, and that sustaining that relationship is essential to success in 2015.

Cameron is known to dislike reshuffles, and yet the 14th and 15th of July saw him radically remodel his Cabinet with the election in mind.

Compare the new set-up to the old. The departure of Michael Gove, for example, was openly motivated by a desire to shed baggage among key electorates like teachers and parents. The swift rise of several female ministers – such as Liz Truss and Nicky Morgan – was about picking the voices and faces of the election campaign as much as about chasing a gender target.

Then there are the senior campaigning roles – while William Hague left the Foreign Office and is soon to leave the Commons, his position as Leader of the House is unequivocally a campaigning one. Well liked and a good media performer, he will be deployed around the country battling for votes, as well as shielding against incoming fire, like a Yorkshire Iron Dome.

The party chairman, Grant Shapps, defied those who predicted he would lose his post in the reshuffle and will see the party through the campaign. He has secured his position by radically restructuring and revitalising CCHQ so that it lives up to its name – as a campaign headquarters.

THE HEART OF THE MACHINE

CCHQ, long the source of gripes and the target of barbs within the Conservative Party, has upped its game. Out has gone the byzantine structure and wide-ranging policy work, to be replaced by a more targeted campaigning focus.

In February 2014 it also moved to a new home in Matthew Parker Street, bedecked with posters of victorious Tory leaders, presumably in order to set the right tone.

At the top sit Shapps and Crosby, managing the machine and the message respectively. The chairman's office is run by Paul Abbott, his chief of staff, who previously worked for Robert Halfon, the campaigning MP for Harlow.

Four teams make up the sharp end of the operation.

The research department, run by Alex Dawson, generates rapid rebuttal, briefings on key issues and political attack material. Over the coming months, the team will grow beyond its current core in order to deal with the increasing intensity of the campaign. Nick Hargrave, a former speechwriter for Cameron, runs the political section, which is charged with maintaining a detailed, instantly accessible database of quotes and claims from the opposition to use against them.

The press team is led by communications director Giles Kenningham, who impressed after leaving ITV to serve as a special advisor to Eric Pickles. His deputy, Tim Collins, used to be Shapps's chief of staff when in opposition, and then sharpened his skills in the private sector before returning to the fold.

The digital and creative team is headed by digital director Craig Elder and creative director Tom Edmonds, who co-ordinate the party's advertising, produce party political broadcasts, oversee the increasingly important social media campaigns and generate a constant flow of graphics to add punch to the points the press team want to make. Their work obviously overlaps somewhat with that of Jim Messina, the former Obama campaign manager, who was engaged to advise on digital campaigning from his base in the US.

The largest, and most geographically dispersed, team is the campaigning department, led by Stephen Gilbert and deputy Darren Mott. This is the point of connection between the agents, campaign managers, regional directors and candidates and the central operation. They oversee canvassing databases, candidate selections, by-elections, target seats and all the elements that make the machine run around the country.

DOWN AT THE GRASSROOTS

The leadership is all too aware that the dramatic fall in Conservative membership poses a serious problem. You can have as many good brains as you like, and a nice, shiny office, but if there is no one to risk being bitten by dogs when pushing leaflets through letterboxes (or to risk being bitten by voters when knocking on people's doors, for that matter) then it is all for naught.

The challenge of restoring the party to its former mass membership status will take far longer than one general election campaign, and will require radical change to our idea of what a political party is. In the meantime, the responsibility for stemming the decline and undoing as much of the damage as possible in time for election day has fallen to Shapps.

With a focus on maintaining campaign capacity, his approach revolves around the idea of shock troops. One hundred people giving an hour a week is, in terms of capacity, the same as ten people giving ten hours a week. Therefore, he established Team 2015 last year in order to find, train and direct the people willing to give more than the minimum.

Team 2015 members don't have to join the party. Instead, they simply have to be willing to regularly go above and beyond to canvass voters, either in person or by phone. Nor do they necessarily campaign in their home seat – they are allocated to their nearest target seat, to bolster the campaign there where they are most useful.

Thousands of people are involved already, and Shapps personally presents the latest figures to the Prime Minister on a regular basis, which demonstrates the importance the leadership places on it.

The grassroots have offered their own version of the scheme – RoadTrip2015, which seeks to be a Tory counterweight to the ability of trade unions to bus large numbers of activists into target seats. Founded by Mark Clarke, the former candidate for Tooting, it proved particularly effective in the Newark by-election, generating thousands of canvassing hours in a must-win battle.

It remains to be seen whether the one-day model of the RoadTrip can prove as successful in a general election, when every seat is fought at once, but it's undoubtedly adding force to the effort in target seats.

In terms of the wider decline of party membership, both approaches are to an extent stop-gap measures. But there's a gap that needs stopping right now, so expect both to grow over the coming months.

DEVELOPING POLICY

Of course, a machine is only one part of winning an election. You also need a manifesto for the machine to communicate to voters.

Once upon a time this would have been designed in CCHQ, or the old Conservative Central Office. Now, the process is split between three bodies – the political elements of the Downing Street Policy Unit, the MPs on the Downing Street Policy Board and the five policy committees of the backbench 1922 Committee. Throw in the likely involvement of some of the Chancellor's people, such as former Policy Exchange boss Neil O'Brien, and it isn't the simplest of systems.

Overall, policy is the responsibility of Jo Johnson, the MP for

Orpington and brother of the London Mayor. He leads the Policy Unit and chairs the Policy Board, as well as reviewing submissions from other organisations.

The MPs on the board – including Margot James, Nadhim Zahawi, Jake Berry, George Eustice, Chris Skidmore, Alun Cairns, Nick Gibb and Paul Uppal – all sit in at least one of five working groups, covering the economy, foreign policy, energy and environment, home and constitutional affairs, and public service reform.

Those five groups almost exactly match the structure of the '22's policy committees, which are respectively chaired by John Redwood (Economy), Sir Edward Leigh (Foreign Affairs), Neil Parish (Environment and Local Government), Robert Buckland (Home affairs and the constitution) and Steve Baker (Public Services).

Formally, the idea is for the relevant MPs from the Policy Board, the relevant '22 representative, and a chairing Cabinet minister to meet regularly on each policy area, feeding everyone's ideas into the process and connecting the backbenches with the leadership. Whether it works that smoothly remains to be seen.

Beyond that formal structure, others will undoubtedly have an input, too. The Conservative Policy Forum is meant to gather ideas from the party grassroots, Nadhim Zahawi runs a Business Feedback Group to canvass the views of companies, pollster Andrew Cooper is still in close contact with Downing Street and Oliver Letwin has never been known to walk past a policy discussion in his life.

Finally, regardless of the idea or who is pushing it, all must pass the Crosby Test – if it doesn't fit the strategy, it turns off key voters or it elicits a more explicit comment, it won't be going in.

FORGETTING 2010

Though the true scale of the shortfall at the last election isn't often mentioned, its memory still haunts the Conservative Party. Every hope is that 2015 will banish it for good.

A comparison with last time round gives some cause for hope and some for concern.

There is clearer messaging and more hard-headed strategy, some of it imported from Australia.

The central machine is undoubtedly better suited to the task, with its people better focused on the sharp end of campaigning.

The fruits of the new policy process are yet to be seen, and we'll know more as the manifesto launch approaches, but there are good MPs involved, including some radical voices from the backbenches.

Around the country, the grassroots are much less numerous than we were in 2010 – a serious problem. Those who remain, though, are arguably better organised and more targeted on the must-win seats.

The emergence of fixed-term parliaments has given plenty of time to lay plans. But, as ever, no battle plan survives contact with the enemy completely intact. The big test, of its resilience and flexibility, is yet to come.

Mark Wallace is Executive Editor of ConservativeHome.com.

The Labour Party general election campaign

Paul Richards

For Ed Miliband to enter Downing Street on the morning of Friday 8 May 2015, it will require an astonishing defiance of political gravity. For Labour to win an election just five years after such colossal rejection as in 2010, and to return to office after just one term in opposition, would be unprecedented. This is the challenge Ed Miliband's Labour Party has set itself.

AN UNEXPECTED LEADER

Ed Miliband is the unexpected leader. As the son of a Marxist politics professor, his life-long passion for politics is no surprise. He spent the summer of 1986 in the basement of Tony Benn's Holland Park home, helping to archive old minutes of meetings and notes for speeches. Aside from a spell as an economics lecturer at Harvard, Miliband has worked in and around Westminster all his adult life. He was a special advisor at the Treasury, then an MP in 2005, then a minister in Gordon Brown's government.

His victory in the 2010 leadership contest, beating four other candidates (Andy Burnham, David Miliband, Diane Abbott and Ed Balls) was a shock to many political observers. Ed Miliband won 50.65 per cent of Labour's electoral college, after second, third and fourth preferences votes were counted defeating the last remaining candidate David Miliband by 1.3 per cent. Because Ed Miliband came first only in the trade union section of the electoral college, and came second in the sections for party members and for parliamentarians, his opponents have accused him of being 'in the pockets of the unions', especially the 1.5 million member-strong Unite.

MILIBAND AS LEADER OF THE OPPOSITION

Miliband's five years as Leader of the Opposition have been characterised by a series of bold and eye-catching tactical moves, and a willingness to take tough decisions. The greatest achievement has been to maintain unity in the Labour Party, not noted for outpourings of brotherly love in previous periods of opposition. Those anticipating or even hoping for a blood-bath were disappointed.

One of his first moves as leader was to scrap the Labour Party's custom in opposition of MPs electing the members of the shadow Cabinet. Tony Blair had accommodated this odd ritual between 1994 and 1997. Instead, Miliband appointed the team he wanted, being prepared to sack colleagues. In subsequent reshuffles, he has promoted the younger MPs (especially those who backed him for leader) and brought on new talent from the 2010 intake and the subsequent by-election victors.

This means the Labour goes into the election with a front-bench team which balances the battle-hardened veterans of the Tony Blair and Gordon Brown eras with the energy and enthusiasm of the likes of Luciana Berger, Tristram Hunt, Chuka Umunna, Rachel Reeves, Liz Kendall, Dan Jarvis, Gloria De Piero and Emma Reynolds. His shadow Cabinet even includes one veteran of the Michael Foot era, Labour's deputy leader Harriet Harman.

His period in opposition has been characterised by taking on vested interests, from the Murdoch empire, to the utility companies, to the trade unions. This latter group saw their voting strength inside Labour curtailed at a Special Conference in 2014, so that future leaders will be elected with one-member-one-vote. Whilst not quite amounting to a 'Clause IV moment', the reforms were nonetheless a bold sign of strength, which even Tony Blair had not dared to attempt.

LABOUR'S STANDING IN THE POLLS AND AT THE BALLOT BOX

Labour has been ahead in the opinion polls since 2010, albeit with a gradually diminishing lead since the steady ten-point leads of 2010 and 2011. Worryingly for Labour, Ed Miliband will fight the 2015 election with opinion poll ratings showing his party behind on economic competence, and with him personally behind on leadership. For example, the IPSOS-MORI poll in September 2013 put Labour on minus eighteen on the economy and Miliband on minus two on the net rating of the opposition leader versus the Prime Minister.

Tony Blair's Labour was behind on the economy, just, in the run-up to 1997, but Blair had a leadership rating of plus sixty-one. James Callaghan led Margaret Thatcher on leadership throughout the 1979 election, yet she won a majority of forty-four. At the annual gathering of the New Labour group Progress in May 2014, the pollster Peter Kellner of YouGov suggested that Labour could not secure a mandate whilst being simultaneously behind on leadership and the economy. If Miliband leads Labour to victory, this will be yet another political record he has smashed.

In the by-elections since 2010, Labour has had some solid performances, alongside some disappointments. Current front-benchers and future stars including Dan Jarvis, Seema Malhotra, Jon Ashworth, Andy Sawford and Steve Reed entered Parliament in by-elections. But Labour lost, painfully, in Bradford West to George Galloway, and came fourth in Eastleigh despite a spirited campaign by author John O'Farrell. In the London Mayor elections in 2012, Labour's Ken

Livingstone lost to the Conservative candidate Boris Johnson for a second time.

LABOUR'S SECRET WEAPON

One reason for Labour's optimism, despite the polls, entering the election is its belief in the efficacy of its ground operation. Thanks to the tireless efforts of doughty general secretary Iain McNicol, Labour has placed huge emphasis on developing its local doorstep campaigning (what it calls its 'field operations'), backed by professional organisers in its 106 target (or 'battle-ground') seats, and supported by an army of volunteers. In the New Labour era, the number of Labour officials at party headquarters outnumbered those in the regional offices by two to one. Today's 350 staff are evenly balanced between the party's regional offices and party HQ at Brewer's Green, equidistant between Victoria Station and the Houses of Parliament.

After the 2014 local and European elections, campaign boss Douglas Alexander MP could claim that Labour activists had knocked on seven million doors. As Michael Dugher MP, campaign communications chief, told *The Independent* in November 2013: 'Labour still has its historic competitive advantage – people. Tory Party membership is dying on its arse and no one is joining the Liberal Democrats.'

The party intends to use digital media to reach out to, and interact with, its key audiences. The party has hired Blue State Digital, the company founded by Howard Dean's online campaigners, which went on to deliver the digital campaign for Obama. The link man between Blue State Digital and Labour's Brewer's Green HQ is Matthew McGregor, who has worked on the Obama campaign in 2012 and the less successful Australian Labor Party campaign in 2013.

It seems to be working. In the month after Mr Miliband's pledge to freeze energy bills, Labour's '#freezethatbill' hashtag on Twitter had 13,378 tweets, and Labour reached about 1.2 million people through Facebook in the month after its promise. A Facebook and Twitter

Thunderclap sent by 900 Labour supporters reached 4.5 million potential voters.

Labour's emphasis is on building relationships with the electors, not merely asking for their vote. This entails a huge philosophical shift from Labour's 1990s Millbank operation, modelled on Clinton's Little Rock, which was all about a unified 'air war' and 'ground war', with simple, repeated messages, rapid rebuttal of the opponents' arguments, and a massive 'get out the vote' (GOTV) effort on polling day. Iain McNicol and others have dismissed this as vote harvesting, transactional politics, unsuited to the digital age.

THE AMERICANS HAVE LANDED

The best proof of this shift in thinking is the arrival of Arnie Graf. With a desk at Labour's Brewer's Green headquarters alongside the general secretary, Graf occupies a position at the heart of the campaign. Graf is a down-to-earth community organiser, credited with mentoring a young Barack Obama, with fifty years' experience of mobilising working-class communities in Chicago and New York. He has visited all of the 106 target seats, recruiting new supporters, mobilising networks, building local campaigns, and inspiring people that politics can make a difference. Allied to the Movement for Change, founded in the UK in 2010 as the catalyst for community organising, Arnie Graf has brought the kind of politics which inspired Obama to the streets of British cities.

The evidence is that community organising can be linked to successful electioneering. A poll by Lord Ashcroft after the Wythenshaw & Sale East by-election in February 2014 suggested that residents in that part of Manchester were significantly more likely to say they had received a visit, letter or leaflet from Labour supporters than from those of any other party. The hand of Graf was apparent behind the campaign, and the victor, Cllr Mike Kane, was a member of the Movement for Change.

Labour's campaign was given a vote of confidence in April 2014 with the arrival of David Axelrod, one of the architects of Barack Obama's victories. Labour hired David Axelrod's AKPD for an undisclosed six-figure sum, after successful wooing by Douglas Alexander. Axelrod cut his teeth in Chicago Democrat politics, helping Harold Washington, the first black mayor of Chicago, to victory in 1983. Axelrod, and his colleagues Larry Grisolano and Mike Donilon, will work closely with Labour's campaign director Spencer Livermore, and the veteran US pollster Stan Greenberg. He reports to Ed Miliband and Douglas Alexander.

THE BATTLEGROUND

Labour is targeting 106 parliamentary seats in this election. Party strategists are assuming every Labour MP, or those standing in their seats if they are retiring, will be re-elected. Each of the 106 seats is currently held by another party. Victory in these seats would give Labour a working majority. Four out of every five seats are Tory-held, many by MPs elected for the first time in 2010. Eighty-eight are seats Labour lost in 2010. Fifteen are seats Labour last won in 2001. Three of the seats weren't held at any point between 1997 and 2010. Labour needs to beat Tories, Lib Dems, Plaid Cymru, SNP, Respect and the Green Party.

It is a myth to suggest that Labour must regain seats solely in the southern and south-eastern regions of England to return to government. Equally it is wrong to say Labour can ignore the 'Tory south' and focus on the north and midlands. Labour must win new seats in every nation and region of the UK.

For example, Labour aims to win Lancashire seats such as Rossendale & Darwen, Blackpool North & Cleveleys, Bury North, Burnley and Morecambe & Lunesdale. In Yorkshire, seats such as Elmet & Rothwell, Keighley, Pudsey, Dewsbury and Bradford East must fall to Labour.

In Wales, Labour is targeting Arfon, Cardiff Central, Cardiff North,

Carmarthen West & South Pembrokeshire, Carmarthen East & Dinefwr, Vale of Glamorgan, Aberconwy and Preseli Pembrokeshire.

In Scotland, Labour aims to win Edinburgh West, Argyll & Bute and Dumfriesshire, Clydesdale & Tweeddale.

In London, where Labour did well in the 2014 elections, the party is targeting Battersea, Hornsey & Wood Green, Enfield North, Bermondsey & Old Southwark, Finchley & Golders Green and Croydon Central.

Labour's targets include some notable bellwether seats such as Thurrock, Amber Valley, Carlisle, Lincoln, Brighton Pavilion, Brighton Kemptown, Stevenage, South Basildon & East Thurrock, Cambridge, Watford and Worcester.

Local Labour Parties have selected a range of impressive women candidates in their winnable seats. If Labour does well in 2015, Westminster watchers should look out for the likes of Polly Billington, Mari Williams, Lucy Rigby, Catherine West, Sarah Owen, Rupa Huq, Melanie Ward, Sophy Gardner, Jessica Asato, Jo Stevens, Ruth Smeeth, Rowenna Davis and Anna Turley to be the next generation of ministers.

This may also be the election which sees some famous Labour sons enter Parliament: Stephen Kinnock, son of Neil, and Will Straw, son of Jack; perhaps even Ewan Blair, son of Tony.

As we survey the electoral map, it is clear that Labour must win marginal, and not-so-marginal, seats in every part of the UK – a true test for a One Nation party, and for Ed Miliband's appeal across a broad range of the British electorate.

THE NUMBERS GAME

Pundits and commentators in the run-up to the election speculated that Labour was running a '35 per cent strategy'. In this scenario, it was said, Labour needed to retain its 29 per cent 'core vote', add another 4 per cent of voters drawn from the ranks of disaffected Liberal Democrats, and add 1 per cent from other parties and non-voters. This gives Labour 35 per cent of the electorate, and enough to squeak a win at the election.

No senior party figure ever publicly advocated such a strategy. Indeed, the absence of the need to switch any voters from the Conservatives inherent in any such strategy flies in the face of the need to win seats in the south east such as Brighton, Basildon, Dover or Hastings.

Others talked of a '40 per cent strategy'. Marcus Roberts for the Fabian Society wrote 'Labour's Next Majority' in 2014 which suggested:

> If Labour scored 40 per cent nationally and this was reflected in its 106 target constituencies then the party would enjoy a majority of 20. Such a result can be achieved by holding onto the vast majority of Labour's 2010 voters (some 27.5 per cent after churn), taking 6.5 points off the Liberal Democrats, adding 5 points of new voters and 1 point from Conservative 2010 voters.

The results of the European elections in 2014 opened up the possibility of a four-way split in terms of vote share. UKIP, the Conservatives and the Labour Party won around a quarter of the votes each, with the remaining quarter shared by the Greens and Liberal Democrats. The reason why Labour may have cause to hope is that if the right-wing vote in the UK, historically the preserve of the Conservative Party, is split between the Tories and UKIP, then a combination of Labour and disgruntled Lib Dem voters, along with other switchers and non-voters persuaded to vote, may be enough to see Ed Miliband into No. 10.

Although no senior figure will admit it, there is also the possibility of a coalition with what remains of the Liberal Democrat parliamentary party after 2015, on condition that Nick Clegg is removed. Labour knows, though, that it must have the discipline to ignore overtures, and refuse to make any, until after polling day.

LABOUR'S CAMPAIGN STRUCTURE

In October 2013, Labour announced its General Election Strategy Committee. This high-level grouping is designed to take the big decisions, rather than the tactical day-to-day decisions, in the heat and smoke of the campaign itself.

This group includes Douglas Alexander (chair of the election campaign), Ed Balls, Yvette Cooper, Michael Dugher, Caroline Flint, Harriet Harman, Sadiq Khan, Ivan Lewis, Gloria De Piero, Rachel Reeves, Chuka Umunna and Chief Whip Rosie Winterton.

The day-to-day running of the campaign rests with a senior team including the general secretary Iain McNicol, Spencer Livermore and Douglas Alexander. In November 2013, the party's staff were given the outline of the campaign structure and reporting lines, including seven taskforces, organised around a central HQ war room. At the heart of the campaign will be the Attack and Rebuttal Unit and the Digital Taskforce.

ISSUES AND THEMES

As the Labour Party enters the election campaign its foremost challenge is to persuade the electorate of its economic competence. The causes of the crash in 2007 may be traced to decisions made by American politicians, bankers and millions of debt-ridden consumers, but because it happened on Labour's watch, Labour still gets the blame. Coalition ministers' mantra, from June 2010 onwards, has been that they are 'cleaning up the mess left behind by Labour'. It is clear that much of the mud has stuck.

So Labour's campaign in 2015 will be built around the theme of One Nation, and practical ways to tackle the 'cost of living crisis.' After some false starts (Blue Labour, Pre-Distribution, responsible capitalism), One Nation is the attempt by Ed Miliband to brand his style of social-democratic politics. It represents a neat catch-all for the policies which will appear in the One Nation manifesto, written by Jon Crud-das MP, from regional banks to jobs guarantees for young people, from the merging of health and social care to more house building.

Like New Labour in 1997, One Nation Labour will offer specific poli-cies pledges which serve as metaphors for bigger reforms. For example, Labour will freeze gas bills for one year, whilst at the same time restruc-turing the energy market to create more choice and lower prices for the consumer. Labour is debating its 'retail offer'. Some believe the offer should be modest, credible, realistic and down-to-earth, addressing head-on anxieties about jobs, wages, crime, immigration and public services. Others want a big, sweeping offer which generates a sense of optimism and hope amidst the post-crash maelstrom.

We can expect a manifesto which couples the grand strategic rhet-oric of Jon Cruddas, with the 'pledge-card' style policies ('see a GP within forty-eight hours') which candidates can sell on the doorstep. In this way, the internal discussions about the size and scope of Labour's 'offer' will be settled.

THE SCALE OF THE CHALLENGE

Labour's campaign has a clear strategy, theme and message. In the TV debates, in the manifesto and on the doorsteps, Labour will have clear policy offers. It has bright, keen candidates in the target seats, unsullied by the Brown era or the expenses scandal. It has a dedicated full-time staff who are working hard. It has the benefit of advice from some of the best political brains in the world.

Labour faces a coalition government comprising a Tory Party which hasn't won for over twenty years, and a Lib Dem Party lead by a leader who has broken the record for unpopularity. David Cameron couldn't win against Gordon Brown in 2010, despite Labour being in power for thirteen years. Tory peer Lord Ashcroft's polling suggests time and time again that Labour is ahead in the marginal seats and heading for victory.

Yet with a year to go before the election, Labour only managed to finish two points ahead of the Tories in the local elections and just one point ahead of the Tories in the European elections. Left-wing parties across Europe are not winning big victories. Austerity is not persuading the voters to become more left-wing. UKIP is leaching Labour votes as well as Tory ones. If Labour wins, or even forms the biggest party in Parliament, it will be an astonishing trick to pull off, and the credit will surely go to Ed Miliband.

Paul Richards is a political consultant and author of Labour's Revival: The Modernisers' Manifesto.

The Liberal Democrat general election campaign

Caron Lindsay

For the first time in living memory, a liberal party will face the United Kingdom electorate to defend its record in a Westminster government. It's worth noting that the date of the election, fixed by legislation, is the fulfillment of a Liberal Democrat manifesto pledge which strips the Prime Minister of the power to call a politically expedient election.

To put it mildly, Labour and the Conservatives want the Liberal Democrats dead as a political force – Labour because they can see the influence the Lib Dems have had on the coalition and want to have things all their own way. The Conservatives because of all the things the Lib Dems have stopped them doing. David Cameron has often been found to say, rather like a Scooby-Doo villain, words to the effect of 'and I could have succeeded if it weren't for those pesky Liberal Democrats'. He has done his best to steal the credit for the raising of the tax threshold, a key Liberal Democrat policy from the front of the manifesto worth £800 a year to those on low and middle incomes.

What judgement will the electorate give on five years in coalition with the Conservatives? How ready is the party to fight the campaign of its life? Let's look at some of the challenges, personalities, battle-fields and prospects for the Liberal Democrats next May.

The 2014 European and local elections were a disaster but not unexpected. If I had been asked to predict the electoral nadir of this parliament for the party, it would have been that set of elections. In 2010, when those mainly metropolitan, Labour-facing elections were last fought, the Lib Dems lost 132 seats. In 2006, when the party was at the height of its popularity post Iraq and had just won a by-election in Gordon Brown's back yard, they had the whopping gain of just two seats.

The Lib Dems were always hanging onto their European seats by their fingertips and a better-than-expected result in 2009, benefitting from Labour meltdown and the Tories being squeezed by UKIP, saved them from heavy losses then. The prospects of a good result in 2014 were always slim.

It's interesting to note that Lord Ashcroft chose the aftermath of the European election campaign to carry out much of the fieldwork in key Liberal Democrat/Conservative marginals. Even that, though, showed that some seats marked as Tory gains were by tiny margins as small as 1 per cent. A projection from *Channel 4 News* on that result still showed the Lib Dems winning as many as forty seats. While the losses hurt the party deeply, the analysis shows brighter prospects ahead.

There are some silver linings from last May's results. In Hull, the party gained a seat from Labour and held out against a massive challenge from them. In the London Borough of Sutton, the Lib Dems actually gained seats. Strong performances in places like Hertfordshire, Southport and Eastleigh show that the party can still pull off good results.

The party can also point to increases in membership in the past four quarters. This is thanks in part to a new scheme that makes it worth the while of local parties to put serious effort into recruiting and retaining members, creating a virtuous cycle that increases their capacity to get things done. It is quite a remarkable turnaround after a decade of continual decline.

What we have to remember is that a year after the last European elections, the Liberal Democrats polled 10 per cent more, despite being heavily squeezed between Conservatives and Labour. It must be possible to at least match or even exceed that this time round.

All the signs from current polling are that nobody is on course to win the next election. Another hung parliament is on the cards. Labour is doing reasonably well in Conservative/Labour marginals and could deny Cameron's party an overall majority but is not performing well enough to get one of their own. In Liberal Democrat/Conservative marginals, it will be critical to persuade Labour voters to vote tactically for the Lib Dems to stop the Tories.

Liberal Democrats went into coalition with the Conservatives in 2010 with their eyes open. The party knew that it was a huge electoral risk, but what do you do when the country needs a stable government? In any event, ducking out would have seen us punished in an election following the failure of a Conservative minority government in the autumn of 2010. An analysis of the successes and failures of Liberal Democrat performance in government would easily take a book in itself, but there are some very immediate actions that we must take. The most important of those is on the party's messaging and communications: how it tells its story.

THE MANIFESTO

The issue of tuition fees casts a very long shadow over the party's time in government. A pledge, ostentatiously signed by most Liberal Democrat MPs, to vote against any rise in university tuition fees and then broken by year's end was a huge political mistake. Nick Clegg's 2012 apology has not yet brought absolution from the electorate. However, a *Financial Times* poll shows the party recovering support amongst students, with even the NUS admitting that students don't choose who to vote for on the basis of one issue. The party needs to show that it has learnt its lesson, but it must also be wary of timidity. An anaemic manifesto that says nothing will not excite and inspire anyone to vote Liberal Democrat.

Over many elections, the party has produced shopping lists of policies – so many thousand more police here, nurses there without a
strong articulation of the values behind them. What it needs to do is
show how the long-held values of the party have been upheld across
government. It needs to show what its ministers have done to work
towards the aim of a fair, free and open society where none shall be
enslaved by poverty, ignorance and conformity.

It's helpful, then, that of the policies implemented by the Lib Dems,
which most show off those values, almost all have been personally
championed by Nick Clegg for his whole political lifetime. His first
major speech as party leader in 2008 was on mental health and he has
made sure that it's been given equal priority with physical health. His
policy of targeting extra funds at kids from disadvantaged backgrounds
in school, which he first wrote about in 2003, will help improve the life
chances of a generation. Shared parental leave and additional childcare
support was done to level the playing field for women in the workplace. Equal marriage is about freedom from conformity. Raising the
tax threshold for workers on low and middle incomes makes the tax
system fairer. One of the coalition's first acts was a Liberal Democrat-
inspired rise in Capital Gains Tax. Both of those measures combined
have helped wipe out the anomaly that Clegg spoke off prior to 2010
whereby a hedge fund manager on a six-figure income paid a lower
marginal rate of tax than his cleaner on the minimum wage. The general public is largely unaware of these things. I know from my many
conversations with voters that telling them what Nick Clegg directly
has done gives the party a foot in the door not least with the people
who supported us in 2010. This sort of message gets them to consider
voting for the party again.

I expect to see the party's communications focus less on impersonal
infographics advertising how many jobs have been created and the like.
It's time to get much more passionate and personal about what the Lib
Dems have done and the lives that have transformed for the better.

Some of the traditional Lib Dem messages need to be retired. Telling people that they have more heart than the Conservatives and more sense than Labour may be very true, but isn't going to change anybody's mind. The Lib Dems need to talk about who they are, not who they are not. Clegg also needs to forget the 'party of protest to party of power' line not least because it directly contradicts the number of times he has stood up to the establishment. It was down to Nick Clegg that there was a judge-led enquiry into phone hacking and a Royal Charter on press regulation, and that we don't have laws empowering the security forces to snoop on all our emails. It was Nick Clegg who produced a blueprint for the first elected second chamber which was derailed by an unholy alliance of Conservative and Labour MPs. Liberal Democrats are reformers at heart and that needs to be communicated more forcefully. That space can't be given to the likes of UKIP.

It's important that the manifesto contains ideas that will invigorate and excite Liberal Democrat members and activists, as well as the electorate, because they are the people who deliver the campaigns on the ground. Nick Clegg needs them much more than Ed Miliband or David Cameron who have the cushion of huge amounts of money to spend on phone banks and direct mail. Nick needs people motivated enough to be knocking on doors or phoning voters from now until next May in key seats. His engagement with the party has been patchy and it's fair to say that some people don't feel that he gets what it's like on the front line. His pained and shell-shocked face the day of the European election results shows that he is actually on the same page as us. He does, though, need to listen to the party and be seen to be doing so.

THE CAMPAIGN

Having set the scene and looked at the messages, we should now look at the nuts and bolts of the campaign. One of Nick Clegg's most sensible acts to date was to put Paddy Ashdown in charge of the election campaign. A popular and charismatic former leader, Ashdown has ensured that key seats have their noses to the grindstone with the result that their organisation and planning for the general election is light years ahead of any election I've known in the last thirty years.

The Liberal Democrats currently have fifty-seven MPs. Of those, eight are retiring. Between them they have almost 200 years of experience and include some of our elder statesmen like Sir Malcolm Bruce and Sir Menzies Campbell. It is acknowledged that incumbency is a positive factor for Liberal Democrats. MPs tend to have significant personal votes. It's therefore a risk to be losing some key figures at this election. However, the party has prepared for this by making sure that candidates are selected early and the sitting MPs are campaigning with them.

It's extremely important for the party's credibility that these candidates are elected. Diversity has always been a problem for us, with no BME faces and only seven women out of fifty-seven, the same number of knights, in our current parliamentary party. Five of the eight new candidates are women and seven are from under-represented groups.

In terms of key battlegrounds, two are in university towns, Cambridge and Edinburgh West, represented since 2010 by Julian Huppert and Mike Crockart respectively. Both MPs voted against raising tuition fees, Crockart resigning his job as Parliamentary Private Secretary to then Secretary of State for Scotland Michael Moore in the process. Both men have been key defenders of civil liberties in Parliament. Crockart has been running a highly popular campaign against nuisance calls which has received backing from a national newspaper and Huppert has been a key expert on science and civil liberties, particularly in the field of digital rights and surveillance.

East Dunbartonshire is a key Liberal Democrat/Labour marginal with an exceptional Liberal Democrat MP in Equalities Minister Jo Swinson. Her local organisation has always been strong and the European election results in her area this year were, remarkably, broadly comparable to those in 2009. Jo is exceptionally popular locally and hasn't stopped campaigning since her election in 2005. She has been responsible for extending consumer rights, cracking down on payday lenders and introducing shared parental leave. If anyone can survive a tight fight like this it's Jo Swinson. Key to that success will be persuading voters that there is absolutely no point in voting Conservative in that seat because they can't win there.

In Eastleigh, Mike Thornton will not have the luxury of the entire party descending on his patch in the way that he did during his by-election in February 2013. It is, however, one of the areas where the party gained ground in May.

Looking beyond the seats that the Lib Dems hold, Oxford West & Abingdon, where PPC Layla Moran is fighting a spirited campaign, and Watford, where Dorothy Thornhill was elected for the fourth time as Mayor in May, are other prospects. Jane Dodds in Montgomeryshire could retake the seat lost by Lembit Opik in 2010.

In this most challenging of elections, it's important that the party can properly support the campaign teams on the ground. Tim Gordon, in his two and a half years as chief executive, has done much to modernise the party organisation. The infrastructure is in better shape and things that should have been sorted out long ago are being tackled. Old databases and tired-looking websites are being replaced by much more useful tools. The party website has been transformed into a bright, engaging and interactive space. The party's election software, Connect, combined with the new Nationbuilder sites, is as good as that which powered the SNP to their Holyrood victory in 2011 and, crucially, is better than those of the other parties. It is up to the campaign teams on the ground to use it to maximum effect.

We know from the Ashcroft polls that we do best when we out-campaign our rivals. The old axiom 'where we work we win' may not always be true, but we surely aren't going to win if we don't work. The beauty of the new technology is that in a fortress election where campaigning activity will be concentrated in the seats the party holds and is trying to gain, it is much easier for people from all over the country to help out. In return for that work, the party will also have to have a strong recovery plan in those areas where it has fallen back, where the party organisation is weaker, to implement after the election.

This time, the Lib Dems will have to do more than simply deliver leaflets. The literature is important, but taking the time to have conversations with voters, to get that foot in the door early, is vital.

There is no doubt that this election is the party's biggest challenge in eighty years. On the positive side, the Lib Dems have committed local MPs who are not just working hard but doing more in terms of voter contact than they have ever done before. There is a good story to tell of liberal values enacted across government. The party is better equipped and organised to get that story across to people. Party activists know that it's possible to do well against both Conservatives and Labour because they have seen recent evidence in places like Hull, Hertfordshire and Eastleigh.

Success in May 2015 will depend on a values-based message and some eye-catching new ideas, boldly presented. The party needs to speak to more voters than ever before and our success depends on how well Nick Clegg can motivate his activists and party members to do that. I can see a path to victory in all of our key seats if the party get these things right.

Caron Lindsay is Co-Editor of Liberal Democrat Voice.

The UKIP general election campaign

Gawain Towler

THE CLAY

The 2015 general election is make-or-break time for UKIP. Never before have the political planets aligned in such a way as they do now, to allow the insurgent, self-styled 'People's Army' a foothold in Westminster. Never before has the situation been more positive for them...

Of course, we heard that in 2014 before the European and local elections; same again in 2013 before the locals, and in 2010 for the general elections.

And of course, there is the argument that getting three seats in the European Parliament back in 1999 was a stroke of good fortune, occasioned by the collapse of the Greens as a political force and by the general post-Blair malaise. Then there were the 2004 Euros. You know, UKIP were damned lucky that they picked up Kilroy-Silk: he boosted their polling by at least 3 per cent, a false positive. And then we hit 'peak UKIP' in 2009: remember, the political class were embroiled in the expenses scandal, and UKIP, not being in Westminster, were clear of the mess and picked up protest votes.

It's all a little bit like walking in the Himalayas, this idea of 'peak UKIP', so fashionable immediately after each electoral success. But with each hill topped, there is a bigger and steeper hill to climb and

UKIP's intrepid band of amateur political hoodlums just gird their loins a little bit tighter, quaff that last ale for the road and set off, generally laughing and whistling a jaunty ditty. Maybe 'Guide Me, O Thou Great Redeemer' or 'I Vow to Thee'.

And since the council elections of 2013 the horrid realisation of the legacy parties is twofold.

Firstly: dammit, they won't go away.

Secondly: what on earth do we do about them?

Of course, just before we've heard before that it is 'make-or-break time' doesn't mean it is untrue now. And Nigel Farage's public announcement after he was selected for the eminently winnable seat of Thanet South in August that he would stand down as party leader if he failed to get elected shows how seriously UKIP's leadership are taking the next election challenge. But as a party of political weebles, we take the knocks and, yes, we get up again.

And boy have there been knocks. Call it special pleading if you like but the level of vitriol and partial reporting focusing on the off-beam comments of various party members has been extraordinary. By any objective view, the attacks on UKIP, and more particularly on its councillors and candidates, have been of a ferocity to surprise even hardened political watchers.

But the impact of the string of revelations about minor party members has had the opposite effect to that intended in the Conservative Attack Unit, which authored and directed many of the attacks (and yes, I do have the evidence that it was orchestrated).

Internally and externally, a funny thing happened. Internally, it created a sometimes slightly paranoid circling of the wagons. UKIP activists began to regard every knocking story as a badge of honour. This does have the downside that many cyber-kippers can act and sound pretty strident on various newspaper and blog comment sections. But it has a very big upside, and that is loyalty. The other thing is that, unlike the old parties, UKIP high command is unusual in politics. We actually like our members. Our default position is to support or defend our members. After all, how many of us, if scrutinised to the forensic degree that many of our candidates have been, would not find an opinion, a statement, a comment, a joke that was a little out of kilter with the currently prescribed and acceptable position? There, but for the grace of Hera, go I. If we find eccentricity, we can live with it; if we discover malice, we deal with it, and fast.

Externally, it had a related effect. The great British public, by and large, are a fair-minded bunch. They recognise weakness, they accept a bit of daftness, they are comfortable with the forthright. What they cannot abide is cant, nastiness and hypocrisy. They find the expectation of moral perfection amongst the elected somewhat absurd. And they know a bully when they see one, and they don't like it. They would prefer, as UKIP does, people who are not constantly checking the 'lines to take', not afraid of their shadow, rather than the cookie-cutter, ineffably interchangeable types served up by the traditional parties.

What the other parties see as 'dangerously off-message' is seen by us as normal. And we believe that people would prefer to be governed by people more like them than by the offerings currently available.

Of course, UKIP live in the real world, and in politics, that is a world circumscribed by the 24-hour media. And so, as we move towards the election, we see that there has been a significant tightening of the selection criteria, and a greater level of ruthlessness. We are not pie-in-the-sky dreamers and do not expect to take all before us in 2015. We have set out a list of target seats, and will do all we can to ensure that those seats are contested fiercely.

This is a change in our traditional approach. In a first-past-the-post system, the market entrant will find things very difficult. It is no surprise that electoral success for UKIP came first through the PR system of the European parliamentary elections. The electoral bar to entry was set lower, and the subject matter was focused on our USP. Withdrawal from the EU was and is our core objective.

The greatest barrier we have faced in general elections has always been the credibility gap.

'Mate,' people would say, 'I agree with you, but if I vote for you, it'll let in Labour' – or Conservatives, or the Lib Dems, or even small reptilian creatures from beyond the stars. This has been both a strategic and a technical stumbling block.

And so, four years ago, when Nigel Farage stood for re-election as the party leader, he made it explicit that he was going to refocus efforts on making the incredible credible. To do so, he and the party have had as lodestars two very different political foci.

In broad terms we have looked to the experience of Preston Manning's Reform Party of Canada. There, a new formation under Manning went from foundation in 1987 to domination of the Canadian political system a mere thirteen years later. Key to this was the election of an Alberta schoolteacher, Deborah Gay, in a 1989 by-election. This proved that Reform was electable and, as importantly, sensible. With the collapse in trust of the pre-existing parties, the way was then open for another party to take centre stage.

In UK terms we have been learning from the Lib Dem handbook. We have taken to pavement politics in a big way. And looking at our council results in the past two years, this change in emphasis is working. Fundamental to this is the impact we are having in local politics. One key aim has been to oppose the 'Cabinet system' in local government. We feel that political exclusivity at local government level is wrong. In an ideal world, local government would be stripped of party labels, but we do not live in an ideal world – however, we have made two things absolutely clear to our councillors and candidates. We believe utterly in the right of recall, and we also believe that there should be no formal whip at that level of governance. We would be disappointed if councillors did not rebel from time to time if it meant that they were representing their constituents. It makes party management difficult, but so what? We are not in politics to represent the party; we are in politics to represent those who have elected us. Telling is that when *The Times* ran a survey into local council attendance, they found that UKIP councillors have the highest attendance rate of any of the major parties.

This doesn't mean that we want to be all things to all people. And make no mistake – when it comes to Westminster candidates, whilst there is policy wriggle room, we expect a greater level of fealty to the policy proscriptions that will be laid out in our upcoming manifesto.

POLICY

On a simple level, UKIP are a classical liberal party. We believe that in a mature society, government should treat people as grown-ups. What is of course interesting is that to try to remove politics from various areas of public life is itself a political act. Vested interests amongst policy monopolists, and the education and health sectors, are two classic examples of producer interest trumping consumer interest. But there is a frightening level of collusion between big corporate interest and legislative power. It is no surprise that some of the greatest cheerleaders for pan-European legislation, particularly at a trade negotiation and workplace regulation level, are the big companies. There has been no greater supporter of EU integration at all levels than the strange coalition of the TUC and the CBI.

It is of course in their interest to ensure that market entry is made as onerous as possible, thus protecting the tired and sclerotic from competition.

So the lodestone by which our policy platform is created is to try and get to the point where people govern their own lives. We are, as Thoreau's aphorism puts it, best governed when least governed.

Of course we have to deal with the world we experience, rather than the one which we would wish to experience, but that simple principle, of trusting people, is our pole star.

TARGETING

It is no secret that UKIP is moving away from its blunderbuss approach into targeting. The research done by Lord Ashcroft has shown that when it comes to embedment on the ground, UKIP are up there with the far more numerously staffed and financed parties when it comes to knocking on doors and face-to-face contact. We may not have the ruinously expensive phone banks of the other parties, but at least people are in a position to say, 'A woman from UKIP knocked on my door last night' – and this is outside the election campaign period.

One of the most unintentionally humorous things that has happened in recent months for us in UKIP has been the discovery, mostly through the hard work of Rob Ford and Matt Goodwin, that UKIP are not the 'Tory Party in exile', as has been the concept of the political class, but a party whose core messages matter more to the blue- rather than the white-collar worker. We have been saying this for years, only to be patted on the head as if we were toddlers. Finally Westminster is waking up to the basic truth. It is not for nothing that the 2014 conference is being held not in a metropolis or a seaside resort, but in Miliband's back yard: Doncaster.

A close look at the results in the past two council elections and the European elections provides us with a solid base from which to work, and the generous work of both Lord Ashcroft and the Goodwin/Ford research team, though not done for our benefit, has given us further data as to demographics and location. However, without a political tribe to call our own as of yet, what will really matter is the quality of the man or woman selected to fight those seats. And it is from a combination of local knowledge, demographic data and polling data that the final decisions will be made on where we target our resources. To do otherwise would be to waste our donors' and members' cash, just at the time we believe we can break through, which would be a dereliction of duty and responsibility.

TEAM

In the last few years UKIP has been putting together a close-knit team to act and implement this basic philosophy.

Obviously the biggest beast has been Nigel Farage, but contrary to many people's impressions he has always been far more a political leader than some sort of creosote bush. Nothing in recent years has given him greater pleasure, and indeed freed up more of his time, than being able to hive off aspects of the party management to others. Today he concentrates on general leadership, rather than the day-to-day minutiae of the party. It was this that allowed him to mastermind the political surprise of the summer, the defection of Douglas Carswell MP, in a way that left the entire Westminster bubble slack-jawed with surprise. The whole process was symptomatic of his approach. As one jaded lobby hack put it at the time, 'Gawain I've been doing political journalism for years now and I don't think I have ever been surprised by an announcement before.' We have had governance by long-trawled, repeated announcements and pre-briefing. UKIP do things differently.

Instead of briefing a few trusted hacks as to the contents of a major speech, the line the press office gives is simple: if you want to know what he is going to say, listen to him say it.

It's a touch scary at times, but it treats all as equals, unlike the situation with the other parties, where it is apparent that there is a secret coterie of those privileged to know in advance.

The back office has in its chairman, Steve Crowther, an old-fashioned liberal with a steely side, and under him a growing team of professionals such as Suzanne Evans, now deputy chairman and a polished media performer in her own right, and Roger Bird, who brings a level of seriousness and stability to day-to-day operations.

The press office, which at times over the years has been a ramshackle operation, has taken on a far more thorough, cohesive, though still small, approach. In the central office there are four staff, who deserve all the plaudits they get. What is remarkable about the team is the pervasive good humour amongst them. The most obvious, regular and telling noise that emanates from the room is laughter. Of course I would say that, wouldn't I, as part of that team, but with Jack Duffin, John Gill and Alex Phillips making up the team it could be nothing but. Though there are specialisations, there are no demarcation disputes, and the team understands each other. It is a happy ship.

One aspect of UKIP's general campaigning which chimes with the way that we see ourselves is that we are rather old-fashioned and enjoy the public meeting. Before both the 2013 and the 2014 elections there has been a traditional speaking tour across the country. To the consternation of political journalists who have turned up at these events, what has been seen is genuine political engagement. In towns and villages across the country, halls have been packed by people who actually want to hear what is being said. The basic premise is the same everywhere. All are welcome, and all are welcome to pose questions. What they expect from UKIP is straight answers to those questions. And if the speaker cannot answer, then so be it. The key detail in all these meetings is that there is no filtering of the audience. These are not highly selected groups of people who can be relied upon to ask useful questions and can be expected to politely or uproariously applaud for the camera. These are ordinary people who just want to find out what the fuss is about.

And these meetings work. I will give an example. It was a wet Wednesday night in Sidmouth during the Euro campaign. I was the draw. Now, to put it frankly, not even my own mother would come out to hear me speak when the gutters ran so deep with rain, but more than sixty turned up. And it wasn't my name on the flyers that brought them, but the rather dubious promise held by the purple-and-yellow branding. Two years earlier Nigel Farage would have been pleased with the turnout; on that night an absolute unknown wannabe was able torque their interest. Did I convince them all? Not in the slightest (particularly not the small group of Tory councillors who heckled me from the back), but afterwards did they feel they had been condescended to? No, they felt included, and part of politics, something the other parties, with their reliance on über computer modelling, have forgotten about.

You can call it outreach, you can call it customer engagement, but basically it's giving a hoot. And it is palpable.

A series of policy committees have been working over the last couple of years, under the guiding hand of Tim Aker. Aker, a former policy wonk with the TaxPayers' Alliance and now an eastern counties MEP, has had the unenviable task of disentangling the well-meaning but sprawling manifesto of 2010 into an independently costed, functional manifesto for 2015. That he has been able to bring together a combination of small-state libertarianism with a social conservatism merely highlights the effort that he has had to put into it. The two poles are never as far apart as some would like to suggest, but with diligence he has been able to knit them together into a cohesive and consistent whole.

From a greater simplification of tax to a firm but fair policy on migration, we can see a single-minded emphasis on the radical within the possible.

As to tactics, well, that would be telling, but we are learning fast on our feet, operating an 'if it isn't broke don't fix it' approach. Thus our use of a hard-hitting poster campaign at the beginning of the electioneering period is, if not a given, quite likely. This of course allows us to hit the ground running and makes it clear to the country at large that we are in the fight to win it.

From such a small team, the online campaigning has been impressive. It is notable that in industry studies, the UKIP brand (and how we hate that word), led by the young Michael Heaver for the past few years, outperforms any other political or lobbying brand to a factor of N2. This is largely because, as can be seen by any cursory glance at the official Facebook page, we offer dialogue. Our dial is set both to receive and to transmit, and thus builds loyalty and inspires activists who know that the management isn't hidden behind serried ranks of firewalls.

There isn't a member of the team who doesn't go out to by-elections. Not to sit behind a desk offering instruction to the indentured volunteer workers, but to actually get their hands dirty, to go knocking on doors. And the members and activists know this, so the team is real rather than imagined.

Somebody once said, 'We are all in this together.' In the case of UKIP this is palpably true, and that authenticity is noticed not only amongst the committed and active, but amongst the general public.

It's going to be a very interesting year.

Gawain Towler is Head of Press at the EFDD Group and UK Independence Party.

Don't blame it on the coalition: how the established parties have failed the test set in 2010

Lord Ashcroft KCMG PC

None of the established parties has passed the test the voters set them in 2010. That is why the result of the next election is so uncertain.

Let's start with a quiz. Shortly after the last election, which clown wrote this?

> Even if the stars had aligned in such a way as to make a minority Conservative government a real possibility, the choice David Cameron made to enter a coalition would still have been the right one, both for the country and for the Conservative Party.

All right, I confess. Enough of you will have read *Minority Verdict* all the way to the end to know that it was me. The contention that forming a coalition was the right thing for the country surely still stands: Britain faced a debt crisis and needed a strong, stable government to restore confidence and put the finances in order. But the right decision for the Conservative Party? With the benefit of hindsight, does that still bear scrutiny?

For many Tories, coalition has been an unhappy experience that they hope never to have to repeat. It has meant compromise and frustration, which some voters share. But if the Conservative Party has been unable to show more voters why it deserves their support, it can hardly point to coalition as the culprit.

After failing to win outright in 2010, the party's political task in this parliament should have been clear. It had to prove to people who had never voted Conservative before what, at best, they had only been able to take on trust: that the party really was on their side, and would look after their public services as well as run the economy and more traditionally Tory issues like immigration. Tories needed to show they could be trusted to govern on their own.

Four years have gone by and there have been some successes. Though most people are yet to feel any personal benefit from the recovery, the Conservatives have established a clear and consistent lead over the other parties when it comes to running the economy. They are more likely than Labour to be thought willing to take tough decisions for the long term, and David Cameron is seen as by far the best available Prime Minister. These are not small things, and in most previous parliaments would have been enough to secure re-election.

Yet despite these twin advantages the party has remained stubbornly behind for most of the parliament. What are the barriers to Tory progress? My national polling has found the Conservative Party is now even less likely than it was in 2010 to be seen to represent the country as a whole, to be on the side of ordinary people, to have its heart in the right place, to stand for fairness, and to be trusted with the NHS. While people think a Conservative government after 2015 is more likely than a Labour one to bring about economic growth and effective welfare reform, they also think it more likely to mean 'higher taxes for people like me'. During the last parliament the party's research would consistently find undecided voters thinking the Tories were best represented by a picture of a posh family standing outside an enormous house. When I repeated the exercise recently, the result was the same.

A certain kind of Tory finds it exasperating to be reminded of this sort of thing. It sounds to them like a lot of touchy-feely nonsense that Conservatives should have no truck with. The trouble is, these perceptions cost the party votes and seats. As Mitt Romney found to his cost, competence is not enough to win if too many think that competence will be deployed in the interests of people other than themselves.

In the same way, the 'modernisation' of the Conservative Party, which many Tories hope they have heard the last of, is not complete, or something that can ever be completed. A modern party is one that is in touch with the times and understands the lives, aspirations and anxieties of the people it hopes to represent.

That has been true of the Conservatives in the past, and David Cameron has made some progress on that front during his nine years in charge. But there remains a gulf. It is one that applies to all parties in differing degrees, but to the Conservatives most of all. To take one example, the party likes to talk about 'the strivers': people of modest means who work hard, try to improve their lot through their own efforts and share what Tories like to think of as Conservative values. But as I found in my *Blue Collar Tories* research, such people do not see the Conservative Party as their natural ally, as they once did. Rather than helping those wanting to get on, the Tories now seemed to be for those who had already made it. By no means did these voters begrudge the rich their success, but in their own lives anxiety and insecurity were as much a force as ambition. Would the party of aspiration be there for them if their fortunes dipped?

As well as re-enlisting people who had once been its natural supporters, to have any hope of a majority the Conservatives needed to reach people who had never even thought of voting Tory. In particular the party needed to win greater support among ethnic minority voters. In *Degrees of Separation* I found that only 4 per cent of black voters identified with the Conservatives, while 55 per cent identified with Labour. Asian voters were nearly twice as likely to say Labour understood minorities than to say the same of the Conservatives; black voters were nearly three times as likely. If this was once just a regrettable fact for the Tories it is fast becoming an urgent problem with electoral consequences: the non-white population of the target seats the Conservatives failed to win in 2010 was well above the national average, especially in London.

The picture is not uniformly bleak for the party: in my research younger Hindus and Sikhs working in the private sector, for example, were comparatively open to the idea of one day switching to the Tories. But are these voters – or people in northern marginals who wanted a change in 2010 but felt Labour's caricature of the Tories was a bit too close to the truth, or aspirational but insecure working-class voters, or those who work in the public sector, or many others who have been put off because they doubted the Tories' priorities – any closer to feeling that the Conservative Party is on their side than they were in May 2010?

I fear they are not. But to go back to my initial question, how much of that is down to the fact of being in coalition? Or to put it another way, would a minority Tory administration have done more to show it was on the side of ordinary people, or win confidence on the NHS, or convince voters from ethnic minorities, or avoid rows about Europe, or even – given the parliamentary maths – do more on immigration or human rights reform?

Ultimately, the question the Tories were unable to answer properly before 2010 – and still are – is this: what is the purpose of a Conservative government? Too many people think the party exists to benefit the few; in government it has had the chance to show it is for those who want to get on, or just get by. The need for austerity and genuinely tough choices have made it a harder test to pass – but for the Tories to blame being in coalition would be a cop-out.

For the Liberal Democrats, the unfamiliar experience of office has posed a different test. Junior coalition partners often struggle to maintain a distinct identity; this has been doubly hard for the Lib Dems because their identity was somewhat hazy to start with. For years they had campaigned as either 'not Labour' or 'not the Tories', as local circumstances required, and they were the most obvious choice for those who wanted 'none of the above'. The ambiguities of equidistance inevitably meant that when they joined a coalition, as they had always wanted, a large chunk of their supporters would react not with rejoicing but with fury: by the end of 2010, the party's poll rating was less than half their general election vote share. Entering office, then, did not so much cause the Lib Dems' weakness as expose it.

That is not to say that joining the coalition was the wrong decision. One of the biggest barriers to supporting the Lib Dems had always been the idea that they were a wasted vote; being offered a share of power and rejecting it would surely prove the case. Indeed what would be the point of a political party that had a chance of governing but turned it down?

Nick Clegg grasped all this, and some of the realities of government, with impressive stoicism: when he was compelled to break his pledge to oppose any rise in tuition fees, he apologised not for the government's policy but for having made such a daft promise in the first place. And on the need for austerity and deficit reduction the Lib Dems have been surprisingly staunch.

These things have not made their electoral position any easier. From the outset, the political temptation for the party would be to try and have things both ways: to be both a responsible party of government capable of dealing with reality, and a party of opposition-in-office, always ready to disown the necessary but unpopular.

But, as I concluded in my research papers *What Future For The Liberal Democrats?* and *What Are The Liberal Democrats For?*, taking an oppositionist approach, trying to burnish their leftist credentials or even leaving the coalition early in an attempt to win back left-wing former supporters is unlikely to succeed. For these people, how the Lib Dems perform in government is beside the point: they blame the party for putting the Conservatives in office and that cannot be pardoned. Many of them would not give the Lib Dems a second look unless they promised never to work with the Tories again – something they can hardly do. For those who are determined to vote for none of the above, the Lib Dems have ruled themselves out indefinitely by becoming very much one of the above.

Nick Clegg's true audience, then, comprises those who want his party to make a constructive contribution to government. That means the Lib Dems' test in this parliament was to play the hand they were dealt as best they could; to use what clout they had to the best possible effect.

It would be hard to argue that they have passed this test. Few think Clegg or his party have exerted any real influence. Though many people (including many Conservative voters) are glad they are there to temper Tory excesses, they struggle to name any concrete Lib Dem achievements.

This is hardly surprising. True, the Lib Dems have had only a limited degree of leverage, but what have they used it to achieve? The pupil premium, for which they like to claim credit, was also in the Conservative manifesto, and there was probably little disagreement between the parties on raising the income tax threshold.

Three things incontrovertibly happened because the Liberal Democrats were in government and would not have happened otherwise: a pointless referendum on the voting system; proposals for an elected House of Lords that went nowhere; and free school meals for primary school children who do not need them. I would like to see all that on their leaflets.

In this parliament the Lib Dems have certainly been in an unenviable position. Perhaps it might have been eased had they chosen to use their share of power to pursue something other than their own obsessions.

Labour's test since 2010 has been to show they have learned the lessons of the last government and that they can be trusted to run the economy. They have not so much failed this test as refused to hand in their homework. The party's response to austerity, which voters largely thought necessary if disagreeable, was to oppose every cut, implying that they would borrow still more – while complaining that the deficit was not falling fast enough. Hardly surprising, then, that the Tories have maintained a clear and consistent lead on economic management, and that the biggest specific concern potential Labour voters have about returning the party to office is that they would once again spend and borrow more than the country can afford.

If the image that defined the Conservative Party in the years before 2010 was a rich family, for Labour it was a fat slob lying on a sofa. He largely symbolised Labour's perceived tendency to indulge those who chose not to work. For all their backroom wonkery on strengthening the contributory principle, the impression the Labour Party has managed to convey on welfare reform – one of the few elements of the government's programme people spontaneously praise – is that they are against it. Not surprisingly, the slob remains Labour's mascot five years later.

Labour's brand was not as badly broken in 2010 as the Tories' was in 1997. People are much more likely to think Labour has its heart in the right place and essentially stands for fairness and helping ordinary people. But many who are tempted to vote Labour in 2015 have real reservations about the party returning to office.

One of these reservations is Ed Miliband. My polling has consistently found less than a third of voters, including those in marginal seats Labour need to win, saying they are dissatisfied with David Cameron's performance and would rather see Miliband in Downing Street. Indeed, only two thirds of Labour voters themselves say this. Most swing voters' reaction is that he is uninspiring, and even four years into his leadership say his brother would have been the better choice.

But doubts about Labour's ability to keep the books in order is just as big a misgiving. My polling has found that while people think a Labour government is more likely than a Tory one to mean more house building, action on the cost of living and improvements in the NHS, it is also more likely to bring more borrowing and debt.

If membership of a coalition government does not excuse the Conservatives and Liberal Democrats their own failures, it is at least a mitigating circumstance. Labour have no such defence. So why have they not confronted people's doubts? After all, Tony Blair would never have risked losing because people thought Labour were on the side of the feckless or were not to be trusted with the public finances; he went out of his way to reassure people every day, even when he was twenty points ahead. Why won't Ed Miliband's Labour do the same? I think there are two reasons: they don't want to, and they don't think they need to.

As I found soon after the election in *What Future For Labour?*, voters who switched away from the party in 2010 thought it had lost because Gordon Brown was not a good Prime Minister, that Labour did not have answers on the most important issues, and that the government had run out of steam. Labour loyalists, meanwhile, thought they had lost because people failed to appreciate what Labour had achieved, credulous voters had been influenced by the right-wing media, and though Labour's policies were right they had been communicated badly. Most thought Labour had not deserved to lose and that the party should defend its record in government – that is, tell the electorate why it had made a mistake – rather than change, let alone apologise.

Most members of the Labour movement also thought the coalition would prove so unpopular that their party would win the next election almost by default. In the first instalment of my *Project Blueprint* research in 2011, I noted that the combination of Labour's core supporters with Lib Dem defectors meant that Ed Miliband could in theory assemble a winning vote share without needing to get out of bed. It is one thing to make this point as an observer, but quite another to use it as an operating assumption. Still, that is what he seems to have done – and that is why we still await his breakthrough.

None of the established parties, then, can truly claim to have met the challenges the voters set them. The Conservatives have not properly shown their purpose to people who do not trust their motives; the Lib Dems have used what power they have to fruitless ends; Labour have complacently declined to tackle the fears people have about putting them back in charge.

All this has created an opportunity for UKIP, which they have taken with some aplomb. The polling for my 2012 study *They're Thinking What We're Thinking: Understanding The UKIP Temptation* found the party's support was based more on outlook than policy. Immigration and the European Union are powerful factors in driving people to UKIP, but so is a wider dissatisfaction with the way they see things going in Britain.

Nigel Farage has converted this disillusionment not just into a significant poll share but into real votes in local elections, by-elections and, most spectacularly, European Parliament elections. Last May, my polling found that six in ten of those who had voted UKIP in the European elections had done so in order to show they were unhappy with their usual party, or as a general protest.

But general elections are different. One of the most important dynamics affecting the result next May will be the extent to which UKIP can maintain momentum and turn disaffection into votes when people have the chance to choose a government, not just send a signal. My polling has found that more than half of all voters think UKIP 'are prepared to say things other parties are scared to say', but they are much less likely to think the party 'reasonable and sensible' – which, despite everything, are qualities people still want in those who govern. Yet my post-Euro election research found that half of UKIP voters – or only half, depending on your point of view – said they would probably vote for the party again in 2015.

In order to maximise their impact, UKIP are likely to target their resources on perhaps twenty-five seats where the demographics and political circumstances work most in their favour.

And because of the national stalemate, the marginals will matter more than ever. My polling in the battleground constituencies will continue up to the end of the campaign, but it has already given us some clues. Labour seem to have the edge over the Conservatives in the most marginal seats they will be contesting directly. The Lib Dems still command a loyal local vote, but only in a few places will this be enough to withstand the national tide against them. UKIP are inflicting damage on all parties, especially the Tories, and have the potential to break through in a handful.

But while there are patterns, swings in constituencies I have polled are very far from uniform; there are big variations between constituencies with similar majorities. In an election whose result will be counted in individual seats, these are the places that will decide the next incumbent of Downing Street.

As for the national battle, will the Tory lead on the economy start to tell in their vote share? Will more good economic news buoy the government, or take the urgency away from economic questions and allow the focus to move to issues like public services, where Labour have the advantage? How will people who prefer Cameron to Miliband but Labour to the Tories resolve their dilemma?

And if, as the signs are, this is the closest election in forty years, will it be because the country is divided between competing visions of Britain – or because it thinks the winner is neither here nor there?

Lord Ashcroft KCMG PC is a businessman, pollster and philanthropist. Full details of the author's research can be found at LordAshcroftPolls.com.

The candidates of 2015

Gareth Knight

There are few things that get politicos as excited as candidate selection regardless of how winnable a seat may be. A candidate at a general election is the focus of every party's campaign – not just a potential future MP, but as the leader of their party's efforts to take the seat. But the excitement of selecting a candidate often belies the fact that in nearly all cases the impact a candidate can have on the result is relatively minimal as people tend to vote with the national swing. Almost everyone involved in politics can tell you stories of popular MPs losing their seats to candidates who never expected to win and unpopular MPs holding their seats against candidates who put in huge efforts to unseat them.

In election agent circles there's a phrase often used to describe the ups and downs of momentum within a campaign bubble – Candidate Syndrome. The theory is that, regardless of party or size of majority to be defended or attacked, every candidate will, at some point in the campaign, be convinced they are going to win and at another point in the campaign, be convinced they are going to lose. Positive words from party activists, a good canvassing session, a good debate in the church hall, and even a Conservative candidate in Knowsley or a Labour candidate in Beckenham will start to think they 'may just pull off the biggest upset of the night'. Equally, a grumpy constituency chairman, indifference on the doorstep and a missed sound bite at a debate and even MPs with rock-solid safe seats will go into a panic.

The decline of party membership in the last twenty years, the growth of pavement politics and the huge resources now available to sitting MPs have turned many general election candidates from being a mere name on a ballot paper to being a person from whom miracles are expected. Candidates are now expected to have casework (something that can almost entirely be blamed on the effective Liberal Democrat style of pavement politics), and many run their local party as de facto chairmen, treasurers, council group leaders, social workers and maintain a job and family while receiving personal and vicious abuse on social media and grumbling and criticism from certain sections of their own local party. A survey conducted by Conservative Home in 2006 showed that at the 2005 general election the average cost of being a winning candidate was £41,550 and for a losing candidate £27,235 including lost income from unpaid holiday from work or lost income from self employment. The direct cost alone, excluding lost income, was £22,020 for winning candidates and £16,070 for losing candidates. When you consider that the national average salary is £26,500, you start to see a problem emerging.

The expectations placed on candidates has inevitably led to the accusation that if you want to be a parliamentary candidate for one of the major political parties you'll probably need to be either cash-rich or time-rich (and ideally both). Those who are not cash-rich or time-rich may also need to be contact-rich. The effect of this is that being a candidate is much more attractive for professional politicians as the investment of emotion, time and money into what will be, in the vast majority of cases, a fruitless cause, is not an attractive prospect. Politics is often said to be inward-looking and insular, and it's difficult to see that changing soon.

CONSERVATIVE PROCEDURES

The introduction of the Priority List ('the A List') before 2010 is still a subject of much bitterness within the party but the basic procedures for selection have remained the same for many years. All candidates must be approved centrally (a process applicants have to pay for, regardless of success) and they are then allowed to apply for seats anywhere or in a particular region or, in some cases, for a specific seat only. The waiting list for a Parliamentary Assessment Board (the assessment day) is notoriously long for some and perceived to be notoriously short for others.

Constituencies advertise their vacancy via the party's candidates department to all on the approved list and applicants submit their CVs. If the local party is small, the candidates department gives the local party a shortlist and if the local party has over 100 members a committee of the local party does the shortlisting. Applicants are whittled down via meetings of the local constituency executive council and the final selection meeting can be a full meeting of the local membership, an open meeting that any constituency can attend and vote at (frequently erroneously referred to as an open primary despite constituents having to pre-register and attend the meeting to be able to vote from a list that has already been sifted) or a full postal ballot to all constituents.

As a broad rule, the more open the selection procedure, the more positive an impact it has on the subsequent election result, with both candidates selected by an all-postal vote of all constituents winning in 2010 (and both, incidentally, were women), but worries about the loss of members' rights and the cost of running such exercises mean all-postal primaries will not become the norm any time soon. Sitting MPs must be readopted as candidates for the following election but they do not need to reapply from scratch. Anne McIntosh and Tim Yeo have been deselected by their local party through this method, and several other MPs have survived concerted attempts by some local activists to deselect them.

LABOUR PROCEDURES

It's no exaggeration to say that selecting candidates in the Labour Party ahead of the 2015 election could result in the biggest shake-up to the party in its history. The selection of a candidate in Falkirk led to Unite the Union – Labour's biggest trade union donor – being surrounded by accusations of signing up scores of party members to influence the selection process. The fallout from Falkirk has directly led to senior Labour figures questioning the very nature of the link between the party and the unions. The knock-on effect of breaking Labour's formal union links could be the loss of a huge proportion of party funding as trade unionists fail to sign up to the party individually and the unions stop giving money to the party directly. The reliance of Labour on union funding combined with the Conservatives' reliance on large donations from wealthy individual donors could speed up moves towards direct state funding of political parties.

Unlike the Conservatives, Labour members may apply to be a candidate providing that, if selected, they are subsequently approved by the central party. Like the Conservatives, the central party maintains a list of approved candidates who may apply at any time. Labour has not embraced the idea of non-members selecting their candidates and there have been accusations of nepotism following the selections of Emily Benn and Will Straw, both descendants of Labour stalwarts – the 'Red Princes' tag just further emphasises the problems parties are having in selecting candidates from a truly diverse range of backgrounds.

All-women shortlists, hugely controversial ahead of the 1997 election and still causing internal argument today, are used in many circumstances as Labour's way of substantially increasing the number of women MPs. While many will question the desirability of discriminating against men as a solution, there is no denying that it has worked in terms of increasing the number of Labour women MPs.

Sitting MPs are subject to a trigger ballot of their local party which decides if the party is to go through a full procedure or simply readopt the MP. Ahead of the 2010 election, Bob Wareing and Anne Moffat were deselected by their local parties.

LIBERAL DEMOCRAT PROCEDURES

The Liberal Democrat candidate selection procedure is quite similar to that of the Conservatives in that to be a candidate you have to be pre-approved by the national party. The process for getting selected to a seat involves a shortlisting process followed by a three-week campaign ahead of a meeting of the full constituency membership which makes it interesting as it's the only one of the three main parties where the way you campaign for yourself to be selected is similar to the way you campaign for yourself to get elected.

In the Liberal Democrats you are therefore less likely to get candidates who are selected on the basis of their speaking skills and ability to duck questions and more likely to get candidates who can devise a strategy for winning the seat. Whether good local campaigners make for better parliamentarians is a matter for debate but given the reputation of the Lib Dems as rabid pavement and pothole politicians who have increased their presence in parliament in the last thirty years, the system works for them.

FUTURE PROBLEMS WITH CANDIDATE SELECTION

The under-representation of women, members of ethnic minority groups and disabled people in parliament will remain a key talking point for the foreseeable future, and barring a significant increase in women on the Liberal Democrat and Conservative benches, it is difficult to see how there will not be further pressure on these parties to more actively address the issue, particularly if the number of women Labour MPs rises.

The cost of being a candidate is the issue none of the parties want to address as they all know how expensive it is, but when standing for parliament for a major political party outside your own area is beyond the financial ability of even relatively wealthy people, the problem will not go away, and parliament will appear even more remote and exclusive.

Transparency of the selection process, as highlighted in Falkirk, is a problem the parties may feel able to address but I do not expect substantial changes. Political parties are extremely controlling and do not yield power over anything without a fight. Historically, national parties will always answer any problem that involves its grassroots with a massive dose of centralisation, and it always makes things even worse.

Recall – nobody ever really believed that MPs would really create a meaningful system of recall, did they? Turkeys will never vote for Christmas.

Primaries – despite the success the Conservatives have had with all-postal primaries, a truly open primary system has three things that make them unattractive prospects for parties: perceived cost (naysayers will never be convinced that a primary is not going to bankrupt the local party); control of who appears on the ballot paper (only Labour – for now – allows people to go through a selection process who have not been pre-approved, a situation that will never change as central parties never devolve power); and how primaries affect sitting MPs (Labour and Conservative MPs are quite well protected, especially compared to politicians in the US. MPs are no more likely to make it easier for them to lose their jobs through open primaries than they are through recall).

The most likely scenario that will see candidate selection change in the coming few years will be a change in leadership of one of the two main parties. The inevitable leadership contest in whichever party loses the general election is likely to hinge on internal democracy, of which candidate selection is key.

A Labour leadership election will be about Falkirk and the relationship with the unions – no Labour leader is going to want to lose among MPs and members and win thanks to the unions again, and talk at the Labour conference will be how they managed to cast aside the highly electable David Miliband and got lumbered with 'Loser Ed'. A separation of Labour from the unions would throw up a big threat to the Conservatives if a new Labour leader can rebuild their party from the ground up (which they would have to do if there was no state funding). Labour has a problem with internal democracy as it is often perceived that the biggest centraliser in the last fifty years was Tony Blair, but he was also the most successful leader in terms of election results.

A Conservative leadership election will be a gory affair as a decade of husky hugging, 'A Lists' and grammar schools but with no election victories to show for it becomes the backdrop for a debate that may resemble a bare-knuckle boxing match. It's practically guaranteed that one of the candidates will run on a democratic renewal mandate, but Conservatives tend to like deference to democracy when it comes to their choice in leader (Ken Clarke in 1997 and David Davis in 2005 were supporters of internal party reform that would have given more power to the members and both were defeated by centralisers in Hague and Cameron).

CANDIDATES OF NOTE

Disappointingly, there aren't many especially notable candidates. Will Straw in Rossendale & Darwen is a name that immediately stands out but his biography makes no mention of his Labour grandee father. A look through the biographies of Labour candidates shows a depressing trend of stereotypes – first in their family to go to university, local councillor, campaigner against a Tory cut of some sort, parliamentary worker, trade union link, public sector employment. As is often the case, some of the more interesting biographies are in the constituencies you cannot imagine Labour winning even with a '97-style landslide. Some candidates even manage to smile for their photos – Ed Miliband's Labour Party is not just for those outraged at the injustice of life! At the time of writing, Labour are well ahead of other parties in terms of candidate selection with over half of all constituencies having an incumbent MP or candidate in place. Even some MPs in safe Conservative seats will have Labour candidates fighting them for nearly a year.

The Conservatives have an equally vanilla set of candidates, though they do have a slightly more varied background than their Labour counterparts and they look unashamedly 'Middle England', like the queue at the cooked meats counter in Waitrose. One of the startling things is that by the end of August, just eight months from polling day, the Conservatives have only selected seventy-five candidates and there are very few in traditionally safe Labour seats.

The Liberal Democrats are, as you would expect, a collection of non-politicians; community activists fighting for post offices and against potholes in the face of these nasty out of touch politicians (it was always going to be their candidates who were most inconvenienced by their party being in government for the first time in decades). If the Conservatives are the queue in Waitrose, the Lib Dems are the queue in Starbucks – an eclectic mix of the professional, the dreamers, the eccentrics and the adorably naive, all swilling down something watery, lacking in bite compared to its competitors and slightly controversial for the last few years.

Perhaps the most notable thing about the likely 2015 intake is how lacking in notability they are. Candidates are largely cut from the same cloth as before, but with less pizzazz. What's frustrating is that we know some of these candidates will become MPs who stand out – the future Dennis Skinners, Jacob Rees-Moggs, Jeremy Thorpes, Teresa Gormans, Lembit Opiks, Diane Abbotts – but in the control-obsessed 2015 election, don't expect many of them to do anything but parrot the party line and be all things to all people.

In 2015, it seems that successful politicians, at the national or constituency level, will not be those who can stir up an interest in politics, policy and issues. They won't show independent thought and communicate with people based on their experience of the world with a real determination to cut through the rhetoric and just get things done. Success will be judged as simply being the least offensive to the most people and performing politics by textbook. And then we wonder why the public holds politicians and politics in such contempt.

Gareth Knight is a psephologist and political consultant.

By-elections in the 2010 parliament

Mike Smithson

By-elections in the current 2010 parliament followed the pattern that we have got used to over the past decade or so – there were far more in Labour-held seats than those of any other party. Thus between May 2010 and September 2014 there had been eighteen contests of which thirteen were in Labour-held seats.

Some of these were prompted by actions of the courts or follow-ups to the MPs' expenses scandal, others by health issues or death and others by MPs deciding to step down to pursue other political opportunities like running for elected mayoral post or the new positions of elected police commissioners.

With two notable exceptions, Oldham East & Saddleworth and Bradford East, the outcomes in almost all of the Labour seats were never really in doubt. Victories on much reduced turnouts appeared to be foregone conclusions with the main interest being, in the period from 2012 onwards in particular, in the rise of the UKIP share of the vote.

Amongst the contests to get most attention there was a dispute over whether the first, at Oldham East & Saddleworth in January 2011, was actually by-election at all because the general election result was voided by order of the courts. The sitting MP Phil Woolas was said to have been personally guilty of 'knowingly making false statements' about the personal character of his Liberal Democrat opponent, Elwyn Watkins, during the general election campaign the previous May. Wilkins took the matter to an election court consisting of High Court judges which ruled in his favour. As a result, Woolas ceased to be an MP from 5 November 2010 and was banned from holding public office for three years.

What made the campaign especially interesting was that this was the first by-election since the formation of the coalition and there was much talk that the Conservatives were not really trying in order to assist the Liberal Democrats. As it turned out, the Conservative vote dropped by 13.6 per cent and Elwyn Wilkins managed to increase his vote by 0.3 per cent. This was not enough and Labour's Debbie Abrahams increased the Labour vote by more than 10 per cent to win comfortably.

The next by-election in the interesting category was more than a year later after the Labour MP for Bradford West, Marsha Singh, had to resign on grounds of ill health. This looked like an easy Labour hold like the contests in Barnsley Central, Leicester South, Inverclyde and Feltham & Heston that had gone before. Then the ex-Labour, then Respect MP George Galloway announced that he was putting his hat into the ring. Few rated his chances and Ladbrokes opened the betting with Galloway at 33/1. Even by election night there was little to suggest that a shock result was in the making. BBC TV did not even mount an overnight by-election result programme.

The result, however, was a sensation. Galloway secured 56 per cent of the votes to Labour's 25 per cent. Ladbrokes, which had reported a spate of big Galloway bets at 5/1 being placed in Bradford betting shops two days beforehand reported that this was their most costly by-election ever.

Six months later, in November 2012, there was a spate of by-elections. Five of them, at Manchester Central, Cardiff South & Penarth,

Middlesbrough, Rotherham and Croydon North were all safe Labour holds on some very small turnouts. The other one, at Corby, was a Tory defence triggered by the resignation of Louise Mensch, who had stepped down for family reasons. Labour managed to offset its Bradford loss with a gain on a 12.7 per cent CON to LAB swing. Ominously for the Conservatives, the UKIP candidate polled 14.3 per cent.

UKIP figured prominently and had their best performance ever in a Westminster seat in the next big really interesting by-election at Eastleigh in February 2013. This had been a key Conservative target in 2010 but had been retained by Chris Huhne for the Liberal Democrats with a majority of nearly 14,000. On 5 February, Huhne, who had been one of the five Liberal Democrats in the first coalition Cabinet, resigned as MP a couple of hours after he had pleaded guilty of lying to police that his then wife and not him had been the driver of his car in 2003 when it was caught speeding. He was later to be jailed.

This was the only hard-fought by-election between the coalition partners during the course the parliament and both parties threw everything at it. It was widely suggested that the UKIP leader, Nigel Farage, who had stood in the seat at a by-election in the 1990s, would be the candidate.

Labour dithered over whether they would fight hard while Diane James for UKIP headed what proved to be a hugely effective UKIP by-election campaign. Her second place share of 27.8 per cent was only 3.3 per cent short of what the Liberal Democrats chalked up in winning the election. The Conservatives were squeezed into third place.

Given how poorly the Liberal Democrats had been performing in the polls and the circumstances of the by-election, Eastleigh was a reminder that it was able to perform reasonably well in its strongholds. They were helped, clearly, by the UKIP performance.

The next contest up was at South Shields where former Labour leadership contender David Miliband stood down to take up an international aid job in New York. After its performance in Eastleigh, it was expected that UKIP would run a high-profile campaign in an area where Labour had a reputation for taking its supporters for granted. For whatever reason, Farage's party did not put the same resources into this battle as they had done three months earlier in Eastleigh but still came a good second on 24.2 per cent to Labour's 50.4 per cent. The Liberal Democrats saw their vote collapse to just 1.4 per cent resulting in another lost deposit during the parliament.

There was a similar outcome in Manchester Wythenshawe & Sale East in February 2014 – a vacancy caused by the death of the popular local MP, Paul Goggins. Again UKIP did not pull all the stops out and ended up in second place on 14.5 per cent and a full forty points behind Labour.

The final by-election, at Newark, was caused by the resignation of the Conservative, Patrick Mercer, following a recommendation from Commons Standard Committee that he be suspended for six months for breach of the paid advocacy rule. This took place just two weeks after the Euro elections in which UKIP had topped the poll with 27.5 per cent of the GB vote. There was a feeling that some of the momentum would carry over particularly because the Conservatives had gone for more than twenty-five years without successfully defending a by-election whilst in office. The UKIP candidate was the seventy-year-old former Conservative MEP, Roger Helmer. Both UKIP and the Conservatives mounted highly intensive campaigns while, strangely, Labour was low-key. Given that in 1997 it had won Newark, albeit on different boundaries, this seemed a strange decision. Opportunities to defeat the Conservatives do not come up very often yet they back-pedalled.

The Conservative won with a 45 per cent share, 9 per cent down on their general election share but nearly 20 per cent ahead of UKIP. The Liberal Democrats, as had become almost the norm, lost another deposit.

Mike Smithson is Editor of PoliticalBetting.com.

BY-ELECTIONS SINCE 2010

Oldham East & Saddleworth – 13 January 2011

(Triggered by a court decision on 5 November 2010 annulling Phil Woolas's general election victory, writ moved on 16 December 2010)

CANDIDATE	PARTY	VOTES	%	CHANGE FROM 2010
Debbie Abrahams	Labour	14,718	42.1%	+10.3%
Elwyn Watkins	Lib Dem	11,160	31.9%	+0.3%
Kashif Ali	Conservative	4,481	12.8%	-13.6%
Paul Nuttall	UKIP	2,029	5.8%	+1.9%
Derek Adams	BNP	1,560	4.5%	-
Peter Allen	Green	530	1.5%	-
Nick 'the Flying Brick' Delves	Monster Raving Loony	145	0.2%	-
Stephen Morris	English Democrats	96	0.4%	-

Majority	3,558 (10.2%)
Total Poll	34,930
Electorate	72,788
Turnout	48%

Barnsley Central – 3 March 2011

(Resignation of Eric Illsley on 9 February 2011, writ moved on 9 February 2011)

CANDIDATE	PARTY	VOTES	%	CHANGE FROM 2010
Dan Jarvis	Labour	14,724	60.8%	+13.5%
Jane Collins	UKIP	2,953	12.2%	+7.5%
James Hockney	Conservative	1,999	8.3%	-9.0%
Enis Dalton	BNP	1,463	6.0%	-2.9%
Dominic Carman	Lib Dem	1,012	4.2%	-13.1%
Tony Devoy	Independent	1,266	5.2%	-
Kevin Riddiough	English Democrats	544	2.2%	-
Howling Laud Hope	Monster Raving Loony	198	0.8%	-
Michael Val Davies	Independent	60	0.2%	-

Majority	11,771 (48.6%)
Total Poll	24,219
Electorate	65,471
Turnout	37%

Leicester South – 5 May 2011

(Resignation of Sir Peter Soulsby on 1 April 2011, writ moved on 5 April 2011)

CANDIDATE	PARTY	VOTES	%	CHANGE FROM 2010
Jonathon Ashworth	Labour	19,771	57.8%	+12.3%
Zuffar Haq	Lib Dem	7,693	22.5%	-4.4%
Jane Hunt	Conservative	5,169	15.1%	-6.2%
Abhijit Pandya	UKIP	994	2.9%	+1.4%
Howling Laud Hope	Monster Raving Loony	553	1.6%	-

Majority	12,078 (35.3%)
Total Poll	34,180
Electorate	77,880
Turnout	43.9%

Belfast West – 9 June 2011

(Resignation of Gerry Adams on 26 January 2011, writ moved on 16 May 2011)

CANDIDATE	PARTY	VOTES	%	CHANGE FROM 2010
Paul Maskey	Sinn Fein	16,211	70.6%	-0.4%
Alex Attwood	SDLP	3,088	13.5%	-2.9%
Gerry Carroll	People Before Profit	1,751	7.6%	-
Brian Kingston	DUP	1,393	6.1%	-1.5%
Bill Manwaring	UUP	386	1.7%	-1.4%
Aaron McIntyre	Alliance	122	0.5%	-

Majority	13,123 (57%)
Total Poll	22,951
Electorate	61,441
Turnout	37.4%

Inverclyde – 30 June 2011

(Death of David Cairns on 9 May 2011, writ moved on 8 June 2011)

CANDIDATE	PARTY	VOTES	%	CHANGE FROM 2010
Iain McKenzie	Labour	15,118	53.8%	-2.2%
Anne McLaughlin	SNP	9.280	33.0%	+15.5%
David Wilson	Conservative	2,784	9.9%	-2.1%
Sophie Bridger	Lib Dem	627	2.2%	-11.1%
Mitch Sorbie	UKIP	288	1.0%	-0.2%

Majority	5,838 (20.8%)
Total Poll	28,097
Electorate	61,856
Turnout	45.4%

Feltham & Heston – 15 December 2011

(Death of Alan Keen on 10 November 2011, writ moved on 24 November 2011)

CANDIDATE	PARTY	VOTES	%	CHANGE FROM 2010
Seema Malhotra	Labour	12,639	54.4%	+10.8%
Mark Bowen	Conservative	6,436	27.7%	-6.3%
Roger Crouch	Lib Dem	1,364	5.9%	-7.9%
Andrew Charalambous	UKIP	1,276	5.5%	+3.5%
David Furness	BNP	540	2.3%	-
Daniel Goldsmith	Green	426	1.8%	-
Roger Cooper	English Democrats	322	1.4%	-
George Hallam	London People Before Profit	128	0.6%	
David Bishop	Bus Pass Elvis	93	0.4%	-

Majority	6,203 (26.7%)
Total Poll	23,224
Electorate	80,813
Turnout	28.7%

Bradford West – 29 March 2012

(Resignation of Marsha Singh on 29 February 2012, writ moved on 6 March 2012)

CANDIDATE	PARTY	VOTES	%	CHANGE FROM 2010
George Galloway	Respect	18,341	55.9%	+52.8%
Imran Hussein	Labour	8,201	25.0	-20.4%
Jackie Whiteley	Conservative	2,746	8.4%	-22.8%
Jeanette Sunderland	Lib Dem	1,505	6.2%	-2.6%
Sonja McNally	UKIP	1,085	3.3%	-
Dawud Islam	Green	481	1.5%	
Neil Craig	Democratic Nationalists	344	1.0%	
Howling Laud Hope	Monster Raving Loony	111	0.3%	

Majority	**10,140 (30.9%)**
Total Poll	**32,814**
Electorate	**64,618**
Turnout	**50.8%**

Cardiff South & Penarth – 15 November 2012

(Resignation of Alun Michael on 22 October, writ moved on 23 October 2012)

CANDIDATE	PARTY	VOTES	%	CHANGE FROM 2010
Stephen Doughty	Labour	9,193	47.3%	+8.4%
Craig Williams	Conservative	3,859	19.9%	-8.4%
Bablin Molik	Lib Dem	2,103	10.8%	-11.4%
Luke Nicholas	Plaid Cymru	1,854	9.5%	+5.4%
Simon Ziegler	UKIP	1,248	6.4%	+2.6%
Anthony Slaughter	Green Party	800	4.1%	-
Andrew Jordan	Socialist Labour	235	1.2%	
Robert Griffiths	Welsh Communist	213	1.1%	

Majority	**5,334 (27.4%)**
Total Poll	**19,436**
Electorate	**75,764**
Turnout	**60.2%**

Corby – 15 November 2012

(Resignation of Louise Mensch on 29 August 2012, writ moved on 23 October 2012)

CANDIDATE	PARTY	VOTES	%	CHANGE FROM 2010
Andy Sawford	Labour	17,267	48.3%	+9.6%
Christine Emmett	Conservative	9,476	26.5%	-15.7%
Margot Parker	UKIP	5,108	14.3%	+14.3%
Jill Hope	Lib Dem	1,770	4.9%	-9.5%
Gordon Riddell	BNP	614	1.7%	-
David Wickham	English Democrats	432	1.2%	
Jonathan Hornett	Green	378	1.1%	
Ian Gillman	Independent	212	0.6%	
Peter Reynolds	Cannabis Law Reform	137	0.4%	
David Bishop	Elvis Loves Pets	99	0.3%	
Mr Mozzarella	Independent	73	0.2%	
Dr Rohen Kapur	Young People's Party UK	39	0.1%	
Adam Lotun	Democracy 2015	35	0.1%	
Chris Scotton	United People's Party	25	0.1%	

Majority	**7,791 (21.8%)**
Total Poll	**35,775**
Electorate	**79,878**
Turnout	**44.8%**

Manchester Central – 15 November 2012

(Resignation of Tony Lloyd on 22 October 2012, writ moved on 23 October 2012)

CANDIDATE	PARTY	VOTES	%	CHANGE FROM 2010
Lucy Powell	Labour	11,507	69.1%	+16.4%
Marc Ramsbottom	Lib Dem	1,571	9.4%	-17.2%
Matthew Sephton	Conservative	754	4.5%	-7.3%
Christopher Cassidy	UKIP	749	4.5%	-
Tom Dylan	Green	652	3.9%	
Eddy O'Sullivan	BNP	492	3.0%	
Loz Kaye	Pirate Party UK	308	1.9%	
Alex Davidson	Trade Unions & Socialist Against Cuts	220	1.3%	
Catherine Higgins	Respect	182	1.1%	
Howling Laud Hope	Monster Raving Loony	78	0.5%	
Lee Holmes	People's Democratic Party	71	0.4%	
Peter Clifford	Communist League	64	0.4%	

Majority	**9,936 (59.7%)**
Total Poll	**16,648**
Electorate	**91,692**
Turnout	**18,2%**

Croydon North – 29 November 2012

(Death of Malcolm Wicks on 29 September 2012, writ moved on 8 November 2012)

CANDIDATE	PARTY	VOTES	%	CHANGE FROM 2010
Steve Reed	Labour	15,898	64.7%	+8.7%
Andrew Stranack	Conservative	4,137	16.8%	-7.3%
Winston McKenzie	UKIP	1,400	5.7%	+4.0%
Marisha Ray	Lib Dem	860	3.5%	-10.5%
Shasha Khan	Green	855	3.5%	
Lee Jasper	Respect	707	2.9%	
Stephen Hammond	Christian People's Alliance	192	0.8%	
Richard Edmonds	National Front	161	0.7%	
Ben Stevenson	Communist	119	0.5%	
John Cartwright	Monster Raving Loony	110	0.4%	
Simon Lane	9/11 was an inside job	66	0.3%	
Robin Smith	Young People's Party	63	0.3%	

Majority	11,761 (47.9%)
Total Poll	24,568
Electorate	93,036
Turnout	26.4%

Middlesbrough – 29 November 2012

(Death of Sir Stuart Bell on 13 October 2012, writ moved on 8 November 2012)

CANDIDATE	PARTY	VOTES	%	CHANGE FROM 2010
Andrew McDonald	Labour	10,201	60.5%	+14.6%
Richard Elvin	UKIP	1,990	11.8%	+8.1%
George Selmer	Lib Dem	1,672	9.9%	-10.0%
Ben Houchen	Conservative	1,063	6.3%	-12.5%
Imdad Hussein	Peace Party	1,060	6.3%	-
Peter Foreman	BNP	328	1.9%	
John Malcolm	Trade Unionist & Socialist Coalition	277	1.6%	
Mark Heslehurst	Independent	275	1.6%	

Majority	8,211 (48.7%)
Total Poll	16,866
Electorate	65,095
Turnout	25.9%

Rotherham – 29 November 2012

(Resignation of Denis MacShane on 5 November 2012, writ moved on 8 November 2012)

CANDIDATE	PARTY	VOTES	%	CHANGE FROM 2010
Sarah Champion	Labour	9,966	46.5%	+1.8%
Jane Collins	UKIP	4,648	21.7%	+15.7%
Marlene Guest	BNP	1,804	8.4%	-2.0%
Yvonne Ridley	Respect	1,778	8.3%	+8.3%
Simon Wilson	Conservative	1,157	5.4%	-11.3%
Michael Beckett	Lib Dem	451	2.1%	-13.9%
David Wildgoose	English Democrats	703	3.3%	-
Simon Copley	Independent	582	2.7%	-
Ralph Dyson	Trade Union & Socialist Coalition	281	1.3%	
Paul Dickson	Independent	51	0.2%	
Clint Bristow	Independent	29	0.1%	

Majority				5,318 (24.8%)
Total Poll				21,450
Electorate				63,420
Turnout				33.8%

Eastleigh – 28 February 2013

(Resignation of Chris Huhne on 5 February 2013, writ moved on 7 February 2013)

CANDIDATE	PARTY	VOTES	%	CHANGE FROM 2010
Mike Thornton	Lib Dem	13,342	32.1%	-14.5%
Diane James	UKIP	11,571	27.8%	+24.2%
Maria Hutchings	Conservative	10,559	25.4%	14.0%
John O'Farrell	Labour	4,088	9.8%	+0.2%
Danny Stupple	Independent	768	1.8%	
Dr Iain Maclennan	National Health Action	392	0.9%	
Ray Hall	Beer, Baccy & Crumpet	235	0.6%	
Kevin Milburn	Christian	163	0.4%	
Howling Laud Hope	Monster Raving Loony	136	0.3%	
Jim Duggan	Peace	128	0.3%	
David Bishop	Elvis Loves Pets	72	0.2%	
Michael Walters	English Democrats	70	0.2%	
Daz Procter	Trade Unionist & Socialist Action	62	0.1%	
Colin Bex	Wessex Regionalists	30	0.1%	

Majority				1,771 (4.3%)
Total Poll				41,616
Electorate				79,004
Turnout				52.7%

Mid Ulster – 7 March 2013

(Resignation of Martin McGuinness on 2 January 2013, writ moved on 11 February 2013)

CANDIDATE	PARTY	VOTES	%	CHANGE FROM 2010
Francie Molloy	Sinn Fein	17,462	46.9%	-5.1%
Nigel Lutton	Independent	12,781	34.4%	-
Patsy McGlone	SDLP	6,478	17.4%	+3.1%
Eric Bullick	Alliance	487	1.3%	+0.3%

Majority	4,681 (12.6%)
Total Poll	37,208
Electorate	67,192
Turnout	55.4%

South Shields – 2 May 2013

(Resignation of David Miliband on 27 March 2013, writ moved on 15 April 2013)

CANDIDATE	PARTY	VOTES	%	CHANGE FROM 2010
Emma Lewell-Buck	Labour	12,493	50.5%	-1.5%
Richard Elvin	UKIP	5,988	24.2%	-
Karen Allen	Conservative	2,857	11.5%	-10%
Ahmed Khan	Independent	1,331	5.4%	-
Phil Brown	Independent Socialist	750	3.0%	-
Dorothy MacBeth Brookes	BNP	711	2.9%	-
Hugh Annand	Lib Dem	352	1.4%	-12.8%
Howling Laud Hope	Monster Raving Loony	197	0.8%	
Thomas Faithful Darwood	Independent	57	0.2%	

Majority	6,505 (26.3%)
Total Poll	24,736
Electorate	64,084
Turnout	57.7%

Wythenshawe & Sale East – 13 February 2014

(Death of Paul Goggins on 7 January 2014, writ moved on 21 January 2014)

CANDIDATE	PARTY	VOTES	%	CHANGE FROM 2010
Michael Kane	Labour	13,261	55.3%	+11.2%
John Bickley	UKIP	4,301	18.0%	+14.5%
Rev Daniel Critchlow	Conservative	3,479	14.5%	-11.0
Mary Di Mauro	Lib Dem	1,176	4.9%	+2.4%
Nigel Woodcock	Green	748	3.1%	-
Eddy O'Sullivan	BNP	700	2.9%	-1.0%
Cpt Chaplington-Smythe	Monster Raving Loony	200	0.8%	-

Majority	8,960 (37.4%)
Total Poll	23,961
Electorate	85,058
Turnout	28.2%

Newark – 5 June 2014

(Resignation of Patrick Mercer on 29 April 2014, writ moved on 1 May 2014)

CANDIDATE	PARTY	VOTES	%	CHANGE FROM 2010
Robert Jennick	Conservative	17,431	45.0%	-8.9%
Roger Helmer	UKIP	10,028	25.9%	+22.1%
Michael Payne	Labour	6,842	17.7%	-4.6%
Paul Baggeley	Independent	1,891	4.9%	-
David Kirwan	Green	1,057	2.7%	-
David Watts	Lib Dem	1,004	2.6%	-17.4%
Nick 'The Flying Brick' Delves	Monster Raving Loony	168	0.4%	-
Andy Hayes	Independent	117	0.3%	
David Bishop	Bus Pass Elvis	87	0.2%	
Dick Rodgers	Stop Commercial Banks	64	0.2%	
Lee Woods	Patriotic Socialist	18	0.0%	

Majority	7,403 (19.1%)
Total Poll	38,703
Electorate	73,486
Turnout	52.7%

Clacton – 9 October 2014

(Resignation of Douglas Carswell on 28 August 2014, writ moved on 2 September 2014)

Result not known at time of going to press.

On Scotland

David Torrance

In May 2014, a year out from the general election, Tom Clark of *The Guardian* listed eight possible outcomes. There were, he argued, many reasons why the Conservatives ought to lose in 2015, and equally other reasons why Labour shouldn't cross the finishing line. There was, however, one relative certainty: the prospect of things being made 'even messier by ramifications from Scotland's looming vote on independence'.

With only one MP north of the border – the Scotland Office minister David Mundell – on the face of it a 'yes' vote would make little difference to the Conservatives' prospects of victory, indeed by removing more than forty Labour MPs from the House of Commons it would, on the contrary, improve the party's chances of a second term (although it would also take out a disproportionate chunk of Liberal Democrat MPs). In the event of a 'no' vote, meanwhile, those Labour MPs look likely to prove crucial to Ed Miliband's chances of forming a majority (or even minority) administration.

Timing is, however, an important factor. Even if a majority of the Scottish electorate answers 'yes' to the referendum question, 'Should Scotland be an independent country?', it would not, of course, result in immediate independence from the rest of the UK. The Scottish government has pencilled in 24 March 2016 as 'independence day', although one constitutional expert has described that eighteen-month timescale as 'risible'. Either way, it looks certain that the general election would take place in the midst of independence negotiations but with Scotland – and its fifty-nine MPs – still part of the United Kingdom of Great Britain and Northern Ireland.

In early 2014 the House of Commons voted on a proposition to ban Scots from taking part in the 2015 general election assuming a 'yes' vote in the referendum. Although the measure failed, the Tory MPs Mark Reckless, Nigel Mills and Nick de Bois all supported it (a majority of Conservative ministers did not take part). Downing Street simply said the Prime Minister was 'focused on making the case for Scotland to remain part of the United Kingdom', but the psephologist Professor John Curtice called it 'one of the unanswered questions and difficulties' about a possible 'yes' vote, suggesting a fresh general election might be necessary in May 2016 (once – and if – Scotland had formally seceded). Angus MacNeil, an SNP MP, even suggested some Scottish (Labour) MPs might try to remain in place *after* independence.

A few months later, a report from the House of Lords Constitution Committee also added its two cents, arguing that MPs representing Scottish constituencies (i.e. Gordon Brown, Alistair Darling and Danny Alexander) should not be allowed to negotiate independence terms on behalf of the rest of the UK. Peers on the committee (chaired by Baroness Jay of Paddington) also said Scottish MPs ought to retain their Commons seats until the actual day of independence, which chimed with the Scottish government's White Paper – *Scotland's Future* – which argued that Scots must continue to be represented in the House of Commons *until* March 2016.

It is often stated that the consequences of Scottish independence would somehow be unprecedented, but in fact the creation of the Irish Free State in 1922 provides some guidance as to likely events nearly a century later. In Ireland the situation was a little more clear-cut, for the last general election contested by every Irish constituency had been in 1918 (when forty-seven Sinn Fein MPs were elected, mostly from prison), and by the time of the next poll in 1922 the Free State had been formed and thus only candidates standing in the six counties of Ulster remained. Thus there was no period of constitutional limbo for Westminster MPs representing Ireland's southern counties.

Independence would also impact on the composition of the Upper House, not hugely important in terms of forming an administration (although any UK government draws on members of both Houses) but perhaps more important thereafter when the House of Lords would be consulted on that government's legislative programme. The Constitution Committee concluded that peers resident in Scotland (of which there are roughly eighty-five) would have to pay tax in the rest of the UK in order to remain on the red benches, and if they did not satisfy that criteria then they would be required to 'retire' from the Lords, although there is currently no easy way to do so.

So let us return to the eight possible scenarios arising from the 2015 general election (I've used Tom Clark's, although my analysis differs in places):

1. A MAJORITY CONSERVATIVE GOVERNMENT

If there's a 'no' vote in September then this is fairly straightforward: the coalition currently has twelve MPs in Scotland (one Tory and eleven Lib Dems) and might expect to retain the majority of those (incumbent Lib Dems will be under less pressure than in England). The Scottish Conservative (and Unionist) Party has set a target of winning four seats (including that which it presently holds), so it's possible – though unlikely on past electoral form – that Scotland, having voted to remain in the UK, might even contribute *more* MPs to a victorious second-term administration.

If, however, Scotland votes 'yes', then the loss of fifty-nine MPs (but just one Tory) in 2016 could actually turn Commons arithmetic in David Cameron's favour by depriving Labour of around forty seats. There is one further consideration: Scotland voting 'yes' could well damage Cameron's electoral chances ahead of the aforementioned election, for he would appear as a 21st-century Lord North.

2. A MAJORITY LABOUR GOVERNMENT

The outcome of the referendum presents the biggest quandary to a potential majority Labour government. If there's a 'no' vote then it's straightforward enough, for Labour's majority will most likely include around forty Scottish MPs, ensuring that an Ed Miliband administration has a strong Scottish flavour, not least in the guise of shadow Foreign Secretary Douglas Alexander, who's also running the party's election campaign.

But if there's a 'yes' vote then a Labour government faces the prospect of losing its majority (assuming it isn't greater than the number of Labour MPs in Scotland) halfway through its term of office, i.e. when Scotland formally secedes from the UK – as the Scottish government plans – in March 2016. Although this would, at least in numerical terms, not be an issue before that point, the prospect of losing its majority would be unhelpful to say the least; indeed, it might even throw into doubt Ed Miliband's ability to form a government after the May 2015 election. In other words, its future, as Tom Clark concluded, 'would be immediately in doubt'.

3. ANOTHER CONSERVATIVE/LIBERAL DEMOCRAT COALITION

If, and there are lots of ifs, the election produces the right parliamentary arithmetic and both David Cameron and Nick Clegg are tempted to give coalition government another bash, then it will still be a minority in a Scottish electoral context. At present the coalition parties have twelve seats between them and, even assuming the Conservatives gain a couple and the Lib Dems – disproportionately represented in terms of Scottish seats – only lose a few, that figure seems unlikely to change by very much.

Assuming a 'no' vote in the referendum then the status quo pretty much applies, although the SNP will no doubt continue to argue that the UK government enjoys a limited mandate north of the border, but if the result's a 'yes' then the withdrawal of Scottish MPs from the House of Commons in March 2016 could, as under the scenario above (though less dramatically), rob a second Tory/Lib Dem coalition of its overall majority. If, however, its majority is big enough, then the loss of a dozen or so coalition MPs in Scotland would only weaken – though not fatally undermine – the administration.

4. CONSERVATIVE MINORITY GOVERNMENT

In a parliament where the Conservatives are the single biggest party then, assuming a poor Liberal Democrat result or its unwillingness to propagate coalition government, a Tory minority administration becomes the most likely option, although not one conducive to delivering either the smack of firm government or more radical Conservative policies.

In the context of the referendum, Scotland has little bearing on this scenario given the slim possibility of there being any more than a few Scottish Tory MPs as a result of the general election. Their withdrawal in March 2016 would obviously make a minority government even more of a minority, but equally it would strengthen the Conservative Party's numerical strength vis-à-vis the opposition, i.e. Labour. Indeed, the anticipation of that altered dynamic could even make forming a minority administration in May 2015 all the more attractive.

5. A LABOUR/LIBERAL DEMOCRAT COALITION

Given that many in both parties reckon this should have been the outcome of the 2010 general election (although it would still have lacked an overall majority), this is another possible outcome of the 2015 electoral contest. Such a coalition would enjoy majority support in Scotland, so in the event of a 'no' vote in the referendum an Ed Mili-band-led Labour/Lib Dem administration would have a great degree of political legitimacy – unlike the present Tory/Lib Dem coalition.

If, however, there's a 'yes' vote, something akin to scenario 2 (above) would apply, with a Labour/Lib Dem coalition government potentially robbed of its majority less than half way through its first parliamen-tary term. Again, this is only an issue if its majority is slim, as the withdrawal of Scottish MPs in 2016 – particularly given the Lib Dems' over-representation north of the border – would markedly diminish both governing parties' strength in the House of Commons.

6. A MINORITY LABOUR GOVERNMENT

If, as might prove to be the case if the Conservatives emerge as the largest single party in 2015, Labour forms a minority government, then again something similar to scenario 2 would apply, for even if a minority administration (with, say, just over 300 MPs) initially looked credible, it would appear much less so following a 'yes' vote and par-ticularly after 'independence day' on 24 March 2016. Assuming a 'no' vote, however, a minority Labour government's relative strength would be unaltered for the duration of the 2015–20 parliament. Indeed, given that Labour has 'won' in Scotland at every Westminster election since 1959, even a minority administration would enjoy a high level of political legitimacy north of the border.

7. A 'RAINBOW' COALITION

As Tom Clark argued in *The Guardian*, after a 'yes' vote 'all sorts of very temporary arrangements could become possible as part of wider negotiations in dissolving the union', although I think it's unlikely SNP MPs would form part of a rainbow coalition at Westminster even were that to be the result of September's referendum.

A similar anti-Tory coalition was, of course, mooted back in 2010, and indeed the SNP leader Alex Salmond was to the fore in talking up such a prospect, although senior Labour figures were equally to the fore in making it clear they'd countenance no such thing. If, however, the Conservatives are the biggest single party following the 2015 contest – even by just one seat – there's an obvious difficulty in depriving it of a chance to form an administration, particularly if that involved factoring in MPs from a part of the UK poised to secede.

If, meanwhile, there is a decisive 'no' vote in the independence referendum, it seems unlikely a (naturally) disappointed SNP would be in any mood to support a Labour government (it certainly wouldn't prop up the Conservatives, for obvious reasons), and while Welsh and Scottish Nationalists have a long-standing parliamentary 'pact' at Westminster, it's more theoretical than real, for the SNP and Plaid Cymru (not to mention the Northern Irish parties) differ on several points of domestic policy. In other words, even were a 'rainbow' coalition to be formed, it would be unlikely to last.

8. A RIGHT-WING COALITION GOVERNMENT

Finally if, as Nigel Farage has predicted, UKIP holds the balance of power following the next general election (as the Liberal Democrats did after 2010), then a coalition of the right is possible, although unlikely given the difficulty of a relatively new party winning under a first-past-the-post system. If necessary, DUP MPs might also end up sheltering under such an umbrella, although this would cause obvious tensions within Northern Ireland.

It would also cause problems north of the border, for all the component parties would be weak in a Scottish context, if they had any representation at all. Although UKIP managed to win a European Parliament seat in Scotland in the most recent elections, it would struggle to gain an MP there (even more so than in England), the DUP obviously doesn't contest elections in Scotland, and the Conservatives cannot hope to win any more than a few Scottish MPs at the next election. Even if there were a 'no' vote, such a scenario would enjoy virtually no legitimacy in Scotland, and if it occurred following a 'yes' vote, it would likely make independence negotiations easier rather than harder.

Obviously some of these eight general election scenarios are much more likely than others but the importance of the Scottish referendum, particularly in the event of a 'yes' vote, is a constant. If there's a 'no' vote then things will rub along much as before but if, although it appears unlikely at the time of writing, a majority of Scots agree with the independence proposition then in the context of the 2015 general election all is changed, to paraphrase W. B. Yeats on Ireland a century ago, changed utterly.

David Torrance is a political writer and author of The Battle for Britain.

The polls in the 2010–15 parliament

Anthony Wells

The biggest and most important shift in the opinion polls of this parliament came almost as soon as it began. The 2010 election was held in the shadow of Cleggmania and for a few days following the first of the leaders' debates Nick Clegg enjoyed record-breaking approval ratings. While the eventual level of Liberal Democrat election support fell short of the pollsters' predictions, the Liberal Democrats receiving 24 per cent of the vote now looks like echo from a different era. Six weeks after the press conference in the Downing Street rose garden, Liberal Democrat support in the polls had been pushed down into the mid-teens. By the end of 2010 they were hovering at around 10 per cent in the polls. The decision to enter into coalition shattered Liberal Democrat support and gave Labour an immediate bonus. It changed the mechanics of mid-term public opinion; it may yet change our party system completely. The story of the polls in the 2015 is both one of very traditional concerns – economic competence and leadership perceptions – and one of something very new, the collapse of the Liberal Democrats and the rise of UKIP.

THE CONSERVATIVES, CUTS AND THE OMNISHAMBLES

The dominant issue at the start of the parliament was naturally the economy and, while the impact of cuts, tax rises and falling living standards hurt the government, support for the government's strategy remained comparatively robust. Within six months, polls tended to find people thought the cuts were unfair, too deep, too fast and not good for the economy. However, they also consistently found that people thought they were necessary, and that they were more the fault of Labour than the coalition. Essentially the public didn't like the government's medicine and weren't sure it was doing any good ... but they saw no alternative but to keep on taking it.

In terms of voting intention, the Conservatives fared better than their coalition partners, enjoying a few months of honeymoon before starting to gradually drop in the polls. David Cameron even managed a brief poll boost from his European 'veto' in December 2011, but it was the 'Omnishambles' Budget of 2012 that really cut into their support. The 2012 Budget managed to bungle on two fronts – it both reinforced the Conservative Party's weaknesses and undermined their strengths. Firstly, George Osborne reduced the top rate of income tax from 50p to 45p. At the simplest level this was an unpopular decision – 61 per cent of people opposed the reduction. There are plenty of governments who've enacted unpopular Budget decisions and got away with them (indeed, one of the strengths of the Conservative Party is that the public perceive it as being far more ready to take 'tough and unpopular decisions'), the problem with the 45p tax rate was that it reinforced existing negative perceptions of the party. The Tories still labour under the public perception that they are the 'party of the rich', and are closer to rich people than ordinary working-class voters. The cut in the top-rate tax band risked reinforcing that, with 48 per cent of people thinking that the biggest gainers from the 2012 Budget were those who were already rich.

The 2012 Budget also risked undermining a key positive for the party, the perception of competence in running the government and economy. The Budget contained changes to tax allowances for pensioners that were dubbed the 'granny tax' and technical changes to VAT on hot food that became the 'pasty tax'. In response to media criticism the government flopped and floundered, David Cameron fluffed questions about when he'd last eaten a pasty, and it ended in an apparent reverse. For a month the government had given the image that they were faffing around about pasties rather than being a serious team making hard economic decisions. Between them, the perceptions of incompetence and favouring the rich resulted in a blow to Conservative poll ratings. The Conservatives dropped from the mid-thirties to around 32 per cent, their lead on the economy evaporated. David Cameron's own approval rating dropped from around minus five to around minus thirty. Throughout the rest of 2012 the Labour lead over the Conservatives averaged at ten points.

THE MILIBAND PARADOX

Labour's increase in support had largely been gifted to them by the rapid collapse of Liberal Democrat support and then by the Omnishambles Budget – they did not have to do much at all in terms of addressing the reasons Labour had been ejected in 2010, they hadn't yet launched popular policies and Ed Miliband's own personal ratings were mediocre. At the same time in 2012 that polls were giving Labour a solid ten-point lead, Ed Miliband had an approval rating of minus twenty-two. Polls since then have consistently showed public perceptions of Miliband as being a weak leader, ineffective and not up to the job of Prime Minister. David Cameron consistently led Ed Miliband on who would be the better PM.

This is not merely a case of it being easier for a politician to look like a credible Prime Minister once they are in the job. While that is undoubtedly true, previous successful Leaders of the Opposition have often had strong leads over the incumbent. As Leaders of the

Opposition, Tony Blair and David Cameron led John Major and Gordon Brown on questions of who would make the best Prime Minister. In opposition in 2008, 49 per cent of people thought that David Cameron looked like a Prime Minister in waiting, but an identical question asked about Ed Miliband in May 2014 found only 15 per cent agreed.

People often say that the Leader of the Opposition does, or does not, 'look like a Prime Minister in waiting'. Do you believe that at the moment David Cameron/Ed Miliband does or does not look like a Prime Minister in waiting?

	DAVID CAMERON – OCT 2008	ED MILIBAND – MAY 2014
Does	49	15
Does not	34	66
Don't know	17	19

(Source: YouGov (October 2008/May 2014))

However, despite Miliband's poor ratings, Labour's lead remained. It was a consistent hope amongst Tory supporters that Miliband's poor ratings would translate into reduced support for Labour. The reality was that while Miliband's poor ratings may well have damaged Labour (we cannot really tell how much larger their lead would have been with a more convincing leader) they did not prevent Labour leading in the polls. A substantial slice of Labour's supporters may have told pollsters that they didn't think Miliband looked like a plausible Prime Minister, or didn't know whether he'd be better than David Cameron … but it did not stop them saying they would vote Labour.

THE VOTELESS RECOVERY?

At the start of 2013, economic optimism began to creep back. In April 2013 just 14 per cent of people thought there were any signs of economic improvement, by July 2014 that had improved to 52 per cent. The increase in economic optimism brought with it increases in perceptions of the government's economic competence. Whether or not the economic recovery was an endorsement of the government's economic decisions, many of the public took them that way. From September 2013, polls started to show that people thought the government's cuts had been good for the economy, and the proportion of people saying that the government had handled the economy well rose from a nadir of 24 per cent in summer 2012 up to the mid-forties. The Conservative lead on which party people most trusted on the economy reasserted itself. Once again, the economy was a strong issue for the Tories.

Thinking about the current state of the economy, which of the following best reflects your view?

	THE ECONOMY IS STILL GETTING WORSE	ECONOMY STOPPED GETTING WORSE, BUT NO SIGNS OF RECOVERY	ECONOMY IN BAD WAY, BUT SIGNS OF RECOVERY	ECONOMY IMPROVING AND ON THE WAY TO RECOVERY	DON'T KNOW
2014					
July 28–29	14	26	34	18	8
April 13–14	16	29	36	11	8
March 13–14	14	32	38	11	6
2013					
December 5–6	22	29	36	7	7
August 22–23	22	36	32	5	6
August 8–9	25	34	30	5	5
April 23–24	43	38	13	1	4

The recovering economy also coincided with a drop in Labour's poll lead. From ten points in 2012 it had fallen to seven points by summer 2013, and four points by summer 2014. The mystery was that this was almost wholly at the expense of the Labour Party, whose support in the polls dropped from 42 per cent to 36 per cent; there was virtually no net increase in the Conservative Party's own support – they averaged 32.4 per cent in all the polls taken in 2012. In the first half of 2014 their average polling figure was 32.5 per cent.

Part of this was probably the nature of the recovery, wage increases remained lower than inflation and this was reflected in the polls: while polls showed people were increasingly optimistic about the economy as a whole, they remained pessimistic about their own personal finances, and still reported feeling worse off than they did a year ago. The recovery in GDP and jobs reported in the media did convince the public that the government were better placed to run the economy than Labour, but a lack of personal feel-good factor perhaps prevented it translating into increased support for the Conservatives.

THE PURPLE REVOLUTION

If Labour support had fallen by six points but the Conservatives were static, where had the support gone? In previous parliaments an unpopular government paired with a lacklustre opposition has normally resulted in increased support for the third party. The nascent SDP–Liberal Alliance soared in the polls in 1981 and 1982 when the Thatcher government struggled and had the doomed Michael Foot as her opponent; their descendants in the Liberal Democrats broke through when New Labour started to hit problems and had Iain Duncan Smith as their main alternative. As part of government the Liberal Democrats were not in any position to capitalise. James Goldsmith once said that when a man marries his mistress he creates a vacancy. By bringing the third party into government, the Conservatives did just that: created a new vacancy for a catch-all protest party, someone to benefit from the votes of those unhappy with both main parties – a vacancy that was ably filled by UKIP.

Of course, there was not a direct transfer of support directly from Labour to UKIP: they took support from all parties (meaning that the Conservatives probably did gain some support from the recovering economy, but saw any gains cancelled out by the growth of UKIP). UKIP support was once characterised as just disaffected right-wing Tories, but this is overly simplistic. Their biggest single chunk of support (typically around 45 per cent of their voters in polls) comes from people who voted Conservative in 2010, but the majority of their voters are not former Tories – they draw support from former Labour voters, former Liberal Democrats, former BNP voters and people who did not previously vote for anyone at all. They are not retired Colonel Blimps in the home counties: their support tends to be elderly but skewed heavily towards the working class, with their strongest clusters of support in rather rundown seaside towns. Neither is the natural assumption that their voters are driven by concern over the European Union directly true: while they are more interested in the issue than most other voters, even amongst UKIP supporters the majority do not consider Europe to be one of the most important issues facing the country. If there is a single issue that has driven UKIP support it has been immigration – 90 per cent or more of UKIP voters name it as one of the biggest issues facing the country. Their support is more than just that of an anti-immigration party, though: it reflects a protest against the government; disillusionment and cynicism with the whole political system and establishment; unhappiness with a metropolitan liberal Britain; and the anger of those who feel left behind or left out of modern Britain. UKIP voters are consistently less trusting of government and the establishment and consistently the most pessimistic about the economy, the country and their place in it.

UKIP's support grew steadily through the parliament, but the underlying drivers of disillusionment with the establishment and opposition to immigration were made reality by the publicity that growing success brought. Each round of success brought a flurry of media coverage and consequential increases in support. After the 2013 county council elections, the Rotherham by-election and the 2014 European elections they saw their support temporarily peak on the back of media coverage before settling again at a new and higher level. The defection of Douglas Carswell in August 2014 and the consequential by-election gave them the chance of another round of publicity to keep their momentum going into 2015.

THE FATE OF THE LIBERAL DEMOCRATS

As for the party that UKIP have eclipsed, polling for the Liberal Democrats has been dire for most of the parliament. The majority of people who voted for them at the last election no longer say they will – after their initial collapse their level of support has been steady at around or just under 10 per cent, and very little they have said or done has made any difference. In July 2012, YouGov found 67 per cent of people were no longer sure what they stood for, 54 per cent thought they had sold out their principles, and 58 per cent believed that they had broken their promises and betrayed their supporters.

	AGREE	DISAGREE	DON'T KNOW
I could never trust the Liberal Democrats, even if they left the coalition	53	28	19
I'm no longer sure what the Liberal Democrats stand for	67	17	16
The Liberal Democrats have sold out their principles by going into coalition with the Conservatives	54	29	17
The Liberal Democrats are propping up an extreme and right-wing government	38	39	21
The Liberal Democrats have broken their promises and betrayed their supporters	58	21	20
By entering coalition the Liberal Democrats have managed to get real Liberal policies put into action	29	53	18
The Liberal Democrats offer different and distinctive policies from the other two parties	27	51	22
The Liberal Democrats have made the coalition government more moderate and centrist	35	44	21
The Liberal Democrats did the responsible thing by entering government at a time of crisis	41	39	20
The Liberal Democrats have shown they are a sensible party of government	23	56	20

(Source: YouGov July 2012)

Barring a dramatic recovery in support over the last few months of the parliament, any vaguely uniform swing will cost the Liberal Democrats most of their parliamentary seats. Their hopes rest upon their incumbent MPs defying the trend. At each round of Lib Dem local election losses this parliament, their spokesmen have pointed to them doing better in areas where they have Members of Parliament, and in some cases this has indeed been true. Their councillors in places like Eastleigh have held firm, but in other places with Liberal Democrat MPs, like Manchester Withington, their councillors have been wiped out.

Polling of some of their marginal seats by Lord Ashcroft highlighted their strengths ... in some areas. A standard voting intention question in the eleven most vulnerable Liberal Democrat v. Conservative marginal seats he polled showed the Liberal Democrats losing every seat (and on a swing that would have lost them many more that Ashcroft did not poll), but when people were asked to consider the situation in their own local constituency and the candidates likely to stand there, his polls found the Liberal Democrats holding three of the seats and tied in one. There was no such reprieve in Liberal Democrat seats vulnerable to Labour – even when respondents were prompted to think of their own local constituency and candidates, Ashcroft's polls showed a crushing swing to Labour. On current polls the Liberal Democrats can expect to be annihilated at the general election in seats where their main opponent is Labour, but we will have to wait until election day to know to what extent their local MPs can resist the tide in seats where they are against the Conservatives.

THE ROUTE TO THE ELECTION

As we move towards the end of the parliament, the polls present an unusual paradox. The underlying figures that normally drive voting intention favour the Conservatives, and increasingly strongly so. The Conservatives have a solid lead as the party that would best handle the growing economy, and if some polls are starting to show the public worry more about immigration than the economy, the Tories lead Labour there too. David Cameron's lead over Ed Miliband on who would make the best Prime Minister seems solid, yet the Conservatives are far short of the sort of lead that would give them a majority.

The reason the Conservatives aren't doing better is perhaps partly the changes to the party system that coalition has wreaked – uniting left-leaning voters more strongly behind Labour while allowing the rise of a party that has disproportionately taken support from the Tories. Another factor may well be the failure of the Conservative Party's modernisation programme to really overcome some of their image problems – they are still seen as a party that is closest to the rich; they are still the party that is most likely to be seen as favouring one part of society rather than governing for everyone.

The final six months of the parliament will show which way that paradox resolves itself. Will voting intention move into line with the underlying figures, or vice versa? Will we see an election where a party wins despite the public neither trusting them on the economy nor thinking their leader would make a decent Prime Minister, or will the Conservative lead on both ultimately give them victory? How many individual Liberal Democrat MPs will resist the tide against them and will UKIP be able to sustain their momentum to the general election and break through the formidable barriers that first-past-the-post places before new parties? There is a temptation to dub every general election the hardest ever to call, but for once it could be true.

Anthony Wells is Editor of UK Polling Report.

When three becomes four: how the media will cover the 2015 general election

Theo Usherwood

Not since the Social Democratic Party roamed the earth thirty-odd years ago has a fourth political party had the popular support needed to decide the outcome of a general election. Now, with the rise and rise of UKIP, we have another major player. Whether you edit a newspaper, run a television news channel, or write for a blog, Nigel Farage's party will command your attention. He is an extrovert. His party is prone to making gaffes on an industrial scale. And the success or failure of Ed Miliband and David Cameron to insulate their parties from the threat posed by UKIP is likely to decide the outcome of the vote in early May 2015. Like him or loathe him, Nigel Farage and his party will dominate the media's coverage of the general election.

In practical terms, UKIP's enhanced status at this election will provide a logistical challenge. There will now be a fourth battle bus to follow from the likes of Southend West, Great Yarmouth and Thanet South. Having already spent a considerable amount of time at the Essex seaside in Clacton reporting on former Tory MP Douglas Carswell's bid to retake the seat as a UKIPcr, I am developing a keen eye for decaying Victorian piers and decrepit arcade halls. This general election will see me in one seaside town after the next, along with many colleagues, conspicuously dressed in our inexpensive suits, waiting for Nigel Farage to arrive and convince an ageing, disgruntled, white working-class population that only UKIP has the answer to the years of social deprivation and neglect suffered by their community.

Now critics will claim, as they have already done, that UKIP spends proportionately too much time in the media glare, given the party will win no more than half a dozen or so seats. However, the reason why Nigel Farage's party will be one, if not the biggest, story of this election is that the party will influence the results in up to 100 constituencies. As UKIP showed in the 2014 local council elections, it can take votes from Labour, as well as the Conservatives. The multi-million-pound question now is: which party will be hardest hit?

If Tony Blair made the 1997 election about 'education, education, education', Nigel Farage will make 2015 about 'immigration, immigration, immigration'. At LBC, where I am political editor, immigration is more important to the majority of our listeners than anything else. The polls show that across the UK, immigration is now the electorate's number one concern. Once a taboo subject, especially amongst left-wing newspapers and broadcasters, looking at and talking about where each of the parties stand on immigration will be unavoidable. For the Tories and Labour, the immigration debate poses a question they cannot answer without advocating the full-scale withdrawal of Britain from the EU. Instead, they would both like to spend more time contesting their respective records on the economy or the NHS in the hope they will divert the agenda away from this very awkward issue.

For political journalists, elections are about personalities more than anything else. This general election will be no different. What captures the imagination of our listeners at LBC, the readers of *The Sun*, or families up and down the country as they sit down to watch the ten o'clock news, is not another row over the latest unemployment figures. No. It is moments when the likes of pensioner and Labour stalwart Gillian Duffy tear into Gordon Brown on the streets of Rochdale at the last election, and the Prime Minister feigns understanding of her concerns before calling her a bigot as he's driven away – Sky's microphone still attached to his lapel. We want to tell the story of the most engaging and entertaining protagonists – those who bring our newspapers, our blogs and our output alive. When it comes to Nigel Farage, there will be a demand to see much more of him standing at a bar holding court, a pint and cigarette in hand. It's an irresistible image for the popular press and one which runs in direct contrast to Ed Miliband. Just as, in 2010, Gordon Brown came to be perceived in the media as a dour and grumpy Scotsman, the media is looking out for the next example of Ed Miliband being weird.

There have already been numerous examples of the brutal criticism awaiting the Labour leader as we count down to polling day. But perhaps the best example of what is in store is the now infamous photo call at New Covent Garden flower market in the run-up to the local elections in May 2014, where Miliband was pictured in various unflattering poses eating a bacon sandwich. I remember speaking to one of Westminster's most respected photographers a couple of years back and even then he said: 'Miliband hasn't got it. He doesn't hold himself like a Prime Minister.' That morning in May 2014, the Labour leader didn't just look weird; he looked scared as he cowered from the cameras. He certainly didn't look like a Prime Minister and his aides only made matters worse as they hopelessly harried around the hordes of photographers, trying and ultimately failing to spare Mr Miliband from yet another set of embarrassing pictures. Tory chief strategist Lynton Crosby will exploit this weakness for maximum effect. David Cameron continues to compare much more favourably to Ed Miliband in US-style approval ratings. Added to that, Mr Miliband's vulnerability plays into the Tories' hands when it comes to tackling the threat posed by UKIP. The Conservative message is simple: 'Vote UKIP, get Miliband.' This is the theme we can expect the right-wing press to run with throughout the election. I can already see one of those pictures of Miliband eating the bacon sandwich appearing on the front page of *The Sun* on election day under the headline 'Is this the man you want to run the country?'

Ed Miliband may take some comfort from the fact he will not be alone when it comes to facing personal media attacks at the election. Nigel Farage and his fellow UKIP parliamentary candidates will also fall under the spotlight. Below ground, both the Tory and Labour press operations will be looking to unearth any unflattering personal stories which may be lurking. I'm sure news editors are already developing further lines on Mr Farage's European parliamentary expenses and allegations of extra-marital affairs – with both stories having already featured prominently in the newspapers during 2014. Meanwhile, investigative journalists will be searching for any whiff of scandal. They'll be checking Twitter feeds and Facebook profiles – both good places to start for casual racist quips and embarrassing photos. And they'll also be looking for any dodgy business dealings, disgruntled ex-lovers and possibly the odd criminal conviction. Journalists will want to keep a keen ear trained on any candidates making outlandish comments which might undermine Mr Farage's insistence that UKIP is a serious alternative. Perhaps the best example in 2014 were claims by UKIP councillor David Silvester, who said severe flooding across the UK was God's retribution for the legalisation of gay marriage. For the main parties, these stories about UKIPers spouting nonsense are gold dust and arguably more effective than any evidence of racism within UKIP. They speak to their hope that the electorate will see UKIP as a bunch of nutters and the idea that while UKIP may be an excusable protest vote in the local and European elections, Farage's party is not a credible option at the general election.

For us in the media, Boris Johnson is catnip and for that reason the London Mayor is another personality who will feature heavily in the media's coverage over the coming months. First you have the colour – the blond mop and the deep bumbling voice. Add to that a bit of showbiz sparkle and the fact that he speaks his mind, and you have an editor's dream. Well, almost. The nugget that really makes the Boris story so absolutely fascinating – that means he will fill the newspapers and the airwaves all the way to polling day and beyond – is that he wants David Cameron's job. Until now the Prime Minister has never really had a proper rival. Unlike Tony Blair, he has enjoyed a productive relationship with his Chancellor (minus a few disagreements here and there), while other attempts by Cabinet members to install themselves as a possible replacement have amounted to nothing. But now we have Boris coming in from City Hall, a man with the popularity to steal the show, the ability to win it for the Tories and the driving ambition to make it to No. 10.

Questions will be asked as to whether the media's obsession with Boris is a little over the top. David Cameron repeatedly refers to the Mayor as the star striker he wants on the pitch scoring goals for the party. But just like any other star striker at a premiership club, Boris doesn't think the rules that apply to lesser mortals also apply to him. He has a habit of straying from the party line and, as a result, the media will spend an unhealthy amount of time scrutinising everything Boris says in the prism of whether it amounts to the London Mayor undermining Cameron's leadership of the Conservatives. It went unnoticed at the time, but moments before he announced his intention to stand during his speech to Bloomberg in August 2014, Boris referred to the Conservative policy to cut net migration to below 100,000 as 'absurd'. In the heat of an election campaign, such a stinging criticism would be seized upon and reported widely. Can David Cameron tame his star striker's maverick tendencies? I am not sure he can. But from speaking to a number of senior Tory MPs, it is clear they will take a very dim view if he undermines their war effort by going rogue. With any bid to take the reins at No. 10 relying heavily on Boris maintaining a strong parliamentary following, the watchful eye of senior backbenchers, many within the 1922 Committee, looks like the best chance Cameron has of keeping Boris on the pitch rather than being forced to banish him to train with the reserves.

When Sky's chief political correspondent Jon Craig wrote this chapter ahead of the 2010 general election, he rightly predicted that if there were televised leaders' debates, they would be key to how the media covered the campaigns. The debates on the BBC, Sky and ITV that materialised did exactly that and all three broadcasters ruled the roost when their turn came. A precedent was set and it looks as if there will be similar debates this time around. But in 2015, I doubt whether the debates will remain the preserve of the main broadcasters. Here at LBC we are looking to get in on the action. We have proved our pedigree. The EU leaders' debates between Nick Clegg and Nigel Farage, as well as countless phone-ins with leading politicians, demonstrate we can produce slick and professional content, not just for radio but for television and online as well. It is also worth noting another bid in the form of a joint venture between Google, the *Telegraph* and *The Guardian*. They have recently appointed the well-respected former Sky executive Chris Birkett to run the project, and an internet-only debate will be tempting for the main parties as there will be the lure of reaching a younger audience, who have historically been so difficult to attract to the ballot box.

While in 2010 we became obsessed with the prospect of televised leaders' debates, this time around the question will be one of who is invited to the party. Whilst perhaps the most salivating prospect is the series of three ninety-minute debates between the UKIP leader, Nick Clegg, David Cameron and Ed Miliband, I am not sure this idea was realistically ever on the table. But if there was ever a minuscule chance, it was extinguished when Farage dispatched the Deputy Prime Minister at the LBC debate on Europe in March 2014. Farage would relish a debate with the Prime Minister and Ed Miliband, who currently argue that as UKIP is not even represented in the House of Commons, it does not deserve a place in the debates. However, at the time of writing this is set to change, with former Tory Douglas Carswell looking increasingly likely to become UKIP's first MP in the Clacton by-election. From the noises being made at No. 10, perhaps the best chance of UKIP involvement will come if one of the debates also involves the Green leader, Natalie Bennett, whose party of course does have an MP in the Commons. The hope here is that Ms Bennett's inclusion dilutes the Farage effect and minimises any chance of him embarrassing Cameron or Miliband.

Up until this point, I have barely mentioned Nick Clegg and the Liberal Democrats and where they will fit into the media's election coverage. That's because they will become less and less important as we get closer to polling day. If there is one story we are interested in, it is how badly the Liberal Democrats will lose. Will the party face obliteration or will Nick Clegg and his team salvage enough votes to save the party from total humiliation? Lib Dem polling is stubbornly low and Lord Ashcroft recently predicted the party could lose seventeen of their fifty-five seats to Labour alone. If that happens, the arithmetic whereby they find themselves as a junior partner in a coalition government looks impossibly tight. This is not lost on many within the party and from talking to some of their special advisors in confidence, they tell me they have already started to put out the feelers for alternative work in the private sector.

Earlier, I touched on one of the defining moments of the 2010 general election when pensioner Gillian Duffy confronted Gordon Brown. Over the past four and a half years, that five-minute clip on YouTube has been viewed fewer than 80,000 times. By way of comparison, Nigel Farage's catastrophic performance during his interview with James O'Brien on LBC in May 2014 has already been watched 326,000 times. The power of Twitter and Facebook is that they allow us to share our best stories with a much wider audience in a matter of seconds. Journalists and the wider public now use social media much more than they did in 2010. There will undoubtedly be a Gillian Duffy moment in 2015. Someone will be lucky enough, or even skilful enough, to capture it in all its glory and they will post it on YouTube without a second thought. It will go viral. How many views will it get? Eight hundred thousand? Eight million? I don't know. But what I do know is that the Gillian Duffy moment of 2015 will be a far bigger news event.

The final word should go to the pollsters, who will tell us which way the wind is blowing on any given issue or following any given event. This election will see more polls on more issues, delivered at greater speed and subject to more in-depth scrutiny than ever before. We will know what the public think of a manifesto pledge or a humiliating gaffe within a matter of hours of either being made. We still do not have a front-runner and the impact of UKIP is far from clear. For that reason, every political journalist will obsess about what the pollsters have to say. We want to know who is up, who is down and ultimately who will win. Whilst the result is uncertain, I am sure we are in for a fascinating few months.

Theo Usherwood is Political Editor at LBC.

2015: The next YouTube/ Twitter/LinkedIn/WhatsApp platform election?

Jag Singh

It wouldn't require very much for an observer of British politics to argue that the role of digital technology and the web has grown at every general election, even if direct engagement by political parties sometimes appears pathetic and banal. We saw in 2010 how campaigns had begun learning to operate within an ecosystem that really wants to be entertained first, and informed second. In subsequent years, campaigns and their managers have become a lot more enthusiastic about the web and social media. A lot has changed since the last election, though, and six key trends look set to shape the next election cycle:

- Voters are increasingly using internet news sites (including social platforms like Twitter) for information. They are not just switching from traditional and print media outlets to the web – they now get this sea of information from a variety of platforms and channels. It's worth noting that the fastest growing segment of the population on the web includes older voters over sixty, and they're spending lots of time online.
- New platforms for social media have given rise to tools and

technologies that allow sophisticated campaigners to mine and extract information about voters and their preferences on a vast scale.

- Mobile apps and ecosystems have become so prevalent that a whole generation of young voters don't even use their desktop computers anymore. These young citizens can be observed oblivious to their surroundings, fixated to screens on their smartphones and tablets and 'phablets' (ridiculous-looking phones the size of mini-tablets).

- Large swathes of voters no longer publicly participate via open social networks and platforms, but instead are now more likely to engage via private platforms like WhatsApp and Snapchat.

- Political parties and their never-ending desire to engage with the public via leaflets and 'knocking on doors' has rendered meaningful two-way dialogue with voters over the internet practically non-existent. Campaigns tend to still only be very interested in the web for pushing out their message and for encouraging people to pass it along to their friends.

- The rise of pressure groups, like 38 Degrees and the TaxPayers' Alliance, who are far more capable of activating their support bases to focus on single-issue campaigns via the web, compared to the traditional political parties and party-affiliated campaign groups. When an entity like 38 Degrees has an email database roughly four times the size of the combined mailing lists of all the major political parties, something interesting is bound to develop out of it.

Many innovations in digital political campaigning are often traced back to the United States, though a comparison to Britain isn't necessarily an apples-to-apples one, given the fixed electoral cycles at all levels of government. There's also the small matter of the eye-watering sums of money donated to (and subsequently spent by) candidates in the US, a stark contrast to the spending limits in place in Britain.

There are two key differences between US and British digital campaigns, and some of this can be attributed to the budget constraints faced by British campaigners. First, in America, the digital team essentially acts as the pillar for an entire campaign team, with technology often baked into the DNA of the campaign's organisation. These teams never operate in isolation from the campaign's various structures, assisting the press, fundraising, field, legal and even research departments. Digital and technology teams are often larger in the US, too, as we discovered in the 2012 presidential campaign – the Obama and Romney teams had an average head count of more than 200 people. Between 2010 and 2014, the major UK political parties' digital teams comprised of fewer than ten staff for each party, and were often siloed within the campaign.

The second key distinction between US and British campaigns remains the attitude of campaign managers toward digital advocacy and tools. An exciting characteristic of the web is the prospect it opens to engage in direct conversation with voters. Technology and digital tools purpose-built for the political process have the potential to transform campaigning into something far more vibrant, and much more analogous to real dialogue, than it was ever before. This dialogue in US campaigns is extended both internally and externally, with technology often radically changing the underlying processes. For the 2012 election cycle, the Obama campaign was lauded in its use of online and mobile technology to support its much-praised 'ground war' efforts. They even launched a dedicated 'travel planner' app for Democratic campaign staff, volunteers and supporters, to help them mobilise and travel across the country, and to easily arrange for accommodation and ride-sharing amongst campaign supporters. Many candidates in the local and state elections used technology and the web to run their campaigns in a more efficient and cost-effective way, but most importantly also tracked volunteers' efforts so as to be able to reward them, and fed all this information back to centralised databases belonging to parties or political action committees (PACs). In Britain, we have seen a degree of coordination between the unions and the Labour Party, and even between the Conservatives and their affiliated pressure groups, for similar efforts, but the degree of sophistication doesn't even come close to matching the way things are done in the US, or even in the commercial sector in the UK for that matter.

Campaigns around the world tend to use the web and digital technology in one of two contexts: messaging or mobilising. The mobilising element involves everything from recruiting and forming a connection with volunteers, donors and voters, to moving them to perform specific actions (online or offline), including donating, phone-banking, canvassing and even simply turning out to vote. The messaging aspect revolves around getting the campaign's key themes out to the right audiences, and is usually either targeted at a broad audience such as all voters in a constituency, or a narrow one such as journalists and bloggers, ethnic minorities, women under thirty, union members, among others. Social media has now begun to play a key role, and many electioneering veterans often point to the consensus that while social media may not win an election campaign, it certainly can keep them from losing.

British campaigns tend to just use their web initiatives mainly as a method of pushing messages out, and there is an often noticeable lack of direct engagement with voters. The top campaign groups rarely, if ever, reply to, comment on, or 'retweet' content to share that didn't originate from within the campaign. This is a marked difference from the offline landscape, where community gatherings and speech introductions often utilise external voices to advocate on behalf of a campaign.

Campaigns in the UK also very clearly attempt to try to control their messaging in ways that bypass the filters of traditional media, but yet still heavily rely on those same media outlets as channels of distribution or even validation. There is a long way to go before they will have eliminated a role for the media. Most campaign websites also still act as the central core of all digital political communication. Even when a voter's journey starts on a campaign's social network page, they frequently find themselves back on the main site, as the primary 'call to action' – a digital-orientated response – such as watching a video, or joining a list, or even donating money, will lead them back at every opportunity. Campaigns in Britain have become a lot better at tracking users' activity and behaviour as we weave in and out of the web, and several roles at the party headquarters are now specifically focused on shoring up their analytics and data-tracking capabilities. Campaign groups are learning to adapt to this environment, too, where messages can be easily tested on small segments of supporters, via the web or email, before being sent out into the wild.

British campaigns and parties have now begun thinking about integrating lots of other data points about people's behavioural and purchasing habits. This information spans everything from the kinds of policy positions they may have publicly supported and the issues they may be passionate about on their private social media channels, to the types of products they buy, to even the job types of their friends and acquaintances on professional social networks like LinkedIn. The main issue at hand is that less than 5 per cent of social network users in the UK have actually directly connected with or befriended political campaigns or candidates on the social web, and while this may not be an insignificant number of people, as a percentage it remains a tiny proportion of the voting population. The parties are acutely aware of this, and frequently aim their content at minority and special interest groups, in the hopes of reaching out to a wider audience. The Conservatives, for instance, have been bombarding different ethnic minority groups on Facebook with messaging revolving around causes or interests aligned with their community, and have seen positive results in their trials. With the right amount of high-quality data, we could easily see our campaigns using advanced statistical modelling techniques to determine how receptive a voter may be to changing their mind based on a campaign's specific pleas.

On a positive note, the campaigners' web and social media strategies are now also increasingly professionalised (or formulaic, depending on how you look at it), and campaign communications gurus are

more effectively integrating social media into the other communications channels within campaigns. There have been several instances
already in the UK of campaigns capturing their opponent's slip-up on
camera and posting it to YouTube, and then following through with
email-blasts comprising various different subject lines and body text
sent out to groups of supporters, with the entire process all taking
place within the space of half an hour. There remains no substitute
however for a highly salient political issue, and we often see limited
take-up of some of the political parties' efforts as a result. Web-chats
and teleconferencing were innovations in the previous election cycle
that became a popular high-tech option for communicating 'personally' with potentially large but targeted groups of voters, but the data
returned after these initiatives were launched showed minimal if not
negative returns on investment.

Most campaigning organisations have now learned to prioritise their
efforts on delivering the right message on the right platform, and the
beauty of web technology is that it allows for actions to be tracked
quite easily, and for the results to be analysed and then understood in
a meaningful way. The results from an email blast aimed at a group of
supporters can be easily compared to a Twitter alert also aimed at the
same group, with the results then influencing the medium to communicate with the wider supporter base. Campaigners in the 'bubble'
however, often forget that they are competing for attention on the web
with porn, cute animal videos, and social interactions between genuine friends and acquaintances, among other things.

Ardent political supporters and volunteers will find themselves in
the euphoric general election 'short campaign' period without apps,
dedicated to assisting with canvassing their neighbours or knocking
on doors within a constituency. Volunteers who do bother to show up
are often still just handed a stack of leaflets and a slip of paper showing
a list of addresses to deliver those leaflets, whereas in the US, activists
and supporters are empowered to use tools that harness all the latest technology and digital knowledge, and tools like canvassing apps

for campaign volunteers offer opportunities to post feedback from the doorstep directly into the campaign headquarters' machinery. Smartphone apps generally still play a relatively minor role in directly connecting voters to campaigns, though, on both sides of the Atlantic.

Social media outreach is commonly aimed at those who are already politically inclined, and British campaigns often forget about the vast majority of users who don't already engage with them on a day-to-day basis. Campaigns and candidates have generally attempted to focus mainly on promoting themselves and their campaign activities, or attacking their opponents by attempting to amplify missteps or gaffes into full-blown memes. Due to the lack of investment over the long term, and in the absence of their own distribution channels, campaigns are forced to give up control of these messages. While they may not have to rely on traditional media outlets to pass them out, some of the 'viral' loops have rapidly fizzled out or taken on a new direction when pushed out into the open web.

In the run-up to the 2010 general election, campaigns became aware that an online army of supporters that isn't limited to any one single geographical location, or a constituency, could often be mobilised as a powerful source of funds and encouragement for areas in other parts of the country. There was a concerted effort to utilise video-based adverts on the web to engage with campaign supporters, though these were almost exclusively aimed at committed party members to encourage a large turnout.

For the 2015 election, Britons can also expect to see targeted ads online aimed at voters. These ads will be delivered across the web by impressive algorithms that within a fraction of a second will have factored in variables including the location of the user and their ward/constituency, their 'persuadability scores' and their past anonymised behavioural data from the campaign's internal data stores.

There are likely to be ads aimed at those who watch the TV debates, and separate sets of ads aimed at those who may have missed the debates, and there will be even be different content within Labour ads aimed at those likely to support the Liberal Democrats at the election. Third-party pressure groups will have the capability to raise large sums of money for specific slates of candidates, having tested numerous subject lines by sending fundraising emails to small groups of supporters and then sending out larger email blasts to their membership lists, and will find ways to better engage with the people who are already part of their team.

Candidates are already trialling technology that allows highly customised and personalised adverts in the local newspaper websites, combined with email lists that offer content highly relevant to their constituents, and this will almost certainly be ramped up in the run-up to the election. Micro-targeting technology affords campaigns the ability to show customised messages to specific types of voters, and is similar to the techniques commercial advertisers use on the web to deliver car rental ads to people who had purchased airline tickets to foreign destinations, the assumption being that once the user had bought a ticket, they'd also be likely to rent a car at their destination. Re-targeting, on the other hand, offers users who may have already visited a page on a campaign site, but failed to fully register their support, to be tracked across the web and served adverts or content on other sites to entice them back to the main page and to complete the process. Both these technologies are currently being trialled by UKIP and the Conservatives on a national level, and it's only a matter of time before local candidates deploy them too.

My verdict for the larger campaigns remains that they've got the basics right, and that they'll just need to incrementally expand their operations to empower the wider community, and not just focus on undecided voters on the web. The challenge for campaigns and candidates will be to find and keep support online, amidst a landscape of decreasing political participation and a loss of trust in the overall political process.

Jag Singh is a co-founder of online political advertising agency MessageSpace.

TV debates: round two?

Joey Jones

DEBATES ARE A GOOD THING

Well I would say that, wouldn't I? I work for Sky News, whose campaigning helped tip the balance to make debates happen last time around. We always felt debates were the best way to allow voters to make an informed decision about the options confronting them, but it needed a bit of a nudge, (specifically the threat of an empty chair in place of any reluctant candidate) to ensure all three party leaders came onside.

But don't take my word for it. 'I think we will have them in every election in the future and I think that it is a really good thing for our democracy,' said a certain David Cameron in 2010. They 'help enable people to make better-informed choices when they cast their votes', according to Ed Miliband. As for Nick Clegg, no surprise: 'The innovation of televised leaders' debates was a good one. I think millions of people found it a good opportunity to see how the party leaders measured up against each other and I think we should repeat them.'

Short of obliging voters to read the parties' election manifestos, sift through those myriad leaflets landing on their doormats or compare and contrast party election broadcasts it is hard to conceive of another way of allowing the political parties to present their cases for government in their own words direct to the electorate. (And there is no perceptible popular clamour for the above proposals.) It is the element of competition, of challenge and counter-challenge that attracts millions of people who are not otherwise greatly politically engaged but may well cast a vote. Above all, it is the element of danger.

DEBATES ARE DANGEROUS

There is one ever-present fear for protagonists. The knockout blow. It is rare, but never out of the question; never to be discounted. Every politician preparing to debate has seen Lloyd Bentsen's killer put-down to vice-presidential challenger Dan Quayle in 1988 – 'Senator, you're no Jack Kennedy' – and every politician has sleepless nights about being similarly floored. The fear infects even the most seasoned performers – think back to David Cameron's frozen, faux-Churchillian visage as the lights came up on the first debate of 2010, his evident nervousness that helped nothing-to-lose Nick Clegg seize the advantage. And let's not kid ourselves – it is that faint chance that a senior politician might find themselves cruelly and suddenly undone that is a key factor in persuading us to watch, and keeping us watching even once they have started reciting page 57 clause 3 of the party constitution.

Danger is the main reason debates did not happen in this country before 2010. Yes, politicians have on occasion chosen to advance arguments to the effect that TV debates are redundant in a country that rejoices in the weekly triumph of light over heat that is Prime Minister's Questions. But ultimately it is a ruthless cost–benefit analysis that has lain behind their reluctance to debate in the past. For a surefire winner (see Tony Blair circa 1997), there is almost only downside. The short-term damage of being labelled frit is massively outweighed by the benefit of avoiding a confrontation where one might throw away the hard-won gains of years of slog with a momentary indiscretion or a renegade bead of sweat.

DEBATES MAKE POLICIES, AND THEY BREAK POLICIES

We are still living with some of the consequences of the 2010 debates in a way that few of us would have predicted at the time. This is particularly clear cut on the issue of universal pensioner benefits. During the Sky News debate, David Cameron looked straight down the barrel of the camera and said: 'I'd like to take this opportunity to say very clearly to any pensioner in the audience, anyone listening at home, that we will keep the free television licence, we'll keep the pension credit, we'll keep the winter fuel allowance, we'll keep the free bus pass – those leaflets you've been getting from Labour are pure and simple lies.'

There are many within the government, and even at the top levels of the Cabinet who now wish the Prime Minister had not made that pledge in that forum. Iain Duncan Smith does not believe wealthy pensioners should still enjoy universal benefits; the Chancellor probably agrees and the Lib Dems have consistently said they must be axed. But the nature of the pledge – eyeball to eyeball with the electorate, as it were – made it instantly irreversible. David Cameron saw what happened to Nick Clegg when he broke his word on tuition fees, and he was not going there. It has meant that every year when the Budget or autumn statement horse-trading has come around, this one area has been strictly off limits.

Debates also brought the politicians to book on what (for them) was the uncomfortable issue of immigration. It is right to pinpoint Gordon Brown's 'Mrs Duffy' remarks as the moment Labour policy on immigration imploded. But even by that point immigration had become central to the debates. The Liberal Democrat policy to offer an amnesty to some illegal immigrants (while insisting it was not an amnesty at all), was progressively unravelling from Debate One, and threw the party into a complete tailspin by the final week of the campaign. Looking back on the 2010 debates from a position where immigration is the forefront of mainstream politicians' preoccupations, we can see the debates (during each of which immigration was raised), exposed a Westminster class that had not yet grasped the anger of the electorate on the issue.

NOVELTY GOES DOWN WELL

In particular, an outsider status is worth prizing. In 2010 it worked for Nick Clegg, who (favoured by the opportunity to kick off the first debate) was able to make his pitch that 'there is an alternative' to the 'two old parties'. The boot was on the other foot for the Liberal Democrat leader when he took on Nigel Farage in the run-up to the 2014 European elections. With the UKIP leader in his familiar role as the anti-politician, Clegg looked the face of the establishment and was correspondingly disadvantaged. On both these occasions, the outsider was also, relatively speaking, the newcomer. Clegg in 2010 and Farage in 2014 were less known than their competitors, and better able to come across as fresh.

If we assume debates in 2015 may have a similar format to the previous election, it is hard to see how any of the party leaders could convincingly project themselves as an outsider. Ed Miliband, whose political thesis is based on the principle of a rupture with a Thatcher–Blair consensus, might have a go, but ultimately any viewer is more likely to be struck by the similarities between the three men. Where Ed Miliband might have a slight edge is in the novelty stakes (though we are talking small margins here). Conventional wisdom about the Labour leader – the *Wallace and Gromit*, geeky caricature that burdens him – might actually be a bit of a gift. It is just the sort of thing an experienced politician should relish the chance to confound.

In a three-way format, therefore, the outsider mantle would be taken up by Alex Salmond and Nigel Farage, who will both cry foul and bemoan an establishment stitch-up. The Scottish First Minister is an old hand at this, and there is no evidence it did him any harm at all in 2010. The danger for the Westminster parties is that locking UKIP out might give their anti-establishment bandwagon rocket-boosters.

A purple bandwagon with rocket-boosters! The stuff of mainstream politicians' nightmares.

A final thought. Some of the techniques that seemed new and fresh last time around risk coming across as laboured and stale in this election. In 2010, Nick Clegg was hailed a genius because he remembered questioners' names and looked at the TV cameras when he spoke. But we are fickle beasts, and there is every chance that this time round a politician attempting to replicate Clegg's skills (quite possibly the Liberal Democrat leader himself) will be criticised as bland and inauthentic. There is a bit of a vogue for shouty politicians right now – think sweaty Farage or 'wildman' Alistair Darling in the first Scottish debate.

2015: CAMERON'S CALL

At the time of writing, there is no certainty debates will happen in the run-up to the 2015 vote. My best guess is that this will remain true at the time of publication, and much of this is because of David Cameron and the Conservatives. The Lib Dems are on board, and Labour's enthusiasm to debate seems wholehearted and genuine. The Tories, however, are not willing to commit.

Part of this goes back to the old dynamic that if you are winning you have more to lose. Not the Conservatives as a party (though the polls may shift), but David Cameron as an individual. He has outpolled his two main rivals right through the parliament and there is no reason to believe that will change. You might think that if the Tories view their leader as a trump card, then they should exploit his strength and drag the party up in his wake. But that was the logic in 2010, and it did not work. Cameron himself was chastened by his inability to impose himself on the debate format, and is correspondingly wary of exposing himself unless he can be more confident of a clear-cut win.

And so Conservatives have increasingly talked up the idea of a head-to-head debate with Ed Miliband. Taking the pesky Lib Dem leader out of the equation makes the dynamic more predictable. 2014 has been a year of head-to-head debates – Clegg/Farage; Darling/Salmond. It has also been a year during which David Cameron has more consistently bettered the Labour leader during Prime Minister's Questions than before. You can see what he might be thinking.

IS THERE A BETTER ALTERNATIVE?

At an on-the-record lunch with Westminster's press corps in late 2012, David Cameron reflected on the shortcomings of the TV debates that had taken place two years earlier. While insisting he remained in favour of the principle of debates, he complained, 'They did take all the life out of the campaign.'

He explained how the debate bubble denied him the cut and thrust of campaigning. 'I like being out there,' he said. 'I like the public meetings, the awkward moments, the difficulties.' This, of course, is complete humbug. While David Cameron's media team are much more adept than their political rivals at giving an impression of spontaneity, his appearances are always meticulously planned and executed. 'Awkward moments', as the Prime Minister puts it, create the same or greater level of panic and dismay in the Cameron camp as with other parties.

Far from a freewheeling, improvised, devil take the hindmost plunge into the bosom of the British electorate, the Cameron view of 'keeping it real' would be (you guessed it) more photo calls, more polite 'Cameron Direct' meetings, fewer journalists on his slimmed-down battle bus. It is an option, and it would undoubtedly play to David Cameron's strengths, but no one should imagine it would be a more democratic option than leaders' debates.

The other possibility is a return to the old favourite of early morning press conferences during which the parties set out their policy du jour to assembled journalists and attempt to dismantle those of their rivals. Again, it could happen, but you know who did most to do away with the system in 2010? David Cameron. Having hired the auditorium in the basement of Millbank Tower and staged an initial press conference with Michael Caine no less, the Conservatives decided they did not fancy such daily events. And once one party decides not to play, there is not much the others can do to make a game of it. Why might this system return nevertheless? Steve Hilton is in America, and the Tories believe their policy/rebuttal team has the firepower to systematically take Labour apart.

David Cameron and his advisors will also weigh up the undoubted damage to his reputation he would suffer by backing away from debates having championed them in the past. We know he does not like his integrity to be questioned. And the Tories will have in the back of their minds the knowledge that if the Prime Minister ducks the challenge, the potent 'empty chair' threat of old could be revived. I might even don my 'Sky News Chicken' suit and harass him on the campaign trail. David Cameron has a big decision to make. And we are all waiting for him.

Joey Jones is Deputy Political Editor of Sky News.

Substance over style: predicting the 2015 manifestos

Nel McDonald

Faced with increasing criticism against his personal leadership, Ed Miliband launched the Labour Party's summer campaign by telling us that 'ideas are the most underrated commodity in politics'. His speech lamented the rising importance of photo ops and lampooned the increasing importance of the artificial, the trivial and the super-ficial in politics. He admitted that he could not compete with David Cameron's slick media persona and promised an election campaign that focused on substance rather than style.

Praising your opponent's natural leadership skills and comparing oneself to Wallace from *Wallace and Gromit* is perhaps an unconventional way to launch an election campaign, however, Miliband's speech seems crafted to counter the oft-repeated tenet that policies no longer matter in politics. The intellectual clashes of the '70s and '80s are long forgotten and the short attention spans of the Buzzfeed generation instead devour only pithy sound bites and listicles. As soon as the party manifestos are published, so too will the editorials lamenting their inconsequentiality.

And yet the publishing of manifestos remains a key part of the election cycle, providing fuel for endless debate in the media. With many political pundits predicting another hung parliament, manifesto

policies become bargaining chips to be swapped, discarded and vocif-
erously defended during negotiations. Whether or not you believe that
manifestos play a key part in the decision-making processes of the
average voter, it is undeniable that the contents of each party's manifesto will play a key part in any future coalition negotiations and,
ultimately, the political landscape for the next five years.

In order to predict the contents of each party's manifesto, it is
first necessary to look at the political environment that has shaped
them. Britain is drastically different today than it was in 2010. The last
election came at the end of thirteen years of consecutive Labour governments and in the middle of a global economic crisis. Faced with
a financial calamity not seen in living memory, the manifestos were
filled with promises to clean up the City and bring the banks into
line. Now we are experiencing economic recovery (however modest), punishing the bankers is no longer rhetoric that resonates with
the electorate. Instead, the discourse has moved towards the cost of
living and how the improved economy translates into real improvements in people's everyday lives.

The Labour Party has been emphatically driving this discourse on
the cost of living, arguing that improvements to the economy have
benefitted a select few and not the majority of people. Labour's position may be justified: according to YouGov figures published in April,
84 per cent of respondents believed that most people's incomes have
not kept pace with rising prices.

To counter the rising cost of living, Labour has mooted a bevy of
policies. Labour seeks to strengthen the national minimum wage,
promote the adoption of a living wage, tackle the abuse of zero-hour
contracts, reintroduce the 50p top tax rate for those earning over
£150,000, repeal the bedroom tax, extend free childcare for three-
and four-year-olds, and tackle rising energy bills by freezing prices
through to 2017.

The Conservatives, however, are strongly denying Labour's accusations that they are unsympathetic to those feeling squeezed.

March's Budget sought to directly address the cost of living by offering enhanced support for childcare and announcing another £500 increase in the income tax personal allowance. We can expect further measures relating to the cost of living to feature in the Conservatives' manifesto, including a freeze in fuel duty.

In addition to the extensive debate on the cost of living, healthcare and education seem to be dominating the policy discussions so far.

The NHS is currently a policy area favoured primarily by Labour and the Lib Dems. A manifesto platform that rests on NHS reform may make sense given that a number of opinion polls indicate that there is strong public support for the NHS. According to a poll carried out for *The Independent*, nearly 60 per cent of people would be willing to pay higher taxes to maintain current services. Similarly, a survey for the *Health Service Journal* shows that almost 90 per cent of people agree that as the economy improves, so too should NHS funding increase.

Labour has been attacking the coalition's health reforms throughout the last term, often criticising the coalition for contracting NHS services to private providers under what Labour has termed the privatisation of the NHS. To counter this, Labour will repeal the Health and Social Care Act 2012. In addition, Labour seeks to integrate health and social care services into a system of 'whole-person care'. This will bring together physical, mental and social care into a more holistic approach to healthcare.

Both Labour and the Lib Dems have promised commitments to improving mental health services. Nick Clegg announced in August that the Lib Dem manifesto will include a pledge to establish a mental health research fund that aims to bring medical understanding of mental health to the same level as physical health and support the development of new treatments. Labour plans on rewriting the NHS constitution (introduced by the coalition) to create a new right to psychological therapies – just as people currently have a right to drugs and medical treatments.

It has been rumoured that both the Lib Dems and Labour are considering hypothecating taxes to boost NHS funding. This idea of earmarking taxes for the NHS was suggested by former Labour minister, Frank Field, earlier in the year and also featured in the Lib Dem's Social Market Foundation report, written by former coalition Health Minister Paul Burstow.

Another key policy area that has attracted significant media attention recently is education. The Conservatives' education reform is perhaps the most well-known policy from their 2010 manifesto and its implementation has been controversial. The government's introduction of Swedish-style free schools has been marred by numerous high-profile scandals.

Michael Gove's ousting from the Cabinet in the July reshuffle has been interpreted by some as an attempt by the Tories to cleanse themselves of their toxic relations with the teaching profession. However, Nicky Morgan has stated that she intends to continue with Gove's overall reform plan and we can expect the 2015 manifesto pledges to largely resemble those of 2010 with regard to education.

Education is one of the areas where coalition tensions have been particularly strong; animosity between Nick Clegg and Michael Gove is well known. A key Lib Dem pledge for the 2015 election will be that all free schools and academies must adhere to the national curriculum and employ staff either already in possession of a teaching qualification or currently working towards a qualification. This could be interpreted as an attempt from the Lib Dems to distance themselves somewhat from their coalition partners.

Another key Lib Dem manifesto commitment is to triple the early-years pupil premium throughout the duration of the next parliament. The early-years pupil premium is currently worth £300 a year for three- and four-year-olds in nursery from disadvantaged backgrounds. The proposed policy would take its value up to £1,000 per child by 2020 and is expected to benefit more than 170,000 children. The pupil premium has been a priority for the Lib Dems since 2010 and this policy area may therefore become a key element in coalition negotiations in the case of another hung parliament.

Labour has announced that no new free schools will be opened under a Labour government although existing ones will be allowed to continue. Other education commitments have focused on apprenticeships and vocational learning. Labour want to introduce a 'Technical Baccalaureate', which would combine vocational qualifications, work experience, and English and maths skills. Labour also intends on building a new post-eighteen apprenticeship and vocational education system.

Perhaps surprising given the recent rise in UKIP's prominence is the lack of discussion regarding Britain's place in the EU. While it is perhaps just a matter of time until more attention is devoted towards European issues, it is certainly the case that recent global crises have complicated the Europe issue. Cameron has never attempted to hide his disdain for the EU and has been happy to grandstand for the Eurosceptics back home while at European summits, often at the expense of his relationships with other EU leaders. But people have been clamouring for action over recent international conflicts, and joint action and solidarity, not grandstanding, is what is required in order to halt ongoing crises. It will be interesting to see how growing global instability, and an increasingly cautious US, will affect Britain's relationship with the EU and other international organisations.

Of course, while it is impossible to predict the content of the manifestos with absolute certainty, what is certain is that this election will be unique due to the rise of UKIP. Earlier in the year, the assumption was that UKIP would win the European Parliament elections but then suffer a sharp drop in support. Similar drops had occurred after the 2004 and 2009 European elections and the pattern was expected (or perhaps hoped) to repeat itself in 2014. But instead UKIP's numbers have held steady and the three main parties are facing the prospect of entering the election season with a fourth dimension at play.

Why has UKIP's support persisted despite expectations to the contrary? There are several possible reasons: surveys show that UKIP voters have become more loyal; the party has not imploded from within as has been the case in the past; and the party has, for the first time, set very clear and realistic goals for the 2015 election. Unlike the 2010 election, when Lord Pearson's stated aim was only to 'influence' the outcome, Farage has announced that for 2015, UKIP intends on winning specific seats. UKIP is therefore running a heavily targeted campaign, focusing on twelve seats where it has a strong presence in local councils and has received a high popular vote in previous elections.

The final reason for UKIP's maintained numbers is that the party is, for the first time, articulating policies in a wide range of areas. Euroscepticism is not enough to maintain continual electoral support and now a genuine attempt is being made to broaden the message.

Tim Aker, UKIP MEP for Eastern Counties, is the man tasked with drafting the UKIP manifesto and while the party has thus far kept relatively quiet about what to expect in the run-up to party conference at the end of September, Aker has said that he's writing a 'blue-collar platform'. Of the policies that have been announced, some of them, such as opposition to the bedroom tax and no tax on the minimum wage, seem orchestrated to undermine Labour support. In fact, UKIP has been demonstrating a clear strategy to get Labour; their annual conference overlaps with Labour's and is being held in Doncaster, practically in the lap of Ed Miliband's seat.

However, nine of the twelve seats earmarked by Farage as key UKIP battlegrounds are currently Tory-held. Add to that the recent defection of a Tory MP and it could be argued that the Conservatives should be equally wary.

Other policies floated by UKIP include substantial cuts to foreign aid, a cut in the size of Whitehall departments, a cut in the top tax rate, and the abolition of the Climate Change Act. It is likely that UKIP's manifesto will end up resembling a smorgasbord of policies from both the left and right. These policies seem designed less to appeal to a specific section on the political spectrum and more to appeal to voters who feel disenchanted with the mainstream parties, left behind by modern politics, and alienated from a political elite who are seemingly determined to give money to foreigners rather than struggling, native, low-skilled workers. While the three main parties have been eagerly announcing numerous policy initiatives, particularly Labour as part of their intense summer offensive, UKIP's policy roster is currently a bit sparse and it will be interesting to see what is included in their final manifesto.

This chapter has focused on policy areas that we know will be important in the manifestos, either because they have been explicitly announced or because they have been key areas for each party over the last five years. I would like to end this chapter with a wildcard addition to these core concerns: public transport. Transport policy is rarely the centrepiece of party policy and while it is unlikely that the election will be won or lost on public transport concerns, the increasingly controversial annual rail fare rises and the immense public outpouring experienced each time shows that transport policy is becoming an increasingly important issue for voters.

As previously stated, Labour is leaning heavily on the cost of living as a key election theme and the rising cost of transport is seen as a central part of that. Labour is promising to cap fares on every route, abolish the 'flex' arrangement whereby train operators can increase particular fares by up to 2 per cent more than the standard formula, and protect and promote provincial bus routes. However, Labour is not the only party that appreciates the importance of affordable public transport. The coalition is not insensitive to the fact that hundreds of thousands of commuters use the trains every day, and last year George Osborne made a last-minute announcement that reduced the permitted rise in rail fares from that which was originally planned by the rail companies. Labour may therefore not be alone in including a reduction in transport costs as a manifesto pledge.

It is unlikely that UKIP's 2010 manifesto pledge to 'encourage a return to the glamour, grace and style of the railway companies of the past' will return for 2015.

Nel McDonald is a blogger and writer.

Guide to political betting

Adam Smith & Stephanie Anderson

UNDER THE BONNET OF POLITICAL BETTING

Betting on elections is as old as the hills. Maybe even older. There are records of wagers placed on the outcome of papal elections dating back to the sixteenth century. The characteristic features of elections lend themselves well to betting – competitive runners, skills on display, old hands versus young pretenders, and a race to the finish to find the victor. Easy bedfellows, you might say.

For the most popular political markets and the biggest political punts, you need look no further than the major, set-piece political events. For Paddy Power historically, that means UK general elections, Irish general elections and US presidential races. The biggest political market in terms of stakes this year will be the Scottish independence referendum.

That said, political betting has never been in the same league as football or horse racing (although there's arguably as much horseshit, dodgy manes and long faces), but it isn't small fry. And it's growing...

Top-grade events like general elections and presidential contests are multi-million-pound markets. It's estimated that the 2015 UK general election will generate an industry turnover of around £30 million.

HOW ARE POLITICAL MARKETS CREATED?

Putting together markets for the major events is relatively straightforward as a vast amount of data exists. Opinion polls, historical voting patterns, constituency information and expert punditry are analysed to calculate what the possible outcomes are, and how likely each is to occur. The general rule in odds compilation is that the more data there is available, the greater their predictive value will be. The same is true for political betting.

So, in a two-horse race like the Scottish independence referendum, aided by regular opinion polls and constant commentary, Paddy Power currently estimates that there is a 23 per cent chance that the Scots will vote 'Yes'. With margin, this means that we offer odds of 2/9.

When looking at opinion polls for the 2015 general election, we note that Labour are ahead, but that the Conservative Party have not dropped to a level that would lose them all of their 2010 gains. So, we estimate that there's a 55 per cent chance of Labour winning the most seats and offer 8/11. Think that's too generous? Or that the economy will win it for the Tories? You can put your money where your mouth is and back David Cameron to return as PM at even money.

Once a market is up and running, then actual bets are used as a form of data too. The flow of cash can affect the odds-on offer, even if none of the original data has changed. For instance, we opened UKIP as 4/7 favourites to win the Clacton by-election. The punters clearly thought the price generous and snapped it up. That weight of opinion, obvious to us in the form of cash being put on UKIP, needed a response. So we brought in a hefty price cut for UKIP and an easing out of the Conservative odds.

After the data has been processed and the market opened for business, a betting line emerges. In major markets, such as those built around the general election, the line represents a strong opinion. Are people more likely to be honest when investing money than when answering a pollster's questions on voting intention? We think so.

The political betting market therefore holds unique predictive value and is often used by journalists to demonstrate what might happen.

This goes some way to explain why many parliamentary candidates keep an eye on the bookies' odds. It isn't unheard of for a candidate to claim that his or her odds should be shorter. The answer to that is always that they should put their money where their mouth is and the price will soon move!

PUNTERS' PICKS

People say you'll never meet a poor bookie, but we have been known to get it wrong. And on some occasions horribly so.

Paddy Power paid out early on Ireland to back the EU Lisbon Treaty in the 2008 referendum, considering a 'Yes' vote a dead cert. The voters opted for a resounding 'No', and Paddy ended up paying out all bets as winners. A great day for the punters.

The 2010 Labour leadership election dominated the media agenda for weeks, not least because of the intriguing family dynamic. A vast amount of information was available and hundreds of thousands of pounds had changed hands. The betting line suggested that David Miliband had a much better chance of winning the leadership than his brother Ed. The betting line was wrong, and the punters who were shrewd enough to back the young pretender at the early stages, when he was available at double-figure prices, collected their reward.

Another figure not on our Christmas card list is George Galloway. At the outset of the 2012 Bradford West by-election, a rank outsider listing of 200/1 was available for Respect to win the seat. Even when Galloway was confirmed as the candidate, the odds only went to 33/1. The punters got stuck in and the price gradually moved in further, but the damage was done. Even though the best information available told us that Labour were still confident on polling day, Galloway beat their candidate into second place by a whopping 35 per cent margin. The bookies were stung, and those who were on at 200/1 really had something to celebrate.

When this happens, we can only laugh at ourselves and admire the punters. We are, after all, in the entertainment business.

MORE THAN JUST THE USUAL MARKETS

Profit and fun are not the only upsides of political betting for the bookie. Elections are headline news, and we certainly don't usually turn down the chance of a front-page mention.

The range of markets is only limited by what we can find results for. Alongside betting on general election outcomes, by-election winners and next party leaders, our politics punters have placed bets on whether or not Barack Obama can quit smoking, how many times John Bercow will interrupt PMQs, what David Cameron will read on holiday, when Cornwall will achieve independence – if the punter is interested in it, we'll endeavour to create a market.

When someone found footage of a young John Bercow appearing in *Crackerjack* we ran a market on the number of times he would be taunted with it in Prime Minister's Questions. When Oliver Letwin chucked away government papers in a St James's Park litter bin we decided to see if anyone knew where such documents would be found next. And when certain Members of Parliament's tax arrangements came to light we made it odds-on that a minister would have to resign because of similarly dodgy accounting.

CONCLUSION

For the UK general election, there will be over 700 markets available to bet on. We'll offer them on as many aspects of the election as we can – from turnout numbers to vote percentages, and tie colours to clichéd speeches – anything that the punter can get interested in.

As for what the future holds beyond 2015, there'll be a never-ending supply of big, small and frankly ridiculous questions for the politico to speculate on. Will there be another Clinton in the White House?

Will Boris manage a U-turn and get his estuary airport? Will it ever come to light just *who* ate Liz Kendall's tuna salad stolen from the House of Commons fridge? In this context, only one thing's for sure – if people are talking about it, the bookies will be pricing it and plenty of people will fancy a flutter.

PADDY'S FAVOURITE POLITICAL MARKETS

Top five most ridiculous political markets

Where would Barack Obama be caught smoking next?
Who will Gillian Duffy vote for?
How many Silvio Berlusconi sex scandals this year?
Decibel level at Prime Minister's Questions?
First Member of Parliament to be rollocked by Speaker Bercow?

Although most people put their money on the major political events we love to make things more interesting by offering a market on the big political event of the day – whatever that may be!

PADDY'S 2015 LOOK AHEAD

Top five most popular general election markets

Most seats
Overall majority
Next government
Prime Minister following election
Constituencies

General elections are big business, and more markets are generated for them than for any other event. For 2015, there will be a market for each of the 650 constituencies as well as one or two hundred other markets such as turnout figures, party seat numbers, government formation and Cabinet membership.

Adam Smith and Stephanie Anderson are Head of External Affairs and Head of Novelties & Politics and Paddy Power.

Election dysfunction? Changes to electoral law since 2010

Donal Blaney

It seems a very long time ago that David Cameron and Nick Clegg consummated their bromance in the Downing Street garden in May 2010. The coalition that ensued has endured a number of rocky moments, few rockier than the collapse of plans for political reform that had been heralded as a key component of the coalition agreement itself.

The coalition agreement promised three things: 'a referendum on electoral reform, much greater cooperation across party lines and changes to our political system to make it far more transparent and accountable'. All were promised because 'we urgently need fundamental political reform'. Sadly, that urgency seems to have been forgotten because few of the changes heralded in the coalition agreement have seen the light of day.

The coalition succeeded in pushing through five-year fixed-term parliaments despite opposition parties' attempts to push for four-year parliaments. Thanks to the Fixed-Term Parliaments Act 2011 (which in essence ended the provisions of the Septennial Act 1715, as amended by the Parliament Act 1911), Parliament will be dissolved on 30 March 2015 and the general election will be held on 7 May 2015. That is, of course, unless Parliament itself orders an earlier date. The coalition agreement had envisaged a 55 per cent threshold for early dissolution but this was increased to two-thirds during the passage of the legislation. A no-confidence motion can still be passed with a simple majority and if fourteen days elapse without a new government being formed and winning a confidence vote in Parliament, an early general election will be called.

There was, of course, a referendum on electoral reform that was held in May 2011 pursuant to the Parliamentary Voting System & Constituencies Act 2011. Only ten of the 440 counting districts recorded 'Yes' votes above 50 per cent and the Alternative Vote system was defeated by a margin of two to one across the country.

The related plan to reduce the number of parliamentary constituencies from 650 to 600 and to ensure that constituency sizes were more even in size was blocked by the Liberal Democrats in a fit of pique after the loss of the AV referendum and a lack of any meaningful reform to the House of Lords. The coalition agreement had promised to establish a committee to bring forward proposals for a wholly or mainly elected upper chamber on the basis of proportional representation. There was no appetite for reform to the House of Lords on the Conservative backbenches and proposals for such reform fell as a result of this opposition.

More equal constituency sizes would have been electorally beneficial to the Conservatives as it would have reduced the number of Labour MPs in some of its Scottish and northern heartlands. The largest electorate in the United Kingdom in 2010 was 110,924 and the smallest was 21,837. Nearly 200 years on from the era of rotten boroughs, this unequal distribution of constituencies remains a stain on the democratic process.

In a potentially innovative move, the coalition had also promised to bring forward early legislation to introduce a power of recall similar to that in the United States which had been invoked successfully in California to the benefit of Arnold Schwarzenegger in 2003. This would have allowed voters to force a by-election where an MP engaged in serious wrongdoing and a petition calling for a by-election had been signed by 10 per cent of that MP's constituents.

The Recall of MPs Draft Bill had proposed that recall petitions could only be triggered if an MP received a custodial sentence or, most controversially, the House of Commons resolved that that MP should face recall. There was a fear that this trigger mechanism could be abused on party political grounds (or, worse, could see MPs protecting one of their own, notwithstanding voters' desire to remove him or her from office). Furthermore, the meaning of 'serious wrongdoing' would have been open to interpretation by the courts, thus impacting upon the sacred principle of parliamentary privilege.

Zac Goldsmith, the independent-minded Conservative MP for Richmond, sought to table a private member's bill to push recall through the House of Commons, but without success. The idea was dropped in February 2014 after the Conservatives and Liberal Democrats were unable to agree on the finer details of the legislation although it was included in the Queen's Speech in June 2014 when the Queen said 'my ministers will introduce legislation on the recall of Members of Parliament'. At the time of writing, no such legislation has been tabled.

Recall became a hot topic of discussion in August 2014 following the Rotherham child abuse scandal. Shaun Wright, the Labour Police & Crime Commissioner for South Yorkshire, had been responsible for children's services in Rotherham for much of the period when this abuse had taken place. The leaders of the main political parties joined the clamour in the media for Mr Wright to resign or to be forced from office, but to no avail. It transpired that the Police Reform & Social Responsibility Act 2011 (which brought in police and crime commissioners) did not include a means by which voters, the courts or the Home Secretary could remove an elected commissioner from office.

A promise in the coalition agreement to fund 200 all-postal primaries targeted at seats that have not changed hands for many years was also quietly dropped. Similarly the promise to ensure that any petition that secures 100,000 signatures would be eligible for formal debate in Parliament has likewise not been translated into any meaningful action to make our political system 'more transparent and account-able', as the coalition agreement had promised.

The Secretary of State for Communities & Local Government, Eric Pickles, had more success in pushing through the coalition's prom-ise to give residents the power to instigate local referendums on any local issue and to give residents the power to veto excessive council tax increases. The Localism Act 2011 is one of the coalition's main successes, notwithstanding that its provisions have not been widely used as yet.

The coalition agreement had also promised to 'reduce electoral fraud by speeding up the implementation of individual voter registration'. The extent of electoral fraud in the United Kingdom was highlighted by the Electoral Commission in January 2014 when it published its final report and recommendations. Among the Electoral Commis-sion's main recommendations were: a call for voters to be required to verify their identities in polling stations to prevent personation; restrictions on the involvement of party political campaigners in absent vote administration processes; and, yes, the introduction of individ-ual voter registration.

The Electoral Registration & Administration Act 2013 replaces householder registration with individual electoral registration. Instead of the head of a household registering eligible voters, individual vot-ers will be required to register themselves, as well as providing their National Insurance number and date of birth on the application form so that their identity can be verified. The Act has been criticised by the Electoral Reform Society, which fears that it may disenfranchise some poorer voters or those from ethnic minority communities. It is anticipated that the Electoral Reform Society will work closely with other self-styled community groups to assist in voter registration drives to compensate for this risk.

Of particular interest was an overt naming-and-shaming exercise whereby the Electoral Commission identified sixteen local author-ity areas where there appears to be a greater risk of cases of electoral fraud being reported. One, Tower Hamlets, is at the time of writing the subject of an election petition in respect of Mayor Lutfur Rahman's re-election in May 2014. The other fifteen local authority areas ought to merit close attention in the 2015 general election. They are Birmingham, Blackburn with Darwen, Bradford, Burnley, Calderdale, Coventry, Derby, Hyndburn, Kirklees, Oldham, Pendle, Peterborough, Slough, Walsall and Woking.

The Electoral Commission did not mince its words when identifying these local authority areas. It said that 'electoral fraud is more likely to be committed by or in support of candidates standing for election in areas which are largely or predominantly populated by some South Asian communities, specifically those with roots in parts of Pakistan or Bangladesh'. That said, *The Guardian* highlighted that the Electoral Commission has only identified ten proven cases of electoral fraud since 2010 such that there are concerns, particularly on the left, that the risks are being overstated for electoral reasons.

In September 2014, the Electoral Commission investigated reports that a voter in the Scottish referendum had sought to sell his vote on eBay. Manifestly, such conduct would be illegal but, at the time of writing, it is not known whether this alleged offence has taken place or not.

While not fraudulent, issues arose concerning the name of a political party that raised concern. It will be recalled that a candidate for the Liberal Democrats secured 10,000 votes in the 1999 European elections and this confusion among electors gave rise to the creation of the Electoral Commission itself. It was therefore of some surprise to see that the Electoral Commission permitted the registration of a political party called An Independence from Europe – with the slogan 'UK Independence Now' – notwithstanding the apparent similarities to the UK Independence Party's own name, slogan and branding. The fact that An Independence from Europe was set up and registered by a former UKIP candidate did not seem to bother the Electoral Commission, even though 23,000 voters chose this hitherto unheard-of political party in the south-west region in the European elections in

2014. Mike Smithson from Political Betting opined that if all of An Independence from Europe's votes (which equated to 1.5 per cent of those cast – more than the British National Party and the English Democrats) had gone to UKIP, Nigel Farage's party would have won two more MEPs.

One case of note merits comment. It concerned prisoners' right to vote following a successful campaign by John Hirst. This Supreme Court case, known catchily as *R (on the application of Chester)* v *The Secretary of State for Justice*, saw claims by a prisoner that his human rights had been infringed by virtue of him being denied his right to vote being dismissed. The blanket ban on prisoners voting was held not to be incompatible with European law. That said, the European Court of Human Rights has made it crystal clear that that blanket ban must go and it is anticipated that an incoming Labour government will be more amenable to acting in accordance with its international obligations than a more Eurosceptic Conservative government would be. Indeed it is the thorny issue of prisoners' votes that has been used as a stick by Eurosceptics to beat the Human Rights Act to greatest effect.

The final word must go to the Transparency of Lobbying, Non-Party Campaigning & Trade Union Administration Act, a piece of legislation that claims to be founded on the principles of transparency and cleaning up politics. This legislation was not mentioned in the coalition agreement. Nor did it merit a mention in any Queen's Speech. In truth it was introduced for naked party political reasons by the Conservative-led coalition in an effort to make political capital out of the Labour Party's over-reliance on trade union funding. The proverbial sledgehammer to crack a nut, the Act risks silencing charities during an election period and the Labour Party has pledged to repeal it if it wins the next general election.

Thus it is that Britain's electoral system, seemingly so stable since the Great Reform Act of 1832 and Gladstone's reforms in the 1870s, now finds itself embroiled in unseemly partisan squabbling more commonplace in a banana republic or an autocracy. It can but be hoped that the 'much greater cooperation across party lines' promised in the coalition agreement resurfaces in the next five years before Britain finds itself enduring the ignominy of UN election observers criticising our own electoral processes. Perhaps the Law Commission's impending consultation on electoral law will bring common sense to bear.

Donal Blaney is principal of the niche litigation law firm, Griffin Law (www.griffinlaw.co.uk).

Target seat data

Edited by Iain Dale

The 400 most marginal seats by majority

The seat ranked 1 has the lowest majority

RANK	CONSTITUENCY	MP ELECTED	1ST	2ND	VOTES	% VOTE
1	Fermanagh & South Tyrone	Michelle Gildernew	SF	IND	4	0.0%
2	Hampstead & Kilburn	Glenda Jackson	LAB	CON	42	0.1%
3	North Warwickshire	Daniel Byles	CON	LAB	54	0.1%
4	Camborne & Redruth	George Eustice	CON	LD	66	0.2%
5	Bolton West	Julie Hilling	LAB	CON	92	0.2%
6	Thurrock	Jackie Doyle-Price	CON	LAB	92	0.2%
7	Oldham East & Saddleworth	Phil Woolas	LAB	LD	103	0.2%
8	Hendon	Matthew Offord	CON	LAB	106	0.2%
9	Sheffield Central	Paul Blomfield	LAB	LD	165	0.4%
10	Solihull	Lorely Burt	LD	CON	175	0.3%
11	Oxford West & Abingdon	Nicola Blackwood	CON	LD	176	0.3%
12	Ashfield	Gloria De Piero	LAB	LD	192	0.4%

RANK	CONSTITUENCY	MP ELECTED	1ST	2ND	VOTES	% VOTE
13	Southampton, Itchen	John Denham	LAB	CON	192	0.4%
14	Cardiff North	Jonathan Evans	CON	LAB	194	0.4%
15	Sherwood	Mark Spencer	CON	LAB	214	0.4%
16	Mid Dorset & North Poole	Annette Brooke	LD	CON	269	0.6%
17	Norwich South	Simon Wright	LD	LAB	310	0.7%
18	Edinburgh South	Ian Murray	LAB	LD	316	0.7%
19	Stockton South	James Wharton	CON	LAB	332	0.7%
20	Lancaster & Fleetwood	Eric Ollerenshaw	CON	LAB	333	0.8%
21	Bradford East	David Ward	LD	LAB	365	0.9%
22	Broxtowe	Anna Soubry	CON	LAB	389	0.7%
23	Truro & Falmouth	Sarah Newton	CON	LD	435	0.9%
24	Swansea West	Geraint Davies	LAB	LD	504	1.4%
25	Newton Abbot	Anne Morris	CON	LD	523	1.1%
26	Wirral South	Alison McGovern	LAB	CON	531	1.3%
27	Amber Valley	Nigel Mills	CON	LAB	536	1.2%
28	Chesterfield	Toby Perkins	LAB	LD	549	1.2%
29	Derby North	Chris Williamson	LAB	CON	613	1.4%
30	Kingston upon Hull North	Diana Johnson	LAB	LD	641	1.9%
31	Dudley North	Ian Austin	LAB	CON	649	1.7%
32	Wolverhampton South	West Paul Uppal	CON	LAB	691	1.7%
33	Great Grimsby	Austin Mitchell	LAB	CON	714	2.2%
34	Waveney	Peter Aldous	CON	LAB	769	1.5%
35	Wells	Tessa Munt	LD	CON	800	1.4%
36	Carlisle	John Stevenson	CON	LAB	853	2.0%
37	Morecambe & Lunesdale	David Morris	CON	LAB	866	2.0%
38	Rochdale	Simon Danczuk	LAB	LD	889	1.9%
39	Telford	David Wright	LAB	CON	978	2.4%
40	Walsall North	David Winnick	LAB	CON	990	2.7%
41	Weaver Vale	Graham Evans	CON	LAB	991	2.3%
42	Harrogate & Knaresborough	Andrew Jones	CON	LD	1,039	2.0%
43	Lincoln	Karl McCartney	CON	LAB	1,058	2.3%
44	Morley & Outwood	Ed Balls	LAB	CON	1,101	2.3%
45	Plymouth, Sutton & Devonport	Oliver Colvile	CON	LAB	1,149	2.6%
46	South Antrim	William McCrea	DUP	UCU	1,183	3.5%
47	Montgomeryshire	Glyn Davies	CON	LD	1,184	3.5%
48	Brighton, Pavilion	Caroline Lucas	GRE	LAB	1,252	2.4%
49	Birmingham, Edgbaston	Gisela Stuart	LAB	CON	1,274	3.1%
50	Stroud	Neil Carmichael	CON	LAB	1,299	2.2%

RANK	CONSTITUENCY	MP ELECTED	1ST	2ND	VOTES	% VOTE
51	St Austell & Newquay	Stephen Gilbert	LD	CON	1,312	2.8%
52	Brighton, Kemptown	Simon Kirby	CON	LAB	1,328	3.1%
53	Brent Central	Sarah Teather	LD	LAB	1,345	3.0%
54	Bedford	Richard Fuller	CON	LAB	1,353	3.0%
55	Watford	Richard Harrington	CON	LD	1,425	2.6%
56	Arfon	Hywel Williams	PC	LAB	1,455	5.6%
57	Halifax	Linda Riordan	LAB	CON	1,472	3.4%
58	Dewsbury	Simon Reevell	CON	LAB	1,526	2.8%
59	Belfast East	Naomi Long	Alliance	DUP	1,533	4.4%
60	Newcastle under Lyme	Paul Farrelly	LAB	CON	1,552	3.6%
61	Warrington South	David Mowat	CON	LAB	1,553	2.8%
62	Plymouth, Moor View	Alison Seabeck	LAB	CON	1,588	3.8%
63	Sutton & Cheam	Paul Burstow	LD	CON	1,608	3.3%
64	Wakefield	Mary Creagh	LAB	CON	1,613	3.6%
65	Newport East	Jessica Morden	LAB	LD	1,650	4.8%
66	Pudsey	Stuart Andrew	CON	LAB	1,659	3.4%
67	Eltham	Clive Efford	LAB	CON	1,663	4.0%
68	Middlesbrough South & East Cleveland	Tom Blenkinsop	LAB	CON	1,677	3.6%
69	Enfield North	Nick de Bois	CON	LAB	1,692	3.8%
70	St Ives	Andrew George	LD	CON	1,719	3.7%
71	Edinburgh North & Leith	Mark Lazarowicz	LAB	LD	1,724	3.6%
72	Walsall South	Valerie Vaz	LAB	CON	1,755	4.3%
73	Nottingham South	Lilian Greenwood	LAB	CON	1,772	4.3%
74	Somerton & Frome	David Heath	LD	CON	1,817	3.0%
75	Burnley	Gordon Birtwistle	LD	LAB	1,818	4.3%
76	Dundee East	Stewart Hosie	SNP	LAB	1,821	4.5%
77	Blackpool South	Gordon Marsden	LAB	CON	1,852	5.3%
78	Gedling	Vernon Coaker	LAB	CON	1,859	3.9%
79	Hove	Mike Weatherley	CON	LAB	1,868	3.7%
80	Na h-Eileanan an Iar	Angus MacNeil	SNP	LAB	1,885	12.8%
81	Manchester, Withington	John Leech	LD	LAB	1,894	4.2%
82	Corby	Louise Bagshawe	CON	LAB	1,895	3.5%
83	Northampton North	Michael Ellis	CON	LAB	1,936	4.8%
84	Brentford & Isleworth	Mary MacLeod	CON	LAB	1,958	3.6%
85	Hastings & Rye	Amber Rudd	CON	LAB	1,993	4.0%
86	Halesowen & Rowley Regis	James Morris	CON	LAB	2,023	4.6%
87	Nuneaton	Marcus Jones	CON	LAB	2,069	4.6%
88	Ipswich	Benedict Gummer	CON	LAB	2,079	4.4%

RANK	CONSTITUENCY	MP ELECTED	1ST	2ND	VOTES	% VOTE
89	Westminster North	Karen Buck	LAB	CON	2,126	5.4%
90	Blackpool North & Cleveleys	Paul Maynard	CON	LAB	2,150	5.3%
91	East Dunbartonshire	Jo Swinson	LD	LAB	2,184	4.6%
92	Belfast North	Nigel Dodds	DUP	SF	2,224	6.0%
93	Bury North	David Nuttall	CON	LAB	2,243	5.0%
94	Bridgend	Madeleine Moon	LAB	CON	2,263	5.9%
95	Delyn	David Hanson	LAB	CON	2,272	6.1%
96	St Albans	Anne Main	CON	LD	2,305	4.4%
97	Luton South	Gavin Shuker	LAB	CON	2,329	5.5%
98	Southampton, Test	Alan Whitehead	LAB	CON	2,413	5.5%
99	Gloucester	Richard Graham	CON	LAB	2,420	4.8%
100	Wirral West	Esther McVey	CON	LAB	2,436	6.2%
101	Kingswood	Chris Skidmore	CON	LAB	2,445	5.1%
102	North East Derbyshire	Natascha Engel	LAB	CON	2,445	5.2%
103	Ynys Môn	Albert Owen	LAB	PC	2,461	7.1%
104	Chippenham	Duncan Hames	LD	CON	2,470	4.7%
105	Hereford & South Herefordshire	Jesse Norman	CON	LD	2,481	5.1%
106	Wolverhampton North East	Emma Reynolds	LAB	CON	2,484	7.1%
107	Erewash	Jessica Lee	CON	LAB	2,501	5.2%
108	Vale of Clwyd	Chris Ruane	LAB	CON	2,509	7.1%
109	Tooting	Sadiq Khan	LAB	CON	2,524	5.0%
110	Scunthorpe	Nick Dakin	LAB	CON	2,549	6.9%
111	City of Chester	Stephen Mosley	CON	LAB	2,583	5.5%
112	Chorley	Lindsay Hoyle	LAB	CON	2,593	5.2%
113	Dagenham & Rainham	Jon Cruddas	LAB	CON	2,630	5.9%
114	Wyre Forest	Mark Garnier	CON	ICHC	2,643	5.2%
115	Gower	Martin Caton	LAB	CON	2,683	6.4%
116	Berwick-upon-Tweed	Alan Beith	LD	CON	2,690	7.0%
117	Weston-super-Mare	John Penrose	CON	LD	2,691	5.1%
118	Exeter	Ben Bradshaw	LAB	CON	2,721	5.2%
119	Stalybridge & Hyde	Jonathan Reynolds	LAB	CON	2,744	6.7%
120	Birmingham, Northfield	Richard Burden	LAB	CON	2,782	6.7%
121	Pontypridd	Owen Smith	LAB	LD	2,785	7.6%
122	Clwyd South	Susan Jones	LAB	CON	2,834	8.2%
123	Croydon Central	Gavin Barwell	CON	LAB	2,879	5.8%
124	Alyn & Deeside	Mark Tami	LAB	CON	2,919	7.3%
125	Keighley	Kris Hopkins	CON	LAB	2,940	6.2%
126	Torridge & West Devon	Geoffrey Cox	CON	LD	2,957	5.4%

RANK	CONSTITUENCY	MP ELECTED	1ST	2ND	VOTES	% VOTE
127	North Cornwall	Dan Rogerson	LD	CON	2,981	6.4%
128	Worcester	Robin Walker	CON	LAB	2,982	6.1%
129	Birmingham, Yardley	John Hemming	LD	LAB	3,002	7.3%
130	Winchester	Steve Brine	CON	LD	3,048	5.4%
131	Penistone & Stocksbridge	Angela Smith	LAB	CON	3,049	6.6%
132	City of Durham	Roberta Blackman-Woods	LAB	LD	3,067	6.6%
133	Hyndburn	Graham Jones	LAB	CON	3,090	7.2%
134	Harrow West	Gareth Thomas	LAB	CON	3,143	6.8%
135	Cannock Chase	Aidan Burley	CON	LAB	3,195	7.0%
136	South East Cornwall	Sheryll Murray	CON	LD	3,220	6.5%
137	Streatham	Chuka Umunna	LAB	LD	3,259	7.0%
138	Cheadle	Mark Hunter	LD	CON	3,272	6.2%
139	Bristol North West	Charlotte Leslie	CON	LD	3,274	6.5%
140	Birmingham, Erdington	Jack Dromey	LAB	CON	3,277	9.2%
141	Angus	Mike Weir	SNP	CON	3,282	8.6%
142	Bury South	Ivan Lewis	LAB	CON	3,292	6.8%
143	Upper Bann	David Simpson	DUP	UCU	3,361	8.1%
144	Darlington	Jenny Chapman	LAB	CON	3,388	7.9%
145	Aberconwy	Guto Bebb	CON	LAB	3,398	11.3%
146	Harrow East	Bob Blackman	CON	LAB	3,403	7.1%
147	Newcastle upon Tyne North	Catherine McKinnell	LAB	LD	3,414	7.8%
148	Carmarthen West & South Pembrokeshire	Simon Hart	CON	LAB	3,423	8.5%
149	Argyll & Bute	Alan Reid	LD	CON	3,431	7.6%
150	Eastbourne	Stephen Lloyd	LD	CON	3,435	6.6%
151	Carmarthen East & Dinefwr	Jonathan Edwards	PC	LAB	3,481	9.2%
152	Birmingham, Selly Oak	Steve McCabe	LAB	CON	3,482	7.5%
153	Aberdeen South	Anne Begg	LAB	LD	3,506	8.1%
154	Warwick & Leamington	Chris White	CON	LAB	3,513	7.2%
155	Newport West	Paul Flynn	LAB	CON	3,544	8.9%
156	South Swindon	Robert Buckland	CON	LAB	3,544	7.5%
157	Hammersmith	Andy Slaughter	LAB	CON	3,549	7.5%
158	Islington South & Finsbury	Emily Thornberry	LAB	LD	3,569	8.2%
159	Stevenage	Stephen McPartland	CON	LAB	3,578	8.0%
160	Pendle	Andrew Stephenson	CON	LAB	3,585	8.0%
161	Don Valley	Caroline Flint	LAB	CON	3,595	8.3%
162	Wrexham	Ian Lucas	LAB	LD	3,658	11.1%
163	West Aberdeenshire & Kincardine	Robert Smith	LD	CON	3,684	8.2%
164	York Outer	Julian Sturdy	CON	LD	3,688	6.9%

RANK	CONSTITUENCY	MP ELECTED	1ST	2ND	VOTES	% VOTE
165	Ealing Central & Acton	Angie Bray	CON	LAB	3,716	7.9%
166	Bristol East	Kerry McCarthy	LAB	CON	3,722	8.3%
167	Loughborough	Nicky Morgan	CON	LAB	3,744	7.1%
168	Brecon & Radnorshire	Roger Williams	LD	CON	3,747	9.6%
169	Birmingham, Hall Green	Roger Godsiff	LAB	RES	3,799	7.8%
170	Edinburgh West	Mike Crockart	LD	LAB	3,803	8.2%
171	Copeland	Jamie Reed	LAB	CON	3,833	9.0%
172	Coventry South	Jim Cunningham	LAB	CON	3,845	8.4%
173	Dudley South	Chris Kelly	CON	LAB	3,856	10.1%
174	Sefton Central	Bill Esterson	LAB	CON	3,862	8.0%
175	Eastleigh	Chris Huhne	LD	CON	3,864	7.2%
176	Glasgow North	Ann McKechin	LAB	LD	3,898	13.2%
177	Norwich North	Chloe Smith	CON	LAB	3,901	9.2%
178	West Dorset	Oliver Letwin	CON	LD	3,923	6.8%
179	Taunton Deane	Jeremy Browne	LD	CON	3,993	6.9%
180	Leicester West	Liz Kendall	LAB	CON	4,017	11.2%
181	Banff & Buchan	Eilidh Whiteford	SNP	CON	4,027	10.5%
182	Merthyr Tydfil & Rhymney	Dai Havard	LAB	LD	4,056	12.6%
183	Torbay	Adrian Sanders	LD	CON	4,078	8.3%
184	Bolton North East	David Crausby	LAB	CON	4,084	9.4%
185	Richmond Park	Zac Goldsmith	CON	LD	4,091	6.9%
186	Stoke-on-Trent South	Robert Flello	LAB	CON	4,130	10.4%
187	Romsey & Southampton North	Caroline Nokes	CON	LD	4,156	8.5%
188	Dumfriesshire, Clydesdale & Tweeddale	David Mundell	CON	LAB	4,194	9.1%
189	Great Yarmouth	Brandon Lewis	CON	LAB	4,276	9.9%
190	Cleethorpes	Martin Vickers	CON	LAB	4,298	9.6%
191	Vale of Glamorgan	Alun Cairns	CON	LAB	4,307	8.8%
192	Ellesmere Port & Neston	Andrew Miller	LAB	CON	4,331	9.8%
193	Worsley & Eccles South	Barbara Keeley	LAB	CON	4,337	10.4%
194	West Lancashire	Rosie Cooper	LAB	CON	4,343	9.0%
195	Perth & North Perthshire	Pete Wishart	SNP	CON	4,379	9.1%
196	Batley & Spen	Mike Wood	LAB	CON	4,406	8.6%
197	Newcastle upon Tyne East	Nicholas Brown	LAB	LD	4,453	11.8%
198	Huddersfield	Barry Sheerman	LAB	CON	4,472	11.0%
199	Rossendale & Darwen	Jake Berry	CON	LAB	4,493	9.5%
200	Elmet & Rothwell	Alec Shelbrooke	CON	LAB	4,521	8.1%
201	Leeds North East	Fabian Hamilton	LAB	CON	4,545	9.6%
202	Workington	Tony Cunningham	LAB	CON	4,575	11.7%

RANK	CONSTITUENCY	MP ELECTED	1ST	2ND	VOTES	% VOTE
203	Cardiff Central	Jenny Willott	LD	LAB	4,576	12.7%
204	Oxford East	Andrew Smith	LAB	LD	4,581	8.9%
205	Preseli Pembrokeshire	Stephen Crabb	CON	LAB	4,605	11.6%
206	Bradford South	Gerry Sutcliffe	LAB	CON	4,622	12.2%
207	Feltham & Heston	Alan Keen	LAB	CON	4,658	9.6%
208	High Peak	Andrew Bingham	CON	LAB	4,677	9.3%
209	Llanelli	Nia Griffith	LAB	PC	4,701	12.5%
210	Cardiff South & Penarth	Alun Michael	LAB	CON	4,709	10.6%
211	Bristol South	Dawn Primarolo	LAB	LD	4,734	9.8%
212	Cardiff West	Kevin Brennan	LAB	CON	4,751	11.6%
213	Foyle	Mark Durkan	SDLP	SF	4,824	12.7%
214	Caithness, Sutherland & Easter Ross	John Thurso	LD	LAB	4,826	16.8%
215	Colne Valley	Jason McCartney	CON	LD	4,837	8.7%
216	Peterborough	Stewart Jackson	CON	LAB	4,861	10.8%
217	North East Somerset	Jacob Rees-Mogg	CON	LAB	4,914	9.6%
218	Cheltenham	Martin Horwood	LD	CON	4,920	9.3%
219	Harlow	Robert Halfon	CON	LAB	4,925	11.2%
220	Totnes	Sarah Wollaston	CON	LD	4,927	10.3%
221	Bosworth	David Tredinnick	CON	LD	5,032	9.3%
222	Chelmsford	Simon Burns	CON	LD	5,110	9.4%
223	Brigg & Goole	Andrew Percy	CON	LAB	5,147	11.7%
224	Stourbridge	Margot James	CON	LAB	5,164	10.9%
225	Ochil & South Perthshire	Gordon Banks	LAB	SNP	5,187	10.3%
226	Portsmouth South	Mike Hancock	LD	CON	5,200	12.6%
227	Milton Keynes South	Iain Stewart	CON	LAB	5,201	9.4%
228	Barrow & Furness	John Woodcock	LAB	CON	5,208	11.8%
229	Redcar	Ian Swales	LD	LAB	5,214	12.4%
230	Bishop Auckland	Helen Goodman	LAB	CON	5,218	12.7%
231	Carshalton & Wallington	Tom Brake	LD	CON	5,260	11.5%
232	Dover	Charlie Elphicke	CON	LAB	5,274	10.5%
233	East Londonderry	Gregory Campbell	DUP	SF	5,355	15.3%
234	Ilford North	Lee Scott	CON	LAB	5,404	11.5%
235	Stafford	Jeremy Lefroy	CON	LAB	5,460	10.9%
236	Dunfermline & West Fife	Thomas Docherty	LAB	LD	5,470	11.2%
237	Hartlepool	Iain Wright	LAB	CON	5,509	14.4%
238	Slough	Fiona Mactaggart	LAB	CON	5,523	11.6%
239	South Ribble	Lorraine Fullbrook	CON	LAB	5,554	10.8%
240	Stoke-on-Trent Central	Tristram Hunt	LAB	LD	5,566	17.1%

RANK	CONSTITUENCY	MP ELECTED	1ST	2ND	VOTES	% VOTE
241	Bournemouth	West Conor Burns	CON	LD	5,583	13.4%
242	Aldershot	Gerald Howarth	CON	LD	5,586	12.3%
243	Moray	Angus Robertson	SNP	CON	5,590	13.6%
244	West Bromwich West	Adrian Bailey	LAB	CON	5,651	15.6%
245	Berwickshire, Roxburgh & Selkirk	Michael Moore	LD	CON	5,675	11.6%
246	Erith & Thamesmead	Teresa Pearce	LAB	CON	5,703	13.4%
247	Salford & Eccles	Hazel Blears	LAB	LD	5,725	13.8%
248	Tynemouth	Alan Campbell	LAB	CON	5,739	10.9%
249	Kingston upon Hull West & Hessle	Alan Johnson	LAB	LD	5,742	18.2%
250	Bradford West	Marsha Singh	LAB	CON	5,763	14.2% RES
251	South Basildon & East Thurrock	Stephen Metcalfe	CON	LAB	5,772	12.9%
252	Hexham	Guy Opperman	CON	LD	5,788	13.3%
253	Sheffield, Heeley	Meg Munn	LAB	LD	5,807	14.2%
254	Finchley & Golders Green	Mike Freer	CON	LAB	5,809	12.3%
255	North Devon	Nick Harvey	LD	CON	5,821	11.3%
256	Redditch	Karen Lumley	CON	LAB	5,821	13.2%
257	Lewisham West & Penge	Jim Dowd	LAB	LD	5,828	12.9%
258	Rother Valley	Kevin Barron	LAB	CON	5,866	12.5%
259	Strangford	Jim Shannon	DUP	UCU	5,876	18.1%
260	Maidstone & The Weald	Helen Grant	CON	LD	5,889	12.0%
261	Belfast South	Alasdair McDonnell	SDLP	DUP	5,926	17.3%
262	Crawley	Henry Smith	CON	LAB	5,928	12.5%
263	South East Cambridgeshire	James Paice	CON	LD	5,946	10.3%
264	Salisbury	John Glen	CON	LD	5,966	12.3%
265	Heywood & Middleton	Jim Dobbin	LAB	CON	5,971	12.9%
266	Battersea	Jane Ellison	CON	LAB	5,977	12.2%
267	Rugby	Mark Pawsey	CON	LAB	6,000	12.6%
268	Northampton South	Brian Binley	CON	LAB	6,004	15.4%
269	Reading West	Alok Sharma	CON	LAB	6,004	12.6%
270	Mansfield Alan	Meale	LAB	CON	6,012	12.4%
271	Southport	John Pugh	LD	CON	6,024	13.8%
272	Poplar & Limehouse	Jim Fitzpatrick	LAB	CON	6,030	12.9%
273	Crewe & Nantwich	Edward Timpson	CON	LAB	6,046	11.8%
274	Canterbury	Julian Brazier	CON	LD	6,048	12.3%
275	Chatham & Aylesford	Tracey Crouch	CON	LAB	6,069	13.9%
276	Tamworth	Chris Pincher	CON	LAB	6,090	13.1%
277	Derby South	Margaret Beckett	LAB	CON	6,122	14.9%
278	Lewisham East	Heidi Alexander	LAB	LD	6,216	14.9%

RANK	CONSTITUENCY	MP ELECTED	1ST	2ND	VOTES	% VOTE
279	Doncaster Central	Rosie Winterton	LAB	CON	6,229	14.9%
280	Coventry North West	Geoffrey Robinson	LAB	CON	6,288	13.5%
281	Burton	Andrew Griffiths	CON	LAB	6,304	12.7%
282	Tewkesbury	Laurence Robertson	CON	LD	6,310	11.7%
283	Dwyfor Meirionnydd	Elfyn Llwyd	PC	CON	6,367	22.0%
284	Hazel Grove	Andrew Stunell	LD	CON	6,371	15.2%
285	Leyton & Wanstead	John Cryer	LAB	LD	6,416	16.0%
286	Clwyd West	David Jones	CON	LAB	6,419	16.8%
287	Calder Valley	Craig Whittaker	CON	LAB	6,431	12.4%
288	York Central	Hugh Bayley	LAB	CON	6,451	13.9%
289	Wolverhampton South East	Pat McFadden	LAB	CON	6,593	19.0%
290	Blyth Valley	Ronnie Campbell	LAB	LD	6,668	17.3%
291	Stockton North	Alex Cunningham	LAB	CON	6,676	16.9%
292	Staffordshire Moorlands	Karen Bradley	CON	LAB	6,689	15.3%
293	West Bromwich	East Tom Watson	LAB	CON	6,696	17.6%
294	Manchester, Gorton	Gerald Kaufman	LAB	LD	6,703	17.5%
295	Sunderland Central	Julie Elliott	LAB	CON	6,725	15.8%
296	Gordon	Malcolm Bruce	LD	SNP	6,748	13.8%
297	West Worcestershire	Harriett Baldwin	CON	LD	6,754	12.5%
298	East Antrim	Sammy Wilson	DUP	UCU	6,770	22.2%
299	Warrington North	Helen Jones	LAB	CON	6,771	15.3%
300	Stockport	Ann Coffey	LAB	CON	6,784	17.3%
301	Cambridge	Julian Huppert	LD	CON	6,792	13.5%
302	Woking	Jonathan Lord	CON	LD	6,807	12.9%
303	Hornsey & Wood Green	Lynne Featherstone	LD	LAB	6,875	12.5%
304	Filton & Bradley Stoke	Jack Lopresti	CON	LAB	6,914	14.3%
305	Nottingham East	Christopher Leslie	LAB	LD	6,969	21.0%
306	Colchester	Bob Russell	LD	CON	6,982	15.1%
307	Leeds West	Rachel Reeves	LAB	LD	7,016	18.1%
308	Wansbeck	Ian Lavery	LAB	LD	7,031	18.4%
309	North Swindon	Justin Tomlinson	CON	LAB	7,060	14.0%
310	Congleton	Fiona Bruce	CON	LD	7,063	13.9%
311	Thornbury & Yate	Steve Webb	LD	CON	7,116	14.8%
312	South Derbyshire	Heather Wheeler	CON	LAB	7,128	14.1%
313	Liverpool, Wavertree	Luciana Berger	LAB	LD	7,167	18.9%
314	Southend West	David Amess	CON	LD	7,270	16.7%
315	Dundee West	Jim McGovern	LAB	SNP	7,278	19.6%
316	Portsmouth North	Penny Mordaunt	CON	LAB	7,289	16.5%

RANK	CONSTITUENCY	MP ELECTED	1ST	2ND	VOTES	% VOTE
317	Broadland	Keith Simpson	CON	LD	7,292	13.8%
318	Mid Sussex	Nicholas Soames	CON	LD	7,402	13.3%
319	South Dorset	Richard Drax	CON	LAB	7,443	14.8%
320	Dumfries & Galloway	Russell Brown	LAB	CON	7,449	14.3%
321	Newcastle upon Tyne Central	Chinyelu Onwurah	LAB	LD	7,466	21.9%
322	North Wiltshire	James Gray	CON	LD	7,483	15.4%
323	North West Leicestershire	Andrew Bridgen	CON	LAB	7,511	14.5%
324	Luton North	Kelvin Hopkins	LAB	CON	7,520	17.5%
325	Poole	Robert Syms	CON	LD	7,541	15.9%
326	Kingston & Surbiton	Edward Davey	LD	CON	7,560	13.2%
327	Wythenshawe & Sale East	Paul Goggins	LAB	CON	7,575	18.6%
328	Reading East	Rob Wilson	CON	LD	7,605	15.2%
329	North West Durham	Pat Glass	LAB	LD	7,612	17.4%
330	South Thanet	Laura Sandys	CON	LAB	7,617	16.6%
331	North Dorset	Robert Walter	CON	LD	7,625	14.1%
332	Enfield, Southgate	David Burrowes	CON	LAB	7,626	17.2%
333	Castle Point	Rebecca Harris	CON	IND	7,632	17.0%
334	Lewes	Norman Baker	LD	CON	7,647	15.3%
335	Bournemouth East	Tobias Ellwood	CON	LD	7,728	17.6%
336	Preston	Mark Hendrick	LAB	LD	7,733	23.8%
337	Guildford	Anne Milton	CON	LD	7,782	14.0%
338	South Cambridgeshire	Andrew Lansley	CON	LD	7,838	13.3%
339	Falkirk	Eric Joyce	LAB	SNP	7,843	15.4%
340	North Somerset	Liam Fox	CON	LD	7,862	13.6%
341	Shrewsbury & Atcham	Daniel Kawczynski	CON	LD	7,944	15.0%
342	Brent North	Barry Gardiner	LAB	CON	8,028	15.4%
343	Scarborough & Whitby	Robert Goodwill	CON	LAB	8,130	16.5%
344	Nottingham North	Graham Allen	LAB	CON	8,138	23.7%
345	Bassetlaw	John Mann	LAB	CON	8,215	16.6%
346	Stoke-on-Trent North	Joan Walley	LAB	CON	8,235	20.5%
347	Stirling	Anne McGuire	LAB	CON	8,304	17.7%
348	Ceredigion	Mark Williams	LD	PC	8,324	21.8%
349	Newry & Armagh	Conor Murphy	SF	SDLP	8,331	18.6%
350	Aberdeen North	Frank Doran	LAB	SNP	8,361	22.2%
351	South Down	Margaret Ritchie	SDLP	SF	8,412	19.8%
352	Edinburgh South West	Alistair Darling	LAB	CON	8,447	18.6%
353	Wallasey	Angela Eagle	LAB	CON	8,507	20.4%
354	Bermondsey & Old Southwark	Simon Hughes	LD	LAB	8,530	19.1%

RANK	CONSTITUENCY	MP ELECTED	1ST	2ND	VOTES	% VOTE
355	Kingston upon Hull East	Karl Turner	LAB	LD	8,597	25.1%
356	Kensington	Malcolm Rifkind	CON	LAB	8,616	24.5%
357	Bolton South East	Yasmin Qureshi	LAB	CON	8,634	21.8%
358	Gillingham & Rainham	Rehman Chishti	CON	LAB	8,680	18.6%
359	Middlesbrough	Stuart Bell	LAB	LD	8,689	26.0%
360	South Suffolk	Tim Yeo	CON	LD	8,689	16.9%
361	Sedgefield	Phil Wilson	LAB	CON	8,696	21.6%
362	Inverness, Nairn, Badenoch & Strathspey	Danny Alexander	LD	LAB	8,765	18.6%
363	Leicester South	Peter Soulsby	LAB	LD	8,808	18.7%
364	Stretford & Urmston	Kate Green	LAB	CON	8,935	19.9%
365	Milton Keynes	North Mark Lancaster	CON	LAB	8,961	16.6%
366	North East Fife	Menzies Campbell	LD	CON	9,048	22.6%
367	Ashton-Under-Lyne	David Heyes	LAB	CON	9,094	23.7%
368	Kettering	Philip Hollobone	CON	LAB	9,094	19.2%
369	Leeds North West	Greg Mulholland	LD	CON	9,103	20.9%
370	East Devon	Hugo Swire	CON	LD	9,114	17.2%
371	Blaydon	David Anderson	LAB	LD	9,117	20.3%
372	Suffolk Coastal	Therese Coffey	CON	LD	9,128	16.6%
373	Edinburgh East	Sheila Gilmore	LAB	SNP	9,181	23.0%
374	Central Devon	Mel Stride	CON	LD	9,230	17.1%
375	Bridgwater & West Somerset	Ian Liddell-Grainger	CON	LD	9,249	17.0%
376	Ealing, Southall	Virendra Sharma	LAB	CON	9,291	21.7%
377	Ealing North	Stephen Pound	LAB	CON	9,301	19.5%
378	Torfaen	Paul Murphy	LAB	CON	9,306	24.7%
379	Gravesham	Adam Holloway	CON	LAB	9,312	19.7%
380	Tiverton & Honiton	Neil Parish	CON	LD	9,320	17.0%
381	Oldham West & Royton	Michael Meacher	LAB	CON	9,352	21.8%
382	Dulwich & West Norwood	Tessa Jowell	LAB	LD	9,365	19.4%
383	The Wrekin	Mark Pritchard	CON	LAB	9,450	20.6%
384	Walthamstow	Stella Creasy	LAB	LD	9,478	23.1%
385	Wycombe	Steve Baker	CON	LD	9,560	19.9%
386	Edmonton	Andy Love	LAB	CON	9,613	23.8%
387	Cynon Valley	Ann Clwyd	LAB	PC	9,617	32.2%
388	Ludlow	Philip Dunne	CON	LD	9,749	20.0%
389	Neath	Peter Hain	LAB	PC	9,775	26.3%
390	Harborough	Edward Garnier	CON	LD	9,797	17.8%
391	Denton & Reddish	Andrew Gwynne	LAB	CON	9,831	26.1%
392	Hemsworth	Jon Trickett	LAB	CON	9,844	22.5%

RANK	CONSTITUENCY	MP ELECTED	1ST	2ND	VOTES	% VOTE
393	Blackburn	Jack Straw	LAB	CON	9,856	21.7%
394	North Herefordshire	Bill Wiggin	CON	LD	9,887	20.8%
395	North Ayrshire & Arran	Katy Clark	LAB	SNP	9,895	21.5%
396	Ayr, Carrick & Cumnock	Sandra Osborne	LAB	CON	9,911	21.6%
397	Orkney & Shetland	Alistair Carmichael	LD	LAB	9,928	51.3%
398	Holborn & St Pancras	Frank Dobson	LAB	LD	9,942	18.2%
399	Shipley	Philip Davies	CON	LAB	9,944	20.1%
400	Skipton & Ripon	Julian Smith	CON	LD	9,950	18.2%

(Source: House of Commons Library)

The 400 most marginal seats by percentage majority

The seat ranked 1 has the lowest % majority

RANK	CONSTITUENCY	MP ELECTED	1ST	2ND	VOTES	% VOTE
1	Fermanagh & South Tyrone	Michelle Gildernew	SF	IND	4	0.0%
2	Hampstead & Kilburn	Glenda Jackson	LAB	CON	42	0.1%
3	North Warwickshire	Daniel Byles	CON	LAB	54	0.1%
4	Camborne & Redruth	George Eustice	CON	LD	66	0.2%
5	Bolton West	Julie Hilling	LAB	CON	92	0.2%
6	Thurrock	Jackie Doyle-Price	CON	LAB	92	0.2%
7	Hendon	Matthew Offord	CON	LAB	106	0.2%
8	Oldham East & Saddleworth	Phil Woolas	LAB	LD	103	0.2%
9	Oxford West & Abingdon	Nicola Blackwood	CON	LD	176	0.3%
10	Solihull	Lorely Burt	LD	CON	175	0.3%
11	Sheffield Central	Paul Blomfield	LAB	LD	165	0.4%
12	Ashfield	Gloria De Piero	LAB	LD	192	0.4%
13	Cardiff North	Jonathan Evans	CON	LAB	194	0.4%
14	Southampton, Itchen	John Denham	LAB	CON	192	0.4%
15	Sherwood	Mark Spencer	CON	LAB	214	0.4%
16	Mid Dorset & North Poole	Annette Brooke	LD	CON	269	0.6%
17	Norwich South	Simon Wright	LD	LAB	310	0.7%
18	Stockton South	James Wharton	CON	LAB	332	0.7%
19	Edinburgh South	Ian Murray	LAB	LD	316	0.7%
20	Broxtowe	Anna Soubry	CON	LAB	389	0.7%
21	Lancaster & Fleetwood	Eric Ollerenshaw	CON	LAB	333	0.8%
22	Truro & Falmouth	Sarah Newton	CON	LD	435	0.9%
23	Bradford East	David Ward	LD	LAB	365	0.9%
24	Newton Abbot	Anne Morris	CON	LD	523	1.1%
25	Amber Valley	Nigel Mills	CON	LAB	536	1.2%

RANK	CONSTITUENCY	MP ELECTED	1ST	2ND	VOTES	% VOTE
26	Chesterfield	Toby Perkins	LAB	LD	549	1.2%
27	Wirral South	Alison McGovern	LAB	CON	531	1.3%
28	Derby North	Chris Williamson	LAB	CON	613	1.4%
29	Swansea West	Geraint Davies	LAB	LD	504	1.4%
30	Wells	Tessa Munt	LD	CON	800	1.4%
31	Waveney	Peter Aldous	CON	LAB	769	1.5%
32	Dudley North	Ian Austin	LAB	CON	649	1.7%
33	Wolverhampton South West	Paul Uppal	CON	LAB	691	1.7%
34	Kingston upon Hull North	Diana Johnson	LAB	LD	641	1.9%
35	Rochdale	Simon Danczuk	LAB	LD	889	1.9%
36	Harrogate & Knaresborough	Andrew Jones	CON	LD	1,039	2.0%
37	Morecambe & Lunesdale	David Morris	CON	LAB	866	2.0%
38	Carlisle	John Stevenson	CON	LAB	853	2.0%
39	Great Grimsby	Austin Mitchell	LAB	CON	714	2.2%
40	Stroud Neil	Carmichael	CON	LAB	1,299	2.2%
41	Weaver Vale	Graham Evans	CON	LAB	991	2.3%
42	Morley & Outwood	Ed Balls	LAB	CON	1,101	2.3%
43	Lincoln	Karl McCartney	CON	LAB	1,058	2.3%
44	Telford	David Wright	LAB	CON	978	2.4%
45	Brighton, Pavilion	Caroline Lucas	GRE	LAB	1,252	2.4%
46	Watford	Richard Harrington	CON	LD	1,425	2.6%
47	Plymouth, Sutton & Devonport	Oliver Colvile	CON	LAB	1,149	2.6%
48	Walsall North	David Winnick	LAB	CON	990	2.7%
49	St Austell & Newquay	Stephen Gilbert	LD	CON	1,312	2.8%
50	Dewsbury	Simon Reevell	CON	LAB	1,526	2.8%
51	Warrington South	David Mowat	CON	LAB	1,553	2.8%
52	Brent Central	Sarah Teather	LD	LAB	1,345	3.0%
53	Somerton & Frome	David Heath	LD	CON	1,817	3.0%
54	Bedford	Richard Fuller	CON	LAB	1,353	3.0%
55	Birmingham, Edgbaston	Gisela Stuart	LAB	CON	1,274	3.1%
56	Brighton, Kemptown	Simon Kirby	CON	LAB	1,328	3.1%
57	Sutton & Cheam	Paul Burstow	LD	CON	1,608	3.3%
58	Halifax	Linda Riordan	LAB	CON	1,472	3.4%
59	Pudsey	Stuart Andrew	CON	LAB	1,659	3.4%
60	South Antrim	William McCrea	DUP	UCU	1,183	3.5%
61	Corby	Louise Bagshawe	CON	LAB	1,895	3.5%
62	Montgomeryshire	Glyn Davies	CON	LD	1,184	3.5%
63	Newcastle under Lyme	Paul Farrelly	LAB	CON	1,552	3.6%

RANK	CONSTITUENCY	MP ELECTED	1ST	2ND	VOTES	% VOTE
64	Middlesbrough South & East Cleveland	Tom Blenkinsop	LAB	CON	1,677	3.6%
65	Wakefield	Mary Creagh	LAB	CON	1,613	3.6%
66	Edinburgh North & Leith	Mark Lazarowicz	LAB	LD	1,724	3.6%
67	Brentford & Isleworth	Mary MacLeod	CON	LAB	1,958	3.6%
68	St Ives	Andrew George	LD	CON	1,719	3.7%
69	Hove	Mike Weatherley	CON	LAB	1,868	3.7%
70	Enfield North	Nick de Bois	CON	LAB	1,692	3.8%
71	Plymouth, Moor View	Alison Seabeck	LAB	CON	1,588	3.8%
72	Gedling	Vernon Coaker	LAB	CON	1,859	3.9%
73	Eltham	Clive Efford	LAB	CON	1,663	4.0%
74	Hastings & Rye	Amber Rudd	CON	LAB	1,993	4.0%
75	Manchester, Withington	John Leech	LD	LAB	1,894	4.2%
76	Walsall South	Valerie Vaz	LAB	CON	1,755	4.3%
77	Nottingham South	Lilian Greenwood	LAB	CON	1,772	4.3%
78	Burnley	Gordon Birtwistle	LD	LAB	1,818	4.3%
79	St Albans	Anne Main	CON	LD	2,305	4.4%
80	Ipswich	Benedict Gummer	CON	LAB	2,079	4.4%
81	Belfast East	Naomi Long	Alliance	DUP	1,533	4.4%
82	Dundee East	Stewart Hosie	SNP	LAB	1,821	4.5%
83	East Dunbartonshire	Jo Swinson	LD	LAB	2,184	4.6%
84	Halesowen & Rowley Regis	James Morris	CON	LAB	2,023	4.6%
85	Nuneaton	Marcus Jones	CON	LAB	2,069	4.6%
86	Chippenham	Duncan Hames	LD	CON	2,470	4.7%
87	Gloucester	Richard Graham	CON	LAB	2,420	4.8%
88	Newport East	Jessica Morden	LAB	LD	1,650	4.8%
89	Northampton North	Michael Ellis	CON	LAB	1,936	4.8%
90	Tooting	Sadiq Khan	LAB	CON	2,524	5.0%
91	Bury North	David Nuttall	CON	LAB	2,243	5.0%
92	Kingswood	Chris Skidmore	CON	LAB	2,445	5.1%
93	Weston-super-Mare	John Penrose	CON	LD	2,691	5.1%
94	Hereford & South Herefordshire	Jesse Norman	CON	LD	2,481	5.1%
95	Wyre Forest	Mark Garnier	CON	ICHC	2,643	5.2%
96	North East Derbyshire	Natascha Engel	LAB	CON	2,445	5.2%
97	Exeter	Ben Bradshaw	LAB	CON	2,721	5.2%
98	Chorley	Lindsay Hoyle	LAB	CON	2,593	5.2%
99	Erewash	Jessica Lee	CON	LAB	2,501	5.2%
100	Blackpool South	Gordon Marsden	LAB	CON	1,852	5.3%
101	Blackpool North & Cleveleys	Paul Maynard	CON	LAB	2,150	5.3%

RANK	CONSTITUENCY	MP ELECTED	1ST	2ND	VOTES	% VOTE
102	Torridge & West Devon	Geoffrey Cox	CON	LD	2,957	5.4%
103	Westminster North	Karen Buck	LAB	CON	2,126	5.4%
104	Winchester	Steve Brine	CON	LD	3,048	5.4%
105	Southampton, Test	Alan Whitehead	LAB	CON	2,413	5.5%
106	Luton South	Gavin Shuker	LAB	CON	2,329	5.5%
107	City of Chester	Stephen Mosley	CON	LAB	2,583	5.5%
108	Arfon	Hywel Williams	PC	LAB	1,455	5.6%
109	Croydon Central	Gavin Barwell	CON	LAB	2,879	5.8%
110	Bridgend	Madeleine Moon	LAB	CON	2,263	5.9%
111	Dagenham & Rainham	Jon Cruddas	LAB	CON	2,630	5.9%
112	Belfast North	Nigel Dodds	DUP	SF	2,224	6.0%
113	Worcester	Robin Walker	CON	LAB	2,982	6.1%
114	Delyn	David Hanson	LAB	CON	2,272	6.1%
115	Keighley	Kris Hopkins	CON	LAB	2,940	6.2%
116	Wirral West	Esther McVey	CON	LAB	2,436	6.2%
117	Cheadle	Mark Hunter	LD	CON	3,272	6.2%
118	North Cornwall	Dan Rogerson	LD	CON	2,981	6.4%
119	Gower	Martin Caton	LAB	CON	2,683	6.4%
120	South East Cornwall	Sheryll Murray	CON	LD	3,220	6.5%
121	Bristol North West	Charlotte Leslie	CON	LD	3,274	6.5%
122	Penistone & Stocksbridge	Angela Smith	LAB	CON	3,049	6.6%
123	Eastbourne	Stephen Lloyd	LD	CON	3,435	6.6%
124	City of Durham	Roberta Blackman-Woods	LAB	LD	3,067	6.6%
125	Birmingham, Northfield	Richard Burden	LAB	CON	2,782	6.7%
126	Stalybridge & Hyde	Jonathan Reynolds	LAB	CON	2,744	6.7%
127	Harrow West	Gareth Thomas	LAB	CON	3,143	6.8%
128	Bury South	Ivan Lewis	LAB	CON	3,292	6.8%
129	West Dorset	Oliver Letwin	CON	LD	3,923	6.8%
130	Taunton Deane	Jeremy Browne	LD	CON	3,993	6.9%
131	Scunthorpe	Nick Dakin	LAB	CON	2,549	6.9%
132	Richmond Park	Zac Goldsmith	CON	LD	4,091	6.9%
133	York Outer	Julian Sturdy	CON	LD	3,688	6.9%
134	Streatham	Chuka Umunna	LAB	LD	3,259	7.0%
135	Berwick-upon-Tweed	Alan Beith	LD	CON	2,690	7.0%
136	Cannock Chase	Aidan Burley	CON	LAB	3,195	7.0%
137	Vale of Clwyd	Chris Ruane	LAB	CON	2,509	7.1%
138	Loughborough	Nicky Morgan	CON	LAB	3,744	7.1%
139	Harrow East	Bob Blackman	CON	LAB	3,403	7.1%

RANK	CONSTITUENCY	MP ELECTED	1ST	2ND	VOTES	% VOTE
140	Wolverhampton North East	Emma Reynolds	LAB	CON	2,484	7.1%
141	Ynys Môn	Albert Owen	LAB	PC	2,461	7.1%
142	Warwick & Leamington	Chris White	CON	LAB	3,513	7.2%
143	Eastleigh	Chris Huhne	LD	CON	3,864	7.2%
144	Hyndburn	Graham Jones	LAB	CON	3,090	7.2%
145	Alyn & Deeside	Mark Tami	LAB	CON	2,919	7.3%
146	Birmingham, Yardley	John Hemming	LD	LAB	3,002	7.3%
147	Birmingham, Selly Oak	Steve McCabe	LAB	CON	3,482	7.5%
148	Hammersmith	Andy Slaughter	LAB	CON	3,549	7.5%
149	South Swindon	Robert Buckland	CON	LAB	3,544	7.5%
150	Argyll & Bute	Alan Reid	LD	CON	3,431	7.6%
151	Pontypridd	Owen Smith	LAB	LD	2,785	7.6%
152	Newcastle upon Tyne North	Catherine McKinnell	LAB	LD	3,414	7.8%
153	Birmingham, Hall Green	Roger Godsiff	LAB	RES	3,799	7.8%
154	Ealing Central & Acton	Angie Bray	CON	LAB	3,716	7.9%
155	Darlington	Jenny Chapman	LAB	CON	3,388	7.9%
156	Pendle	Andrew Stephenson	CON	LAB	3,585	8.0%
157	Sefton Central	Bill Esterson	LAB	CON	3,862	8.0%
158	Stevenage	Stephen McPartland	CON	LAB	3,578	8.0%
159	Elmet & Rothwell	Alec Shelbrooke	CON	LAB	4,521	8.1%
160	Upper Bann	David Simpson	DUP	UCU	3,361	8.1%
161	Aberdeen South	Anne Begg	LAB	LD	3,506	8.1%
162	West Aberdeenshire & Kincardine	Robert Smith	LD	CON	3,684	8.2%
163	Clwyd South	Susan Jones	LAB	CON	2,834	8.2%
164	Edinburgh West	Mike Crockart	LD	LAB	3,803	8.2%
165	Islington South & Finsbury	Emily Thornberry	LAB	LD	3,569	8.2%
166	Bristol East	Kerry McCarthy	LAB	CON	3,722	8.3%
167	Don Valley	Caroline Flint	LAB	CON	3,595	8.3%
168	Torbay	Adrian Sanders	LD	CON	4,078	8.3%
169	Coventry South	Jim Cunningham	LAB	CON	3,845	8.4%
170	Carmarthen West & South Pembrokeshire	Simon Hart	CON	LAB	3,423	8.5%
171	Romsey & Southampton North	Caroline Nokes	CON	LD	4,156	8.5%
172	Batley & Spen	Mike Wood	LAB	CON	4,406	8.6%
173	Angus	Mike Weir	SNP	CON	3,282	8.6%
174	Colne Valley	Jason McCartney	CON	LD	4,837	8.7%
175	Vale of Glamorgan	Alun Cairns	CON	LAB	4,307	8.8%
176	Oxford East	Andrew Smith	LAB	LD	4,581	8.9%
177	Newport West	Paul Flynn	LAB	CON	3,544	8.9%

RANK	CONSTITUENCY	MP ELECTED	1ST	2ND	VOTES	% VOTE
178	Copeland	Jamie Reed	LAB	CON	3,833	9.0%
179	West Lancashire	Rosie Cooper	LAB	CON	4,343	9.0%
180	Perth & North Perthshire	Pete Wishart	SNP	CON	4,379	9.1%
181	Dumfriesshire, Clydesdale & Tweeddale	David Mundell	CON	LAB	4,194	9.1%
182	Carmarthen East & Dinefwr	Jonathan Edwards	PC	LAB	3,481	9.2%
183	Norwich North	Chloe Smith	CON	LAB	3,901	9.2%
184	Birmingham, Erdington	Jack Dromey	LAB	CON	3,277	9.2%
185	Bosworth	David Tredinnick	CON	LD	5,032	9.3%
186	High Peak	Andrew Bingham	CON	LAB	4,677	9.3%
187	Cheltenham	Martin Horwood	LD	CON	4,920	9.3%
188	Chelmsford	Simon Burns	CON	LD	5,110	9.4%
189	Milton Keynes South	Iain Stewart	CON	LAB	5,201	9.4%
190	Bolton North East	David Crausby	LAB	CON	4,084	9.4%
191	Rossendale & Darwen	Jake Berry	CON	LAB	4,493	9.5%
192	Cleethorpes	Martin Vickers	CON	LAB	4,298	9.6%
193	Leeds North East	Fabian Hamilton	LAB	CON	4,545	9.6%
194	Feltham & Heston	Alan Keen	LAB	CON	4,658	9.6%
195	North East Somerset	Jacob Rees-Mogg	CON	LAB	4,914	9.6%
196	Brecon & Radnorshire	Roger Williams	LD	CON	3,747	9.6%
197	Bristol South	Dawn Primarolo	LAB	LD	4,734	9.8%
198	Ellesmere Port & Neston	Andrew Miller	LAB	CON	4,331	9.8%
199	Great Yarmouth	Brandon Lewis	CON	LAB	4,276	9.9%
200	Dudley South	Chris Kelly	CON	LAB	3,856	10.1%
201	Ochil & South Perthshire	Gordon Banks	LAB	SNP	5,187	10.3%
202	Totnes Sarah	Wollaston	CON	LD	4,927	10.3%
203	South East Cambridgeshire	James Paice	CON	LD	5,946	10.3%
204	Stoke-on-Trent South	Robert Flello	LAB	CON	4,130	10.4%
205	Worsley & Eccles South	Barbara Keeley	LAB	CON	4,337	10.4%
206	Dover	Charlie Elphicke	CON	LAB	5,274	10.5%
207	Banff & Buchan	Eilidh Whiteford	SNP	CON	4,027	10.5%
208	Cardiff South & Penarth	Alun Michael	LAB	CON	4,709	10.6%
209	South Ribble	Lorraine Fullbrook	CON	LAB	5,554	10.8%
210	Peterborough	Stewart Jackson	CON	LAB	4,861	10.8%
211	Stafford	Jeremy Lefroy	CON	LAB	5,460	10.9%
212	Tynemouth	Alan Campbell	LAB	CON	5,739	10.9%
213	Stourbridge	Margot James	CON	LAB	5,164	10.9%
214	Huddersfield	Barry Sheerman	LAB	CON	4,472	11.0%
215	Wrexham	Ian Lucas	LAB	LD	3,658	11.1%

RANK	CONSTITUENCY	MP ELECTED	1ST	2ND	VOTES	% VOTE
216	Dunfermline & West Fife	Thomas Docherty	LAB	LD	5,470	11.2%
217	Leicester West	Liz Kendall	LAB	CON	4,017	11.2%
218	Harlow	Robert Halfon	CON	LAB	4,925	11.2%
219	Aberconwy	Guto Bebb	CON	LAB	3,398	11.3%
220	North Devon	Nick Harvey	LD	CON	5,821	11.3%
221	Carshalton & Wallington	Tom Brake	LD	CON	5,260	11.5%
222	Ilford North	Lee Scott	CON	LAB	5,404	11.5%
223	Slough	Fiona Mactaggart	LAB	CON	5,523	11.6%
224	Berwickshire, Roxburgh & Selkirk	Michael Moore	LD	CON	5,675	11.6%
225	Cardiff West	Kevin Brennan	LAB	CON	4,751	11.6%
226	Preseli Pembrokeshire	Stephen Crabb	CON	LAB	4,605	11.6%
227	Workington	Tony Cunningham	LAB	CON	4,575	11.7%
228	Tewkesbury	Laurence Robertson	CON	LD	6,310	11.7%
229	Brigg & Goole	Andrew Percy	CON	LAB	5,147	11.7%
230	Newcastle upon Tyne East	Nicholas Brown	LAB	LD	4,453	11.8%
231	Barrow & Furness	John Woodcock	LAB	CON	5,208	11.8%
232	Crewe & Nantwich	Edward Timpson	CON	LAB	6,046	11.8%
233	Maidstone & The Weald	Helen Grant	CON	LD	5,889	12.0%
234	Bradford South	Gerry Sutcliffe	LAB	CON	4,622	12.2%
235	Battersea	Jane Ellison	CON	LAB	5,977	12.2%
236	Canterbury	Julian Brazier	CON	LD	6,048	12.3%
237	Salisbury	John Glen	CON	LD	5,966	12.3%
238	Aldershot	Gerald Howarth	CON	LD	5,586	12.3%
239	Finchley & Golders Green	Mike Freer	CON	LAB	5,809	12.3%
240	Calder Valley	Craig Whittaker	CON	LAB	6,431	12.4%
241	Mansfield	Alan Meale	LAB	CON	6,012	12.4%
242	Redcar	Ian Swales	LD	LAB	5,214	12.4%
243	Crawley	Henry Smith	CON	LAB	5,928	12.5%
244	West Worcestershire	Harriett Baldwin	CON	LD	6,754	12.5%
245	Hornsey & Wood Green	Lynne Featherstone	LD	LAB	6,875	12.5%
246	Rother Valley	Kevin Barron	LAB	CON	5,866	12.5%
247	Llanelli	Nia Griffith	LAB	PC	4,701	12.5%
248	Portsmouth South	Mike Hancock	LD	CON	5,200	12.6%
249	Reading West	Alok Sharma	CON	LAB	6,004	12.6%
250	Rugby	Mark Pawsey	CON	LAB	6,000	12.6%
251	Merthyr Tydfil & Rhymney	Dai Havard	LAB	LD	4,056	12.6%
252	Burton	Andrew Griffiths	CON	LAB	6,304	12.7%
253	Cardiff Central	Jenny Willott	LD	LAB	4,576	12.7%

RANK	CONSTITUENCY	MP ELECTED	1ST	2ND	VOTES	% VOTE
254	Bishop Auckland	Helen Goodman	LAB	CON	5,218	12.7%
255	Foyle	Mark Durkan	SDLP	SF	4,824	12.7%
256	Na h-Eileanan an Iar	Angus MacNeil	SNP	LAB	1,885	12.8%
257	Woking	Jonathan Lord	CON	LD	6,807	12.9%
258	South Basildon & East Thurrock	Stephen Metcalfe	CON	LAB	5,772	12.9%
259	Poplar & Limehouse	Jim Fitzpatrick	LAB	CON	6,030	12.9%
260	Lewisham West & Penge	Jim Dowd	LAB	LD	5,828	12.9%
261	Heywood & Middleton	Jim Dobbin	LAB	CON	5,971	12.9%
262	Tamworth	Chris Pincher	CON	LAB	6,090	13.1%
263	Glasgow North	Ann McKechin	LAB	LD	3,898	13.2%
264	Redditch	Karen Lumley	CON	LAB	5,821	13.2%
265	Kingston & Surbiton	Edward Davey	LD	CON	7,560	13.2%
266	Mid Sussex	Nicholas Soames	CON	LD	7,402	13.3%
267	South Cambridgeshire	Andrew Lansley	CON	LD	7,838	13.3%
268	Hexham	Guy Opperman	CON	LD	5,788	13.3%
269	Bournemouth West	Conor Burns	CON	LD	5,583	13.4%
270	Erith & Thamesmead	Teresa Pearce	LAB	CON	5,703	13.4%
271	Coventry North West	Geoffrey Robinson	LAB	CON	6,288	13.5%
272	Cambridge	Julian Huppert	LD	CON	6,792	13.5%
273	North Somerset	Liam Fox	CON	LD	7,862	13.6%
274	Moray	Angus Robertson	SNP	CON	5,590	13.6%
275	Southport	John Pugh	LD	CON	6,024	13.8%
276	Salford & Eccles	Hazel Blears	LAB	LD	5,725	13.8%
277	Gordon	Malcolm Bruce	LD	SNP	6,748	13.8%
278	Broadland	Keith Simpson	CON	LD	7,292	13.8%
279	Chatham & Aylesford	Tracey Crouch	CON	LAB	6,069	13.9%
280	York Central	Hugh Bayley	LAB	CON	6,451	13.9%
281	Congleton	Fiona Bruce	CON	LD	7,063	13.9%
282	Guildford	Anne Milton	CON	LD	7,782	14.0%
283	North Swindon	Justin Tomlinson	CON	LAB	7,060	14.0%
284	North Dorset	Robert Walter	CON	LD	7,625	14.1%
285	South Derbyshire	Heather Wheeler	CON	LAB	7,128	14.1%
286	Bradford West	Marsha Singh	LAB	CON	5,763	14.2%
287	Sheffield, Heeley	Meg Munn	LAB	LD	5,807	14.2%
288	Dumfries & Galloway	Russell Brown	LAB	CON	7,449	14.3%
289	Filton & Bradley Stoke	Jack Lopresti	CON	LAB	6,914	14.3%
290	Hartlepool	Iain Wright	LAB	CON	5,509	14.4%
291	North West Leicestershire	Andrew Bridgen	CON	LAB	7,511	14.5%

RANK	CONSTITUENCY	MP ELECTED	1ST	2ND	VOTES	% VOTE
292	Thornbury & Yate	Steve Webb	LD	CON	7,116	14.8%
293	South Dorset	Richard Drax	CON	LAB	7,443	14.8%
294	Derby South	Margaret Beckett	LAB	CON	6,122	14.9%
295	Lewisham East	Heidi Alexander	LAB	LD	6,216	14.9%
296	Doncaster Central	Rosie Winterton	LAB	CON	6,229	14.9%
297	Shrewsbury & Atcham	Daniel Kawczynski	CON	LD	7,944	15.0%
298	Isle of Wight	Andrew Turner	CON	LD	10,527	15.0%
299	Colchester	Bob Russell	LD	CON	6,982	15.1%
300	Hazel Grove	Andrew Stunell	LD	CON	6,371	15.2%
301	Reading East	Rob Wilson	CON	LD	7,605	15.2%
302	Staffordshire Moorlands	Karen Bradley	CON	LAB	6,689	15.3%
303	Lewes	Norman Baker	LD	CON	7,647	15.3%
304	Warrington North	Helen Jones	LAB	CON	6,771	15.3%
305	East Londonderry	Gregory Campbell	DUP	SF	5,355	15.3%
306	Brent North	Barry Gardiner	LAB	CON	8,028	15.4%
307	North Wiltshire	James Gray	CON	LD	7,483	15.4%
308	Northampton South	Brian Binley	CON	LAB	6,004	15.4%
309	Falkirk	Eric Joyce	LAB	SNP	7,843	15.4%
310	West Bromwich	West Adrian Bailey	LAB	CON	5,651	15.6%
311	Sunderland Central	Julie Elliott	LAB	CON	6,725	15.8%
312	Poole	Robert Syms	CON	LD	7,541	15.9%
313	Leyton & Wanstead	John Cryer	LAB	LD	6,416	16.0%
314	Scarborough & Whitby	Robert Goodwill	CON	LAB	8,130	16.5%
315	Portsmouth North	Penny Mordaunt	CON	LAB	7,289	16.5%
316	Bassetlaw	John Mann	LAB	CON	8,215	16.6%
317	South Thanet	Laura Sandys	CON	LAB	7,617	16.6%
318	Suffolk Coastal	Therese Coffey	CON	LD	9,128	16.6%
319	Milton Keynes North	Mark Lancaster	CON	LAB	8,961	16.6%
320	Southend West	David Amess	CON	LD	7,270	16.7%
321	Caithness, Sutherland & Easter Ross	John Thurso	LD	LAB	4,826	16.8%
322	Clwyd West	David Jones	CON	LAB	6,419	16.8%
323	South Suffolk	Tim Yeo	CON	LD	8,689	16.9%
324	Stockton North	Alex Cunningham	LAB	CON	6,676	16.9%
325	Castle Point	Rebecca Harris	CON	IND	7,632	17.0%
326	Bridgwater & West Somerset	Ian Liddell-Grainger	CON	LD	9,249	17.0%
327	Tiverton & Honiton	Neil Parish	CON	LD	9,320	17.0%
328	Central Devon	Mel Stride	CON	LD	9,230	17.1%
329	Stoke-on-Trent Central	Tristram Hunt	LAB	LD	5,566	17.1%

RANK	CONSTITUENCY	MP ELECTED	1ST	2ND	VOTES	% VOTE
330	East Devon	Hugo Swire	CON	LD	9,114	17.2%
331	Enfield, Southgate	David Burrowes	CON	LAB	7,626	17.2%
332	Blyth Valley	Ronnie Campbell	LAB	LD	6,668	17.3%
333	Belfast South	Alasdair McDonnell	SDLP	DUP	5,926	17.3%
334	Stockport	Ann Coffey	LAB	CON	6,784	17.3%
335	North West Durham	Pat Glass	LAB	LD	7,612	17.4%
336	Luton North	Kelvin Hopkins	LAB	CON	7,520	17.5%
337	Manchester, Gorton	Gerald Kaufman	LAB	LD	6,703	17.5%
338	Bournemouth East	Tobias Ellwood	CON	LD	7,728	17.6%
339	West Bromwich East	Tom Watson	LAB	CON	6,696	17.6%
340	Stirling	Anne McGuire	LAB	CON	8,304	17.7%
341	Harborough	Edward Garnier	CON	LD	9,797	17.8%
342	Strangford	Jim Shannon	DUP	UCU	5,876	18.1%
343	Leeds West	Rachel Reeves	LAB	LD	7,016	18.1%
344	Skipton & Ripon	Julian Smith	CON	LD	9,950	18.2%
345	Holborn & St Pancras	Frank Dobson	LAB	LD	9,942	18.2%
346	Kingston upon Hull West & Hessle	Alan Johnson	LAB	LD	5,742	18.2%
347	Wansbeck	Ian Lavery	LAB	LD	7,031	18.4%
348	Newry & Armagh	Conor Murphy	SF	SDLP	8,331	18.6%
349	Gillingham & Rainham	Rehman Chishti	CON	LAB	8,680	18.6%
350	Edinburgh South West	Alistair Darling	LAB	CON	8,447	18.6%
351	Wythenshawe & Sale East	Paul Goggins	LAB	CON	7,575	18.6%
352	Inverness, Nairn, Badenoch & Strathspey	Danny Alexander	LD	LAB	8,765	18.6%
353	Leicester South	Peter Soulsby	LAB	LD	8,808	18.7%
354	Liverpool, Wavertree	Luciana Berger	LAB	LD	7,167	18.9%
355	Wolverhampton South East	Pat McFadden	LAB	CON	6,593	19.0%
356	Bermondsey & Old Southwark	Simon Hughes	LD	LAB	8,530	19.1%
357	Folkestone & Hythe	Damian Collins	CON	LD	10,122	19.2%
358	Kettering	Philip Hollobone	CON	LAB	9,094	19.2%
359	Dulwich & West Norwood	Tessa Jowell	LAB	LD	9,365	19.4%
360	Ealing North	Stephen Pound	LAB	CON	9,301	19.5%
361	Dundee West	Jim McGovern	LAB	SNP	7,278	19.6%
362	Gravesham	Adam Holloway	CON	LAB	9,312	19.7%
363	South Down	Margaret Ritchie	SDLP	SF	8,412	19.8%
364	Wycombe	Steve Baker	CON	LD	9,560	19.9%
365	South Norfolk	Richard Bacon	CON	LD	10,940	19.9%
366	Stretford & Urmston	Kate Green	LAB	CON	8,935	19.9%
367	Huntingdon	Jonathan Djanogly	CON	LD	10,819	19.9%

RANK	CONSTITUENCY	MP ELECTED	1ST	2ND	VOTES	% VOTE
368	Ludlow	Philip Dunne	CON	LD	9,749	20.0%
369	Shipley	Philip Davies	CON	LAB	9,944	20.1%
370	Blaydon	David Anderson	LAB	LD	9,117	20.3%
371	Twickenham	Vincent Cable	LD	CON	12,140	20.3%
372	East Renfrewshire	Jim Murphy	LAB	CON	10,420	20.4%
373	Wallasey	Angela Eagle	LAB	CON	8,507	20.4%
374	Stoke-on-Trent	North Joan Walley	LAB	CON	8,235	20.5%
375	Horsham	Francis Maude	CON	LD	11,460	20.5%
376	Bristol West	Stephen Williams	LD	LAB	11,366	20.5%
377	The Wrekin	Mark Pritchard	CON	LAB	9,450	20.6%
378	Rochester & Strood	Mark Reckless	CON	LAB	9,953	20.7%
379	North Herefordshire	Bill Wiggin	CON	LD	9,887	20.8%
380	Newbury	Richard Benyon	CON	LD	12,248	20.9%
381	Leeds North West	Greg Mulholland	LD	CON	9,103	20.9%
382	Nottingham East	Christopher Leslie	LAB	LD	6,969	21.0%
383	Bury St Edmunds	David Ruffley	CON	LD	12,380	21.1%
384	South West Wiltshire	Andrew Murrison	CON	LD	10,367	21.1%
385	Spelthorne	Kwasi Kwarteng	CON	LD	10,019	21.2%
386	Dartford	Gareth Johnson	CON	LAB	10,628	21.2%
387	Gainsborough	Edward Leigh	CON	LD	10,559	21.4%
388	North Ayrshire & Arran	Katy Clark	LAB	SNP	9,895	21.5%
389	Ayr, Carrick & Cumnock	Sandra Osborne	LAB	CON	9,911	21.6%
390	Sedgefield	Phil Wilson	LAB	CON	8,696	21.6%
391	Blackburn	Jack Straw	LAB	CON	9,856	21.7%
392	Ealing, Southall	Virendra Sharma	LAB	CON	9,291	21.7%
393	Ceredigion	Mark Williams	LD	PC	8,324	21.8%
394	Oldham West & Royton	Michael Meacher	LAB	CON	9,352	21.8%
395	Bolton South East	Yasmin Qureshi	LAB	CON	8,634	21.8%
396	Newcastle upon Tyne Central	Chinyelu Onwurah	LAB	LD	7,466	21.9%
397	Bromsgrove	Sajid Javid	CON	LAB	11,308	21.9%
398	Dwyfor Meirionnydd	Elfyn Llwyd	PC	CON	6,367	22.0%
399	Ilford South	Mike Gapes	LAB	CON	11,287	22.0%
400	Aberdeen North	Frank Doran	LAB	SNP	8,361	22.2%

(Source: House of Commons Library)

Top 75 Conservative target seats

RANK	SEAT	% SWING REQUIRED	INCUMBENT PARTY
1	Hampstead & Kilburn	Majority 42 (0.1%)	LAB
2	Bolton West	Majority 92 (0.2%)	LAB
3	Solihull	Majority 175 (0.3%)	LIB
4	Southampton, Itchen	Majority 192 (0.4%)	LAB
5	Mid Dorset & North Poole	Majority 269 (0.6%)	LIB
6	Wirral South	Majority 531 (1.3%)	LAB
7	Derby North	Majority 613 (1.4%)	LAB
8	Wells	Majority 800 (1.4%)	LIB
9	Dudley North	Majority 649 (1.7%)	LAB
10	Great Grimsby	Majority 714 (2.2%)	LAB
11	Morley & Outwood	Majority 1101 (2.3%)	LAB
12	Telford	Majority 978 (2.4%)	LAB
13	Walsall North	Majority 990 (2.7%)	LAB
14	St Austell & Newquay	Majority 1312 (2.8%)	LIB
15	Somerton & Frome	Majority 1817 (3%)	LIB
16	Birmingham, Edgbaston	Majority 1274 (3.1%)	LAB
17	Sutton & Cheam	Majority 1608 (3.3%)	LIB
18	Halifax	Majority 1472 (3.4%)	LAB
19	Newcastle under Lyme	Majority 1552 (3.6%)	LAB
20	Middlesbrough South & East Cleveland	Majority 1677 (3.6%)	LAB
21	Wakefield	Majority 1613 (3.6%)	LAB
22	St Ives	Majority 1719 (3.7%)	LIB
23	Plymouth Moor View	Majority 1588 (3.8%)	LAB
24	Gedling	Majority 1859 (3.9%)	LAB
25	Eltham	Majority 1663 (4%)	LAB
26	Walsall South	Majority 1755 (4.3%)	LAB
27	Nottingham South	Majority 1772 (4.3%)	LAB
28	Chippenham	Majority 2470 (4.7%)	LIB
29	Tooting	Majority 2524 (5%)	LAB
30	Chorley	Majority 2593 (5.2%)	LAB
31	North East Derbyshire	Majority 2445 (5.2%)	LAB
32	Exeter	Majority 2721 (5.2%)	LAB
33	Blackpool South	Majority 1852 (5.3%)	LAB
34	Westminster North	Majority 2126 (5.4%)	LAB
35	Oldham East & Saddleworth	Majority 103 (5.4%)	LAB
36	Southampton, Test	Majority 2413 (5.5%)	LAB
37	Luton South	Majority 2329 (5.5%)	LAB
38	Bridgend	Majority 2263 (5.9%)	LAB

39	Dagenham & Rainham	Majority 2630 (5.9%)	LAB
40	Delyn	Majority 2272 (6.1%)	LAB
41	Cheadle	Majority 3272 (6.2%)	LIB
42	North Cornwall	Majority 2981 (6.4%)	LIB
43	Gower	Majority 2683 (6.4%)	LAB
44	Norwich South	Majority 310 (6.4%)	LIB
45	Penistone & Stocksbridge	Majority 3049 (6.6%)	LAB
46	Eastbourne	Majority 3435 (6.6%)	LIB
47	Birmingham, Northfield	Majority 2782 (6.7%)	LAB
48	Stalybridge & Hyde	Majority 2744 (6.7%)	LAB
49	Bury South	Majority 3292 (6.8%)	LAB
50	Harrow West	Majority 3143 (6.8%)	LAB
51	Bradford East	Majority 365 (6.9%)	LIB
52	Taunton Deane	Majority 3993 (6.9%)	LIB
53	Scunthorpe	Majority 2549 (6.9%)	LAB
54	Berwick-upon-Tweed	Majority 2690 (7%)	LIB
55	Vale of Clwyd	Majority 2509 (7.1%)	LAB
56	Wolverhampton North East	Majority 2484 (7.1%)	LAB
57	Eastleigh	Majority 3864 (7.2%)	LIB
58	Hyndburn	Majority 3090 (7.2%)	LAB
59	Alyn & Deeside	Majority 2919 (7.3%)	LAB
60	Birmingham, Selly Oak	Majority 3482 (7.5%)	LAB
61	Hammersmith	Majority 3549 (7.5%)	LAB
62	Argyll & Bute	Majority 3431 (7.6%)	LIB
63	Brighton, Pavilion	Majority 1252 (7.6%)	GRE
64	Darlington	Majority 3388 (7.9%)	LAB
65	Sefton Central	Majority 3862 (8%)	LAB
66	Aberdeenshire West & Kincardine	Majority 3684 (8.2%)	LIB
67	Clwyd South	Majority 2834 (8.2%)	LAB
68	Bristol East	Majority 3722 (8.3%)	LAB
69	Don Valley	Majority 3595 (8.3%)	LAB
70	Torbay	Majority 4078 (8.3%)	LIB
71	Coventry South	Majority 3845 (8.4%)	LAB
72	Batley & Spen	Majority 4406 (8.6%)	LAB
73	Angus	Majority 3282 (8.6%)	LIB
74	Newport West	Majority 3544 (8.9%)	LAB
75	Copeland	Majority 3833 (9%)	LAB

(Source: UK Polling Report)

Top 100 Labour target seats

RANK	SEAT	% SWING REQUIRED	INCUMBENT PARTY
1	North Warwickshire	Majority 54 (0.1%)	CON
2	Thurrock	Majority 92 (0.2%)	CON
3	Hendon	Majority 106 (0.2%)	CON
4	Cardiff North	Majority 194 (0.4%)	CON
5	Sherwood	Majority 214 (0.4%)	CON
6	Norwich South	Majority 310 (0.7%)	LIB
7	Stockton South	Majority 332 (0.7%)	CON
8	Broxtowe	Majority 389 (0.7%)	CON
9	Lancaster & Fleetwood	Majority 333 (0.8%)	CON
10	Bradford East	Majority 365 (0.9%)	LIB
11	Amber Valley	Majority 536 (1.2%)	CON
12	Waveney	Majority 769 (1.5%)	CON
13	Wolverhampton South West	Majority 691 (1.7%)	CON
14	Morecambe & Lunesdale	Majority 866 (2%)	CON
15	Carlisle	Majority 853 (2%)	CON
16	Stroud	Majority 1299 (2.2%)	CON
17	Weaver Vale	Majority 991 (2.3%)	CON
18	Lincoln	Majority 1058 (2.3%)	CON
19	Brighton, Pavilion	Majority 1252 (2.4%)	GRE
20	Plymouth Sutton & Devonport	Majority 1149 (2.6%)	CON
21	Dewsbury	Majority 1526 (2.8%)	CON
22	Warrington South	Majority 1553 (2.8%)	CON
23	Brent Central	Majority 1345 (3%)	LIB
24	Bedford	Majority 1353 (3%)	CON
25	Brighton, Kemptown	Majority 1328 (3.1%)	CON
26	Pudsey	Majority 1659 (3.4%)	CON
27	Corby	Majority 1895 (3.5%)	CON
28	Brentford & Isleworth	Majority 1958 (3.6%)	CON
29	Hove	Majority 1868 (3.8%)	CON
30	Enfield North	Majority 1692 (3.8%)	CON
31	Hastings & Rye	Majority 1993 (4%)	CON
32	Manchester, Withington	Majority 1894 (4.2%)	LIB
33	Burnley	Majority 1818 (4.3%)	LIB
34	Ipswich	Majority 2079 (4.4%)	CON
35	Dundee East	Majority 1821 (4.5%)	LIB
36	East Dunbartonshire	Majority 2184 (4.6%)	LIB
37	Halesowen & Rowley Regis	Majority 2023 (4.6%)	CON
38	Nuneaton	Majority 2069 (4.6%)	CON

39	Gloucester	Majority 2420 (4.8%)	CON
40	Northampton North	Majority 1936 (4.8%)	CON
41	Bury North	Majority 2243 (5%)	CON
42	Kingswood	Majority 2445 (5.1%)	CON
43	Erewash	Majority 2501 (5.3%)	CON
44	Blackpool North & Cleveleys	Majority 2150 (5.3%)	CON
45	City of Chester	Majority 2583 (5.5%)	CON
46	Arfon	Majority 1455 (5.6%)	GRE
47	Croydon Central	Majority 2879 (5.8%)	CON
48	Worcester	Majority 2982 (6.1%)	CON
49	Keighley	Majority 2940 (6.2%)	CON
50	Wirral West	Majority 2436 (6.2%)	CON
51	Cannock Chase	Majority 3195 (7%)	CON
52	Loughborough	Majority 3744 (7.1%)	CON
53	Harrow East	Majority 3403 (7.1%)	CON
54	Warwick & Leamington	Majority 3513 (7.2%)	CON
55	Birmingham, Yardley	Majority 3002 (7.3%)	LIB
56	South Swindon	Majority 3544 (7.5%)	CON
57	Ealing Central & Acton	Majority 3716 (7.9%)	CON
58	Pendle	Majority 3585 (8%)	CON
59	Stevenage	Majority 3578 (8%)	CON
60	Elmet & Rothwell	Majority 4521 (8.1%)	CON
61	Edinburgh West	Majority 3803 (8.2%)	LIB
62	Watford	Majority 1425 (8.2%)*	CON
63	Carmarthen West & South Pembrokeshire	Majority 3423 (8.5%)	CON
64	Vale of Glamorgan	Majority 4307 (8.9%)	CON
65	Argyll & Bute	Majority 3431 (8.9%)*	LIB
66	Dumfriesshire, Clydesdale & Tweeddale	Majority 4194 (9.1%)	CON
67	Carmarthen East & Dinefwr	Majority 3481 (9.2%)	GRE
68	Norwich North	Majority 3901 (9.2%)	CON
69	High Peak	Majority 4677 (9.3%)	CON
70	Milton Keynes South	Majority 5201 (9.4%)	CON
71	Rossendale & Darwen	Majority 4493 (9.5%)	CON
72	Cleethorpes	Majority 4298 (9.6%)	CON
73	North East Somerset	Majority 4914 (9.6%)	CON
74	Great Yarmouth	Majority 4276 (9.9%)	CON
75	Dudley South	Majority 3856 (10.1%)	CON
76	Dover	Majority 5274 (10.5%)	CON
77	Colne Valley	Majority 4837 (10.6%)*	CON
78	South Ribble	Majority 5554 (10.8%)	CON

79	Peterborough	Majority 4861 (10.8%)	CON
80	Stafford	Majority 5460 (10.9%)	CON
81	Stourbridge	Majority 5164 (10.9%)	CON
82	Harlow	Majority 4925 (11.2%)	CON
83	Aberconwy	Majority 3398 (11.3%)	CON
84	Ilford North	Majority 5404 (11.5%)	CON
85	Preseli Pembrokeshire	Majority 4605 (11.6%)	CON
86	Brigg & Goole	Majority 5147 (11.7%)	CON
87	Crewe & Nantwich	Majority 6046 (11.8%)	CON
88	Bristol North West	Majority 3274 (12%)*	CON
89	Battersea	Majority 5977 (12.3%)	CON
90	Finchley & Golders Green	Majority 5809 (12.3%)	CON
91	Calder Valley	Majority 6431 (12.4%)	CON
92	Redcar	Majority 5214 (12.4%)	LIB
93	Crawley	Majority 5928 (12.5%)	CON
94	Hornsey & Wood Green	Majority 6875 (12.5%)	LIB
95	Reading West	Majority 6004 (12.6%)	CON
96	Rugby	Majority 6000 (12.6%)	CON
97	Burton	Majority 6304 (12.7%)	CON
98	Cardiff Central	Majority 4576 (12.7%)	LIB
99	Na h-Eileanan an Iar (Western Isles)	Majority 1885 (12.8%)	LIB
100	South Basildon & East Thurrock	Majority 5772 (12.9%)	CON

(Source: UK Polling Report)

Top 30 Liberal Democrat target seats

RANK	SEAT	% SWING REQUIRED	INCUMBENT PARTY
1	Camborne & Redruth	Majority 66 (0%)	CON
2	Oldham East & Saddleworth	Majority 103 (0%)	LAB
3	Oxford West & Abingdon	Majority 176 (0%)	CON
4	Sheffield Central	Majority 165 (0%)	LAB
5	Ashfield	Majority 192 (0%)	LAB
6	Edinburgh South	Majority 316 (1%)	LAB
7	Truro & Falmouth	Majority 435 (1%)	CON
8	Newton Abbot	Majority 523 (1%)	CON
9	Chesterfield	Majority 549 (1%)	LAB
10	Swansea West	Majority 504 (1%)	LAB
11	Hampstead & Kilburn	Majority 42 (0%)*	LAB
12	Kingston-upon-Hull North	Majority 641 (2%)	LAB
13	Rochdale	Majority 889 (2%)	LAB
14	Harrogate & Knaresborough	Majority 1039 (2%)	CON

15	Watford	Majority 1425 (3%)	CON
16	Montgomeryshire	Majority 1184 (4%)	CON
17	Edinburgh North & Leith	Majority 1724 (4%)	LAB
18	St Albans	Majority 2305 (4%)	CON
19	Newport East	Majority 1650 (5%)	LAB
20	Derby North	Majority 613 (1%)*	LAB
21	Weston-super-Mare	Majority 2691 (5%)	CON
22	Hereford & South Herefordshire	Majority 2481 (5%)	CON
23	West Devon and Torridge	Majority 2957 (5%)	CON
24	Winchester	Majority 3048 (5%)	CON
25	Northampton North	Majority 1936 (5%)	CON
26	South East Cornwall	Majority 3220 (6%)	CON
27	Bristol North West	Majority 3274 (7%)	CON
28	City of Durham	Majority 3067 (7%)	LAB
29	West Dorset	Majority 3923 (7%)	CON
30	Richmond Park	Majority 4091 (7%)	CON

*Lib Dems in third place
(Source: UK Polling Report)

Top 20 SNP target seats

RANK	SEAT	% SWING REQUIRED	INCUMBENT PARTY
1	Ochil & South Perthshire	0.74	Lab
2	Dundee West	7.28	Lab
3	Kilmarnock & Loudoun	9.80	Lab
4	Aberdeen North	10.08	Lab
5	Argyll & Bute	10.49	Lib
6	Edinburgh East	11.51	Lab
7	Linlithgow & East Falkirk	12.07	Lab
8	Stirling	12.49	Lab
9	North Ayrshire & Arran	12.98	Lab
10	Paisley & Renfrewshire North	13.45	Lab
11	Lanark & Hamilton East	14.14	Lab
12	East Lothian	14.19	Lab
13	Dunfermline & West Fife	14.25	Lab
14	Midlothian	14.26	Lab
15	Glenrothes	14.27	Lab
16	Glasgow North	14.50	Lab
17	Gordon	14.53	Lab
18	Edinburgh South West	14.60	Lab
19	Falkirk	14.73	Lab
20	Livingston	14.77	Lab

Top 10 Plaid Cymru target seats

RANK	SEAT	% SWING REQUIRED	INCUMBENT PARTY
1	Ceredigion	0.31	Lib
2	Arfon	0.91	Lab
3	Ynys Môn	1.75	Lab
4	Llanelli	10.23	Lab
5	Aberconwy	15.06	Lab
6	Carmarthen West & South Pembrokeshire	15.84	Lab
7	Cardiff West	15.97	Lab
8	Gower	17.69	Lab
9	Neath	17.74	Lab
10	Clwyd South	17.89	Lab

(Source: UK Polling Report)

Top UKIP target seats

Editor's note: It is impossible to compile tables like the above for UKIP target seats because they would be utterly meaningless if we just used voting data from the 2010 election. Robert Ford and Matthew Goodwin, however, have come to our rescue. Read on…

In our recent book, *Revolt on the Right*, we compiled a list of the most demographically receptive seats in the country for UKIP. This allowed us to rank all seats according to how favourable their populations are for UKIP, using the most recent census data.

UKIP's ideal seats share key characteristics. Firstly, they have lots of 'left-behind' voters who we also know from our research are the most receptive to UKIP and its policies. Second, these seats also have very low numbers of voters who tend to remain resistant to UKIP, including university graduates, ethnic minorities and people in professional and economically secure occupations. This is a useful first exercise in filtering through all seats to find those where, if UKIP stood a candidate and knocked on doors, they would probably find lots of receptive voters.

Clearly, we are not saying that UKIP will enjoy strong support in all of these seats. It might be that they simply do not target these seats, or the local Conservative MP has a formidable majority that makes a UKIP insurgence unlikely. In order to find seats that UKIP actually has a chance of winning, you would need to look at *both* demography and the local political context, such as whether the vote is split across three parties, whether UKIP is targeting the seat and has been recruiting support through local elections.

Take the seat of Knowsley as an example. This is the fifth most UKIP-friendly seat in the country, but it will be incredibly difficult for UKIP to win the seat because of the very large Labour majority (over 25,000). In fact, even whilst most of the most demographically favourable seats for UKIP have Labour incumbents, they are often protected by large majorities.

The most potent UKIP challenges to Labour come in seats such as Great Grimsby, where the radical right insurgents have already put in strong local showings, and the local Labour Party has a smaller majority to fall back on.

However, even a large majority may not provide total safety from a strong local UKIP candidate. Clacton was the number one most UKIP-favourable seat on our measures prior to Douglas Carswell's defection. His strong local profile certainly contributes to his apparent ability to bring most Conservative voters with him to his new party, but their sympathies for UKIP's policies no doubt play a part too.

While Labour MPs in the safe seats near the top of this list would be unlikely to jump ship, the overnight disappearance of a 12,000 vote Conservative majority in Clacton should give them pause. Their seats have almost as many voters from UKIP-sympathising groups as Douglas Carswell's has.

The overall ranking of each seat in the full *Revolt on the Right* database is provided in the final column.

Dr Matthew Goodwin and Dr Robert Ford are the authors of Revolt on the Right.

Labour

RANK	SEAT	REGION	LABOUR MAJORITY (VOTES)	LABOUR MAJORITY (%)	UKIP VOTE 2010	OVERALL RANKING IN REVOLT ON THE RIGHT
1	Rhondda	Wales	11,553	37.2	1.2	2
2	Blaenau Gwent	Wales	10,516	32.5	1.5	3
3	Kingston upon Hull East	Yorkshire and the Humber	8,597	25.1	8	4
4	Easington	North East	14,982	42.9	4.7	5
5	Knowsley	North West	25,690	57.5	2.5	6
6	Barnsley East	Yorkshire and the Humber	11,090	28.9	4.5	7
7	Aberavon	Wales	11,039	35.7	1.6	8
8	Merthyr Tydfil & Rhymney	Wales	4,056	12.6	2.7	9
9	Doncaster North	Yorkshire and the Humber	10,909	26.3	4.3	10
10	Liverpool, Walton	North West	19,818	57.7	2.6	11
11	Normanton, Pontefract & Castleford	Yorkshire and the Humber	10,979	23.7	Did not stand	12
12	Great Grimsby	Yorkshire and the Humber	714	2.2	6.2	13
13	Ashfield	East Midlands	192	0.4	1.9	14
14	Bolsover	East Midlands	11,182	25.4	3.9	15
15	Cynon Valley	Wales	29,876	32.2	3.4	17
16	Wentworth & Dearne	Yorkshire and the Humber	13,920	33.1	8.1	18
17	Houghton & Sunderland South	North East	10,990	28.9	2.7	20
18	Ogmore	Wales	13,246	38.2	2.3	22
19	Walsall North	West Midlands	990	2.7	4.8	23
20	Islwyn	Wales	12,215	35.2	2.7	24
21	Stoke-on-Trent North	West Midlands	8,235	20.5	6.2	25
22	Washington & Sunderland West	North East	11,458	30.7	3.3	26
23	Hartlepool	North East	5,509	14.4	7	27
24	Blackpool South	North West	1,852	5.3	3.8	29
25	Barnsley Central	Yorkshire and the Humber	11,771	30.0	12.2	30
26	Bishop Auckland	North East	5,218	12.7	2.7	31
27	Plymouth, Moor View	South West	1,588	3.8	7.7	33
28	Hemsworth	Yorkshire and the Humber	9,844	22.4	Did not stand	34
29	Stoke-on-Trent South	West Midlands	4,130	10.4	3.4	35
30	Bootle	North West	21,181	51.3	6.1	36
31	Torfaen	Wales	9,306	24.7	2.3	37
32	Mansfield	East Midlands	6,012	12.4	6.2	38
33	Workington	North West	4,575	11.7	2.2	39

RANK	SEAT	REGION	LABOUR MAJORITY (VOTES)	LABOUR MAJORITY (%)	UKIP VOTE 2010	OVERALL RANKING IN REVOLT ON THE RIGHT
34	South Shields*	North East	6,505	25.8	24.2	41
35	Don Valley	Yorkshire and the Humber	3,595	8.3	4.4	43
36	Neath	Wales	9,775	26.3	2.2	46
37	Halton	North West	15,504	37.5	3	47
38	Kingston upon Hull West & Hessle	Yorkshire and the Humber	5,740	18.2	5.4	48
39	Stockton North	North East	6,676	16.9	3.9	49
40	Swansea East	Wales	10,838	33.2	2.6	50
41	Scunthorpe	Yorkshire and the Humber	2,549	6.9	4.6	51
42	Jarrow	North East	12,908	33.3	Did not stand	52
43	Liverpool, West Derby	North West	18,467	51.6	3.1	54
44	North Durham	North East	12,076	29.5	3.3	56
45	Llanelli	Wales	4,701	12.6	2.8	58
46	Sedgefield	North East	8,696	21.6	3.7	59
47	St Helens North	North West	13,101	29.4	4.7	60
48	St Helens South & Whiston	North West	14,122	30.6	2.7	61
49	Wigan	North West	10,487	23.8	5.7	63
50	Blyth Valley	North East	6,668	17.3	4.3	64
51	Bassetlaw	East Midlands	8,215	16.6	3.6	65
52	Rotherham*	Yorkshire and the Humber	5,318	24.5	21.8	66
53	Nottingham North	East Midlands	8,138	23.7	3.9	68
54	Birkenhead	North West	15,395	43.6	Did not stand	69
55	Caerphilly	Wales	10,755	27.6	2.4	70
56	Wansbeck	North East	7,031	18.4	2.5	72
57	Makerfield	North West	12,490	28.5	Did not stand	75
58	Clwyd South	Wales	2,834	8.2	2.4	77
59	Vale of Clwyd	Wales	2,509	7.1	1.4	78
60	Middlesbrough South & East Cleveland	North East	1,677	3.6	4.1	79
61	North West Durham	North East	7,612	17.4	2.9	86
62	Barrow & Furness	North West	5,208	11.8	1.9	89
63	North Tyneside	North East	12,884	27.8	2.8	90
64	Copeland	North West	389	9.0	2.3	91
65	Denton & Reddish	North West	9,831	26.1	5.5	93
66	Gateshead	North East	12,549	32.8	2.9	94
67	Rother Valley	Yorkshire and the Humber	5,866	12.6	5.6	96

RANK	SEAT	REGION	LABOUR MAJORITY (VOTES)	LABOUR MAJORITY (%)	UKIP VOTE 2010	OVERALL RANKING IN REVOLT ON THE RIGHT
68	Wallasey	North West	8,507	20.4	2.9	97
69	Chesterfield	East Midlands	549	1.2	3.1	100
70	North East Derbyshire	East Midlands	2,445	5.2	5.6	103
71	Garston & Halewood	North West	16,877	39.4	3.6	104
72	Blaydon	North East	2,277	20.3	Did not stand	105
73	Dudley North	West Midlands	649	1.7	8.5	106
74	Delyn	Wales	2,272	6.1	1.8	107
75	Telford	West Midlands	981	2.4	5.9	108
76	West Bromwich West	West Midlands	5,651	15.6	4.3	109
77	Ynys Mon	Wales	2,461	7.1	3.5	113
78	Ashton-under-Lyne	North West	9,094	23.7	4.4	115
79	Leigh	North West	12,011	27.1	3.5	116
80	Middlesbrough	North East	8,211	26.0	11.8	119
81	Darlington	North East	3,388	7.9	2.8	120
82	Alyn and Deeside	Wales	2,919	7.3	2.5	122
83	Sheffield South East	Yorkshire and the Humber	10,505	25.4	4.6	131
84	Doncaster Central	Yorkshire and the Humber	6,229	14.9	3.4	132
85	Stoke-on-Trent Central	West Midlands	5,566	17.1	4.3	134
86	Newport East	Wales	1,650	4.8	2	135
87	Wolverhampton North East	West Midlands	2,484	7.1	3.3	138
88	Worsley & Eccles South	North West	4,337	10.4	4.9	141
89	Sunderland Central	North East	6,725	15.8	2.6	143
90	Ellesmere Port & Neston	North West	4,331	9.8	3.7	146
91	Kingston upon Hull North	Yorkshire and the Humber	641	1.9	4.1	147
92	Heywood & Middleton	North West	5,971	12.9	2.6	148
93	Sheffield, Heeley	Yorkshire and the Humber	5,807	14.2	3.7	150
94	Wrexham	Wales	3,658	11.1	2.3	151
95	Corby*	East Midlands	7,791	21.8	14.3	155
96	Stalybridge & Hyde	North West	2,744	6.7	3.3	157
97	Penistone & Stocksbridge	Yorkshire and the Humber	3,049	6.5	4.2	158
98	Birmingham Northfield	West Midlands	2,782	6.7	3.3	164
99	Wakefield	Yorkshire and the Humber	1,613	3.7	Did not stand	165
100	Sheffield Brightside & Hillsborough	Yorkshire and the Humber	13,632	35.0	4.1%	166

* and bold text indicates figures are from by-election results

Conservative

RANK	SEAT	REGION	CON MAJORITY	CON MAJORITY (%)	UKIP VOTE 2010	RANK IN REVOLT ON THE RIGHT
1	Clacton	Eastern	22,867	28	-	1
2	Boston & Skegness	East Midlands	21,325	28.8	9.5	16
3	Great Yarmouth	Eastern	4,276	9.9	4.8	21
4	Waveney	Eastern	769	1.5	5.2	28
5	Louth & Horncastle	East Midlands	13,871	27.5	4.3	32
6	Amber Valley	East Midlands	536	1.2	2	40
7	Blackpool North and Cleveleys	North West	2,150	5.3	4.1	42
8	North East Cambridgeshire	Eastern	16,425	31.4	5.7	44
9	Cleethorpes	Yorkshire	18,939	9.6	7.1	45
10	South Holland & the Deepings	East Midlands	21,880	43.6	6.5	54
11	Cannock Chase	West Midlands	3,195	7	3.5	55
12	North West Norfolk	Eastern	14,810	31	3.9	58
13	Dudley South	West Midlands	3,856	10.1	8.2	67
14	Brigg & Goole	Yorkshire	5,147	11.7	4	71
15	Castle Point	Eastern	7,632	16.9	-	74
16	South West Norfolk	Eastern	13,140	26.7	6.2	76
17	Erewash	East Midlands	2,501	5.3	1.8	80
18	Carlisle	North West	853	2	2.3	81
19	North Warwickshire	West Midlands	54	0.1	2.8	82
20	Sherwood	East Midlands	214	0.4	3	84
21	Yorkshire East	Yorkshire	13,486	26.3	4.2	85
22	Scarborough & Whitby	Yorkshire	8,130	16.5	3	87
23	Bridgwater & West Somerset	South West	9,249	17	4.8	88
24	North Thanet	South East	13,528	31.2	6.5	92
25	Sittingbourne & Sheppey	South East	12,383	25.5	5.4	95
26	Camborne & Redruth	South West	66	0.2	5.1	98
27	Wyre Forest	West Midlands	2,643	5.2	2.9	102
28	Morecambe & Lunesdale	North West	866	2	4.2	110
29	Staffordshire Moorlands	West Midlands	6,689	15.3	8.2	111
30	Dover	South East	5,274	10.5	3.5	114
31	Preseli Pembrokeshire	Wales	4,605	11.6	2.3	117
32	Isle of Wight	South East	10,527	15	3.5	118
33	Norwich North	Eastern	3,901	9.2	4.4	121

RANK	SEAT	REGION	CON MAJORITY	CON MAJORITY (%)	UKIP VOTE 2010	RANK IN REVOLT ON THE RIGHT
34	Aldridge-Brownhills	West Midlands	15,256	39.5	-	123
35	Montgomeryshire	Wales	1,184	3.5	3.3	124
36	Mid Norfolk	Eastern	13,856	27.3	5.5	125
37	Havant	South East	12,160	27.7	5.9	126
38	Carmarthen W & S Pembrokeshire	Wales	3,423	8.4	2.8	128
39	Bognor Regis & Littlehampton	South East	13,063	27.9	6.5	129
40	South Basildon & East Thurrock	Eastern	5,772	12.9	5.9	133
41	Tamworth	West Midlands	6,090	13.1	4.9	136
42	Halesowen & Rowley Regis	West Midlands	2,023	4.6	6.4	139
43	Torridge & West Devon	South West	2,957	5.3	5.5	140
44	Thanet South	South East	7,617	16.6	5.5	142
45	Clwyd West	Wales	6,419	16.8	2.3	144
46	Tiverton & Honiton	South West	9,320	17	6	145
47	Nuneaton	West Midlands	2,069	4.6	0	149
48	Forest of Dean	South West	11,064	22.7	5.2	153
49	Aberconwy	Wales	3,398	11.3	2.1	154
50	Penrith & the Border	North West	11,241	24.9	2.8	156
51	North West Leicestershire	East Midlands	7,511	14.5	2.2	159
52	Christchurch	South West	15,410	31.2	8.5	160
53	Gainsborough	East Midlands	10,559	21.4	4.2	163
54	Newton Abbot	South West	523	1.1	6.4	168
55	Hastings & Rye	South East	1,993	4	2.8	169
56	South Dorset	South West	7,443	14.8	4	170
57	Broadland	Eastern	7,292	13.8	4.5	171
58	Stourbridge	West Midlands	5,164	10.9	4.5	173
59	North Shropshire	West Midlands	15,828	30.5	4.7	174
60	Thirsk & Malton	Yorkshire	11,281	29.6	6.6	175
61	South East Cornwall	South West	3,220	6.8	6.2	176
62	Weston-super-Mare	South West	2,691	5.1	2.7	177
63	Hereford & South Herefordshire	West Midlands	2,481	5.1	3.4	179
64	Bosworth	East Midlands	5,032	9.3	2	181
65	Totnes	South West	4,927	10.3	6	182
66	Ludlow	West Midlands	9,749	20	4.4	183
67	Folkestone & Hythe	South East	10,122	19.2	4.6	185

RANK	SEAT	REGION	CON MAJORITY	CON MAJORITY (%)	UKIP VOTE 2010	RANK IN REVOLT ON THE RIGHT
68	Suffolk Coastal	Eastern	9,128	16.6	5.7	187
69	Crewe & Nantwich	North West	6,046	11.8	2.8	188
70	Wellingborough	East Midlands	11,787	22.8	3.2	192
71	Beverley & Holderness	Yorkshire	12,987	24.4	3.5	193
72	Grantham & Stamford	East Midlands	14,826	28.1	3	195
73	Burton	West Midlands	6,304	12.7	2.9	197
74	Chatham & Aylesford	South East	13.9	13.9	3	198
75	Gosport	South East	14,413	30.7	3.2	199
76	Portsmouth North	South East	7,289	16.5	4.1	200
77	Bexhill & Battle	South East	12,880	23.6	0	201
78	Rossendale & Darwen	North West	4,493	9.5	3.4	202
79	South Suffolk	Eastern	8,689	16.9	7.1	203
80	Harlow (Essex)	South East	4,925	11.2	3.6	204
81	Sleaford & North Hykeham	East Midlands	19,905	33.4	3.6	206
82	Rochford & Southend East	Eastern	11,050	26.5	5.8	207
83	New Forest West	South East	16,896	35.5	5.9	209
84	Redditch	West Midlands	5,821	13.2	3.4	210
85	Kingswood	South West	2,445	5.1	3.2	211
86	Harwich & North Essex	Eastern	11,447	23.4	5.2	212
87	New Forest East	South East	11,307	22.6	5	214
88	South West Wiltshire	South West	10,367	21.1	5.5	215
89	Lincoln	East Midlands	1,058	2.1	2.2	216
90	South Staffordshire	West Midlands	16,590	32.9	5.5	217
91	Braintree	Eastern	16,121	32.8	5	220
92	Kettering	East Midlands	9,094	19.2	-	221
93	West Suffolk	Eastern	13,050	27.1	6.4	222
94	East Worthing & Shoreham	South East	11,105	22.9	6.2	223
95	Weaver Vale	North West	991	2.3	2.3	224
96	Basildon Billericay	Eastern	12,398	29.7	3.8	226
97	North Herefordshire	West Midlands	9,887	20.8	5.7	227
98	Rayleigh & Wickford	Eastern	22,338	42.7	4.2	228
99	South Derbyshire	East Midlands	7,128	14.1	2.4	230
100	Worthing West	South East	11,729	23.9	6	232

Liberal Democrat

RANK	SEAT	REGION	LD MAJORITY	LD MAJORITY (%)	UKIP VOTE 2010 (%)	RANK IN REVOLT ON THE RIGHT
1	Redcar	North East	5,214	12.4	4.5	19
2	North Norfolk	Eastern	11,626	23.4	5.4	62
3	St Austell & Newquay	South West	1,312	2.8	3.7	73
4	Torbay	South West	4,078	8.3	5.3	99
5	North Cornwall	South West	3,076	5.5	5.5	101
6	Berwick-upon-Tweed	North East	2,690	7	3.2	127
7	North Devon	South West	5,821	11.3	7.2	130
8	Burnley	North West	1,818	4.3	2.2	137
9	Yeovil	South West	13,036	22.8	4.1	152
10	St Ives	South West	1,719	3.7	5.6	161
11	Brecon & Radnorshire	Wales	3,747	9.6	2.3	162
12	Wells	South West	800	1.4	3.1	190
13	Somertone & Frome	South West	1,817	3	3.2	219
14	Eastbourne	South East	3,435	6.6	2.5	225
15	Westmorland & Lonsdale	North West	12,264	23.8	1.6	250
16	Taunton Deane	South West	3,993	6.9	3.6	261
17	Mid Dorset & Poole North	South West	269	0.6	4.5	264
18	Hazel Grove	North West	6,371	15.2	5.1	269
19	Ceredigion	Wales	8,324	21.8	2.6	287
20	Lewes	South East	7,647	15.3	3.4	303

50 facts about the 2010 election

Compiled by Iain Dale

1. 650 MPs were elected, 306 of them Conservative, 258 Labour and 57 Lib Dem.

2. The Conservatives gained 10.7 million votes (36.1 per cent), Labour 8.6 million (29.0 per cent), Lib Dems 6.8 million (23.0 per cent).

3. The Conservatives had net gains of 96 seats, Labour lost 90 and the Lib Dems were down 5.

4. In Northern Ireland the DUP won 8 seats (-1), Sinn Fein 5 (-), the SDLP 3 (-) and the Alliance 1 (+1). Lady Sylvia Hermon was elected as an Independent. Sinn Fein polled the most votes.

5. Caroline Lucas became Britain's first Green MP in Brighton Pavilion.

6. Turnout at the election was 3.7 per cent higher than in 2005, at 65.1 per cent.

7. The 2010 election was the first time no party had gained an overall majority since February 1974.

8. The Conservatives and Lib Dems won 59.1 per cent of the popular vote, the largest of any government since the Second World War.

9. Labour's vote share (29 per cent) was their lowest since 1983, and was down 6.3 per cent on 2005.

10. 35 per cent voted for parties other than Labour and the Conservatives, more than at any election since 1918.

11. The swing from Labour to the Conservatives was 4.9 per cent.

12. A total of 29.7 million people cast valid votes.

13. The safest seat in percentage terms is in Liverpool Walton, where Labour's Steve Rotheram enjoys a 57.7 per cent majority. The largest in terms of actual votes – 27,826 – is Labour's Stephen Timms in East Ham.

14. Of the 200 safest seats, 106 are held by the Conservatives, 83 by Labour, 4 by the Lib Dems and 7 by others.

15. The seats with the two smallest majorities are Fermanagh & South Tyrone, where Sinn Fein's Michelle Gildernew has a majority of 4, and Hampstead & Highgate, where Labour's Glenda Jackson has a majority of 42.

16. Of the 200 seats with the smallest majorities, the Conservatives hold 83, Labour 80, the Lib Dems 27 and others 10.

17. The Conservatives are second in 79 of the 200 most marginal seats, Labour in 73, the Lib Dems in 40 and others in 8.

18. 117 seats changed hands, which amounts to 18 per cent of the total seats.

19. 38 per cent of men voted Conservative, 28 per cent voted Labour, 22 per cent Lib Dem.

20. 36 per cent of women voted Conservative, 31 per cent voted Labour, 26 per cent Lib Dem.

21. 4,150 candidates stood at the 2010 election, 596 more than in 2005. The previous record was 3,725 in 1997.

22. At the 2010 election 21 per cent of the candidates were women, up from 20.3 per cent in 2005 and 19.3 per cent in 2001.

23. The youngest candidate at the election was the independent candidate in Erewash, Luke Wilkins, who was eighteen years and thirty-six days old on election day.

24. The oldest candidate was 95-year-old Robert Leaky who stood in Skipton & Ripon for the Virtue Currency Cognitive Appraisal Party. He had also been the oldest candidate at the 2005 election.

25. The Liberal Democrats had the most second- and third-placed candidates.

26. 81 female Labour MPs were elected, 49 Conservatives, 7 Lib Dems, 1 Green, 1 SNP, 1 SDLP, 1 Sinn Fein, 1 Alliance and 1 Green, making a total of 143.

27. Labour MPs elected in 2010 were on average four years older than Conservatives.

28. The oldest MP is Sir Peter Tapsell (Con, Louth & Horncastle) who was born on 1 February 1930.

29. The youngest MP is Pamela Nash, Labour MP for Airdrie & Shotts, who was twenty-five years old at the last election.

30. 48 per cent of Conservative MPs were first elected at the 2010 election.

31. 7 per cent of all MPs were first elected at a by-election.

32. 54 per cent of Conservative MPs, 14 per cent of Labour MPs and 39 per cent of Liberal Democrats were educated at private schools.

33. 75 per cent of MPs went to university.

34. Twenty MPs, nineteen of whom are Conservatives, went to Eton. The other one is a Liberal Democrat.

35. 14 per cent of MPs are lawyers, 8 per cent are teachers, and 35 per cent have a professional background.

36. 41 per cent of Conservative MPs have a business background, as do 8 per cent of Labour MPs and 19 per cent of Liberal Democrats.

37. 14 per cent of MPs went into Parliament having spent all their careers in politics. In 1983 that figure was 3 per cent.

38. Only 4 per cent of MPs are manual workers, compared to 16 per cent in 1979.

39. The total electorate at the 2010 election numbered 45,597,461.

40. The average Conservative seat had 72,418 voters. For Labour the figure is 68,487 and for the Liberal Democrats it's 69,440. The average constituency had 70,150 voters.

41. Turnout in Conservative-won seats was 7.3 per cent higher than in seats which elected a Labour MP.

42. The first three Muslim female MPs were elected in 2010 – Shabana Mahmood in Birmingham Ladywood, Rushanara Ali in Bethnal Green & Bow and Yasmin Qureshi in Bolton SE.

43. Eighty-nine Muslim candidates fought this election, the highest ever.

44. Five MPs came back to the Commons after having been previously defeated – Stephen Twigg, John Cryer, Geraint Davies, Jonathan Evans and Chris Leslie.

45. There were fourteen by-elections in the 2005–10 parliament. Eight were due to the deaths of sitting MPs and six were caused by resignations.

46. The first seat to declare its result on election night was Houghton & Sunderland South, at 10.52 p.m.

47. The final seat to declare its result was Devon West & Torridge, at 5.06 p.m.

48. For the first time, TV debates were held between the three party leaders. The three debates attracted audiences of 9.9 million (ITV), 4.6 million (Sky) and 8.3 million (BBC).

49. There were only seven constituencies where one of the major parties lost their deposits – five Labour and two Conservative.

50. Sixteen Labour ministers were defeated at the 2010 election, compared to 1997, when a record-breaking thirty-five Conservative ministers lost their seats.

With thanks to Rallings & Thrasher for much of this information.

25 pieces of election trivia

Compiled by Iain Dale

1. At the 2005 election, 1,385 candidates lost their deposits, including five Conservatives and one Liberal Democrat.

2. At the last election there were 14,901 overseas voters.

3. The largest majority ever received by a successful candidate was when the Conservative Sir A. C. Lawson won Brighton in 1931 with a stunning majority of 62,253. He also holds the record for the most votes ever received in a general election, with a massive 75,205 in the same election.

4. The smallest general election majority was two votes, achieved by Mark Oaten in Winchester in 1997 and A. J. Flint in Ilkeston North in 1931.

5. The smallest number of votes ever cast for a candidate in a general election was one – for Ms C. Taylor-Dawson, who stood in Cardiff North in 2005. Presumably she voted for herself.

6. The highest turnout in an individual seat in a general election was 93.4 per cent in Fermanagh & South Tyrone in 1951.

7. The lowest turnout was in Lambeth in 1918, when only 29.7 per cent of the electorate bothered to vote.

8. The highest number of candidates to stand in seat at a general election is fifteen, in Sedgefield, Tony Blair's former seat, in 2005.

9. The average size of a constituency is 60,000–70,000 voters. But in 1935, in the constituency of Romford there were 167,939 voters on the electoral register.

10. Southwark North holds the record for the smallest number of voters on the register in a single-member seat, with 14,108 in 1945.

11. In 1992 the Lib Dems won Inverness, Nairn & Lochaber with only 26 per cent of the vote. A mere 1,741 votes separated the winner from the fourth-placed candidate.

12. When the Conservatives won the Crewe & Nantwich by-election in May 2008, it was their first by-election gain from Labour since 1978.

13. The highest number of recounts at a general election count is seven, held by Brighton Kemptown in 1964 (Labour's D. H. Hobden won with a majority of seven) and Peterborough in 1966, where Sir Harmer Nicholls was returned with a majority of three votes.

14. The record for the longest count is held by Derbyshire North East. At the 1922 election the count took eighteen and a quarter hours.

15. In Harlow in 2005 the result was not announced until 11.40 a.m. on the Saturday following the election. There had been three recounts and the counting agents were exhausted.

16. Screaming Lord Sutch fought forty-one different elections and by-elections between 1963 and 1997. In 1992 he fought in the seats of all three party leaders.

17. Jennie Lee holds the record for the most number of elections contested by a female candidate – thirteen.

18. James Maxton retained his Glasgow Bridgeton seat in 1935 by spending only £54 – a record low.

19. At the Haltemprice & Howden by-election in 2006, twenty-three of the twenty-six candidates lost their deposits.

20. The highest turnout at a by-election occurred in Ashton-under-Lyne on 29 October 1928, when 89.1 per cent of the electorate voted.

21. At five general elections between 1922 and 1931 in Darwen, the turnout always exceeded 90 per cent.

22. In 2015, around 4.5 per cent of the electorate will be voting for the first time. Of this number, 82.7 per cent will be white, 3.9 per cent will be mixed race, 2.1 per cent Indian, 2.5 per cent Pakistani, 1.1 per cent Bangladeshi, 0.8 per cent Chinese and 4.2 per cent black.

23. The lowest ever turnout at a UK election was in 2012, when only 15 per cent of the population voted for their police & crime commissioners.

24. The last UK general election not to be held on a Thursday was on Tuesday 27 October 1931.

25. That was also the last time any party (Stanley Baldwin's Conservatives) gained over 50 per cent of the vote.

Election 2010 statistics

Compiled by Iain Dale

How Britain voted in 2010

	CON	LAB	LIB	OTH	CON LEAD	TURNOUT	LAB-CON SWING
All	37	30	24	10	7	65%	5.0
Male	38	28	22	12	10	66%	5.0
Female	36	31	26	8	4	64%	5.5
18–24	30	31	30	9	-2	44%	4.5
25–34	35	30	29	7	5	55%	9.0
35–44	34	31	26	9	4	66%	8.5
45–54	34	31	26	12	6	69%	5.0
55–64	38	28	23	12	10	73%	1.0
65+	44	31	16	9	13	76%	3.5
AB1	39	26	29	7	13	76%	2.0
C1	39	28	24	9	11	66%	3.0
C2	37	29	22	12	8	58%	7.5
DE	31	40	17	12	-10	57%	7.0
Houseowners	45	24	21	11	21	74%	3.0
Mortgage	36	29	26	9	7	66%	6.0
Social renter	24	47	19	11	-23	55%	8.0
Private renter	35	29	27	9	6	55%	7.5

(Courtesy of IPSOS-MORI)

Summary of electoral statistics in 2010 general election in England

	CON	LAB	LD	OTHER	TOTAL
Seats won	297	191	43	2	533
Change	+91	-87	-4	0	0
Votes (000s)	9.908.0	7.039.4	6,075.6	2,058.2	25,081.3
% vote	39.5	28.1	24.2	8.2	100
Change	+3.8	-7.4	+1.3	+2.3	0
Candidates	532	532	532	1,829	3,425
Deposits lost	0	5	0	1,633	1,638

Summary of electoral statistics in 2010 general election in Scotland

	CON	LAB	LD	SNP	OTHER	TOTAL
Seats won	1	41	11	6	0	59
Change	0	+1	0	0	-1	0
Votes (000s)	412.9	1,035.5	465.5	491.4	60.5	2,465.8
% vote	16.7	42.0	18.9	19.9	2.5	100
Change	+0.9	+3.1	-3.7	+2.3	-2.6	0
Candidates	59	59	59	59	113	349
Deposits lost	2	0	0	0	110	112

Summary of electoral statistics in 2010 general election in Wales

	CON	LAB	LD	PC	OTHER	TOTAL
Seats won	8	26	3	3	0	40
Change	+5	-4	-1	+1	-1	0
Votes (000s)	382.7	531.6	295.2	165.4	91.8	1,466.7
% vote	26.1	36.2	20.1	11.3	6.3	100
Change	+4.7	-6.5	+1.7	-1.3	+1.3	0
Candidates	40	40	40	40	108	268
Deposits lost	0	0	0	11	103	114

Summary of electoral statistics in 2010 general election in Northern Ireland

	DUP	SF	SDLP	UCU	ALL	OTHERS	TOTAL
Seats won	8	5	3	0	1	1	18
Change	-1	0	0	-1	+1	+1	0
Votes (000s)	168.2	171.9	111.0	102.4	42.8	77.6	673.9
% vote	25.0	25.5	16.5	15.2	6.3	11.5	100
Change	-8.7	+1.2	-1.0	-2.6	+2.4	+8.8	0
Candidates	16	17	18	17	18	22	108
Deposits lost	0	4	2	2	10	11	29

Summary of electoral statistics in 2010 general election in the North East

(Tyne & Wear, Cleveland, Durham, Northumberland)

	CON	LAB	LD	OTHER	TOTAL
Seats won	2	25	2	0	29
Change	+1	-2	+1	0	0
Votes (000s)	282.3	518.3	280.5	108.8	1,189.9
% vote	23.7	43.6	23.6	9.1	100
Change	+4.2	-9.3	+0.2	+4.9	0
Candidates	29	29	29	86	173
Deposits lost	0	0	0	72	72

Summary of electoral statistics in 2010 general election in the North West

(Lancashire, Merseyside, Cheshire, Cumbria, Greater Manchester)

	CON	LAB	LD	OTHER	TOTAL
Seats won	22	47	6	0	75
Change	+12	-13	+1	0	0
Votes (000s)	1,038.8	1,289.9	707.8	236.5	3,273.0
% vote	31.7	39.4	21.6	7.2	100
Change	+3.0	-5.7	+0.3	+2.4	0
Candidates	75	75	75	220	445
Deposits lost	0	1	0	197	198

Summary of electoral statistics in 2010 general election in Yorkshire and the Humber

(North Yorkshire, South Yorkshire, West Yorkshire, Humberside)

	CON	LAB	LD	OTHER	TOTAL
Seats won	19	32	3	0	54
Change	+10	-9	-1	0	0
Votes (000s)	790.1	826.5	551.7	237.2	2,405.6
% vote	32.8	34.4	22.9	9.9	100
Change	+3.7	-9.2	+2.3	+3.2	0
Candidates	54	54	54	176	338
Deposits lost	0	0	0	144	144

Summary of electoral statistics in 2010 general election in the East Midlands

(Nottinghamshire, Leicestershire, Lincolnshire, Derbyshire, Northamptonshire)

	CON	LAB	LD	OTHER	TOTAL
Seats won	31	15	0	0	46
Change	+12	-11	-1	0	0
Votes (000s)	915.9	661.9	463.1	183.4	2,224.3
% vote	41.2	29.8	20.8	8.2	100
Change	+4.1	-9.2	+2.4	+2.8	0
Candidates	46	46	46	147	285
Deposits lost	0	0	0	132	132

Summary of electoral statistics in 2010 general election in the West Midlands

(West Midlands, Warwickshire, Hereford & Worcester, Shropshire, Staffordshire)

	CON	LAB	LD	OTHER	TOTAL
Seats won	33	24	2	0	59
Change	+15	-14	0	-1	0
Votes (000s)	1,044.1	808.1	540.3	248.1	2,640.6
% vote	39.5	30.6	20.5	9.4	100
Change	+4.5	-8.1	+1.9	+1.7	0
Candidates	59	59	59	183	360
Deposits lost	0	0	0	153	153

Summary of electoral statistics in 2010 general election in the Eastern Region

(Norfolk, Suffolk, Essex, Bedfordshire, Cambridgeshire, Hertfordshire)

	CON	LAB	LD	OTHER	TOTAL
Seats won	52	2	4	0	58
Change	+10	-11	+1	0	0
Votes (000s)	1,356.7	564.6	692.9	264.8	2,879.0
% vote	47.1	19.6	24.1	9.2	100
Change	+3.8	-10.2	+2.2	+4.2	0
Candidates	58	58	58	207	381
Deposits lost	0	0	0	182	182

Summary of electoral statistics in 2010 general election in London

	CON	LAB	LD	OTHER	TOTAL
Seats won	28	38	7	0	73
Change	+7	-6	0	-1	0
Votes (000s)	1,174.5	1,245.6	751.6	229.6	3,401.3
% vote	34.5	36.6	22.1	6.7	100
Change	+2.6	-2.3	+0.2	-0.5	0
Candidates	73	73	73	345	564
Deposits lost	0	0	0	335	335

Summary of electoral statistics in 2010 general election in the South East

	CON	LAB	LD	OTHER	TOTAL
Seats won	74	4	4	2	84
Change	+13	-13	-2	+2	0
Votes (000s)	2,118.0	697.6	1,124.8	353.8	4,294.2
% vote	49.3	16.2	26.2	8.2	100
Change	+4.4	-8.1	+0.8	+3.0	0
Candidates	83	83	83	293	542
Deposits lost	0	2	0	267	269

Summary of electoral statistics in 2010 general election in the South West

	CON	LAB	LD	OTHER	TOTAL
Seats won	36	4	15	0	55
Change	+11	-8	-3	0	0
Votes (000s)	1,187.6	426.9	963.0	195.9	2,773.4
% vote	42.8	15.4	34.7	7.1	100
Change	+4.2	-7.4	+2.2	+1.0	0
Candidates	55	55	55	172	337
Deposits lost	0	2	0	151	153

Candidates by party and finishing position

	FIRST	SECOND	THIRD	FOURTH	FIFTH/LOWER	TOTAL
Conservative	306	190	100	33	2	631
Labour	258	159	208	6	0	631
Lib Dem	57	243	298	33	0	631
Other	29	58	44	577	1,549	2,257

Age of MPs elected at the 2010 election by party

	AVERAGE	YOUNGEST	OLDEST
Conservative	48	James Wharton (26)	Sir Peter Tapsell (80)
Labour	52	Pamela Nash (25)	Sir Gerald Kaufman (79)
Lib Dem	50	Jo Swinson (30)	Sir Menzies Campbell (68)
Other	51	Jonathan Edwards (33)	Pat Doherty (64)

MPs elected at the 2010 election by date first elected

	CON	LAB	LIB	OTHER	TOTAL
1959	1	0	0	0	1
1964	0	0	0	0	0
1966	0	1	0	0	1
1970	2	3	1	0	6
1974f	3	0	0	0	3
1974o	1	3	0	0	4
1979	2	7	1	0	10
1983	18	9	3	2	32
1987	9	20	1	0	30
1992	21	26	2	1	50
1997	26	59	13	3	101
2001	22	30	9	9	70
2005	54	37	17	7	115
2010	147	63	10	7	227

Top ten largest electorates in 2010

Isle of Wight	109,922
East Ham	90,674
Manchester Central	90,110
NW Cambridgeshire	88,851
Holborn & St Pancras	88,563
Milton Keynes S	86,559
Oxford W & Abingdon	86,458
Ilford S	86,220
West Ham	85,313
Croydon N	85,216

Top ten smallest electorates in 2010

Na h-Eileanan an Iar	21,780
Orkney & Shetland	33,085
Arfon	41,198
Aberconwy	44,593
Dwyfor Meironnydd	45,354
Caithness, Sutherland & Easter Ross	47,263
Montgomeryshire	48,730
Ynys Mon	50,075
Cynon Valley	50,650
Aberavon	50,838

Highest turnouts at the 2010 general election

East Renfrewshire	77.3%
Westmorland & Lonsdale	76.9%
Richmond Park	76.2%
Winchester	75.8%
Central Devon	75.7%
NE Somerset	75.4%
St Albans	75.4%
Kenilworth & Southam	75.2%
Thornbury & Yate	75.2%
E Dunbartonshire	75.2%

Lowest turnouts at the 2010 general election

Manchester Central	44.3%
Leeds Central	46.0%
Birmingham Ladywood	48.7%
Glasgow NE	49.1%
Blackley & Broughton	49.2%
Thirsk & Malton	49.9%
Manchester Gorton	50.5%
Kingston upon Hull E	50.6%
East Antrim	50.7%
Glasgow Central	50.9%

Top ten most marginal seats by number of votes

Fermanagh & S Tyrone	4
Hampstead & Kilburn	42
N Warwickshire	54
Camborne & Redruth	66
Bolton W	92
Thurrock	92
Oldham E & Saddleworth	103
Hendon	106
Solihull	175
Oxford W & Abingdon	176

Top ten safest seats

Liverpool Walton	19,818	57.7%
Knowsley	25,686	57.5%
East Ham	27,826	55.2%
Belfast W	17,579	54.7%
Glasgow NE	15,942	54.2%
Liverpool, West Derby	18,467	51.6%
Orkney & Shetland	9,928	51.3%
Bootle	21,181	51.3%
Kirkcaldy & Cowdenbeath	23,009	50.2%
Coatbridge, Chryston & Bellshill	20,714	49.8%

Seats with highest Conservative vote share

Richmond (Yorkshire)	62.8%
Beaconsfield	61.1%
Windsor	60.8%
NE Hampshire	60.6%
Chelsea & Fulham	60.5%
Chesham & Amersham	60.4%
Maldon	59.8%
Orpington	59.7%
Maidenhead	59.5%
Aldridge Brownhills	59.3%

Seats with highest Labour vote share

Liverpool Walton	72.0%
Knowsley	70.9%
East Ham	70.4%
Glasgow NE	68.3%
Coatbridge, Chryston & Bellshill	66.6%
Bootle	66.4%
Kirkcaldy & Cowdenbeath	64.5%
Liverpool, West Derby	64.1%
West Ham	62.7%
Birkenhead	62.5%

Seats with highest Liberal Democrat vote share

Orkney & Shetland	62.0%
Westmorland & Lonsdale	60.0%
Bath	56.6%
Yeovil	55.7%
N Norfolk	55.0%
Twickenham	54.4%
Sheffield Hallam	53.4%
Ross, Skye & Lochaber	52.6%
Lewes	52.0%
Thornbury & Yate	51.9%

Seats with lowest Conservative vote share

Na h-Eileanan an Iar	4.4%
Glasgow E	4.5%
Glasgow NE	5.3%
Rhondda	6.4%
Liverpool Walton	6.5%
Glasgow SW	6.6%
Dunfermline & West Fife	6.8%
Blaenau Gwent	7.0%
Glasgow N	7.1%
Glasgow C	7.1%

Seats with lowest Labour vote share

Westmorland & Lonsdale	2.2%
N Cornwall	4.2%
Newbury	4.3%
Somerton & Frome	4.4%
Eastbourne	4.8%
Lewes	5.0%
Richmond Park	5.0%
Guildford	5.1%
Taunton Deane	5.1%
Cheltenham	5.1%

Seats with lowest Liberal Democrat vote share

Glasgow E	5.0%
Kilmarnock & Loudoun	7.3%
Na h-Eileanan an Iar	7.5%
Ynys Mon	7.5%
Glenrothes	7.7%
Glasgow NE	7.7%
Airdrie & Shotts	8.1%
West Dunbartonshire	8.1%
Barking	8.2%
Coatbridge, Chryston & Bellshill	8.5%

Ten most improved Conservative vote shares

Hartlepool	16.7
Montgomeryshire	13.8
Esher & Walton	13.2
Crewe & Nantwich	12.9
Cardiff C	12.3
Camborne & Redruth	12.0
Basingstoke	11.7
St Ives	11.7
Devon SW	11.6
Ynys Mon	11.4

Ten most improved Labour vote shares

Blaenau Gwent	20.1
East Ham	16.8
West Ham	10.9
Glenrothes	10.4
Dunbartonshire W	9.4
Edinburgh W	9.1
Bethnal Green & Bow	8.5
Paisley & Renfrewshire N	8.3
Paisley & Renfrewshire S	7.0
East Renfrewshire	6.9

Ten most improved Liberal Democrat vote shares

Redcar	25.0
Ashfield	19.5
Merthyr Tydfil	17.0
Dunfermline & West Fife	14.9
Westmorland & Lonsdale	14.1
Ceredigion	13.5
Maidstone & The Weald	13.2
Brent C	13.1
Burnley	12.0
Bosworth	11.7

Ten largest Green Party vote shares

Brighton, Pavilion	31.3
Norwich S	14.9
Cambridge	7.6
Lewisham Deptford	6.7
Brighton Kemptown	5.5
Hove	5.2
Edinburgh E	5.1
Leeds W	4.7
Hackney N & Stoke Newington	4.6
Lancaster & Fleetwood	4.4

Ten largest UKIP vote shares

Buckingham	17.4
Boston & Skegness	9.5
Christchurch	8.5
Spelthorne	8.5
Dudley N	8.5
Walsall S	8.4
Cambridgeshire NW	8.3
Dudley S	8.2
Devon E	8.2
Staffordshire Moorlands	8.2

Ten largest BNP vote shares

Barking	14.6
Dagenham & Rainham	11.2
Rotherham	10.4
Stoke-on-Trent S	9.4
West Bromwich W	9.4
Burnley	9.0
Barnsley C	8.9
Barnsley E	8.6
Normanton, Pontefract & Castleford	8.4
Leeds C	8.2

Ten largest SNP vote shares

Na h-Eileanan an Iar	45.7
Banff & Buchan	41.3
Moray	39.7
Perth & N Perthshire	39.6
Angus	39.6
Dundee E	37.8
Falkirk	30.3
Dundee W	28.9
Ochil & S Perthshire	27.6
Kilmarnock & Loudoun	26

Ten largest Plaid Cymru vote shares

Dwyfor & Meirionnydd	44.3
Arfon	36.0
Carmarthen E & Dinefwr	35.6
Llanelli	29.9
Ceredigion	28.3
Ynys Mon	26.2
Cynon Valley	20.3
Neath	19.9
Rhondda	18.1
Aberconwy	17.8

Seats where major parties lost their deposits

4.8%	Eastbourne	Labour
4.5%	Glasgow E	Conservative
4.4%	Somerton & Frome	Labour
4.4%	Na h-Eileanan an Iar	Conservative
4.3%	Newbury	Labour
4.2%	Cornwall N	Labour
2.2%	Westmorland & Lonsdale	Labour

Women candidates at the 2005 and 2010 elections

	CONSERVATIVE	LABOUR	LIB DEMS
2005	122 (19%)	166 (26%)	145 (23%)
2010	153 (22%)	191 (30%)	134 (20%)

Ten quickest declarations in 2010

Houghton & Sunderland South	10.52 p.m.
Washington & Sunderland West	11.26 p.m.
Sunderland Central	11.41 p.m.
West Tyrone	12.36 a.m.
North Antrim	12.39 a.m.
Darlington	12.48 a.m.
Thornbury & Yate	12.48 a.m.
Belfast East	12.48 a.m.
Durham North	12.49 a.m.
Lagan Valley	12.58 a.m.

Ten latest declarations in 2010

Devon West & Torridge	5.06 p.m.
Lancaster & Fleetwood	3.37 p.m.
Dudley North	3.31 p.m.
Morecambe & Lunesdale	3.15 p.m.
Amber Valley	3.14 p.m.
St Ives	3.10 p.m.
Hackney South & Shoreditch	3.07 p.m.
Fermanagh & South Tyrone	3.02 p.m.
Hackney North & Stoke Newington	2.33 p.m.
Penrith & The Border	2.30 p.m.

Newspaper endorsements at the 2010 election

Daily Express	Conservative
Daily Telegraph	Conservative
Daily Mail	Conservative
Daily Mirror	Labour
Daily Record	Labour
Financial Times	Conservative
Mail on Sunday	Conservative
The Sun	Conservative
The Guardian	Liberal Democrat
The Independent	Liberal Democrat/Labour
News of the World	Conservative
The Observer	Liberal Democrat
Scotland on Sunday	Liberal Democrat
Sunday Mirror	Labour
Sunday Telegraph	Conservative
Sunday Times	Conservative
The Times	Conservative

*All other papers decided not to endorse any political party

Historical election data

Results of general elections 1832–2010

ELECTION	CON%	CON SEATS	LAB%	LAB SEATS	LIB%	LIB SEATS	OTHER %	SEATS
1832	28.9	147			71.1	408		
1835	42.8	238			57.2	317		
1837	48.2	284			51.8	271		
1841	52.7	326			47.2	229	0.1	
1847	43.1	285			56.2	267	0.6	1
1852	40.8	290			58.9	261	0.3	
1857	31.0	222			68.9	329	0.1	
1859	33.4	245			66.6	306		
1865	40.0	244			60.0	311		
1868	38.6	234			61.4	321		
1874	44.6	319			55.4	232		
1880	42.7	214			57.3	337		
1885	45.6	233			51.8	319	2.6	17
1886	51.2	376			48.6	192	0.2	1
1892	49.5	292			49.6	272	1.0	5
1895	50.5	392			48.0	176	1.5	1
1900	51.0	383	1.9	2	46.5	182	0.6	2
1906	43.0	141	5.8	29	49.6	396	1.7	3
1910j	47.1	253	7.8	40	44.1	273	1.0	3
1910d	47.0	254	7.4	42	45.3	271	0.3	2
1918	39.5	359	23.0	57	28.6	163	8.8	27
1922	38.0	334	29.9	142	29.2	115	2.9	12
1923	37.7	248	31.0	191	30.1	158	1.2	6
1924	45.9	400	34.0	151	18.2	40	1.9	12
1929	37.5	250	37.8	287	23.5	59	1.2	7
1931	60.9	512	31.1	52	6.9	36	1.2	3
1935	47.8	419	38.6	154	6.7	21	1.5	9
1945	39.3	202	48.8	393	9.2	12	2.6	21
1950	43.0	288	46.8	315	9.3	6	0.9	1
1951	47.8	312	49.4	295	2.6	6	0.3	0
1955	49.3	335	47.4	277	2.8	6	0.6	0
1959	48.8	353	44.6	258	6.0	6	0.6	1
1964	42.9	292	44.8	317	11.4	9	0.9	0
1966	41.4	242	48.8	364	8.6	12	1.1	0
1970	46.2	322	43.9	288	7.6	6	2.3	2
1974f	38.8	297	38.0	301	19.8	14	3.4	11
1974o	36.7	277	40.2	319	18.8	13	4.3	14

ELECTION	CON%	CON SEATS	LAB%	LAB SEATS	LIB%	LIB SEATS	OTHER %	SEATS
1979	44.9	339	37.8	269	14.1	11	3.2	4
1983	43.5	397	28.3	209	26.0	23	2.2	4
1987	43.3	376	31.5	229	23.1	22	2.1	6
1992	42.8	336	35.2	271	18.3	20	3.7	7
1997	31.5	165	44.3	418	17.2	46	7.0	12
2001	32.7	166	42.0	412	18.8	52	6.5	11
2005	33.2	198	36.1	355	22.6	62	8.0	13
2010	36.9	306	29.7	258	23.6	57	9.9	11

Votes for parties 1983–2010

	2010	2005	2001	1997	1992	1987	1983
Con	10,703,654	8,784,915	8,357,615	9,600,943	14,093,007	13,760,583	13,012,316
Lab	8,606,517	9,552,436	10,724,953	13,518,167	11,560,484	10,029,807	8,456,934
Lib	6,836,248	5,985,454	4,814,321	5,242,947	5,999,606	7,341,633	7,780,949
SNP	491,386	412,267	464,314	621,550	629,564	416,473	331,975
PC	165,394	174,838	195,893	161,030	154,947	123,599	125,309
UKIP	919,471	605,973	390,563	105,722	0	0	0
Green	285,612	283,414	166,477	63,991	171,927	89,753	53,848
BNP	564,321	192,745	47,129	35,832	7,005	0	0
UUP	102,361	127,414	216,839	258,349	271,049	276,230	259,952
DUP	168,216	241,856	181,999	107,348	103,039	85,642	152,749
SDLP	110970	125,726	169,865	190,814	184,445	154,087	137,012
SF	171,942	174,530	175,933	126,921	78,291	83,389	102,701

Seats won by party 1983–2010

	2010	2005	2001	1997	1992	1987	1983
Con	306	198	166	165	336	376	397
Lab	258	355	412	418	271	229	209
Lib	57	62	52	46	20	22	23
SNP	6	6	5	6	3	3	2
PC	3	3	4	4	4	3	2
UUP	0	1	6	10	9	9	11
DUP	8	9	5	2	3	3	3
SDLP	3	3	3	3	4	3	1
SF	5	5	4	2	0	1	1
Others	4	4	2	3	1	1	1
Total	650	646	659	659	651	650	650

Vote share by party 1983–2010 (excl. Northern Ireland)

	2010	2005	2001	1997	1992	1987	1983
Con	36.9	33.2	32.7	31.5	42.8	43.3	43.5
Lab	29.7	36.1	42.0	44.3	34.4	31.5	28.3
Lib	23.6	22.6	18.8	17.2	17.8	23.1	26.0
SNP % in Scotland	19.9	17.7	20.1	22.1	21.5	14	11.8
PC % in Wales	11.3	11.3	12.6	14.3	9.9	8.9	7.3
UKIP	3.1	2.2	1.5	0.3	0	0	0
Green	1.0	1.0	0.6	0.2	0.5	0.3	0.2
Others		2.4	1.7	4.0	3.0	0.1	0.4

Number of seats up for election at each election since 1945

1945	640
1950	625
1951	625
1955	630
1959	630
1964	630
1966	630
1970	630
1974 Feb	635

1974 Oct	635
1979	635
1983	650
1987	650
1992	651
1997	659
2001	659
2005	646
2010	650
2015	650

Votes per seat won 1979–2010

	CON	LAB	LIB	PC	SNP
1979	40,407	42,871	392,164	66,272	252,130
1983	36,597	40,464	338,302	62,655	165,988
1987	36,597	43,798	333,711	41,200	138,824
1992	41,811	42,659	299,980	38,737	209,855
1997	58,128	32,340	113,977	40,258	103,592
2001	50,332	26,031	92,583	48,973	92,863
2005	44,335	26,908	96,539	58,279	68,711
2010	34,979	33,359	119,934	55,131	81,898

Seat gains and losses by party 1979–2010

	CON	LAB	LIB	OTHERS (ALL NET)
1979	55	-40	-3	-12
1983*	7	-5	-2	-
1987	-17	21	-5	1
1992*	-41	42	-2	1
1997	-178	146	28	4
2001*	1	-6	6	-1
2005	33	-47	11	3
2010*	97	-91	-5	-1

* Affected by boundary changes. Figs used only reflect seats with no or minor changes

Voter turnout 1970–2010

1970	72.0%
1974 Feb	78.8%
1974 Oct	72.8%
1979	76.0%
1983	72.7%
1987	75.3%
1992	77.7%
1997	71.4%
2001	59.4%
2005	61.4%
2010	65.1%

Number of postal votes cast 1979–2010

1979	846,335
1983	757,604
1987	947,948
1992	835,074
1997	937,205
2001	1,758,055
2005	5,362,501
2010	6,996,006

Number of spoilt ballot papers 1974–2010

1974 Feb	42,252
1974 Oct	37,706
1979	117,848
1983	51,104
1987	36,945
1992	39,726
1997	93,408
2001	100,005
2005	85,038
2010	81,879

Average number of candidates per seat 1970–2010

1970	2.9
1974 Feb	3.4
1974 Oct	3.5
1979	4.1
1983	4.0
1987	3.6
1992	4.5
1997	5.7
2001	5.0
2005	5.5
2010	6.4

Quickest results 1959–2010

1959	Billericay	9.57 p.m.
1964	Cheltenham	10.00 p.m.
1966	Cheltenham	10.04 p.m.
1970	Guildford	11.10 p.m.
1974 Feb	Guildford	11.10 p.m.
1974 Oct	Guildford	11.10 p.m.
1979	Glasgow Central	11.34 p.m.
1983	Torbay	11.10 p.m.
1987	Torbay	11.02 p.m.
1992	Sunderland South	11.06 p.m.
1997	Sunderland South	10.46 p.m.
2001	Sunderland South	10.41 p.m.
2005	Sunderland South	10.43 p.m.
2010	Houghton & Sunderland South	10.52 p.m.

Swings between the major parties 1950–2010

1950	2.9 Con
1951	1.1 Con
1955	1.8 Con
1959	1.2 Con
1964	3.1 Lab
1966	2.8 Lab
1970	4.9 Con
1974 Feb	0.8 Lab
1974 Oct	2.2 Lab
1979	5.3 Con
1983	4.1 Con
1987	1.7 Lab
1992	2.1 Lab
1997	10.2 Lab
2001	1.8 Con
2005	3.1 Con
2010	5.0 Con

Women candidates and MPs elected 1970–2010

	MPS	% OF ALL MPS	CANDIDATES	% OF ALL CANDIDATES
1970	26	4.1	99	5.4
1974 Feb	23	3.6	143	6.7
1974 Oct	27	4.3	161	7.1
1979	19	3.0	216	8.4
1983	23	3.5	280	10.9
1987	41	6.3	329	14.2
1992	60	9.2	571	19.3
1997	120	18.2	672	18.0
2001	126	17.9	636	19.2
2005	128	19.8	720	20.3
2010	143	22.0	874	21.1

Black and ethnic minority candidates 1979–2010

	CON CAND.	MPS	LABOUR CAND	MPS	LIB DEM CAND	MPS	TOTAL CAND.	TOTAL MPS
1979	2	0	1	0	2	0	5	0
1983	4	0	6	0	8	0	18	0
1987	6	0	14	4	9	0	29	4
1992	8	1	9	5	5	0	22	6
1997	9	0	13	9	17	0	39	9
2001	16	0	21	12	29	0	66	12
2005	41	2	32	13	40	0	113	15
2010	44	11	49	16	43	0	136	27

Average age of MPs 1979–2010

1979	49.6
1983	48.8
1987	49.0
1992	50.0
1997	49.3
2001	50.3
2005	51.2
2010	50.1

The Green Party vote 1979–2010

ELECTION	CANDIDATES	MPS ELECTED	LOST DEPOSITS	TOTAL VOTES	%
1979	53	0	53	39,918	0.1
1983	108	0	108	53,848	0.2
1987	133	0	133	89,753	0.3
1992	256	0	256	171,927	0.5
1997	95	0	95	63,991	0.2
2001	145	0	135	166,477	0.6
2005	203	0	179	283,414	1.0
2010	335	1	328	285,612	1.0

The British National Party vote 1992–2010

ELECTION	CANDIDATES	MPS ELECTED	LOST DEPOSITS	TOTAL VOTES	%
1992	13	0	13	7,005	0.0
1997	57	0	54	35,832	0.1
2001	33	0	28	47,129	0.2
2005	119	0	85	192,745	0.7
2010	338	0	266	564,321	1.9

The United Kingdom Independence Party (UKIP) vote 1997–2010

ELECTION	CANDIDATES	MPS ELECTED	LOST DEPOSITS	TOTAL VOTES	%
1997	183	0	192	105,722	0.3
2001	428	0	422	390,563	1.5
2005	496	0	458	605,973	2.2
2010	558	0	459	919,471	3.1

Overseas electors 1987–2010

1987	11,100
1992	31,942
1997	23,583
2001	12,936
2005	18,975
2010	14,901

Spoilt ballot papers 1979–2010*

	TOTAL	AVERAGE PER CONSTITUENCY
1979	117,848	186
1983	51,104	79
1987	36,945	57
1992	39,726	61
1997	93,408	142
2001	100,005	152
2005	85,038	129
2010	81,879	126

*A ballot paper is spoilt if it doesn't have an official watermark, someone has voted for more than one candidate, written something which could identify the voter or is unmarked or void for uncertainty.

Candidates who have fought the most elections

41	Screaming Lord Sutch
26	W. G. Boaks
26	William Ewart Gladstone
17	Tony Benn

Jennie Lee holds the record for the most elections fought by a woman – 13

The demographics of the 2015 general election

Compiled by Robert Waller

Twenty constituencies with highest proportion of voters over 65 years old

	%	PARTY HOLDING SEAT
Christchurch	36.0	C
Clacton	35.0	C
North Norfolk	34.1	LD
New Forest West	33.9	C
East Devon	31.7	C
Bexhill & Battle	31.3	C
West Dorset	31.1	C
Totnes	30.9	C
Louth & Horncastle	30.5	C
Worthing West	30.1	C
Dwyfor Meirionnydd	30.0	Plaid Cymru
Suffolk Coastal	29.7	C
Tiverton & Honiton	29.2	C
Chichester	28.9	C
Westmorland & Lonsdale	28.8	LD
Lewes	28.6	LD
West Worcestershire	28.5	C
Aberconwy	28.4	C
Arundel & South Downs	28.3	C
Brecon & Radnorshire	28.2	LD

It might be thought that there are few interesting features among the constituencies with the highest proportion of pensioners, as many of them have traditionally been safe Conservative seats, but in fact not only are there several Liberal Democrat strongholds, including the Westmorland seat of party president Tim Farron, but in general this list could provide hope for UKIP, a resurgent party whose strength has grown dramatically since the last general election in 2010.

Ten constituencies with lowest proportion of voters over 65 years old

	%	PARTY HOLDING SEAT
Poplar & Limehouse	6.9	Lab
Bermondsey & Old Southwark	8.2	LD
Bethnal Green & Bow	8.3	Lab
East Ham	8.4	Lab
Vauxhall	8.4	Lab
Bristol West	8.5	LD
West Ham	8.6	Lab
Hackney North & Stoke Newington	8.6	Lab
Lewisham Deptford	8.9	Lab
Battersea	9.1	C

Ten constituencies with highest proportion of residents born in Africa

	%	PARTY HOLDING SEAT
Camberwell & Peckham	16.6	Lab
Erith & Thamesmead	14.4	Lab
Harrow East	13.9	C
Leicester East	13.3	Lab
Edmonton	12.5	Lab
West Ham	12.0	Lab
Brent North	11.5	Lab
Brent Central	11.4	LD
Greenwich & Woolwich	11.4	Lab
Croydon North	11.3	Lab

This list actually includes two distinct groups – those in the London boroughs of Hendon and Brent and in Leicester will include many of South Asian ancestry who came to Britain after being expelled from Kenya and Uganda in the 1960s and 1970s, while those in seats in south and east London and Edmonton will mainly be more recent 'Afro-Caribbean' immigrants from West Africa and Somalia. Commonwealth citizens can vote in general elections.

Twenty constituencies with highest proportion of black residents

	%	PARTY HOLDING SEAT
Camberwell & Peckham	37.4	Lab
Croydon North	31.5	Lab
Lewisham Deptford	28.9	Lab
Edmonton	27.3	Lab
Hackney South & Shoreditch	26.9	Lab
Tottenham	26.7	Lab
Lewisham East	25.8	Lab
Erith & Thamesmead	25.7	Lab
Brent Central	25.5	LD
Dulwich & West Norwood	25.0	Lab
Vauxhall	24.7	Lab
Streatham	24.3	Lab
West Ham	23.1	Lab
Birmingham Ladywood	22.6	Lab
Lewisham West & Penge	22.4	Lab
Barking	20.2	Lab
Bermondsey & Old Southwark	20.1	LD
Greenwich & Woolwich	20.1	Lab
Hackney North & Stoke Newington	19.6	Lab
Walthamstow	18.9	Lab

Some interesting features:

- Nineteen of the twenty seats are within the boundaries of Greater London – the only exception is Birmingham Ladywood.
- There are no constituencies with a black majority, whereas there are six with an Asian majority.
- Eighteen of the top twenty seats are held by Labour, and two by the Liberal Democrats – though Sarah Teather's retirement in Brent Central means that one of those will almost certainly be gained by Labour.
- There are no Conservative seats in the top twenty; the highest in the list is Enfield North (15.5 per cent) at number twenty-five.
- Only three of the top twenty have black MPs at present: Tottenham (David Lammy), Streatham (Chuka Umunna) and Hackney North & Stoke Newington (Diane Abbott).

- The increases in percentage of black (Afro-Caribbean) residents between 2001 and 2011 were largely due to the rise in the number of those of African origin, not Caribbean – for example, in Erith & Thamesmead, where the proportion born in Africa at 14.4 per cent is the highest of any seat.

Twenty constituencies with lowest proportion of white residents

	%	PARTY HOLDING SEAT
East Ham	23.1	Lab
Ilford South	24.2	Lab
Brent North	26.6	Lab
Birmingham Ladywood	27.3	Lab
Ealing Southall	30.4	Lab
Leicester East	31.4	Lab
West Ham	34.5	Lab
Croydon North	35.2	Lab
Birmingham Hall Green	35.5	Lab
Birmingham Hodge Hill	35.7	Lab
Bradford West	37.1	Respect
Brent Central	38.8	LD
Harrow East	39.2	C
Birmingham Perry Barr	39.7	Lab
Harrow West	40.1	Lab
Hayes & Harlington	43.4	Lab
Poplar & Limehouse	43.5	Lab
Camberwell & Peckham	44.8	Lab
Feltham & Heston	44.9	Lab
Slough	45.1	Lab

Some interesting features:

- Although boundary changes make exact comparisons impossible, it is fairly clear that the percentage of white residents dropped in every one of the above constituencies between the 2001 and 2011 censuses.
- In 2001 there were ten seats with a white minority; in 2011 there were twenty-seven.
- The greatest fall, of over 20 per cent, was in Ilford South – as recently as 1992 a highly marginal seat, gained then by Labour from the Conservatives by only 402 votes.

Ten constituencies with highest proportion of residents born in Poland

	%	PARTY HOLDING SEAT
Ealing North	8.5	Lab
Ealing Central & Acton	6.5	C
Slough	6.0	Lab
Luton South	5.5	Lab
Tottenham	5.4	Lab
Southampton Test	5.0	Lab
Mitcham & Morden	4.9	Lab
Brentford & Isleworth	4.5	C
Brent Central	4.4	LD
Peterborough	4.1	C

Though EU citizens, people born in Poland (and Romania, below) may well not be eligible to vote in general elections, unless they have UK nationality, but where there is such a concentration it may of course impact the choices of those who do have a vote – and there are several key marginals in the list above, with Brent Central a labour target from the Liberal Democrats and Ealing Central & Acton and Peterborough from the Conservatives, while Southampton Test and Luton South are Conservative targets from Labour.

Five constituencies with highest proportion of residents born in Romania

	%	PARTY HOLDING SEAT
Harrow East	3.3	C
Brent North	2.9	Lab
Hendon	2.4	C
Leyton & Wanstead	1.9	Lab
Walthamstow	1.8	Lab

It should be remembered that these figures are from the 2011 census, before immigration restrictions on Romanians were eased, but it is likely that any influx would be most concentrated where existing communities are located, such as in north and east London boroughs as above.

Both Harrow East and Hendon are key Labour targets that they must gain to become the largest party nationally, never mind win an overall majority. If there has been an increase in Romanian immigration since 2013 that could affect the votes of the rest of the electorate in these constituencies.

Twenty constituencies with highest proportion of voters with degrees

	%	PARTY HOLDING SEAT
Battersea	57.4	C
Richmond Park	55.2	C
Cities of London & Westminster	54.5	C
Wimbledon	54.4	C
Hampstead & Kilburn	54.0	Lab
Chelsea & Fulham	53.7	C
Kensington	52.2	C
Hornsey & Wood Green	52.0	LD
Putney	51.6	C
Tooting	51.4	Lab
Twickenham	49.5	LD
Islington North	48.8	Lab
Vauxhall	48.7	Lab
Ealing Central & Acton	48.5	C
Dulwich & West Norwood	47.6	Lab
Hammersmith	47.5	Lab
Islington South & Finsbury	47.4	Lab
Westminster North	47.3	Lab
Bristol West	47.2	LD
Edinburgh South	46.9	Lab

Twenty constituencies with highest proportion of full-time students

	%	PARTY HOLDING SEAT
Sheffield Central	38.1	Lab
Nottingham South	34.5	Lab
Cardiff Central	33.9	LD
Newcastle upon Tyne East	31.4	Lab
Liverpool Riverside	30.9	Lab
Manchester Central	29.1	Lab
Leeds North West	28.6	LD
Oxford East	27.7	Lab
Cambridge	27.5	LD
Manchester Gorton	26.3	Lab
Glasgow Central	25.2	Lab
Glasgow North	25.0	Lab
Leeds Central	24.9	Lab
Leicester South	24.8	Lab
Swansea West	24.7	Lab
Bristol West	24.3	LD
Portsmouth South	24.2	(LD)
Coventry South	24.2	Lab
Canterbury	24.0	C
Birmingham Ladywood	23.3	Lab

Some interesting features:

- Following Nick Clegg's perceived change of position on student fee increases, it is often said that the Liberal Democrats, who have done well in recent elections in constituencies influenced by universities, would suffer greatly at the 2015 election. It is true that five of the top twenty seats by proportion of full-time students aged 16–24 were won by Liberal Democrats (including Portsmouth South, where Mike Hancock was suspended and then resigned the whip in 2014). However, apart from this seat, the others are held by large majorities that suggests support from beyond the student community, and these seem safe, apart from Cardiff Central where a Labour gain is on the cards.
- Some present Lib Dem seats widely predicted to fall to Labour because of the 'student swing', notably Manchester Withington and Norwich South, are not in fact on this top twenty list.
- However, it is also true that several of the Liberal Democrat target

seats from Labour have a high proportion of students, and this suggests that seats above such as Sheffield Central, Swansea West and Oxford East are even less likely to change hands in 2015.

- Conservatives traditionally do not do well among students, but the list above shows this should not be critical in the 2015 election, with no Tory marginals or targets on the list.

Twenty constituencies with lowest proportion of voters with degrees

	%	PARTY HOLDING SEAT
Birmingham Hodge Hill	12.1	Lab
Walsall North	12.2	Lab
Hull East	12.7	Lab
Glasgow East	12.7	Lab
West Bromwich West	13.1	Lab
Nottingham North	13.3	Lab
Liverpool Walton	13.3	Lab
Clacton	13.4	C
Stoke-on-Trent North	13.7	Lab
Wolverhampton South East	13.9	Lab
Rhondda	14.0	Lab
Great Yarmouth	14.2	C
Knowsley	14.3	Lab
Rotherham	14.3	Lab
Doncaster North	14.3	Lab
Boston & Skegness	14.6	C
Great Grimsby	14.6	Lab
Blackpool South	14.6	Lab
Castle Point	14.6	C
Ashfield	14.6	Lab

The most interesting theme running through this surprisingly disparate list is: the United Kingdom Independence Party.

As well as the perhaps expected selection of very safe Labour industrial seats, including that of party leader Ed Miliband in Doncaster North, there are four Conservative seats on the east coast where UKIP have done exceptionally well in local and European elections in 2013–14, including some touted as candidates for a possible Westminster gain in 2015 – such as Great Yarmouth, where they won most of the seats in recent council elections, and Boston & Skegness, with its large eastern European immigration. It might also be remembered that Castle Point may have a claim to being UKIP's first seat, as Bob Spink briefly defected from the Conservatives in 2008 before standing in 2010 as an Independent Green Belt candidate.

Also on the east coast is Great Grimsby, where Lord Ashcroft's marginal polling has suggested UKIP could well challenge in a marginal Labour seat being vacated by the veteran Austin Mitchell – a target the Conservatives need to win if they are to form a majority government in 2015. What is more, another Labour seat where UKIP has done exceptionally well recently is shadow spokesperson Gloria de Piero's Ashfield in Nottinghamshire.

There does, therefore, appear to be a correlation between some of UKIP's best chances and those seats with the fewest voters with degrees.

Twenty constituencies with highest proportion of single parents

	%	PARTY HOLDING SEAT
Belfast West	19.1	Sinn Fein
Edmonton	15.3	Lab
Barking	14.6	Lab
Foyle	14.5	SDLP
Croydon North	14.5	Lab
Nottingham North	14.2	Lab
Belfast North	13.8	DUP
Tottenham	13.6	Lab
Liverpool Walton	13.0	Lab
Enfield North	12.8	C
Erith & Thamesmead	12.7	Lab
Knowsley	12.7	Lab
Birmingham Hodge Hill	12.6	Lab
Glasgow East	12.5	Lab
Croydon Central	12.2	C
Birmingham Erdington	12.2	Lab
Liverpool West Derby	12.2	Lab
Camberwell & Peckham	12.1	Lab
Dagenham & Rainham	12.1	Lab
Birkenhead	12.0	Lab

An interesting mixture of types of seat: predominantly white working-class areas, such as those in Nottingham and Merseyside; those with a substantial Afro-Caribbean population, such as Edmonton, Tottenham and Erith & Thamesmead; and seats in Northern Ireland and Scotland.

The two Conservative marginals on this list, Enfield North and Croydon Central, have moved up the rank order significantly between the 2001 and 2011 censuses, and this suggest social changes that will make them very difficult to hold in 2015, especially given Labour's strong performance in London boroughs and the European election in the capital in 2014.

Twenty constituencies with highest proportion of social rented housing

	%	PARTY HOLDING SEAT
Camberwell & Peckham	50.6	Lab
Hackney South & Shoreditch	50.1	Lab
Glasgow North East	49.0	Lab
Islington South & Finsbury	43.7	Lab
Bermondsey & Old Southwark	43.5	LD
Glasgow East	43.3	Lab
Bethnal Green & Bow	42.7	Lab
Holborn & St Pancras	41.8	Lab
Vauxhall	41.2	Lab
Glasgow South West	39.8	Lab
Greenwich & Woolwich	39.3	Lab
Birmingham Ladywood	38.2	Lab
Motherwell & Wishaw	37.6	Lab
Sheffield Brightside & Hillsborough	37.5	Lab
Hackney North & Stoke Newington	37.3	Lab
Blackley & Broughton	37.3	Lab
West Dunbartonshire	37.3	Lab
Glasgow North West	36.9	Lab
Nottingham North	36.8	Lab

Social rented housing (formerly local authority or council housing) has long been an even better predictor of how a constituency votes than social class, especially due to the 'neighbourhood' or environmental effect: working-class voters in a strongly social rented area tend to be more likely to vote Labour than in other types of neighbourhood.

It is also generally true that the 'better' (in the sense of perceived as more desirable) council housing estates have seen more private sales than others. Therefore it is no surprise that almost all of the constituencies on this list are safe for the Labour party, with the notable exception of Bermondsey, which, with some boundary changes, Simon Hughes has managed to hold for the Liberal Democrats and their predecessors for over thirty years since his initial by-election victory in February 1983.

Council housing has for many decades been generally more prevalent in Scotland, and the SNP have on occasion challenged in some of the seats on this list, most particularly Glasgow East, which they held from a 2008 by-election until it was regained for Labour by Margaret Curran in the 2010 general election.

Twenty constituencies with highest proportion of owner-occupied housing

	%	PARTY HOLDING SEAT
Sefton Central	87.2	Lab
Rayleigh & Wickford	86.0	C
Cheadle	85.9	LD
East Dunbartonshire	85.8	LD
Wyre & Preston North	85.2	C
Haltemprice & Howden	84.4	C
Charnwood	83.5	C
Castle Point	83.4	C
Sutton Coldfield	82.4	C
Solihull	82.1	LD
Mid Derbyshire	82.1	C
South Leicestershire	82.1	C
Bromsgrove	82.1	C
East Renfrewshire	82.0	Lab
York Outer	81.9	C
North Somerset	81.7	C
Staffordshire Moorlands	81.5	C
Harborough	81.3	C
Maldon	81.3	C
Old Bexley & Sidcup	81.3	C

Sources: Anthony Wells, UK Polling Report, and House of Commons Library Research Paper RP 14/10, Census 2011 Constituency Results, United Kingdom.

Some interesting features:

- While high owner occupation is usually a positive feature for Conservatism (remember Mrs Thatcher's sale of council housing), the table shows that this is not universally so. Two Labour seats appear in the top twenty, including the top one in this category, Sefton Central (which includes Formby, Maghull and the northern part of Crosby, famously won by Shirley Williams in 1982), plus Wirral South is at number twenty-one. The point is that these three are all in regions where the Conservative Party has become unpopular – Merseyside (Sefton Central and Wirral South) and Scotland (Jim Murphy's East Renfrewshire). Region can trump housing tenure as a determinant of political preference.

- There are also three Liberal Democrat seats. One, Cheadle in Greater Manchester, is a long-term Liberal stronghold going back all the way to Michael Winstanley's election in 1966, but it has been a triumph for Lorely Burt to win Solihull in the West Midlands twice narrowly, and it would be similarly unlikely for her to make it a hat-trick in 2015. In the third, East Dunbartonshire, Jo Swinson is also under great pressure – but, because this is Scotland, from Labour.

- Only one of the seats above is in Greater London – Old Bexley & Sidcup, the linear descendant of the constituency held by Edward Heath from 1950 to 2001.

Ten constituencies with highest proportion of voters in same-sex civil partnerships

	%	PARTY HOLDING SEAT
Bermondsey & Old Southwark	3.2	LD
Brighton Kemptown	3.2	C
Cities of London & Westminster	3.0	C
Brighton, Pavilion	2.9	Green
Islington South & Finsbury	2.7	Lab
Holborn & St Pancras	2.6	Lab
Lewisham Deptford	2.6	Lab
Camberwell & Peckham	2.6	Lab
Hove	2.4	C
Dulwich & Norwood	2.4	Lab

These figures are from reported returns from the 2011 census, so pre-date the institution of same-sex marriage.

They also should not be taken as an indicator of 'percentage gay/lesbian', which would include many not in same-sex civil partnerships or not reporting to the official government census.

However, the list does still have political interest, as probably including the greatest variety of constituency patterns of contest of any of our lists. It includes the only Green seat (Caroline Lucas in Brighton Pavilion, a multi-way marginal); two Conservative seats vulnerable to Labour (Hove and Brighton Kemptown); a safe Tory stronghold (the Cities of London & Westminster); several safe Labour constituencies in London; and finally the seat of the Liberal Democrat Simon Hughes who is also the only gay MP for any of the top ten seats in this category.

The seats with the lowest percentage of civil partnerships recorded in England and Wales are at 0.4 per cent: Castle Point in Essex, which includes Canvey Island (safe Conservative, but with a likely strong UKIP presence); Harrow East (a Conservative seat vulnerable to Labour); and the Liberal Democrats' safe Thornbury and Yate in Gloucestershire.

Twenty constituencies with highest proportion of higher professional and managerial workers

	%	PARTY HOLDING SEAT
Wimbledon	24.0	C
Cities of London & Westminster	23.8	C
Battersea	23.4	C
Richmond Park	23.3	C
Chelsea & Fulham	22.6	C
Hampstead & Kilburn	21.2	Lab
Kensington	20.7	C
Wokingham	20.5	C
Putney	20.4	C
Twickenham	20.2	LD
South Cambridgeshire	19.9	C
St Albans	19.8	C
Hitchin & Harpenden	19.8	C
Esher & Walton	19.8	C
North East Hampshire	19.5	C
Sheffield Hallam	19.2	LD
Islington South & Finsbury	19.1	Lab
Maidenhead	19.1	C
Westminster North	18.9	Lab
Altrincham & Sale West	18.8	C

Class has for many decades been regarded as the strongest single predictor of voting patterns, and although class-based voting has been in decline in Britain since about 1960, it still is. However, it is by no means the be-all-and-end-all as far as constituencies are concerned, as shown by the presence in the above list of three Labour seats inclined to the left – and also by the fact that Wimbledon, Battersea, Putney and St Albans were all won by Labour in 1997 and 2001.

Besides the presence of two current Liberal Democrat seats, those of Nick Clegg and Vince Cable, Richmond Park was also theirs until lost in 2010. So it can be said that having a very high percentage of senior managers and professionals is not necessarily a sign of strong Conservatism.

Twenty constituencies with lowest proportion of higher professional and managerial workers

	%	PARTY HOLDING SEAT
Birmingham Hodge Hill	2.9	Lab
Liverpool Walton	3.6	Lab
Glasgow East	3.8	Lab
Rhondda	3.8	Lab
Belfast West	3.9	Sinn Fein
Nottingham North	4.0	Lab
Blaenau Gwent	4.0	Lab
Middlesbrough	4.1	Lab
Hull East	4.1	Lab
Great Grimsby	4.1	Lab
Wolverhampton South East	4.2	Lab
Glasgow North East	4.3	Lab
West Bromwich West	4.3	Lab
Walsall North	4.3	Lab
Glenrothes	4.4	Lab
Wolverhampton North East	4.4	Lab
Glasgow South West	4.4	Lab
Blackpool South	4.5	Lab
Merthyr Tydfil & Rhymney	4.5	Lab
Knowsley	4.5	Lab

The list of seats with the lowest proportion of senior managers and professionals in Britain is in general strongly correlated with great Labour strength, though it should be noted that Glasgow East was held by the SNP from 2008 to 2010, Blackpool South is on the Conservative target list, and Great Grimsby is regarded as a genuine three-way marginal with the Tories only 714 votes behind in 2010.

Generally the constituencies are in the category of 'white working class', as those with more recent patterns of immigration tend also to have more aspirational characteristics, with more educational qualifications and often in large cities which themselves host more professionals and managers. However, right at the top of this list, as of others, is Birmingham Hodge Hill, which has a Muslim and Asian majority, and very high unemployment as well as other indices of social and economic deprivation.

List of retiring MPs

At the time this book went to press, 67 sitting MPs had announced they were standing down at the 2010 election. This compares to 149 MPs who retired at the 2010 election and 86 at the 2005 election.

CONSERVATIVES (25)

Bexhill & Battle – Greg Barker
Boston & Skegness – Mark Simmonds
Bury St Edmunds – David Ruffley
Cannock Chase – Aiden Burley
Cardiff North – Jonathan Evans
Croydon South – Sir Richard Ottaway
Dudley South – Chris Kelly
Erewash – Jessica Lee
Havant – David Willetts
Hertsmere – James Clappison
Hove – Mike Weatherley
Louth & Horncastle – Sir Peter Tapsell
Mid Worcestershire – Sir Peter Luff
North East Hampshire – James Arbuthnot
North Oxfordshire – Sir Tony Baldry
North Warwickshire – Dan Byles
North West Hampshire – Sir George Young
Northampton South – Brian Binley
Richmond (Yorks) – William Hague

South Cambridgeshire – Andrew Lansley
South East Cambridgeshire – Sir Jim Paice
South Ribble – Lorraine Fullbrook
South Suffolk – Tim Yeo
South Thanet – Laura Sandys
Tonbridge & Malling – Sir John Stanley
Uxbridge & Ruislip South – Sir John Randall
Wealden – Charles Hendry

LABOUR (30)

Aberavon – Hywel Francis
Aberdeen North – Frank Doran
Ashton Under Lyne – David Heyes
Batley & Spen – Mike Wood
Blackburn – Jack Straw
Bootle – Joe Benton
Bradford South – Gerry Sutcliffe
Bristol South – Dame Dawn Primarolo
Coventry North East – Bob Ainsworth
Cynon Valley – Ann Clwyd
Dulwich & West Norwood – Dame Tessa Jowell
Ellesmere Port & Neston – Andrew Miller
Falkirk – Eric Joyce*
Glenrothes – Lindsay Roy
Gower – Martin Caton
Great Grimsby – Austin Mitchell
Greenwich & Woolwich – Nick Raynsford
Hampstead & Kilburn – Glenda Jackson
Leeds East – George Mudie
Lewisham, Deptford – Dame Joan Ruddock
Neath – Peter Hain
Salford & Eccles – Hazel Blears

Sheffield, Brightside & Hillsborough – David Blunkett
Sheffield, Heeley – Meg Munn
Southampton, Itchen – John Denham
St Helens South & Whiston – Shaun Woodward
Stirling – Anne McGuire
Stoke-on-Trent North – Joan Walley
Swansea East – Sian James
Workington – Sir Tony Cunningham

Eric Joyce was elected as a Labour MP but resigned from the Labour party in 2012 after pleading guilty to four charges of assault.

LIBERAL DEMOCRAT (9)

Bath – Don Foster
Berwick-upon-Tweed – Sir Alan Beith
Brent Central – Sarah Teather
Gordon – Sir Malcolm Bruce
Hazel Grove – Sir Andrew Stunell
Mid Dorset and North Poole – Annette Brooke
North East Fife – Sir Menzies Campbell
Redcar – Ian Swales
Somerton & Frome – David Heath

PLAID CYMRU (1)

Dwyfor Meirionnydd – Elfyn Lloyd

List courtesy of UK Polling Report & Anthony Wells. Correct at 28 August 2014.

What will happen to the Liberal Democrat vote: a seat-by-seat prediction

Iain Dale

I got myself into a lot of trouble on election night in 2010 when I promised to run down Whitehall naked if the Lib Dems only won fifty-nine seats, which was the BBC projection. When I interviewed Danny Alexander he said he'd join me. They actually only won fifty-seven, albeit with 23 per cent of the vote. I have yet to make good on my promise – and I won't be doing so! I think the only way to gauge how many seats the Lib Dems will win in 2015 is to go through their MPs, seat by seat, and analyse the probable result. So, here goes…

A few months ago I posted a prediction that the Lib Dems would win thirty to thirty-five seats at the next election. I went through each Lib Dem seat and predicted what would happen to it. To read the original predictions, visit my website. Clearly, any such exercise is fraught with difficulty, and I freely admitted that many would disagree with the conclusions. Reading through the comments of that blogpost, the consensus seemed to be that I had been too kind to the Lib Dems in Scotland but too hard on them in the south west. That was, of course, before the European and local elections, when the Lib

Dems performed far worse than I think even their worst enemy had wished. They came fifth in the popular vote in the European elections, behind the Greens, polling only 6.87 per cent of the popular vote.

Four months ago, I predicted that of the fifty-seven seats, thirty-five would remain Lib Dem, fourteen would fall to the Conservatives and eight to Labour. But of the thirty-five Lib Dem holds, I reckoned only thirteen were dead-certs, nine hot bets, eight probable and five were rated as possible, but by no means definite.

My new prediction is that of the fifty-seven seats, twenty-eight will remain Lib Dem, seventeen will fall to the Conservatives, eleven to Labour and one to the SNP.

I remain of the view that Labour will be the beneficiaries of most of the decline in Lib Dem votes across the country, but that the Conservatives might benefit a little in the south and south west. The big unknown factor here is how the size of the UKIP vote might affect existing Conservative vote levels in many of these seats. I have tried not to make these predictions through blue-tinted spectacles, but it may be that I will have underestimated the impact of UKIP, especially bearing in mind their performance in the May elections. I have also assumed that the Lib Dems will not win a single one of their top twenty target seats. Even if that proves to be wrong, looking through the list it is hard to see more than a handful of even remotely possible gains based on the way things look at the moment.

Inverness, Nairn, Badenoch & Strathspey

Danny Alexander
Majority: 8,765 over Labour
Prediction: **PROBABLE LIB DEM HOLD**

Lewes

Norman Baker
Majority: 7,647
Prediction: **PROBABLE LIB DEM HOLD**
If Labour takes enough votes from the Lib Dems it could let the Conservatives in, and Lewes used to be a safe
Tory seat. Baker's local popularity should see him through but with a much smaller majority.

Berwick-upon-Tweed

Sir Alan Beith (retiring – Julie Pörksen selected)
Majority: 2,690 over the Conservatives
Prediction: **PROBABLE CONSERVATIVE GAIN**
The Conservative candidate Anne-Marie Trevelyan stood in 2010 and if her vote holds up, she only needs Labour
to take a small proportion of the Lib Dem vote. Beith's incumbency will also disappear.

Burnley

Gordon Birtwistle
Majority: 1,818 over Labour
Prediction: **LABOUR GAIN**
Birtwistle is a straight-talking northerner and speaks out against what he views as wishy-washy liberalism.
He's very popular but it would be a major shock if he held on to the seat he snatched from Labour in 2010.

Carshalton & Wallington

Tom Brake
Majority: 5,260 over the Conservatives
Prediction: **POSSIBLE CONSERVATIVE GAIN**
Somewhat charismatically challenged Brake is nevertheless a very good constituency MP and this could see
him through, but the Labour vote here is bound to recover. However, I'd say this was a 50/50 prediction and
could easily go the other way. This would be the sixth time Brake has fought the seat and that counts for a lot.

Mid Dorset & North Poole

Annette Brooke (retiring – Vikki Slade selected)
Majority: 269
Prediction: **CONSERVATIVE GAIN**
It was a shock this seat didn't go Tory last time. With Annette Brooke standing down, the Lib Dems will have
to perform miracles to keep this seat.

Taunton Deane

Jeremy Browne
Majority: 3,993 over the Conservatives
Prediction: **POSSIBLE CONSERVATIVE GAIN – 50/50**
Boundary changes last time increased Browne's majority from just over 500. I don't know how popular he is locally. Seen as a very good minister it was a shock when he was sacked by Clegg. Might he stand down? I'd say this was a 50/50 call.

Gordon

Sir Malcolm Bruce (retiring – Christine Jardine selected)
Majority: 6,748 over the SNP
Prediction: **PROBABLE SNP GAIN**

Sutton & Cheam

Paul Burstow
Majority: 1,608
Prediction: **PROBABLE CONSERVATIVE GAIN**
The Labour vote has halved to 7.7 per cent since 1997 and will inevitably rise in 2015. Paul Burstow is standing again and incumbency could play a vital role if he is to retain his seat, but if the Tory vote holds up, he may have a problem.

Solihull

Lorely Burt
Majority: 175
Prediction: **CONSERVATIVE GAIN**
Lorely Burt did very well to hang onto her seat last time (she won it in 2005 with a majority of 279) and confounded all expectations. The Labour vote has gone down from 25 per cent to 8 per cent and if Labour takes just a thousand votes from the Lib Dems the Conservatives will win a seat many think they should never have lost.

Twickenham

Vince Cable
Majority: 12,140
Prediction: **DEAD-CERT LIB DEM HOLD**

North East Fife

Sir Menzies Campbell (retiring)
Majority: 9.348
Prediction: **LIB DEM HOLD**
The Conservatives will be targeting this seat but it's a remote hope for them. The new Lib Dem candidate may suffer a dent in their majority but unless Ming Campbell's personal vote is more than the norm, this seat should stay Liberal Democrat.

Orkney & Shetland

Alistair Carmichael
Majority: 9,928
Prediction: **DEAD-CERT LIB DEM HOLD**
None of the other parties come close – the Lib Dems won 62 per cent of the vote in 2010. Jo Grimond's legacy is safe!

Sheffield Hallam

Nick Clegg
Majority: 15,284
Prediction: **DEAD-CERT LIB DEM HOLD**
This used to be a Tory seat, but it would take a political earthquake for them to take it off Nick Clegg. Interestingly the Labour vote has started to rise, but not enough to cause the Lib Dems to panic.

Edinburgh West

Michael Crockart
Majority: 3,803
Prediction: **PROBABLE LIB DEM HOLD**
This seat went Lib Dem in 1997 and although the Lib Dem majority plummeted by 10,000 last time it is difficult to see them losing. Prior to 1997 it was a Tory seat, but last time Labour beat the Tories into second place. A Labour victory is not impossible to imagine, but still rather unlikely.

Kingston & Surbiton

Edward Davey
Majority: 7,560
Prediction: **LIB DEM HOLD**
Ed Davey won this seat in 1997 with a wafer-thin majority of fifty-six, which rose to more than 15,000 in 2001. But, since then the Conservative vote has been on the rise. Davey has only managed to win with such handsome majorities because he has squeezed the Labour vote from 23 per cent down to 9 per cent. If that trend reverses, the Conservatives could squeak it, but it's highly unlikely.

Westmorland & Lonsdale

Tim Farron
Majority: 12,264
Prediction: **DEAD-CERT LIB DEM HOLD**
Tim Farron has 60 per cent of the vote and while the Conservatives held this seat as recently as 2001, they have zero chance of winning it back in 2015. Why? Because it's a two-horse race. In 1997 the Labour vote was more than 20 per cent. In 2010 it was 2 per cent.

Hornsey & Wood Green

Lynne Featherstone
Majority: 6,875
Prediction: **POSSIBLE LABOUR GAIN**
Since 1997 Lynne Featherstone has built up the Lib Dem vote from 5,000 to 25,000 so as a constituency campaigner she is hard to beat. Meanwhile the Labour vote has declined from 31,000 to 18,000. The Conservatives have gone down from 21,000 to 9,000. This is a difficult one to call, but I now think Labour are edging ahead.

Bath

Don Foster (retiring)
Majority: 11,883
Prediction: **LIB DEM HOLD**
The Conservatives have been desperate to win this seat back since Chris Patten lost it in 1992, but it's extremely unlikely to revert to the fold despite the fact that Don Foster is standing down.

St Ives

Andrew George
Majority: 1,719
Prediction: **POSSIBLE CONSERVATIVE GAIN**
The Tories got a 10.39 per cent swing last time and took a huge chunk out of Andrew George's 11,000 majority. This time George will be hoping UKIP's vote reduces Tory potency. His incumbency and local popularity could see Andrew George home, but four months on from my last prediction, I now think the Tories may make it.

St Austell & Newquay

Stephen Gilbert
Majority: 1,312
Prediction: **POSSIBLE CONSERVATIVE GAIN**
This seat could go either way. Labour are nowhere with only 7 per cent of the vote. If UKIP does well in the south west, the Lib Dems win here, if they don't, they won't.

Cheltenham

Martin Horwood
Majority: 4,920
Prediction: **PROBABLE LIB DEM HOLD**
A Liberal Democrat seat since 1992, this is one that the Conservatives had expected to take back in both 2005 and 2010, but it wasn't to be. The Labour vote has been squeezed to just 5 per cent. Martin Horwood is extremely popular and will have built up a high personal vote. On a catastrophic night for the Lib Dems it's easy to see Cheltenham falling, but not otherwise.

Portsmouth South

Mike Hancock (deselected)
Majority: 5,200
Prediction: **POSSIBLE CONSERVATIVE GAIN**
This seat has never had a huge Lib Dem majority since it was won by Mike Hancock in 1997. It's always ranged between three and six thousand. It's difficult to assess the impact of the groping scandal, but on top of their national woes, it could be that the Tories win back what was once for them a safe seat. Hancock has failed to squeeze the Labour vote as much as some of his colleagues, and not so long ago they managed a healthy 25 per cent. If they return to those levels the Tories will win.

North Devon

Nick Harvey
Majority: 5,821
Prediction: **PROBABLE LIB DEM HOLD**
Ever since this seat was wrested back from the Conservatives in 1992, pundits have predicted it would return to the Tories, but astute constituency campaigning by Nick Harvey has prevented this from happening. I don't see this changing. This seat has a strong UKIP vote which inevitably depresses that of the Conservatives.

Somerton & Frome

David Heath (retiring)
Majority: 1,817
PREDICTION: **PROBABLE CONSERVATIVE GAIN**
Lib Dem HQ must have been tearing their hair out when David Heath announced his retirement, as he stood the best prospect of retaining this seat. His current majority is the largest he has ever enjoyed, but that is largely because at the last election the UKIP vote doubled to nearly 2,000. If they do the same in 2015 they could deny the Conservatives again what they thought they had in the bag last time.

Birmingham Yardley

John Hemming
Majority: 3,002
Prediction: **PROBABLE LABOUR GAIN**
Hemming is a maverick and I wouldn't bet against him pulling off a surprise, but if Labour is to form a government it's this kind of seat they need to take back.

Chippenham

Duncan Hames
Majority: 2,470
Prediction: **POSSIBLE CONSERVATIVE GAIN**
Although his majority isn't big, Duncan Hames has dug himself in since winning the seat in 2010 and will be difficult to shift. But the Tory candidate Michelle Donelan is a good campaigner. Yet again, her success depends on warding off UKIP and encouraging Lib Dems to vote Labour.

Bermondsey & Old Southwark

Simon Hughes
Majority: 8,530
Prediction: **PROBABLE LIB DEM HOLD**
I had thought this would be a dead-cert hold for Simon Hughes but increasingly I am wondering if I am right. Labour seem very confident they can take this.

Eastleigh

Mike Thornton
Majority: 1,771
Prediction: **POSSIBLE CONSERVATIVE GAIN**
The Conservatives thought they would win this seat back at each of the last two general elections, but each time Chris Huhne pulled through. At the by-election they came third, with UKIP almost pipping the rather monochrome Mike Thornton. It's highly unlikely UKIP's vote will hold up, so the outcome of this seat may depend on where UKIP's voters put their cross. If enough of them return to the Conservative fold, it could be enough to see the Conservative home.

Cheadle

Mark Hunter
Majority: 3,272
Prediction: **PROBABLE LIB DEM HOLD**
Apart from a narrow majority of thirty-three in 1997, the Lib Dems have had a majority of three or four thousand in this seat ever since. As long as the slightly resurgent Labour vote doesn't gain too much traction, I think Mark Hunter will be safe.

Cambridge

Julian Huppert
Majority: 6,792
Prediction: **PROBABLE LABOUR GAIN**
If you look at the size of the Lib Dem majority here, Julian Huppert ought to be considered very safe, but this is a seat that swings with the wind, and if the wind is blowing towards Labour you can see it returning to them. It obviously has a high student vote and this may determine the outcome. However, Huppert has been a strong performer both locally and in parliament and if anyone can hold this seat for the Lib Dems, he can. Bearing in mind the Lib Dems' calamitous results in May, however, I've now changed my mind and think Labour will win here.

Ross, Skye & Lochaber

Charles Kennedy
Majority: 13,070
Prediction: **DEAD-CERT LIB DEM HOLD**
Out on his own, and despite an invisible presence in this parliament, there would need to be a miracle to shift Charles Kennedy.

North Norfolk

Norman Lamb
Majority: 11,626
Prediction: **DEAD-CERT LIB DEM HOLD**
Lamb's majority is even bigger than the one he had over me in 2005. Although I think it will reduce in 2010 due to the crumbling Lib Dem local organisation and the resurgent North Norfolk Labour Party, he will still win handsomely.

Yeovil

David Laws
Majority: 13,036
Prediction: **DEAD-CERT LIB DEM HOLD**

Manchester Withington

John Leech
Majority: 1,894
Prediction: **LABOUR GAIN**
Although John Leech trebled his majority last time, I fear the bell tolls for him unless UKIP can take a lot of votes from Labour.

Eastbourne

Stephen Lloyd
Majority: 3,435
Prediction: **PROBABLE CONSERVATIVE GAIN**
Won in 2010 from Nigel Waterson, Stephen Lloyd may hang on, but I'd expect the Labour vote to at least double at the expense of the Lib Dems so, yet again, a lot depends on how many votes the Tories lose to UKIP.

Berwickshire, Roxburgh & Selkirk

Michael Moore
Majority: 5,675
Prediction: **LIB DEM HOLD**
David Steel's old seat – it's never been 100 per cent safe, but it would be a major shock for the Conservatives to take this seat.

Leeds North West

Greg Mulholland
Majority: 9,103
Prediction: **DEAD-CERT LIB DEM HOLD**
A Labour seat as recently as 2005, Labour has now slipped to third place. With a classic split-opposition situation it would be a brave man who would vote against a third term for Greg Mulholland.

Wells

Tessa Munt
Majority: 800
Prediction: **PROBABLE CONSERVATIVE GAIN**
The former seat of David Heathcoat-Amory, Tessa Munt won Wells in 2010. The Tories will make every effort to regain it and will be devastated if they don't pull it off.

Southport

John Pugh
Majority: 6,024
Prediction: **LIB DEM HOLD**
It's difficult to see this as anything other than a Lib Dem win.

Argyll & Bute

Alan Reid
Majority: 3,431
Prediction: **POSSIBLE LIB DEM HOLD**
A four-way marginal, this could go to any of the main parties. If the Lib Dems lose, my guess is that it would go to Labour, even though they were in third place in 2010.

North Cornwall

Dan Rogerson
Majority: 2,981
Prediction: **PROBABLE CONSERVATIVE GAIN**
A seat where the Lib Dem majority has been on the slide in every election since 1997's highpoint of more than 13,000. If UKIP hadn't existed, the Conservatives would have won this seat in 2010. So the key question is whether they will eat further into the Conservative vote in 2015. If so, the Lib Dems will hang on, otherwise this is a pretty safe bet for the Tories.

Colchester

Sir Bob Russell
Majority: 6,982
Prediction: **LIB DEM HOLD**
Difficult to see anything other than another home run for Sir Bob!

Torbay

Adrian Sanders
Majority: 4,078
Prediction: **POSSIBLE LIB DEM HOLD**
Regarded as a sure-fire Tory gain in 2010, it didn't happen, and in all honesty Adrian Sanders has built up a strong personal vote which may carry him through once again.

West Aberdeenshire & Kincardine

Sir Robert Smith
Majority: 3,684
Prediction: **POSSIBLE CONSERVATIVE GAIN**
The Lib Dem majority was halved last time, and it's very possible to see how rises in the Labour and SNP votes could see this seat return to the Conservative fold.

Hazel Grove

Andrew Stunell (retiring – Lisa Smart selected)
Majority: 6,371
Prediction: **PROBABLE LIB DEM HOLD**
The Lib Dem majority has fallen in every election since 1997 but the Tories haven't been able to capitalise. And I don't see them bucking the trend in 2015.

Redcar

Ian Swales
Majority: 5,214
Prediction: **LABOUR GAIN**
This was a very surprising result last time and was due in large part to massive job losses on Teesside. On that basis, the seat may return to its natural fold.

East Dunbartonshire

Jo Swinson
Majority: 2,184
Prediction: **LABOUR GAIN**
Jo Swinson is popular but all the political portents are against her. She will be a major loss to the Lib Dems.

Brent Central

Sarah Teather (retiring)
Majority: 1,345
Prediction: **DEAD-CERT LABOUR GAIN**
If the Lib Dems retain this seat it will be miracle of all miracles.

Caithness, Sutherland & Easter Ross

John Thurso
Majority: 4,828
Prediction: **LIB DEM HOLD**
A small electorate, Thurso should hold the seat he won in 2001.

Bradford East

David Ward
Majority: 365
Prediction: **DEAD-CERT LABOUR GAIN**
One of the nastier Lib Dem MPs, few will shed tears at his demise.

Thornbury & Yate

Steve Webb
Majority: 7,116
Prediction: **DEAD-CERT LIB DEM HOLD**

Norwich South

Simon Wright
Majority: 310
Prediction: **DEAD-CERT LABOUR GAIN**
Student fees will do it for Simon Wright due to the large university vote. Of all the seats the Lib Dems are slated to lose, this is the deadest cert of dead-certs.

Ceredigion

Mark Williams
Majority: 8,324
Prediction: **DEAD-CERT LIB DEM HOLD**

Brecon & Radnorshire

Roger Williams
Majority: 3,747
Prediction: **POSSIBLE CONSERVATIVE GAIN**
A Conservative gain here is possible but not definite. One of the tightest results in 2015, I'd think.

Bristol West

Stephen Williams
Majority: 11.336
Prediction: **DEAD-CERT LIB DEM HOLD**

Cardiff Central

Jenny Willott
Majority: 4,576
Prediction: **PROBABLE LABOUR GAIN**
Labour have their sights on this one. Assuming no Lib Dem poll bounce, I now think they will take this.

REGIONAL & CONSTITUENCY PROFILES

Regional Profiles by Robert Waller

Constituency Profiles by Daniel Hamilton

Election Data Tables by Greg Callus

South West England

In most of the regions, we have not spent significant time discussing Liberal Democrat hopes of gains in the 2015 general election. This is, we hope, forgivable given the dramatic decline since 2010 of the junior coalition party in opinion polls and also real elections. The Lib Dems have lost hundreds of local council seats each May since they joined the coalition government, and in the European Parliament election of 2014 their share of the vote more than halved to 6.6 per cent across the nation, and their tally of MEPs fell from eleven to just one. Due to the incumbency effect and their concentration of resources, they should hold more of their existing Westminster MPs in 2015 than expected, maybe many more; their performance in local government by-elections has held up well where they have been in contention to hold or even gain wards. It should come as no surprise if they retain as many as forty or even forty-five constituencies, and they could very well be in contention for negotiations with major parties to form another coalition in the event of a hung parliament. But fresh gains seem unlikely – and perhaps their best chance of these comes in the South West region.

Cornwall is always a hard county to predict. This county at the far end of the south-western peninsula beyond the river Tamar is independently minded and does not always follow national trends. In 2005 the Liberal Democrat party won all five seats in Cornwall. Then in 2010, when the county's allocation was increased to six, it lost half of them in the Conservative revival. It is by no means impossible that at least some of the lost three may be recovered: Camborne & Redruth and

Truro & Falmouth both need a swing of under 1 per cent, and South East Cornwall, where the Lib Dems were weakened by the retirement of Colin Breed in 2010, still only needs 3 per cent. Cornwall's idiosyncrasies, based on traditional nonconformity, a distance from and distrust of London and its government, and a determination to 'do different' means that almost anything may happen here.

Altogether seven of the top fifteen Liberal Democrat targets from the Conservatives are in this South West region. Three of the others have been won by the party in the last ten years: Newton Abbot (formerly named Teignbridge), Weston-super-Mare and Torridge & West Devon. In another, the urban Bristol North West, they made an advance in 2010, increasing their share by over 10 per cent as Labour slipped from first to third. Two final constituencies are very much at the outer edges of possibility as gains: Oliver Letwin's West Dorset, and Totnes, where the Conservative MP Dr Sarah Wollaston has used her 'open primary' method of selection as a springboard to an unusually independent contribution in the Commons, which is likely to go down better with the electors than with her party's establishment.

If the South West includes some of the best chances for Liberal Democrat gains, it is also likely to see some losses. It has been often stated that their MPs build up much larger personal votes than those of larger parties, but when they retire this leaves their seats particularly vulnerable. An unusually large number of Lib Dem members are retiring in 2015. At least nine had announced their intention to stand down by August 2014, compared with a final total of seven in 2010 (in five of these cases their nominated successors could not hold the seat). In two seats in the region this makes the Conservatives favourites for a gain – Mid Dorset & North Poole (Annette Brooke) and Somerton & Frome (David Heath). In Bath, Don Foster is also going, twenty-three years after he ousted the Tory chairman Chris Patten, but he has built up a large enough majority to be passed on. However, the Liberal Democrats only just held on to their other three seats in Cornwall in 2010, and only just gained Wells in Somerset and Chippenham in

Wiltshire by a somewhat larger margin, so a lot of constituencies may change hands – and not all in one direction.

As in other parts of the south outside London, Labour is a relatively minor party in this region, winning only four of the fifty-one divisions at the last general election. However, it should be remembered that this region as defined for European elections includes Gloucestershire and Wiltshire, where Labour lost half a dozen seats in 2010. Some of these, like North Swindon, seem beyond their reach now, but the unexpectedly industrial Stroud needs a swing of only 1.1 per cent to be regained, while Gloucester would fall on 2.5 per cent, Kingswood on 3 per cent and South Swindon on 4 per cent – all in line with most national opinion polls in 2014. One seat in Devon is also in the 'relatively easily regained' list – Plymouth Sutton & Devonport, whose names recall a number of high-profile if very varied MPs including David Owen and Alan Clark.

None of Labour's four seats could be described as very safe, but there is the feeling that if the Conservatives could not take Exeter, Plymouth Moor View (the working-class north of the city), or either Bristol South or East from Labour's tired government in 2010, they will not do so now. David Cameron's hopes of an overall majority rest mainly on biting into the fifteen seats of his partner Nick Clegg's party.

A final joker in the pack is UKIP. In the European elections the Eurosceptic (some would say Europhobic) party easily topped the poll, with a 33 per cent share, and finished first in many local authorities – and hence Westminster constituencies – in the region. They were assisted by the higher age profile in the region, which includes Christchurch, the seat with the highest proportion of pensioners, and the long south-western coastline. But this cannot be taken as an indicator that they will actually win, or even come close to winning, seats when voters are choosing an actual government for the United Kingdom alone. However, UKIP will receive hundreds of thousands of votes in the region, and there is an unanswered question about where these might come from. Unless they are drawn fairly equally from

Conservative, Labour, Liberal Democrat, other and none, a differential impact will be made. But the interpretation that Europe 2014 and Westminster 2015 are very different contests strongly influences this regional survey, as is demonstrated by the amount of attention paid to the Liberal Democrats' chances above – when they actually finished fifth in the Euro elections, behind the Greens as well as UKIP, Conservative and Labour. As traditionally the second party in the South West of England, they must hope they do very, very much better.

Bath

LIB DEM HOLD	PARTY	2010 CANDIDATE	2010 VOTES	2010 % VOTE	PPC FOR 2015
Majority	Lib Dem	Don Foster MP	26,651	56.6	Steve Bradley
11,883	Conservative	Fabian Richter	14,768	31.4	Ben Howlett
Turnout	Labour	Hattie Ajderian	3,251	6.9	Ollie Middleton
70.61%	Others		2,416	5.1	

Bournemouth East

CONSERVATIVE HOLD	PARTY	2010 CANDIDATE	2010 VOTES	2010 % VOTE	PPC FOR 2015
Majority	Conservative	Tobias Ellwood MP	21,320	48.4	Tobias Ellwood MP
7,728	Lib Dem	Lisa Northover	13,592	30.9	
Turnout	Labour	David Stokes	5,836	13.3	
61.90%	Others		3,276	7.4	

Bournemouth West

CONSERVATIVE HOLD	PARTY	2010 CANDIDATE	2010 VOTES	2010 % VOTE	PPC FOR 2015
Majority	Conservative	Conor Burns	18,808	45.1	Conor Burns MP
5,583	Lib Dem	Alasdair Murray	13,225	31.7	
Turnout	Labour	Sharon Carr-Brown	6,171	14.8	David Stokes
58.06%	Others		3,455	8.3	

Bridgwater & West Somerset

CONSERVATIVE HOLD	PARTY	2010 CANDIDATE	2010 VOTES	2010 % VOTE	PPC FOR 2015
Majority	Conservative	Ian Liddell-Grainger MP	24,675	45.3	Ian Liddell-Grainger MP
9,249	Lib Dem	Theo Butt Philip	15,426	28.3	Justine Baker
Turnout	Labour	Kathy Pearce	9,332	17.1	Michael Lerry
66.31%	Others		5,060	9.3	

Bristol East

LABOUR HOLD	PARTY	2010 CANDIDATE	2010 VOTES	2010 % VOTE	PPC FOR 2015
Majority	Labour	Kerry McCarthy MP	16,471	36.6	Kerry McCarthy MP
3,722	Conservative	Adeela Shafi	12,749	28.3	Theodora Clarke
Turnout	Lib Dem	Michael Popham	10,993	24.4	Abdul Malik
64.82%	Others		4,804	10.7	

Bristol North West

CONSERVATIVE GAIN FROM LABOUR	PARTY	2010 CANDIDATE	2010 VOTES	2010 % VOTE	PPC FOR 2015
Majority	Conservative	Charlotte Leslie	19,115	38.0	Charlotte Leslie MP
3,274	Lib Dem	Paul Harrod	15,841	31.5	
Turnout	Labour	Sam Townend	13,059	25.9	Darren Jones
68.51%	Others		2,321	4.6	

Majority 3274 (12%)

The subject of significant boundary changes prior to the 2010 general election, the seat was won by Conservative Charlotte Leslie. The constituency is a diverse social mix, encompassing wealthy commuter suburbs such as Westbury-on-Trym and Stoke Bishop, which favour the Conservatives, and areas of genuine deprivation around the industrial Avonmouth Docks. Levels of owner occupation here are, at 65.5 per cent, significantly below average with one in five homes council-owned. The Conservatives performed robustly in the 2014 local elections, polling 33.6 per cent of the vote in the constituency to Labour's 24.5 per cent. The Liberal Democrats polled just 17.4 per cent of the vote, roughly half of the 31 per cent they secured at the 2010 election. The Labour candidate will be local solicitor Darren Jones.

Bristol South

LABOUR HOLD	PARTY	2010 CANDIDATE	2010 VOTES	2010 % VOTE	PPC FOR 2015
Majority	Labour	Dawn Primarolo MP	18,600	38.4	Karin Smyth
4,734	Lib Dem	Mark Wright	13,866	28.7	Mark Wright
Turnout	Conservative	Mark Lloyd Davies	11,086	22.9	Isobel Grant
61.56%	Others		4,825	10.0	

Bristol West

LIB DEM HOLD	PARTY	2010 CANDIDATE	2010 VOTES	2010 % VOTE	PPC FOR 2015
Majority	Lib Dem	Stephen Williams MP	26,593	48.0	Stephen Williams MP
11,366	Labour	Paul Smith	15,227	27.5	Thangam Debbonaire
Turnout	Conservative	Nick Yarker	10,169	18.4	Claire Hiscott
66.90%	Others		3,358	6.1	

Camborne & Redruth

CONSERVATIVE WIN (NEW SEAT)	PARTY	2010 CANDIDATE	2010 VOTES	2010 % VOTE	PPC FOR 2015
Majority	Conservative	George Eustace	15,969	37.6	George Eustace MP
66	Lib Dem	Julia Goldsworthy MP	15,903	37.4	Julia Goldsworthy
Turnout	Labour	Jude Robinson	6,945	16.3	Michael Foster
66.42%	Others		3,676	8.7	

Majority 66 (0%)

Located 250 miles from central London and formed from parts of the existing Falmouth & Camborne and Truro & St Austell constituencies, Camborne and Redruth is one of the United Kingdom's most westerly constituencies. This is the Liberal Democrats' number one national target seat. All three main political parties are competitive here, with Labour, the Conservatives and Liberal Democrats having each won an edition of the parliamentary constituency since 1997. Labour's support is greatest in the former tin- and copper-mining town of Redruth, the Liberal Democrats dominate in Cornwall's largest town, Camborne, and the Conservatives are strongest in the rural areas surrounding both towns. The sitting Conservative MP and Environment Minister George Eustice will face a challenge from former Liberal Democrat MP Julia Goldsworthy who represented Falmouth and Camborne from 2005 to 2010.

Cheltenham

LIB DEM HOLD	PARTY	2010 CANDIDATE	2010 VOTES	2010 % VOTE	PPC FOR 2015
Majority	Lib Dem	Martin Horwood MP	26,659	50.5	Martin Horwood MP
4,920	Conservative	Mark Coote	21,739	41.2	Alex Chalk
Turnout	Labour	James Green	2,703	5.1	
66.82%	Others		1,685	3.2	

Chippenham

LIB DEM WIN (NEW SEAT)	PARTY	2010 CANDIDATE	2010 VOTES	2010 % VOTE	PPC FOR 2015
Majority	Lib Dem	Duncan Hames	23,970	45.8	Duncan Hames MP
2,470	Conservative	Wilfred Emmanuel-Jones	21,500	41.0	Michelle Donelan
Turnout	Labour	Greg Lovell	3,620	6.9	Andy Newman
72.65%	Others		3,295	6.3	

Christchurch

CONSERVATIVE HOLD	PARTY	2010 CANDIDATE	2010 VOTES	2010 % VOTE	PPC FOR 2015
Majority	Conservative	Christopher Chope MP	27,888	56.4	Christopher Chope MP
15,410	Lib Dem	Martyn Hurll	12,478	25.3	
Turnout	Labour	Robert Deeks	4,849	9.8	Andrew Satherley
71.76%	Others		4,201	8.5	

North Cornwall

LIB DEM HOLD	PARTY	2010 CANDIDATE	2010 VOTES	2010 % VOTE	PPC FOR 2015
Majority	Lib Dem	Dan Rogerson MP	22,512	48.1	Dan Rogerson MP
2,981	Conservative	Siân Flynn	19,531	41.7	Scott Mann
Turnout	UKIP	Miriel O'Connor	2,300	4.9	
68.95%	Others		2,501	5.3	

South East Cornwall

CONSERVATIVE GAIN FROM LIB DEM	PARTY	2010 CANDIDATE	2010 VOTES	2010 % VOTE	PPC FOR 2015
Majority	Conservative	Sheryll Murray	22,390	45.1	Sheryll Murray MP
3,220	Lib Dem	Karen Gillard	19,170	38.6	Phil Hutty
Turnout	Labour	Michael Sparling	3,507	7.1	
69.52%	Others		4,550	9.2	Stephanie McWilliam (UKIP)

The Cotswolds

CONSERVATIVE HOLD	PARTY	2010 CANDIDATE	2010 VOTES	2010 % VOTE	PPC FOR 2015
Majority	Conservative	Geoffrey Clifton-Brown MP	29,075	53.0	Geoffrey Clifton-Brown MP
12,864	Lib Dem	Mike Collins	16,211	29.6	Paul Hodgkinson
Turnout	Labour	Mark Dempsey	5,886	10.7	
71.46%	Others		3,660	6.7	

Devizes

CONSERVATIVE HOLD	PARTY	2010 CANDIDATE	2010 VOTES	2010 % VOTE	PPC FOR 2015
Majority	Conservative	Claire Perry	25,519	55.1	Claire Perry MP
13,005	Lib Dem	Fiona Hornby	12,514	27.0	
Turnout	Labour	Junab Ali	4,711	10.2	Chris Watts
68.78%	Others		3,596	7.8	

Central Devon

CONSERVATIVE WIN (NEW SEAT)	PARTY	2010 CANDIDATE	2010 VOTES	2010 % VOTE	PPC FOR 2015
Majority	Conservative	Mel Stride	27,737	51.5	Mel Stride MP
9,230	Lib Dem	Phil Hutty	18,507	34.4	
Turnout	Labour	Moira Macdonald	3,715	6.9	Lynne Richards
75.66%	Others		3,914	7.3	

East Devon

CONSERVATIVE HOLD	PARTY	2010 CANDIDATE	2010 VOTES	2010 % VOTE	PPC FOR 2015
Majority	Conservative	Hugo Swire MP	25,662	48.3	Hugo Swire MP
9,114	Lib Dem	Paul Robathan	16,548	31.2	
Turnout	Labour	Gareth Manson	5,721	10.8	Jessica Pearce
72.62%	Others		5,161	9.7	

North Devon

LIB DEM HOLD	PARTY	2010 CANDIDATE	2010 VOTES	2010 % VOTE	PPC FOR 2015
Majority	Lib Dem	Nick Harvey MP	24,305	47.4	Nick Harvey MP
5,821	Conservative	Philip Milton	18,484	36.0	Peter Heaton-Jones
Turnout	UKIP	Steve Crowther	3,720	7.2	Steve Crowther
68.88%	Others		4,812	9.4	Mark Cann (Labour)

South West Devon

CONSERVATIVE HOLD	PARTY	2010 CANDIDATE	2010 VOTES	2010 % VOTE	PPC FOR 2015
Majority	Conservative	Gary Streeter MP	27,908	56.0	Gary Streeter MP
15,874	Lib Dem	Anna Pascoe	12,034	24.1	Tom Davies
Turnout	Labour	Luke Pollard	6,193	12.4	Chaz Singh
70.41%	Others		3,725	7.5	

Torridge & West Devon

CONSERVATIVE HOLD	PARTY	2010 CANDIDATE	2010 VOTES	2010 % VOTE	PPC FOR 2015
Majority	Conservative	Geoffrey Cox MP	25,230	45.7	Geoffrey Cox MP
2,957	Lib Dem	Adam Symons	22,273	40.3	Paula Dolphin
Turnout	UKIP	Robin Julian	3,021	5.5	
71.43%	Others		4,733	8.6	

Mid Dorset & North Poole

LIB DEM HOLD	PARTY	2010 CANDIDATE	2010 VOTES	2010 % VOTE	PPC FOR 2015
Majority	Lib Dem	Annette Brooke MP	21,100	45.1	Vikki Slade
269	Conservative	Nick King	20,831	44.5	Michael Tomlinson
Turnout	Labour	Darren Brown	2,748	5.9	
72.36%	Others		2,109	4.5	

Majority 269 (0.6%)

A cumbersomely, yet precisely-named seat, Dorset Mid and Poole North was gained from the Conservatives by Liberal Democrat Annette Brooke at the 2001 general election after years of domination on a local government level. This is an attractive part of the world with extremely high levels of owner occupation, low unemployment and a substantial elderly population. There are no particularly large towns in the seat, the largest settlements being Corfe Mullen and Upton with less than 10,000 residents. The Conservatives, who were only 269 votes away from victory in 2010, are fielding barrister Michael Tomlinson. With Annette Brooke opting for retirement, the Liberal Democrat candidate will be Vikki Slade.

North Dorset

CONSERVATIVE HOLD	PARTY	2010 CANDIDATE	2010 VOTES	2010 % VOTE	PPC FOR 2015
Majority	Conservative	Robert Walter MP	27,640	51.1	Robert Walter MP
7,625	Lib Dem	Emily Gasson	20,015	37.0	Hugo Mieville
Turnout	Labour	Mike Bunney	2,910	5.4	Kim Fendley
73.42%	Others		3,576	6.6	

South Dorset

CONSERVATIVE GAIN FROM LABOUR	PARTY	2010 CANDIDATE	2010 VOTES	2010 % VOTE	PPC FOR 2015
Majority	Conservative	Richard Drax	22,667	45.1	Richard Drax MP
7,443	Labour	Jim Knight MP	15,224	30.3	Simon Bowkett
Turnout	Lib Dem	Ros Kayes	9,557	19.0	
68.58%	Others		2,862	5.7	

Majority 7443 (14.8%)

Gained from Labour by incumbent Conservative MP Richard Drax at the 2010 general election, the South Dorset constituency is one of the few true Conservative–Labour marginal in this part of south-west England. The fortunes of Weymouth, the constituency's largest town, have closely mirrored decline of British coastal tourism. Tourism does, however, remain a substantial local employer in Weymouth itself and along the stunning Jurassic Coast. The seat itself is politically polarised with Labour dominating the political landscape in Weymouth and the Conservatives running up overwhelming margins in the inland, rural portions of the constituency. Having been entirely wiped out in the 2009 county council elections, Labour staged a comeback here in 2013 – winning five seats in the Weymouth and Portland portion of the seat. Almost entirely white, a fifth of residents have no qualifications, although rates of home ownership are high at 72.7 per cent. The Labour candidate will be Simon Bowkett, a Weymouth & Portland councillor.

West Dorset

CONSERVATIVE HOLD	PARTY	2010 CANDIDATE	2010 VOTES	2010 % VOTE	PPC FOR 2015
Majority	Conservative	Oliver Letwin MP	27,287	47.6	Oliver Letwin MP
3,923	Lib Dem	Sue Farrant	23,364	40.7	Ros Kayes
Turnout	Labour	Steve Rick	3,815	6.7	Rachel Rogers
74.59%	Others		2,871	5.0	

Exeter

LABOUR HOLD	PARTY	2010 CANDIDATE	2010 VOTES	2010 % VOTE	PPC FOR 2015
Majority	Labour	Ben Bradshaw MP	19,942	38.2	Ben Bradshaw MP
2,721	Conservative	Hannah Foster	17,221	33.0	Dominic Morris
Turnout	Lib Dem	Graham Oakes	10,581	20.3	
67.71%	Others		4,503	8.6	

Filton & Bradley Stoke

CONSERVATIVE HOLD	PARTY	2010 CANDIDATE	2010 VOTES	2010 % VOTE	PPC FOR 2015
Majority	Conservative	Jack Lopresti	19,686	40.8	Jack Lopresti MP
6,914	Labour	Ian Boulton	12,772	26.4	
Turnout	Lib Dem	Peter Tyzack	12,197	25.3	
70.00%	Others		3,646	7.5	

Majority 6914 (14.3%)

Located just to the north of Bristol, Filton and Bradley Stoke is essentially a dormitory suburb for those working in the city. Much of the housing in the constituency is fairly newly built, with the Bradley Stoke housing estate having only been completed in the late 1980s. Filton is strongly inclined towards the Labour Party while the Conservatives rack up comfortable margins in the South Gloucestershire villages of Almondsbury, Stoke Gifford and Winterbourne. Aside from commuters travelling to white-collar jobs in Bristol, there is a vibrant hi-tech aviation manufacturing sector. The Conservative incumbent Jack Lopresti will be challenged by Labour's Ian Boulton.

Forest of Dean

CONSERVATIVE HOLD	PARTY	2010 CANDIDATE	2010 VOTES	2010 % VOTE	PPC FOR 2015
Majority	Conservative	Mark Harper MP	22,853	46.9	Mark Harper MP
11,064	Labour	Bruce Hogan	11,789	24.2	Steve Parry-Hearn
Turnout	Lib Dem	Christopher Coleman	10,676	21.9	
71.27%	Others		3,445	7.1	

Gloucester

CONSERVATIVE GAIN FROM LABOUR	PARTY	2010 CANDIDATE	2010 VOTES	2010 % VOTE	PPC FOR 2015
Majority	Conservative	Richard Graham	20,267	39.9	Richard Graham MP
2,420	Labour	Parmjit Dhanda MP	17,847	35.2	Sophy Gardner
Turnout	Lib Dem	Jeremy Hilton	9,767	19.2	
64.00%	Others		2,883	5.7	

Majority 2420 (4.8%)

Situated on the banks of the River Severn some ninety miles from London, Conservative Richard Graham seized this seat from Labour in 1997. Gloucester is a key regional business centre with many people travelling from miles around to the town's shopping facilities. Aside from the large service sector, the town's largest employer is the Cheltenham and Gloucester building society which is headquartered here. A relatively compact constituency, Labour is strongest in the central wards of Gloucester town while the Conservatives perform strongly in the southerly Quedgeley wards. The seat is home to a small yet growing Asian population and has an owner occupation rate of around 75 per cent. The Labour candidate here will be Sophy Gardner, a former Royal Air Force Officer.

Kingswood

CONSERVATIVE GAIN FROM LABOUR	PARTY	2010 CANDIDATE	2010 VOTES	2010 % VOTE	PPC FOR 2015
Majority	Conservative	Chris Skidmore	19,362	40.4	Chris Skidmore MP
2,445	Labour	Roger Berry MP	16,917	35.3	Jo McCarron
Turnout	Lib Dem	n/a	8,072	16.8	
72.19%	Others		3,555	7.4	

Majority 2445 (5.1%)

Four miles east of Bristol city centre and formed out of the former Bristol South East constituency once represented until 1983 by Tony Benn, Kingswood was won by Conservative historian Chris Skidmore at the 2010 general election. The bulk of the constituency is heavily inclined towards the Labour Party, with Kingswood having once been a coal-mining and shoe-manufacturing town. Industry remains important in the town with its excellent transport links and proximity to pleasant countryside, making it an attractive place for businesses to locate. There is a considerable amount of residual Conservative support here with the party holding strong leads in the commuter suburbs of Longwell Green, Bitton and Stoke Gifford whose numerous new housing developments favour the party. Jo McCarron will be the Labour candidate.

Newton Abbot

CONSERVATIVE GAIN FROM LIB DEM	PARTY	2010 CANDIDATE	2010 VOTES	2010 % VOTE	PPC FOR 2015
Majority	Conservative	Anne-Marie Morris	20,774	43.0	Anne-Marie Morris MP
523	Lib Dem	Richard Younger-Ross MP	20,251	41.9	Richard Younger-Ross
Turnout	Labour	Patrick Canavan	3,387	7.0	
69.65%	Others		3,871	8.0	

Majority 523 (1%)

Gained from the Liberal Democrats by Conservative Anne-Marie Morris at the 2010 general election, this seat includes the Devon towns of Teignmouth, Kingsteington and Dawlish and substantial parts of the Dartmoor National Park. This constituency is generally middle-class in nature with a high number of second home owners. At 77.3 per cent, levels of owner occupation here are extremely high, as is the proportion of those over the age of sixty (28.1 per cent). Agriculture and tourism are the constituency's two largest employers. Given the closeness of the 2010 general election where the Tories triumphed by just 523 votes, it was no surprise that the 2013 county council elections resulted in a virtual score draw with the Lib Dems outpacing the Conservatives by a 33 per cent to 31 per cent margin. Despite their resilience at a local government level, polling conducted by Lord Ashcroft in June 2014 showed the Conservatives ahead on 39 per cent of the vote with UKIP and the Lib Dems tied on 20 per cent. The Liberal Democrat challenger will be former MP Richard Younger-Ross who represented the seat from 2001 to 2010.

Plymouth, Moor View

LABOUR HOLD	PARTY	2010 CANDIDATE	2010 VOTES	2010 % VOTE	PPC FOR 2015
Majority	Labour	Alison Seabeck MP	15,433	37.2	Alison Seabeck MP
1,588	Conservative	Matthew Groves	13,845	33.3	Johnny Mercer
Turnout	Lib Dem	Stuart Bonar	7,016	16.9	
61.01%	Others		5,232	12.6	

Majority 1588 (3.8%)

A constituency that could more logically be described as Plymouth North, Labour's Alison Seabeck held off a strong Conservative challenge in 2010 by 1,588 votes. Moor View is a tough, working class constituency which enjoys little of the historical prestige of the neighbouring Sutton and Devonport seat: almost four in five have residents have no qualifications, a third of properties are council-owned and unemployment is considerably higher than the national average. There are no particularly strong areas for the Conservatives in this constituency, yet the party is broadly tied with Labour in the Budshead, Eggbuckland and Southway areas in the north of the seat. Labour dominates, with insurmountable leads in Honicknowle and St Budeaux – home to large council estates with considerable crime and social problems. Seabeck will be challenged by Conservative Johnny Mercer.

Plymouth, Sutton and Devonport

CONSERVATIVE WIN (NEW SEAT)	PARTY	2010 CANDIDATE	2010 VOTES	2010 % VOTE	PPC FOR 2015
Majority	Conservative	Oliver Colville	15,050	34.3	Oliver Colville MP
1,149	Labour	Linda Gilroy MP	13,901	31.7	Luke Pollard
Turnout	Lib Dem	Judy Evans	10,829	24.7	
60.18%	Others		4,114	9.4	

Majority 1149 (2.6%)

No other constituency is so steeped in Britain's maritime tradition in quite the same way as Plymouth Sutton and Devonport; the staging point of Francis Drake's victories, home of the world's largest naval base and haven for small manufacturing industries serving the shipping industry. Despite having the same name as the constituency once represented by Tory diarist Alan Clark, the present make-up constituency shares little real resemblance to it and is largely urban in composition. At 54.8 per cent, owner-occupation levels in the constituency are high, with 20.4 per cent of homes privately rented – perhaps unsurprising given the transitory residence status of many of the military families who move to the area. Seized by the Conservative Oliver Colville at the 2010 general election, the seat has seen a substantial surge in support for UKIP in recent years, the party winning several seats on Plymouth City Council. The Labour candidate will be Luke Pollard.

Poole

CONSERVATIVE HOLD	PARTY	2010 CANDIDATE	2010 VOTES	2010 % VOTE	PPC FOR 2015
Majority	Conservative	Robert Syms MP	22,532	47.5	Robert Syms MP
7,541	Lib Dem	Philip Eades	14,991	31.6	Philip Eades
Turnout	Labour	Jason Sanderson	6,041	12.7	
65.30%	Others		3,872	8.2	

Salisbury

CONSERVATIVE HOLD	PARTY	2010 CANDIDATE	2010 VOTES	2010 % VOTE	PPC FOR 2015
Majority	Conservative	John Glen	23,859	49.2	John Glen MP
5,966	Lib Dem	Nick Radford	17,893	36.9	Reetendranath Banerji
Turnout	Labour	Tom Gann	3,690	7.6	Thomas Corbin
71.90%	Others		3,039	6.3	

North Somerset

CONSERVATIVE HOLD	PARTY	2010 CANDIDATE	2010 VOTES	2010 % VOTE	PPC FOR 2015
Majority	Conservative	Liam Fox MP	28,549	49.3	Liam Fox MP
7,862	Lib Dem	Brian Mathew	20,687	35.7	
Turnout	Labour	Steve Parry-Hearn	6,448	11.1	
74.95%	Others		2,257	3.9	

North East Somerset

CONSERVATIVE GAIN FROM LABOUR	PARTY	2010 CANDIDATE	2010 VOTES	2010 % VOTE	PPC FOR 2015
Majority	Conservative	Jacob Rees-Mogg	21,130	41.3	Jacob Rees-Mogg MP
4,914	Labour	Dan Norris MP	16,216	31.7	Todd Foreman
Turnout	Lib Dem	Gail Coleshill	11,433	22.3	
75.43%	Others		2,424	4.7	

Majority 4914 (9.6%)

Previously known as Wansdyke, North East Somerset has been represented since 2010 by the flamboyant Conservative MP Jacob Rees-Mogg. The seat is a curious mixture of solidly Conservative countryside areas in the Chew Valley that are in commuting distance of Bristol and neighbouring Bath, and Labour-inclined areas such as Keynsham and Midsomer Norton, which previously formed part of the Somerset coal field. Overall, the demographic make-up of this constituency is as you would expect for this affluent part of the South West with low levels of local authority housing and an overwhelmingly white population. Rees-Mogg will face a challenge from Labour's Todd Foreman.

Somerton & Frome

LIB DEM HOLD	PARTY	2010 CANDIDATE	2010 VOTES	2010 % VOTE	PPC FOR 2015
Majority	Lib Dem	David Heath MP	28,793	47.5	n/s
1,817	Conservative	Annunziata Rees-Mogg	26,976	44.5	David Warburton
Turnout	Labour	David Oakensen	2,675	4.4	David Oakensen
74.33%	Others		2,168	3.6	

Majority 1817 (3%)

Seized from the Conservatives by Liberal Democrat David Heath in 1997, this seat has remained stubbornly marginal, recording majorities of 130, 668, 812 and 1,817 in the past four elections. A largely rural constituency, the seat contains the market town of Frome and the Royal Naval Air Station at Yeovilton. A Lord Ashcroft poll commissioned in June 2014 showed the Conservatives comfortably ahead of the Liberal Democrats by a 41 per cent to 29 per cent margin. This follows the 2013 local elections where the Conservatives led the Lib Dems by a 39 per cent to 30 per cent margin. The Conservative candidate will be David Warburton. The Liberal Democrats will select a replacement for the retiring Heath later this year.

St Austell & Newquay

LIB DEM WIN (NEW SEAT)	PARTY	2010 CANDIDATE	2010 VOTES	2010 % VOTE	PPC FOR 2015
Majority	Lib Dem	Stephen Gilbert	20,189	42.7	Stephen Gilbert MP
1,312	Conservative	Caroline Righton	18,877	40.0	Steve Double
Turnout	Labour	Lee Jameson	3,386	7.2	Deborah Hopkins
62.75%	Others		4,786	10.1	

Majority 1312 (2.8%)

A newly-created constituency at the 2010 general election, St Austell and Newquay is comprised of roughly half of the current Truro and St Austell, a quarter of Cornwall North and a tenth of the Cornwall South East constituencies. With around 20,000 residents apiece, both St Austell and Newquay are vibrant towns whose populations can grow dramatically during the summer months as thousands of tourists visit the area's attractive beach resorts. Unsurprisingly, tourism is the largest local employer here although agriculture dominates when one travels inland. The sitting Liberal Democrat MP Stephen Gilbert will face a challenge from Conservative Steve Double.

St Ives

LIB DEM HOLD	PARTY	2010 CANDIDATE	2010 VOTES	2010 % VOTE	PPC FOR 2015
Majority	Lib Dem	Andrew George MP	19,619	42.7	Andrew George MP
1,719	Conservative	Derek Thomas	17,900	39.0	Derek Thomas
Turnout	Labour	Phillippa Latimer	3,751	8.2	Cornelius Oliver
68.60%	Others		4,651	10.1	

Majority 1719 (3.7%)

Located at the south-western extremity of Cornwall, the St Ives constituency is England's most westerly constituency. The seat itself contains some of England's best-known tourist destinations, including the Scilly Isles, Lands End and Penzance. With an above-average retired population and large number of second home-owners, the Labour Party has little cache here. After several election cycles in which the Liberal Democrats dominated play locally, the Conservatives secured a 10.4 per cent in 2010 – bringing them 1,719 votes from victory. The Conservatives were the victors here in the 2013 local elections, winning 26 per cent of the vote to UKIP's 19 per cent and the Lib Dems' 13 per cent. The 2015 election will see a rematch between long-serving Liberal Democrat MP Andrew George and Conservative Derek Thomas. A June 2014 poll from Lord Ashcroft confirmed the election will be a tight fight with the Conservatives and Lib Dem tied on 30 per cent and 29 per cent apiece with UKIP close behind on 21 per cent.

Stroud

CONSERVATIVE GAIN FROM LABOUR	PARTY	2010 CANDIDATE	2010 VOTES	2010 % VOTE	PPC FOR 2015
Majority	Conservative	Neil Carmichael	23,679	40.8	Neil Carmichael MP
1,299	Labour	David Drew MP	22,380	38.6	David Drew
Turnout	Lib Dem	Dennis Andrewartha	8,955	15.4	
74.05%	Others		2,959	5.1	

Majority 1299 (2.2%)

Nestled at the foot of the Cotwold Hills in the attractive Gloucestershire countryside, even the most optimistic of Labour strategists could never have predicted Stroud would ever fall to Labour in 1997. Indeed, it is a mark of the town's long-term political shift that sitting Conservative MP Neil Carmichael could only secure a 1,299 majority in 2010 in a seat his party had won by 13,000 in 1992. Stroud is an attractive market town originally built around the cloth trade which has in recent years become a centre for light industry and manufacturing. Stroud has marketed itself as a 'book town' and is home to a substantial left-leaning literary community, evident in the success of the Green Party in capturing council seats locally. Three-quarters of homes here are owner-occupied and an above-average number of residents hold university degrees. The 2014 local elections were essentially a draw with the Conservatives winning twenty-two seats to Labour's twenty. The Labour candidate will be former MP David Drew.

North Swindon

CONSERVATIVE GAIN FROM LABOUR	PARTY	2010 CANDIDATE	2010 VOTES	2010 % VOTE	PPC FOR 2015
Majority	Conservative	Justin Tomlinson	22,408	44.6	Justin Tomlinson MP
7,060	Labour	Victor Agarwal	15,348	30.5	Mark Dempsey
Turnout	Lib Dem	Jane Lock	8,668	17.2	
64.16%	Others		3,871	7.7	

Majority 7060 (14%)

Located in north-east Wiltshire, Swindon enjoys excellent railway and road links to London, the Midlands and the West Country. Swindon North is the more working class of the town's two seats yet enjoys low unemployment as a result of significant investment from service industries in the last two decades. While some of Swindon's poorest wards are found within the boundaries of this seat, the proportion of middle-class professionals making their homes here can only be expected to grow in the coming years as the construction of upscale private estates close on the cusp of the Wiltshire countryside continues at fever-pitch. While the Conservatives have lost ground on a local government level since 2010 in many 'new town' constituencies, the party remains firmly in control of Swindon Borough Council. The seat was won in 2010 by Conservative Justin Tomlinson who will face Labour candidate Mark Dempsey in 2015.

South Swindon

CONSERVATIVE GAIN FROM LABOUR	PARTY	2010 CANDIDATE	2010 VOTES	2010 % VOTE	PPC FOR 2015
Majority	Conservative	Robert Buckland	19,687	41.8	Robert Buckland MP
3,544	Labour	Anne Snelgrove MP	16,143	34.3	Anne Snelgrove
Turnout	Lib Dem	Damon Hooton	8,305	17.6	
64.89%	Others		2,984	6.3	

Majority 3544 (7.5%)

Stretching from the centre of the former railway town to the wilds of rural Wiltshire, both major parties have areas of considerable residual strength here. Labour dominate in the Central and Parks wards, home to much of the town's decaying council housing stock, while the Conservatives lead convincingly in the rural Wroughton and Chiseldon area. With a number of large technology and service-sector firms based here, unemployment is not a problem. The Conservatives continue to be in a dominant position here on a local government level, expanding their majority on Swindon Borough Council at the 2014 local elections. Welsh-born barrister Robert Buckland captured the seat for the Conservatives in 2010. He faces a rematch with former Labour MP Anne Snelgrove.

Taunton Deane

LIB DEM HOLD	PARTY	2010 CANDIDATE	2010 VOTES	2010 % VOTE	PPC FOR 2015
Majority	Lib Dem	Jeremy Browne MP	28,531	49.1	Jeremy Browne MP
3,993	Conservative	Mark Formosa	24,538	42.2	Rebecca Pow
Turnout	Labour	Martin Jevon	2,967	5.1	Neil Guild
70.48%	Others		2,114	3.6	Laura Bailhache (UKIP)

Tewkesbury

CONSERVATIVE HOLD	PARTY	2010 CANDIDATE	2010 VOTES	2010 % VOTE	PPC FOR 2015
Majority	Conservative	Laurence Robertson MP	25,472	47.2	Laurence Robertson MP
6,310	Lib Dem	Alistair Cameron	19,162	35.5	
Turnout	Labour	Stuart Emmerson	6,253	11.6	
70.39%	Others		3,074	5.7	

Thornbury & Yate

LIB DEM HOLD	PARTY	2010 CANDIDATE	2010 VOTES	2010 % VOTE	PPC FOR 2015
Majority	Lib Dem	Steve Webb MP	25,032	51.9	Steve Webb MP
7,116	Conservative	Matthew Riddle	17,916	37.2	Luke Hall
Turnout	Labour	Roxanne Egan	3,385	7.0	
75.24%	Others		1,893	3.9	

Tiverton & Honiton

CONSERVATIVE HOLD	PARTY	2010 CANDIDATE	2010 VOTES	2010 % VOTE	PPC FOR 2015
Majority	Conservative	Neil Parish	27,614	50.3	Neil Parish MP
9,320	Lib Dem	Jon Underwood	18,294	33.3	
Turnout	Labour	Vernon Whitlock	4,907	8.9	Caroline Kolek
71.47%	Others		4,079	7.4	

Torbay

LIB DEM HOLD	PARTY	2010 CANDIDATE	2010 VOTES	2010 % VOTE	PPC FOR 2015
Majority	Lib Dem	Adrian Sanders MP	23,126	47.0	Adrian Sanders MP
4,078	Conservative	Marcus Wood	19,048	38.7	Kevin Foster
Turnout	Labour	David Pedrick-Friend	3,231	6.6	Sue Maddock
64.54%	Others		3,805	7.7	

Totnes

CONSERVATIVE HOLD	PARTY	2010 CANDIDATE	2010 VOTES	2010 % VOTE	PPC FOR 2015
Majority	Conservative	Sarah Wollaston	21,940	45.9	Sarah Wollaston MP
4,927	Lib Dem	Julian Brazil	17,013	35.6	Julian Brazil
Turnout	Labour	Carol Whitty	3,538	7.4	
70.40%	Others		5,352	11.2	

Truro & Falmouth

CONSERVATIVE WIN (NEW SEAT)	PARTY	2010 CANDIDATE	2010 VOTES	2010 % VOTE	PPC FOR 2015
Majority	Conservative	Sarah Newton	20,349	41.7	Sarah Newton MP
435	Lib Dem	Terrye Teverson	19,914	40.8	Simon Rix
Turnout	Labour	Charlotte MacKenzie	4,697	9.6	Hanna Toms
69.08%	Others		3,808	7.8	

Majority 435 (1%)

A newly formed constituency at the 2010 general election, the seat was won by Conservative Sarah Newton. Employment in both towns has traditionally revolved around industry – mining in Truro and docking in Falmouth – but the tourist-driven service sector now dominates. At 27.1 per cent, the proportion of pensioners here is well above average. Polling conducted by Lord Ashcroft in June 2014 showed the Conservatives leading the field with 33 per cent, with UKIP on 22 per cent, Labour on 18 per cent and the Liberal Democrats in fourth place on 16 per cent – less than half of their 41 per cent vote share in 2010. The Liberal Democrat candidate will be local councillor Simon Rix.

Wells

LIB DEM GAIN FROM CONSERVATIVE	PARTY	2010 CANDIDATE	2010 VOTES	2010 % VOTE	PPC FOR 2015
Majority	Lib Dem	Tessa Munt	24,560	44.0	Tessa Munt MP
800	Conservative	David Heathcoat-Amory MP	23,760	42.5	James Heappey
Turnout	Labour	Andy Merryfield	4,198	7.5	Chris Inchley
70.33%	Others		3,346	6.0	

Majority 800 (1.4%)

A long-term Liberal Democrat target, the party finally succeeded in ousting Conservative MP David Heathcoat-Amory by exactly 800 votes at the 2010 election following his involvement in the expenses scandal. A predominantly rural seat, the constituency takes in the picturesque cathedral city of Wells itself, the site of the famous music festival at Glastonbury and scores of villages nestled in the Mendip Hills. The Conservatives were big winners here in the 2013 county council elections, leading the Liberal Democrats by a 40 per cent to 24 per cent margin. A June 2014 poll from Lord Ashcroft showed the Conservatives ahead of the Liberal Democrats here by a 34 per cent to 29 per cent margin, with UKIP on 16 per cent. The sitting MP Tessa Munt will be challenged by Conservative James Heappey.

Weston-super-Mare

CONSERVATIVE HOLD	PARTY	2010 CANDIDATE	2010 VOTES	2010 % VOTE	PPC FOR 2015
Majority	Conservative	John Penrose MP	23,356	44.3	John Penrose MP
2,691	Lib Dem	Mike Bell	20,665	39.2	
Turnout	Labour	David Bradley	5,772	10.9	Tim Taylor
67.17%	Others		2,923	5.5	

North Wiltshire

CONSERVATIVE HOLD	PARTY	2010 CANDIDATE	2010 VOTES	2010 % VOTE	PPC FOR 2015
Majority	Conservative	James Gray MP	25,114	51.6	James Gray MP
7,483	Lib Dem	Mike Evemy	17,631	36.2	Brian Mathew
Turnout	Labour	Jason Hughes	3,239	6.7	Peter Baldrey
73.44%	Others		2,715	5.6	

South West Wiltshire

CONSERVATIVE HOLD	PARTY	2010 CANDIDATE	2010 VOTES	2010 % VOTE	PPC FOR 2015
Majority	Conservative	Andrew Murrison MP	25,321	51.7	Andrew Murrison MP
10,367	Lib Dem	Trevor Carbin	14,954	30.5	
Turnout	Labour	Rebecca Rennison	5,613	11.5	
68.42%	Others		3,130	6.4	

Yeovil

LIB DEM HOLD	PARTY	2010 CANDIDATE	2010 VOTES	2010 % VOTE	PPC FOR 2015
Majority	Lib Dem	David Laws MP	31,843	55.7	David Laws MP
13,036	Conservative	Kevin Davis	18,807	32.9	Marcus Fysh
Turnout	Labour	Lee Skevington	2,991	5.2	Martin Jevon
69.44%	Others		3,519	6.2	

South East England

The largest – and some would say most impersonal and unwieldy – of all the European Parliament regions in the United Kingdom, the South East has ten MEPs representing well over six million voters in nine counties. It is also the most strongly Conservative at Westminster, as they won seventy-four of the eighty-four seats in 2010.

This does, of course, leave the dominant party with limited opportunities for further gains in 2015. However, the Tories do have their eyes on perhaps halving the paltry handful (four each, in fact) of Liberal Democrat and Labour constituencies. For their coalition partners, only Norman Baker's Lewes can be regarded as truly safe, although when Eastleigh fell vacant following the guilty plea in Chris Huhne's case regarding the concealment of violating speed limits, the Conservatives only managed to reduce the Lib Dem lead from 7.2 per cent to 4.3 per cent. If they could not make a gain in such circumstances, the Tories may well not be favourites in the general election. They probably have a better chance in Eastbourne, against Stephen Lloyd, who pulled off a surprise gain in 2010. However their highest hopes of all rest with Flick Drummond in Portsmouth South, where the long-serving MP Mike Hancock has had multiple difficulties culminating in his switch from Liberal Democrat to independent in 2014; he also lost his Portsmouth city council ward of Fratton to UKIP in May that year.

The two Labour seats the Conservatives hope to take are both in Southampton. In Test, the western of these two constituencies, they require a swing of 3 per cent. However in Itchen to the east, the Labour majority is only 192 or 0.4 per cent, and the popular MP John Denham is retiring. What is more, the series of opinion polls in marginal constituencies taken for Lord Ashcroft shows the Tories performing far more competitively in Itchen than in almost any of the others, level pegging in late August 2014, for example. If Labour were to lose the two Southamptons, they would only hold Oxford East and Slough in the entire region – very untypical seats, for different reasons: the former with one of the highest proportions of students in the country, and the latter which is now majority non-white.

However if Labour were to be further reduced, they would have no chance of forming a government. To do so, they will have to gain a number of constituencies which *are* typical of this huge and populous region. This should not be impossible. They won thirteen seats in Kent and Sussex alone in 1997 and 2001, and held twelve of these in 2005 when Tony Blair's overall majority was more than halved. Success in the South East was a keystone of these three New Labour triumphs. Then in 2010 things went badly wrong. All of the twelve seats were lost, some after adverse boundary changes, and mostly with very large swings that mean they seem out of reach now – for example, Gillingham & Rainham now has a Tory majority of 8,650 and would need a 10 per cent swing. The only seat in Kent which is remotely winnable for Labour is Dover, and that has a majority for Charlie Elphicke of over 5,000.

The three best Labour chances to regain some ground are all in Sussex. Swings to the Conservatives were lower in the Brighton and Hove area, and both Brighton Kemptown and Hove would be recovered on a 2 per cent swing, as would the rather 'odd couple' Hastings & Rye. This is also probably the place to mention the most central of Brighton's three seats, Pavilion, which produced one of the most remarkable results of the 2010 general election. Caroline Lucas won for the Greens with over 16,000 votes, followed by Labour with 15,000 and the Conservatives with 12,000. For the Greens to win any representation under the first-past-the-post system is quite an achievement, and Caroline Lucas – the best known spokesperson and face in the party – has a good chance of repeating her success, though Labour present the greater threat.

There may just be another remarkable result in the South East in 2015, occasioned by the success of another, if very different kind of 'minor' party – though there has been nothing minor about the impact of UKIP in recent years. In the 2014 European elections, they were the most major party of all, including finishing top in the South East and taking four of its ten seats. At the top of their list here was Nigel Farage, and in August 2014 he finally announced that he will contest South Thanet in the general election (as he did in 2005). Kent (though not the Isle of Thanet) is his place of origin, but there had been speculation that he would stand elsewhere – in the 2014 Newark by-election, for example – and in 2010 he opposed the Speaker John Bercow in Buckingham. Back in 2005 Farage only polled 2,079 votes in South Thanet, just on the deposit retention line of 5 per cent, but he will undoubtedly do much better in 2015. This was one of many areas where UKIP amassed more votes than anyone else in the 2014 European elections, and there are very solid bases of support in parts of the seat such as Cliftonville, which is affected by eastern European immigration in its western part. Although the seat was held by Labour from 1997 to 2010, they then fell over 7,500 votes behind the Conservative Laura Sandys – and neither she nor the former Labour MP Stephen Ladyman are standing next time. If Nigel Farage does not win South Thanet, he may well poll up to 25 or 30 per cent and possibly beat Labour into second place.

UKIP are likely to increase their vote substantially in many other seats across the South East, and while the first-past-the-post system means it is unlikely they will win any seats, their impact on the other parties' shares is unclear, and will add to the interest in this otherwise rather monolithically Conservative region.

Aldershot

CONSERVATIVE HOLD	PARTY	2010 CANDIDATE	2010 VOTES	2010 % VOTE	PPC FOR 2015
Majority	Conservative	Gerald Howarth MP	21,203	46.7	Gerald Howarth MP
5,586	Lib Dem	Adrian Collett	15,617	34.4	Alan Hiliar
Turnout	Labour	Jonathan Slater	5,489	12.1	Gary Puffett
63.51%	Others		3,075	6.8	

Arundel & South Downs

CONSERVATIVE HOLD	PARTY	2010 CANDIDATE	2010 VOTES	2010 % VOTE	PPC FOR 2015
Majority	Conservative	Nick Herbert MP	32,333	57.8	Nick Herbert MP
16,691	Lib Dem	Derek Deedman	15,642	27.9	
Turnout	Labour	Tim Lunnon	4,835	8.6	
72.86%	Others		3,172	5.7	

Ashford

CONSERVATIVE HOLD	PARTY	2010 CANDIDATE	2010 VOTES	2010 % VOTE	PPC FOR 2015
Majority	Conservative	Damian Green MP	29,878	54.1	Damian Green MP
17,297	Lib Dem	Chris Took	12,581	22.8	
Turnout	Labour	Chris Clark	9,204	16.7	
67.90%	Others		3,522	6.4	

Aylesbury

CONSERVATIVE HOLD	PARTY	2010 CANDIDATE	2010 VOTES	2010 % VOTE	PPC FOR 2015
Majority	Conservative	David Lidington MP	27,736	52.2	David Lidington MP
12,618	Lib Dem	Steven Lambert	15,118	28.4	
Turnout	Labour	Kathryn White	6,695	12.6	William Cass
68.29%	Others		3,613	6.8	

Banbury

CONSERVATIVE HOLD	PARTY	2010 CANDIDATE	2010 VOTES	2010 % VOTE	PPC FOR 2015
Majority	Conservative	Tony Baldry MP	29,703	52.8	Tony Baldry MP
18,227	Lib Dem	David Rundle	11,476	20.4	
Turnout	Labour	Leslie Sibley	10,773	19.2	Sean Woodcock
66.65%	Others		4,289	7.6	

Basingstoke

CONSERVATIVE HOLD	PARTY	2010 CANDIDATE	2010 VOTES	2010 % VOTE	PPC FOR 2015
Majority	Conservative	Maria Miller MP	25,590	50.5	Maria Miller MP
13,176	Lib Dem	John Shaw	12,414	24.5	Janice Spalding
Turnout	Labour	Funda Pepperell	10,327	20.4	Paul Harvey
67.12%	Others		2,323	4.6	

Beaconsfield

CONSERVATIVE HOLD	PARTY	2010 CANDIDATE	2010 VOTES	2010 % VOTE	PPC FOR 2015
Majority	Conservative	Dominic Grieve MP	32,053	61.1	Dominic Grieve MP
21,782	Lib Dem	John Edwards	10,271	19.6	
Turnout	Labour	Jeremy Miles	6,135	11.7	
70.00%	Others		4,031	7.7	

Bexhill & Battle

CONSERVATIVE HOLD	PARTY	2010 CANDIDATE	2010 VOTES	2010 % VOTE	PPC FOR 2015
Majority	Conservative	Gregory Barker MP	28,147	51.6	n/s
12,880	Lib Dem	Mary Varrall	15,267	28.0	
Turnout	Labour	James Royston	6,524	12.0	Michelle Thew
67.36%	Others		4,649	8.5	

Bognor Regis & Littlehampton

CONSERVATIVE HOLD	PARTY	2010 CANDIDATE	2010 VOTES	2010 % VOTE	PPC FOR 2015
Majority	Conservative	Nick Gibb MP	24,087	51.4	Nick Gibb MP
13,063	Lib Dem	Simon McDougall	11,024	23.5	Francis Oppler
Turnout	Labour	Michael Jones	6,580	14.0	Alan Butcher
66.16%	Others		5,161	11.0	

Bracknell

CONSERVATIVE HOLD	PARTY	2010 CANDIDATE	2010 VOTES	2010 % VOTE	PPC FOR 2015
Majority	Conservative	Philip Lee	27,327	52.4	Philip Lee MP
15,704	Lib Dem	Ray Earwicker	11,623	22.3	
Turnout	Labour	John Piasecki	8,755	16.8	James Walsh
67.81%	Others		4,431	8.5	

Brighton, Kemptown

CONSERVATIVE GAIN FROM LABOUR	PARTY	2010 CANDIDATE	2010 VOTES	2010 % VOTE	PPC FOR 2015
Majority	Conservative	Simon Kirby	16,217	38.0	Simon Kirby MP
1,328	Labour	Simon Burgess	14,889	34.9	Nancy Platts
Turnout	Lib Dem	Juliet Williams	7,691	18.0	
64.69%	Others		3,908	9.2	

Majority 1328 (3.1%)

Arguably the less bohemian of the two Brighton city constituencies, Kemptown is considerably more residential in composition than neighbouring Pavilion. Taking in wards in the east of the city, the constituency also includes the Conservative strongholds of Peacehaven and Telscombe Cliffs which are every bit the sleepy Sussex stereotype. Labour support is strongest in the Brighton city wards with the tough Moulsecoomb and Whitehawk estates resulting in more than a fifth of the constituency's residents living in social housing. The Green Party, whilst weaker here than in neighbouring Pavilion, holds council seats in Queen's Park and runs a minority administration at the Town Hall. Won for the Conservatives in 2010 by local businessman and former nightclub operator Simon Kirby, the Labour candidate will be Nancy Platts.

Brighton, Pavilion

GREEN GAIN FROM LABOUR	PARTY	2010 CANDIDATE	2010 VOTES	2010 % VOTE	PPC FOR 2015
Majority	Green	Caroline Lucas	16,238	31.3	Caroline Lucas MP
1,252	Labour	Nancy Platts	14,986	28.9	Purna Sen
Turnout	Conservative	Charlotte Vere	12,275	23.7	Clarence Mitchell
70.04%	Others		8,335	16.1	

Majority 1252 (2.4%)

Brighton Pavilion made history in 2010 by electing the United Kingdom's first-ever Green Member of Parliament in the form of Dr Caroline Lucas. The city's famous Marine Parade, the University of Sussex and quirky shopping areas are all found within the constituency's boundaries. For years a Conservative stronghold, the changing demographics and social outlook of the seat saw Labour win by more than 13,000 votes in 1997 before shifting to the Greens in 2010. Polling conducted by Lord Ashcroft in June 2014 showed Labour and the Greens effectively tied locally – 33 per cent to 32 per cent – with the Conservatives way back on 18 per cent. Labour are fielding Purna Sen while the Conservative candidate will be former BBC broadcaster Clarence Mitchell.

Buckingham

SPEAKER (FORMERLY CONSERVATIVE)	PARTY	2010 CANDIDATE	2010 VOTES	2010 % VOTE	PPC FOR 2015
Majority	Speaker	John Bercow MP	22,860	47.3	John Bercow MP
12,529	BCD	John Stevens	10,331	21.4	
Turnout	UKIP	Nigel Farage	8,410	17.4	
64.47%	Others		6,743	13.9	

Canterbury

CONSERVATIVE HOLD	PARTY	2010 CANDIDATE	2010 VOTES	2010 % VOTE	PPC FOR 2015
Majority	Conservative	Julian Brazier MP	22,050	44.8	Julian Brazier MP
6,048	Lib Dem	Guy Voizey	16,002	32.5	James Flanaghan
Turnout	Labour	Jean Samuel	7,940	16.1	Hugh Lanning
66.39%	Others		3,217	6.5	

Chatham & Aylesford

CONSERVATIVE GAIN FROM LABOUR	PARTY	2010 CANDIDATE	2010 VOTES	2010 % VOTE	PPC FOR 2015
Majority	Conservative	Tracey Crouch	20,230	46.2	Tracey Crouch MP
6,069	Labour	Jonathan Shaw MP	14,161	32.3	Tristan Osborne
Turnout	Lib Dem	John McClintock	5,832	13.3	
64.46%	Others		3,584	8.2	

Majority 6069 (13.9%)

Forty minutes by train from central London, the Chatham and Aylesford constituency is quite literally split down the middle – by both the M2 motorway and its diverse social mix. The former naval dockyard town of Chatham, which has struggled for years with high unemployment and urban decay, provides the base of Labour's support while Walderslade and Aylesford towards the south of the seat are firmly part of the Conservative-inclined commuter belt. Being so close to London, the population of the area is predicted to grow significantly in the coming years as new housing developments continue to spring up at a frantic pace. Held since 2010 by independently minded Conservative Tracey Crouch, the Labour candidate will be Tristan Osborne.

Chesham & Amersham

CONSERVATIVE HOLD	PARTY	2010 CANDIDATE	2010 VOTES	2010 % VOTE	PPC FOR 2015
Majority	Conservative	Cheryl Gillan MP	31,658	60.4	Cheryl Gillan MP
16,710	Lib Dem	Tim Starkey	14,948	28.5	
Turnout	Labour	Anthony Gajadsarsingh	2,942	5.6	
74.57%	Others		2,896	5.5	

Chichester

CONSERVATIVE HOLD	PARTY	2010 CANDIDATE	2010 VOTES	2010 % VOTE	PPC FOR 2015
Majority	Conservative	Andrew Tyrie MP	31,427	55.3	Andrew Tyrie MP
15,877	Lib Dem	Martin Lury	15,550	27.4	Andrew Smith
Turnout	Labour	Simon Holland	5,937	10.5	
69.61%	Others		3,873	6.8	

Crawley

CONSERVATIVE GAIN FROM LABOUR	PARTY	2010 CANDIDATE	2010 VOTES	2010 % VOTE	PPC FOR 2015
Majority	Conservative	Henry Smith	21,264	44.8	Henry Smith MP
5,928	Labour	Chris Oxlade	15,336	32.3	Chris Oxlade
Turnout	Lib Dem	John Vincent	6,844	14.4	
65.27%	Others		4,060	8.5	

Majority 5928 (12.5%)

After failing to gain the seat from Labour by only thirty-seven votes in 2005, former West Sussex County Council leader Henry Smith finally seized Crawley for the Conservatives by a 5,928 margin at the 2010 general election. Previously represented by outsize Conservative Nicholas Soames, the constituency encompasses concrete-dominated Crawley town, Gatwick Airport and the Conservative bastions of Maidenbower, Pound Hill and Worth. It has amongst the highest ethnic minority populations of any southern seat. Despite having control of Crawley Borough Council from 2007 to 2014, the Conservatives lost ground on a local level last year, with Labour now holding a twenty-seat-to-sixteen margin at the town hall. The Labour candidate will be Chris Oxslade.

Dartford

CONSERVATIVE GAIN FROM LABOUR	PARTY	2010 CANDIDATE	2010 VOTES	2010 % VOTE	PPC FOR 2015
Majority	Conservative	Gareth Johnson	24,428	48.8	Gareth Johnson MP
10,628	Labour	John Adams	13,800	27.6	Simon Thompson
Turnout	Lib Dem	James Willis	7,361	14.7	
65.66%	Others		4,491	9.0	

Dover

CONSERVATIVE GAIN FROM LABOUR	PARTY	2010 CANDIDATE	2010 VOTES	2010 % VOTE	PPC FOR 2015
Majority	Conservative	Charlie Elphicke	22,174	44.0	Charlie Elphicke MP
5,274	Labour	Gwyn Prosser MP	16,900	33.5	Clair Hawkins
Turnout	Lib Dem	John Brigden	7,962	15.8	Sarah Smith
70.14%	Others		3,349	6.6	

Majority 5274 (10.5%)

The centre of the British cross-channel ferry industry, the Dover constituency was won from Labour by Conservative Charlie Elphicke on a 10.4 per cent swing in 2010. As one might expect, support for Labour is robust in Dover Town, a mix of elegant regency properties and rapidly decaying tenement blocks which were thrown up in the aftermath of World War Two bomb damage. Labour is also strong in rural Aylesham, home to the former Betteshanger Colliery which closed in 1989. While the coastal town of Deal is fairly evenly politically divided the rest of the constituency is far more favourable to the Conservatives with villages such as River, Kearsney and Temple Ewell backing the party by landslide margins. Labour clawed back significant lost ground here at the 2013 county council elections, taking back seats in Dover and Deal from the Conservatives and narrowly missing topping the poll across the constituency amidst a UKIP surge. The Labour candidate will be Clair Hawkins.

Eastbourne

LIB DEM GAIN FROM CONSERVATIVE	PARTY	2010 CANDIDATE	2010 VOTES	2010 % VOTE	PPC FOR 2015
Majority	Lib Dem	Stephen Lloyd	24,658	47.3	Stephen Lloyd MP
3,435	Conservative	Nigel Waterson MP	21,223	40.7	Caroline Ansell
Turnout	Labour	Dave Brinson	2,497	4.8	
66.96%	Others		3,746	7.2	

Eastleigh

LIB DEM HOLD	PARTY	2010 CANDIDATE	2010 VOTES	2010 % VOTE
Majority	Lib Dem	Chris Huhne MP	24,966	46.5
3,864	Conservative	Maria Hutchings	21,102	39.3
Turnout	Labour	Leo Barraclough	5,153	9.6
69.28%	Others		2,429	4.5

Eastleigh (2013 by-election)

LIB DEM HOLD	PARTY	2013 CANDIDATE	2013 VOTES	2013 % VOTE	PPC FOR 2015
Majority	Lib Dem	Mike Thornton	13,342	32.1	Mike Thornton MP
1,771	UKIP	Diane James	11,571	27.8	
Turnout	Conservative	Marie Hutchings	10,559	25.4	Mims Davies
53.74%	Others		6,144	14.8	

Epsom & Ewell

CONSERVATIVE HOLD	PARTY	2010 CANDIDATE	2010 VOTES	2010 % VOTE	PPC FOR 2015
Majority	Conservative	Chris Grayling MP	30,868	56.2	Chris Grayling MP
16,134	Lib Dem	Jonathan Lees	14,734	26.8	
Turnout	Labour	Craig Montgomery	6,538	11.9	Sheila Carson
68.77%	Others		2,815	5.1	

Esher & Walton

CONSERVATIVE HOLD	PARTY	2010 CANDIDATE	2010 VOTES	2010 % VOTE	PPC FOR 2015
Majority	Conservative	Dominic Raab	32,134	58.9	Dominic Raab MP
18,593	Lib Dem	Lionel Blackman	13,541	24.8	
Turnout	Labour	Francis Eldergill	5,829	10.7	
72.40%	Others		3,039	5.6	

Fareham

CONSERVATIVE HOLD	PARTY	2010 CANDIDATE	2010 VOTES	2010 % VOTE	PPC FOR 2015
Majority	Conservative	Mark Hoban MP	30,037	55.3	Mark Hoban MP
17,092	Lib Dem	Alex Bentley	12,945	23.8	
Turnout	Labour	James Carr	7,719	14.2	
71.59%	Others		3,644	6.7	

Faversham & Mid Kent

CONSERVATIVE HOLD	PARTY	2010 CANDIDATE	2010 VOTES	2010 % VOTE	PPC FOR 2015
Majority	Conservative	Hugh Robertson MP	26,250	56.2	Hugh Robertson MP
17,088	Lib Dem	Dave Naghi	9,162	19.6	
Turnout	Labour	Ashok Rehal	7,748	16.6	
67.84%	Others		3,552	7.6	

Folkestone & Hythe

CONSERVATIVE HOLD	PARTY	2010 CANDIDATE	2010 VOTES	2010 % VOTE	PPC FOR 2015
Majority	Conservative	Damian Collins	26,109	49.4	Damian Collins MP
10,122	Lib Dem	Lynne Beaumont	15,987	30.3	Lynne Beaumont
Turnout	Labour	Donald Worsley	5,719	10.8	Claire Jeffrey
67.69%	Others		4,985	9.4	

Gillingham & Rainham

CONSERVATIVE GAIN FROM LABOUR	PARTY	2010 CANDIDATE	2010 VOTES	2010 % VOTE	PPC FOR 2015
Majority	Conservative	Rehman Chishti	21,624	46.2	Rehman Chishti MP
8,680	Labour	Paul Clark MP	12,944	27.7	Paul Clark
Turnout	Lib Dem	Andrew Stamp	8,484	18.1	
66.07%	Others		3,734	8.0	

Gosport

CONSERVATIVE HOLD	PARTY	2010 CANDIDATE	2010 VOTES	2010 % VOTE	PPC FOR 2015
Majority	Conservative	Caroline Dinenage	24,300	51.8	Caroline Dinenage MP
14,413	Lib Dem	Rob Hylands	9,887	21.1	
Turnout	Labour	Graham Giles	7,944	16.9	
64.46%	Others		4,808	10.2	

Gravesham

CONSERVATIVE HOLD	PARTY	2010 CANDIDATE	2010 VOTES	2010 % VOTE	PPC FOR 2015
Majority	Conservative	Adam Holloway MP	22,956	48.5	Adam Holloway MP
9,312	Labour	Kathryn Smith	13,644	28.8	Tanmanjeet Singh Dhesi
Turnout	Lib Dem	Anna Arrowsmith	6,293	13.3	
67.39%	Others		4,410	9.3	

Guildford

CONSERVATIVE HOLD	PARTY	2010 CANDIDATE	2010 VOTES	2010 % VOTE	PPC FOR 2015
Majority	Conservative	Anne Milton MP	29,618	53.3	Anne Milton MP
7,782	Lib Dem	Sue Doughty	21,836	39.3	Kelly-Marie Blundell
Turnout	Labour	Tim Shand	2,812	5.1	Richard Wilson
72.09%	Others		1,301	2.3	

East Hampshire

CONSERVATIVE HOLD	PARTY	2010 CANDIDATE	2010 VOTES	2010 % VOTE	PPC FOR 2015
Majority	Conservative	Damian Hinds	29,137	56.8	Damian Hinds MP
13,497	Lib Dem	Adam Carew	15,640	30.5	
Turnout	Labour	Jane Edbrooke	4,043	7.9	
71.02%	Others		2,497	4.9	

North East Hampshire

CONSERVATIVE HOLD	PARTY	2010 CANDIDATE	2010 VOTES	2010 % VOTE	PPC FOR 2015
Majority	Conservative	James Arbuthnot MP	32,075	60.6	Ranil Jayawardena
18,597	Lib Dem	Denzil Coulson	13,478	25.5	
Turnout	Labour	Barry Jones	5,173	9.8	
73.33%	Others		2,213	4.2	

North West Hampshire

CONSERVATIVE HOLD	PARTY	2010 CANDIDATE	2010 VOTES	2010 % VOTE	PPC FOR 2015
Majority	Conservative	George Young MP	31,072	58.3	Kit Malthouse
18,583	Lib Dem	Tom McCann	12,489	23.4	
Turnout	Labour	Sarah Evans	6,980	13.1	
69.49%	Others		2,751	5.2	

Hastings & Rye

CONSERVATIVE GAIN FROM LABOUR	PARTY	2010 CANDIDATE	2010 VOTES	2010 % VOTE	PPC FOR 2015
Majority	Conservative	Amber Rudd	20,468	41.1	Amber Rudd MP
1,993	Labour	Michael Foster MP	18,475	37.1	Sarah Owen
Turnout	Lib Dem	Nick Perry	7,825	15.7	Nick Perry
64.67%	Others		3,046	6.1	

Majority 1993 (4%)

Gained by Conservative Amber Rudd at the 2010 general election, the incumbent currently serves as Minister at the Department for Energy & Climate Change. The town of Hastings, located just over 60 miles from London and home to the bulk of the constituency's population, has long suffered from a lack of inward investment partly caused by its woeful road and rail links. The town has long been a Labour bastion with low owner occupation rates (65.8 per cent) and a third of residents having no qualifications. At the other end of the social spectrum, the genteel town of Rye with its cobbled streets, ornate churches and medieval lanes is similarly loyal to the Conservatives. The Labour candidate will be Sarah Owen, a former political advisor to Lord Alan Sugar.

Havant

CONSERVATIVE HOLD	PARTY	2010 CANDIDATE	2010 VOTES	2010 % VOTE	PPC FOR 2015
Majority	Conservative	David Willetts MP	22,433	51.1	n/s
12,160	Lib Dem	Alex Payton	10,273	23.4	
Turnout	Labour	Robert Smith	7,777	17.7	
63.02%	Others		3,420	7.8	

Henley

CONSERVATIVE HOLD	PARTY	2010 CANDIDATE	2010 VOTES	2010 % VOTE	PPC FOR 2015
Majority	Conservative	John Howell MP	30,054	56.2	John Howell MP
16,588	Lib Dem	Andy Crick	13,466	25.2	
Turnout	Labour	Richard McKenzie	5,835	10.9	Sam Juthani
73.19%	Others		4,165	7.8	

Horsham

CONSERVATIVE HOLD	PARTY	2010 CANDIDATE	2010 VOTES	2010 % VOTE	PPC FOR 2015
Majority	Conservative	Francis Maude MP	29,447	52.7	Francis Maude MP
11,460	Lib Dem	Godfrey Newman	17,987	32.2	
Turnout	Labour	Andrew Skudder	4,189	7.5	
71.99%	Others		4,218	7.6	

Hove

CONSERVATIVE GAIN FROM LABOUR	PARTY	2010 CANDIDATE	2010 VOTES	2010 % VOTE	PPC FOR 2015
Majority	Conservative	Mike Weatherley	18,294	36.7	Graham Cox
1,868	Labour	Celia Barlow MP	16,426	33.0	Peter Kyle
Turnout	Lib Dem	Paul Elgood	11,240	22.6	Lev Eakins
69.46%	Others		3,859	7.7	

Majority 1868 (3.8%)

Despite this seat being almost entirely contiguous with Brighton, Hove residents go to very great lengths to assert Hove's asymmetry from the remainder of the city's urban sprawl. Hove, with its beautifully manicured gardens and large elderly population is much closer to the stereotype of a sleepy Sussex seaside town than the remainder of the city. The constituency is, however, still home to a large transient population with more than a fifth of residents living in privately rented accommodation and some areas of real poverty. Labour support is strongest in the Portslade area in the west of the constituency while the Conservatives dominate in Stanford & Westbourne, home to one of the country's largest Jewish communities. Won by Conservative businessman Mike Weatherley in 2010, he is stepping down after just one term. The Labour candidate will be charity worker Peter Kyle.

Isle of Wight

CONSERVATIVE HOLD	PARTY	2010 CANDIDATE	2010 VOTES	2010 % VOTE	PPC FOR 2015
Majority	Conservative	Andrew Turner MP	32,810	46.7	Andrew Turner MP
10,527	Lib Dem	Jill Wareham	22,283	31.7	
Turnout	Labour	Mark Chiverton	8,169	11.6	Stewart Blackmore
63.92%	Others		7,002	10.0	

Lewes

LIB DEM HOLD	PARTY	2010 CANDIDATE	2010 VOTES	2010 % VOTE	PPC FOR 2015
Majority	Lib Dem	Norman Baker MP	26,048	52.0	Norman Baker MP
7,647	Conservative	Jason Sugarman	18,401	36.7	Maria Caulfield
Turnout	Labour	Hratche Koundarjian	2,508	5.0	Lloyd Russell-Mole
72.90%	Others		3,131	6.3	

Maidenhead

CONSERVATIVE HOLD	PARTY	2010 CANDIDATE	2010 VOTES	2010 % VOTE	PPC FOR 2015
Majority	Conservative	Theresa May MP	31,937	59.5	Theresa May MP
16,769	Lib Dem	Tony Hill	15,168	28.2	Tony Hill
Turnout	Labour	Pat McDonald	3,795	7.1	Charlie Smith
73.75%	Others		2,820	5.2	

Maidstone & The Weald

CONSERVATIVE HOLD	PARTY	2010 CANDIDATE	2010 VOTES	2010 % VOTE	PPC FOR 2015
Majority	Conservative	Helen Grant	23,491	48.0	Helen Grant MP
5,889	Lib Dem	Peter Carroll	17,602	36.0	Jasper Gerard
Turnout	Labour	Rav Seeruthun	4,769	9.7	Allen Simpson
68.87%	Others		3,066	6.3	

Meon Valley

CONSERVATIVE WIN (NEW SEAT)	PARTY	2010 CANDIDATE	2010 VOTES	2010 % VOTE	PPC FOR 2015
Majority	Conservative	George Hollingbery	28,818	56.2	George Hollingbery MP
12,125	Lib Dem	Liz Leffman	16,693	32.6	
Turnout	Labour	Howard Linsley	3,266	6.4	
72.69%	Others		2,461	4.8	

Milton Keynes North

CONSERVATIVE HOLD	PARTY	2010 CANDIDATE	2010 VOTES	2010 % VOTE	PPC FOR 2015
Majority	Conservative	Mark Lancaster MP	23,419	43.5	Mark Lancaster MP
8,961	Labour	Andrew Pakes	14,458	26.8	Emily Darlington
Turnout	Lib Dem	Jill Hope	11,894	22.1	
65.37%	Others		4,117	7.6	

Majority 8961 (16.6%)

The more rural and safer for the Tories of the two Milton Keynes constituencies, Milton Keynes North (formerly Milton Keynes North East) has been held by Conservative Mark Lancaster since 2005. Labour is strongest in the urban southern portions of the seat while the Conservatives dominate in the villages of Linford and Hanslope Park. With a high proportion of residents who commute to London or work locally in white-collar professions, the constituency has a higher income and less social housing than the national average. The Labour candidate will be Emily Darlington, a trade union official.

Milton Keynes South

CONSERVATIVE GAIN FROM LABOUR	PARTY	2010 CANDIDATE	2010 VOTES	2010 % VOTE	PPC FOR 2015
Majority	Conservative	Iain Stewart	23,034	41.6	Iain Stewart MP
5,201	Labour	Phyllis Starkey MP	17,833	32.2	Andrew Pakes
Turnout	Lib Dem	n/a	9,787	17.7	
63.93%	Others		4,679	8.5	

Majority 5201 (9.4%)

Since the division in 1992 of the town of Milton Keynes into two parliamentary constituencies, the southern portion of the town has always been the more favourable seat for Labour. This seat is a classic urban/rural split with the city centre areas favouring Labour and southern villages feeling every bit the Buckinghamshire Tory stronghold. For a South East constituency, the proportion of residents living in social housing is high (22.5 per cent) yet the managerial and professional class is also large here. The sitting Conservative Member of Parliament Iain Stewart will face a challenge from Labour's Andrew Pakes.

Mole Valley

CONSERVATIVE HOLD	PARTY	2010 CANDIDATE	2010 VOTES	2010 % VOTE	PPC FOR 2015
Majority	Conservative	Paul Beresford MP	31,263	57.5	Paul Beresford MP
15,653	Lib Dem	Alice Humphreys	15,610	28.7	Paul Kennedy
Turnout	Labour	James Dove	3,804	7.0	
75.14%	Others		3,647	6.7	

New Forest East

CONSERVATIVE HOLD	PARTY	2010 CANDIDATE	2010 VOTES	2010 % VOTE	PPC FOR 2015
Majority	Conservative	Julian Lewis MP	26,443	52.8	Julian Lewis MP
11,307	Lib Dem	Terry Scriven	15,136	30.3	
Turnout	Labour	Peter Sopowski	4,915	9.8	Andrew Pope
68.68%	Others		3,542	7.1	

New Forest West

CONSERVATIVE HOLD	PARTY	2010 CANDIDATE	2010 VOTES	2010 % VOTE	PPC FOR 2015
Majority	Conservative	Desmond Swayne MP	27,980	58.8	Desmond Swayne MP
16,896	Lib Dem	Mike Plummer	11,084	23.3	
Turnout	Labour	Janice Hurne	4,666	9.8	Lena Samuels
69.62%	Others		3,842	8.1	

Newbury

CONSERVATIVE HOLD	PARTY	2010 CANDIDATE	2010 VOTES	2010 % VOTE	PPC FOR 2015
Majority	Conservative	Richard Benyon MP	33,057	56.4	Richard Benyon MP
12,248	Lib Dem	David Rendel	20,809	35.5	Judith Bunting
Turnout	Labour	Hannah Cooper	2,505	4.3	
74.03%	Others		2,218	3.8	

Oxford East

LABOUR HOLD	PARTY	2010 CANDIDATE	2010 VOTES	2010 % VOTE	PPC FOR 2015
Majority	Labour	Andrew Smith MP	21,938	42.5	Andrew Smith MP
4,581	Lib Dem	Steve Goodard	17,357	33.6	Mark Mann
Turnout	Conservative	Ed Argar	9,727	18.8	
63.06%	Others		2,629	5.1	

Oxford West & Abingdon

CONSERVATIVE GAIN FROM LIB DEM	PARTY	2010 CANDIDATE	2010 VOTES	2010 % VOTE	PPC FOR 2015
Majority	Conservative	Nicola Blackwood	23,906	42.3	Nicola Blackwood MP
176	Lib Dem	Evan Harris MP	23,730	42.0	Layla Moran
Turnout	Labour	Richard Stevens	5,999	10.6	Sally Copley
65.33%	Others		2,845	5.0	

Majority 176 (0%)

A Tory seat since its inception, years of dominance on a local government level helped Liberal Democrat Dr Evan Harris snatch this seat from Conservatives at the 1997 general election before surprisingly returning to the Conservative column in 2010. Located to the east of the Prime Minister's Witney constituency, the seat contains the bulk of Oxford's 'picture postcard' areas including the university, city walls and attractive market town of Abingdon. While demographically this may appear to be a Tory seat, the city's urban-based academic community and large student population tended to favour the Liberal Democrats in pre-coalition days while Conservative support is greatest in the towns of Kidlington and Abingdon. Polling conducted in June 2014 by Conservative peer Lord Ashcroft showed the Conservatives ahead of the Lib Dems by a 36 per cent to 25 per cent margin, with Labour on 18 per cent – considerably up on their 2010 showing. The Conservative incumbent Nicola Blackwood will face a challenge from Liberal Democrat Layla Moran.

Portsmouth North

CONSERVATIVE GAIN FROM LABOUR	PARTY	2010 CANDIDATE	2010 VOTES	2010 % VOTE	PPC FOR 2015
Majority	Conservative	Penny Mordaunt	19,533	44.3	Penny Mordaunt MP
7,289	Labour	Sarah McCarthy-Fry MP	12,244	27.8	John Ferrett
Turnout	Lib Dem	Darren Sanders	8,874	20.1	
62.73%	Others		3,467	7.9	

Majority 7289 (16.5%)

Located in the northern part of the city of Portsmouth, this is one of the most densely populated constituencies in the south-east of England. Historically, much of the employment in this constituency has revolved around the town's Royal Navy base and associated military manufacturing industries, yet the town's insurance sector has grown dramatically in recent times. While the seat has a lower than average income for a south-east of England seat and is plagued by poor quality housing, its military tradition has seen it lean strongly towards the Conservatives. The Conservatives were the winners of the 2014 local elections, taking 28 per cent of the vote to the UK Independence Party's 23 per cent. Labour, who are the main challengers on a parliamentary level and held the seat from 1997 to 2010, took just 19.5 per cent of the vote. Penny Mordaunt, the Conservative Member of Parliament here since 2010, will be challenged by John Ferrett.

Portsmouth South

LIB DEM HOLD	PARTY	2010 CANDIDATE	2010 VOTES	2010 % VOTE	PPC FOR 2015
Majority	Lib Dem	Mike Hancock MP	18,921	45.9	n/s
5,200	Conservative	Flick Drummond	13,721	33.3	Flick Drummond
Turnout	Labour	John Ferrett	5,640	13.7	Sue Castillon
58.75%	Others		2,982	7.2	

Reading East

CONSERVATIVE HOLD	PARTY	2010 CANDIDATE	2010 VOTES	2010 % VOTE	PPC FOR 2015
Majority	Conservative	Rob Wilson MP	21,269	42.6	Rob Wilson MP
7,605	Lib Dem	Gareth Epps	13,664	27.3	
Turnout	Labour	Anneliese Dodds	12,729	25.5	Matt Rodda
66.71%	Others		2,323	4.6	

Majority 7605 (17.1%)

Stretching from Reading town centre and out to the town's eastern suburbs of Woodley, the constituency was won from Labour by Conservative Rob Wilson at the 2005 general election. The seat is home to a diverse social mix, with a large middle-class population who commute to London and work in many of the hi-tech industrial parks located in the seat, as well as poorer areas of central Reading which possess large ethnic minority populations. Labour were the narrow winners here in the 2014 local elections, outpacing the Conservatives by a 31.8 per cent to 27.5 per cent margin. The Liberal Democrats, who were once a considerable force here on a local government level, have faded in recent years. The Labour candidate here will be Matt Rodda.

Reading West

CONSERVATIVE GAIN FROM LABOUR	PARTY	2010 CANDIDATE	2010 VOTES	2010 % VOTE	PPC FOR 2015
Majority	Conservative	Alok Sharma	20,523	43.2	Alok Sharma MP
6,004	Labour	Naz Sarkar	14,519	30.5	Victoria Groulef
Turnout	Lib Dem	Daisy Benson	9,546	20.1	
65.90%	Others		2,942	6.2	

Majority 6004 (12.6%)

A middle-class seat which stretches from the urban wards of Battle, Norcot and Minister out to prosperous Pangbourne and Purley-on-Thames in rural West Berkshire, Reading West returned Conservative Alok Sharma at the 2010 general election. The seat is largely middle class in nature, containing Conservative-inclined Pangbourne and Theale that are every bit the archetypal picture of rural West Berkshire as well as Labour-leaning urban areas such as Southcote and Whitley where deprivation is about the national average. Labour was the easy victor at the 2014 local elections, easily outpacing the Conservatives in the Reading Borough Council portion of the seat – yet elections did not take place in the West Berkshire portion of the constituency from where Mr Sharma draws much of his support. Labour has selected Victoria Groulef.

Reigate

CONSERVATIVE HOLD	PARTY	2010 CANDIDATE	2010 VOTES	2010 % VOTE	PPC FOR 2015
Majority	Conservative	Crispin Blunt MP	26,688	53.4	Crispin Blunt MP
13,591	Lib Dem	Jane Kulka	13,097	26.2	
Turnout	Labour	Robert Hull	5,672	11.3	
69.80%	Others		4,521	9.0	

Rochester & Strood

CONSERCATIVE GAIN FROM LABOUR	PARTY	2010 CANDIDATE	2010 VOTES	2010 % VOTE	PPC FOR 2015
Majority	Conservative	Mark Reckless	23,604	49.2	Mark Reckless MP
9,953	Labour	Teresa Murray	13,651	28.5	Naushabah Khan
Turnout	Lib Dem	Geoff Juby	7,800	16.3	
65.04%	Others		2,916	6.1	

Romsey & Southampton North

CONSERVATIVE WIN (NEW SEAT)	PARTY	2010 CANDIDATE	2010 VOTES	2010 % VOTE	PPC FOR 2015
Majority	Conservative	Caroline Nokes	24,345	49.7	Caroline Nokes MP
4,156	Lib Dem	Sandra Gidley MP	20,189	41.3	Ben Nicholls
Turnout	Labour	Aktar Beg	3,116	6.4	Darren Paffey
71.80%	Others		1,289	2.6	

Runnymede & Weybridge

CONSERVATIVE HOLD	PARTY	2010 CANDIDATE	2010 VOTES	2010 % VOTE	PPC FOR 2015
Majority	Conservative	Philip Hammond MP	26,915	55.9	Philip Hammond MP
16,509	Lib Dem	Andrew Falconer	10,406	21.6	
Turnout	Labour	Paul Greenwood	6,446	13.4	
66.35%	Others		4,383	9.1	

Sevenoaks

CONSERVATIVE HOLD	PARTY	2010 CANDIDATE	2010 VOTES	2010 % VOTE	PPC FOR 2015
Majority	Conservative	Michael Fallon MP	28,076	56.8	Michael Fallon MP
17,515	Lib Dem	Alan Bullion	10,561	21.4	Alan Bullion
Turnout	Labour	Gareth Siddorn	6,541	13.2	
71.00%	Others		4,230	8.6	

Sittingbourne & Sheppey

CONSERVATIVE GAIN FROM LABOUR	PARTY	2010 CANDIDATE	2010 VOTES	2010 % VOTE	PPC FOR 2015
Majority	Conservative	Gordon Henderson	24,313	50.0	Gordon Henderson MP
12,383	Labour	Angela Harrison	11,930	24.6	Guy Nicholson
Turnout	Lib Dem	Keith Nevols	7,943	16.4	
64.04%	Others		4,392	9.0	

Slough

LABOUR HOLD	PARTY	2010 CANDIDATE	2010 VOTES	2010 % VOTE	PPC FOR 2015
Majority	Labour	Fiona Mactaggart MP	21,884	45.8	Fiona Mactaggart MP
5,523	Conservative	Diana Coad	16,361	34.3	
Turnout	Lib Dem	Chris Tucker	6,943	14.5	
61.62%	Others		2,554	5.3	

Southampton, Itchen

LABOUR HOLD	PARTY	2010 CANDIDATE	2010 VOTES	2010 % VOTE	PPC FOR 2015
Majority	Labour	John Denham MP	16,326	36.8	Rowenna Davis
192	Conservative	Royston Smith	16,134	36.3	Royston Smith
Turnout	Lib Dem	David Goodall	9,256	20.8	
59.59%	Others		2,696	6.1	

Majority 192 (0.4%)

Historically the safer of the two Southampton constituencies for Labour, former Communities Secretary John Denham held off a challenge from Conservative candidate and then Southampton City Council leader Royston Smith by only 192 votes in 2010. This constituency includes the majority of Southampton's recognisable areas including town centre, docks and new shopping developments at Banana Wharf. At one in ten, the proportion of residents in full-time education is lower here than in neighbouring Test. With many large council estates and higher than average levels of unemployment, the residents of this constituency have long been well disposed towards Labour. Despite losing ground on a local government level in many marginal across the country since 2010, the Conservatives successfully held their ground and outpolled Labour in Itchen at the 2014 local elections. Royston Smith will once again stand for the Conservatives. With Denham opting for retirement, the Labour candidate will be Peckham Councillor Rowenna Davis.

Southampton, Test

LABOUR HOLD	PARTY	2010 CANDIDATE	2010 VOTES	2010 % VOTE	PPC FOR 2015
Majority	Labour	Alan Whitehead MP	17,001	38.5	Alan Whitehead MP
2,413	Conservative	Jeremy Moulton	14,588	33.0	Jeremy Moulton
Turnout	Lib Dem	Dave Callaghan	9,865	22.3	
61.43%	Others		2,733	6.2	

Spelthorne

CONSERVATIVE HOLD	PARTY	2010 CANDIDATE	2010 VOTES	2010 % VOTE	PPC FOR 2015
Majority	Conservative	Kwasi Kwarteng	22,261	47.1	Kwasi Kwarteng MP
10,019	Lib Dem	Mark Chapman	12,242	25.9	
Turnout	Labour	Adam Tyler-Moore	7,789	16.5	
67.12%	Others		5,012	10.6	

East Surrey

CONSERVATIVE HOLD	PARTY	2010 CANDIDATE	2010 VOTES	2010 % VOTE	PPC FOR 2015
Majority	Conservative	Sam Gyimah	31,007	56.7	Sam Gyimah MP
16,874	Lib Dem	David Lee	14,133	25.9	David Lee
Turnout	Labour	Matthew Rodda	4,925	9.0	
71.09%	Others		4,575	8.4	

Surrey Heath

CONSERVATIVE HOLD	PARTY	2010 CANDIDATE	2010 VOTES	2010 % VOTE	PPC FOR 2015
Majority	Conservative	Michael Gove MP	31,326	57.6	Michael Gove MP
17,289	Lib Dem	Alan Hilliar	14,037	25.8	
Turnout	Labour	Matt Willey	5,552	10.2	Laween Atroshi
69.58%	Others		3,432	6.3	

South West Surrey

CONSERVATIVE HOLD	PARTY	2010 CANDIDATE	2010 VOTES	2010 % VOTE	PPC FOR 2015
Majority	Conservative	Jeremy Hunt MP	33,605	58.7	Jeremy Hunt MP
16,318	Lib Dem	Mike Simpson	17,287	30.2	
Turnout	Labour	Richard Mollet	3,419	6.0	
74.85%	Others		2,948	5.1	

Mid Sussex

CONSERVATIVE HOLD	PARTY	2010 CANDIDATE	2010 VOTES	2010 % VOTE	PPC FOR 2015
Majority	Conservative	Nicholas Soames MP	28,329	50.7	Nicholas Soames MP
7,402	Lib Dem	Serena Tierney	20,927	37.5	
Turnout	Labour	David Boot	3,689	6.6	Greg Mountain
72.35%	Others		2,910	5.2	

North Thanet

CONSERVATIVE HOLD	PARTY	2010 CANDIDATE	2010 VOTES	2010 % VOTE	PPC FOR 2015
Majority	Conservative	Roger Gale MP	22,826	52.7	Roger Gale MP
13,528	Labour	Michael Britton	9,298	21.5	Frances Rehal
Turnout	Lib Dem	Laura Murphy	8,400	19.4	George Cunningham
63.18%	Others		2,819	6.5	

South Thanet

CONSERVATIVE GAIN FROM LABOUR	PARTY	2010 CANDIDATE	2010 VOTES	2010 % VOTE	PPC FOR 2015
Majority	Conservative	Laura Sandys	22,043	48.0	Craig Mackinlay
7,617	Labour	Stephen Ladyman MP	14,426	31.4	Will Scobie
Turnout	Lib Dem	Peter Bucklitsch	6,935	15.1	Russ Timpson
65.58%	Others		2,529	5.5	

Majority 7617 (16.6%)

Located on the East Kent coastline, the voters of South Thanet shocked the political establishment by electing Labour's Steve Ladyman at the 1997 general election. It took until 2010 for the Conservative Party's Laura Sandys to take the seat back for the Conservatives. The largest town in the constituency is the port of Ramsgate, a socially deprived area that struggles from high unemployment and has long been Labour-inclined. The second largest settlement is Broadstairs, a pleasant town characterised by its elderly population and elegant regency properties that is more closely associated with the Conservatives. Outside of Ramsgate and Broadstairs, the Conservatives pile up the votes in picturesque East Kent villages like Wingham and Sandwich. UKIP were the big winners here at the 2013 county council elections, seizing all by one of the constituency's eight seats. With its elderly population, almost entirely white ethnic profile and staunch Eurosceptic tendencies, it is no surprise that UKIP leader Nigel Farage will stand here. The Conservative candidate will be Medway Councillor and former UKIP deputy leader Craig Mackinlay.

Tonbridge & Malling

CONSERVATIVE HOLD	PARTY	2010 CANDIDATE	2010 VOTES	2010 % VOTE	PPC FOR 2015
Majority	Conservative	John Stanley MP	29,723	57.9	Tom Tugendhat
18,178	Lib Dem	Liz Simpson	11,545	22.5	
Turnout	Labour	Daniel Griffiths	6,476	12.6	
71.48%	Others		3,570	7.0	

Tunbridge Wells

CONSERVATIVE HOLD	PARTY	2010 CANDIDATE	2010 VOTES	2010 % VOTE	PPC FOR 2015
Majority	Conservative	Greg Clark MP	28,302	56.2	Greg Clark MP
15,576	Lib Dem	David Hallas	12,726	25.3	
Turnout	Labour	Gary Heather	5,448	10.8	
68.13%	Others		3,844	7.6	

Wantage

CONSERVATIVE HOLD	PARTY	2010 CANDIDATE	2010 VOTES	2010 % VOTE	PPC FOR 2015
Majority	Conservative	Ed Vaizey MP	29,284	52.0	Ed Vaizey MP
13,547	Lib Dem	Alan Armitage	15,737	27.9	
Turnout	Labour	Steven Mitchell	7,855	13.9	
70.03%	Others		3,465	6.2	

Wealden

CONSERVATIVE HOLD	PARTY	2010 CANDIDATE	2010 VOTES	2010 % VOTE	PPC FOR 2015
Majority	Conservative	Charles Hendry MP	31,090	56.6	Nusrat Ghani
17,179	Lib Dem	Chris Bowers	13,911	25.3	
Turnout	Labour	Lorna Blackmore	5,266	9.6	
71.82%	Others		4,702	8.6	

Winchester

CONSERVATIVE GAIN FROM LIB DEM	PARTY	2010 CANDIDATE	2010 VOTES	2010 % VOTE	PPC FOR 2015
Majority	Conservative	Steve Brine	27,155	48.5	Steve Brine MP
3,048	Lib Dem	Martin Tod	24,107	43.1	Jackie Porter
Turnout	Labour	Patrick Davies	3,051	5.5	
75.81%	Others		1,642	2.9	

Windsor

CONSERVATIVE HOLD	PARTY	2010 CANDIDATE	2010 VOTES	2010 % VOTE	PPC FOR 2015
Majority	Conservative	Adam Afriyie MP	30,172	60.8	Adam Afriye MP
19,054	Lib Dem	Julian Tisi	11,118	22.4	
Turnout	Labour	Amanjit Jhund	4,910	9.9	Fiona Dent
71.34%	Others		3,388	6.8	

Witney

CONSERVATIVE HOLD	PARTY	2010 CANDIDATE	2010 VOTES	2010 % VOTE	PPC FOR 2015
Majority	Conservative	David Cameron MP PM	33,973	58.8	David Cameron MP PM
22,740	Lib Dem	Dawn Barnes	11,233	19.4	
Turnout	Labour	Joe Goldberg	7,511	13.0	Duncan Enright
73.34%	Others		5,052	8.7	

Woking

CONSERVATIVE HOLD	PARTY	2010 CANDIDATE	2010 VOTES	2010 % VOTE	PPC FOR 2015
Majority	Conservative	Jonathan Lord	26,551	50.3	Jonathan Lord MP
6,807	Lib Dem	Rosie Sharpley	19,744	37.4	Chris Took
Turnout	Labour	Tom Miller	4,246	8.0	
71.49%	Others		2,245	4.3	

Wokingham

CONSERVATIVE HOLD	PARTY	2010 CANDIDATE	2010 VOTES	2010 % VOTE	PPC FOR 2015
Majority	Conservative	John Redwood MP	28,754	52.7	John Redwood MP
13,492	Lib Dem	Prue Bray	15,262	28.0	Clive Jones
Turnout	Labour	George Davidson	5,516	10.1	
71.38%	Others		4,996	9.2	

East Worthing & Shoreham

CONSERVATIVE HOLD	PARTY	2010 CANDIDATE	2010 VOTES	2010 % VOTE	PPC FOR 2015
Majority	Conservative	Tim Loughton MP	23,458	48.5	Tim Loughton MP
11,105	Lib Dem	James Doyle	12,353	25.5	Jemima Bland
Turnout	Labour	Emily Benn	8,087	16.7	
65.40%	Others		4,499	9.3	

Worthing West

CONSERVATIVE HOLD	PARTY	2010 CANDIDATE	2010 VOTES	2010 % VOTE	PPC FOR 2015
Majority	Conservative	Peter Bottomley MP	25,416	51.7	Peter Bottomley MP
11,729	Lib Dem	Hazel Thorpe	13,687	27.9	Hazel Thorpe
Turnout	Labour	Ian Ross	5,800	11.8	
64.68%	Others		4,220	8.6	

Wycombe

CONSERVATIVE HOLD	PARTY	2010 CANDIDATE	2010 VOTES	2010 % VOTE	PPC FOR 2015
Majority	Conservative	Steve Baker	23,423	48.6	Steve Baker MP
9,560	Lib Dem	Steve Guy	13,863	28.8	
Turnout	Labour	Andrew Lomas	8,326	17.3	
64.92%	Others		2,539	5.3	

London

With seventy-three parliamentary seats to be contested, the nation's growing and vibrant capital will once again be a key battleground in the 2015 election. With nine gains, it provided a fair share of the Conservative advance that enabled David Cameron to become Prime Minister in 2010, but there are signs that it may not bring such happy news as he endeavours to strengthen his position in government and party next time.

The recent electoral news in London has not been good for the Tories, with the exception of Boris Johnson's re-election as London Mayor in 2012 (which may not actually be the best personal news for Mr Cameron, especially with Boris likely to be returning to the Commons in 2015 as a London MP). In May 2014 this was without doubt the region where Labour's vote held up the best in their disappointing European elections, as they took four of the eight seats with over 36 per cent of the vote, an increase of no less than 15.5 per cent on 2009. Without London they would have finished third nationally behind the Conservatives as well as UKIP. At the same time, Labour made advances in the four-yearly all-out London borough elections, taking control of several councils such as Hammersmith & Fulham, Croydon and Merton. London's growing population has rapidly become even more cosmopolitan and multi-ethnic since the turn of the century, and the perception of the Tories as 'tough on immigration' as well as the large proportion of public sector workers and 'chattering classes' may all hinder further progress for the centre-right party.

Labour on the other hand have high hopes of reversing the defeat in 2010. Taking local election evidence into account, their top targets look eminently winnable. Hendon (in the borough of Barnet, where they made nine gains in May 2014 and fell just short of council control) requires a swing of just a tenth of 1 per cent. Brentford & Isleworth in Hounslow, west London, has a majority of under 2,000, and Labour did very well in the by-election for the other Hounslow constituency, Feltham & Heston, just before Christmas 2011. Some observers tip the third on the list, Enfield North, also needing a swing of around 2 per cent, to be one of Labour's most likely gains in the whole country. A significant proportion of the capital's population growth since the 2001 census has been caused by immigration from Africa, and over 10 per cent of Enfield North's population in 2011 was born there. Croydon Central is a classic marginal sandwiched between the solidly Labour north of the borough and the Conservative south – and, as stated above, the marginal Croydon wards fell to Labour in 2014. Harrow East must also be a realistic prospect. A glance at the lists of the top ten or twenty seats in various categories elsewhere in this book shows how well Bob Blackman did to make a gain in 2010. Harrow East is by far the most 'non-white' constituency in the UK to be held by the Conservatives, and the only one in their column without a white majority. Also well within Labour's grasp are Ealing Central & Acton (swing required 4 per cent), and Ilford North (6 per cent), another seat displaying evidence of rapid social change.

Furthermore, Labour can pick up seats from the Liberal Democrats, who have been imploding in most parts of London. For example, their vote in the European elections in 2014 was more than halved to under 7 per cent. The most certain prediction of a change of hands of all parliamentary seats is Brent Central, which was only won by the Lib Dems in 2010 because Sarah Teather was standing – and now she is not, expressing herself disillusioned. Lynne Featherstone has a comfortable looking 6,875 majority in Hornsey & Wood Green, but her party was devastated in the 2014 Haringey borough elections, losing fourteen councillors to Labour. This is one of the places where the Liberal Democrat membership of a Conservative-led coalition is not favourably received. Labour were even ahead in 2014 in the vote tally in the seat Simon Hughes has held for over thirty years, now named Bermondsey & Old Southwark, but that long-tended personal vote should enable him to hold on.

The Conservatives also intend to fight hard to make gains from their coalition partners. One bright spot in the May 2014 London borough elections was that they gained Kingston upon Thames from the Lib Dems, and that must make the Cabinet minister Ed Davey uncomfortable, though again, as with so many MPs from his party, incumbency will enable him to have a much better chance of winning than national opinion polls suggest. But other evidence is not such good news for the Tories in the borough of Sutton, where they perennially hope to gain Sutton & Cheam and Carshalton & Wallington. This was the one local authority where the Liberal Democrats improved in 2014, strengthening their already massive grip on the council.

The top Conservative target held by Labour is the remarkable constituency of Hampstead & Kilburn, where the redoubtable Glenda Jackson held on by forty-two votes in 2010, with the Liberal Democrats also within a thousand. Now seventy-eight years of age, the Oscar-winner turned politician is now retiring, but the seat remains very hard to call. This seat on London's commanding northern heights lies in the top ten both for higher professional and managerial workers and educational qualifications, and perhaps its cultural affinity for liberalism with a small 'l' may keep it once again out of the Tory grasp. A very different kind of seat is next on the Tory hit list, Eltham in south-east London, needing a swing of 2 per cent from Labour MP Clive Efford, who is a former taxi driver. Then comes Tooting – despite its plebeian reputation very much part of the gentrified borough of Wandsworth (it lies tenth in the order of constituencies for residents with degrees) – and then Westminster North, where Karen Buck did well to hold on by over 2,000 at the last general election.

The last word should be reserved for 'other' parties. London is UKIP's weakest area, as its multi-national nature may explain, but in the heart of the East End lies the borough of Tower Hamlets, whose politics can only be described as 'one-off'. In 2010, Rushanara Ali convincingly regained Bethnal Green & Bow from Respect, for whom George Galloway had himself taken the seat from Labour's Oona King in a highly charged 2005 campaign. Galloway did not stand here at the last general election (though he reappeared in the Commons less than two years later, see Yorkshire & the Humber region, Bradford West) and Respect has subsequently lost its presence in Tower Hamlets. However the same section of the vote he had courted, largely among the Bangladeshi community, is still very evident in the success of the Tower Hamlets First candidate Lutfur Rahman in the direct mayoral elections in 2010 and 2014, despite controversy both about his administration and the conduct of the most recent elections. THF candidates also won in some wards in the borough, and if the group contests either of the Tower Hamlets seats in 2015, more drama may be expected.

Barking

LABOUR HOLD	PARTY	2010 CANDIDATE	2010 VOTES	2010 % VOTE	PPC FOR 2015
Majority	Labour	Margaret Hodge MP	24,628	54.3	Margaret Hodge MP
16,555	Conservative	Simon Marcus	8,073	17.8	Mina Rahman
Turnout	BNP	Nick Griffin	6,620	14.6	
61.38%	Others		6,022	13.3	

Battersea

CONSERVATIVE GAIN FROM LABOUR	PARTY	2010 CANDIDATE	2010 VOTES	2010 % VOTE	PPC FOR 2015
Majority	Conservative	Jane Ellison	23,103	47.3	Jane Ellison MP
5,977	Labour	Martin Linton MP	17,126	35.1	Will Martindale
Turnout	Lib Dem	n/a	7,176	14.7	
65.66%	Others		1,387	2.8	

Majority 5977 (12.3%)

Home to the seemingly permanently derelict power station, parts of Clapham Common and Europe's busiest railway station at Clapham Junction, Battersea was won by the now Conservative Health Minister Jane Ellison at the 2010 general election. The Tories dominate at a local government level, easily topping the poll at the 2010 mayoral elections and 2014 local elections where they outpaced Labour by 12 per cent in the popular vote. While the seat remained resistant to Conservative advances until 1987 and was regained by Labour on a below-average swing at the 1997 election, the long-term demographics here do not favour Labour. Indeed, the seat has undergone a rapid transformation from working-class Labour bastion to bastion of moneyed young professionals. The Labour candidate will be Will Martindale.

Beckenham

CONSERVATIVE HOLD	PARTY	2010 CANDIDATE	2010 VOTES	2010 % VOTE	PPC FOR 2015
Majority	Conservative	Bob Stewart	27,597	57.9	Bob Stewart
17,784	Lib Dem	Stephen Jenkins	9,813	20.6	
Turnout	Labour	Damien Egan	6,893	14.5	
72.01%	Others		3,383	7.1	

Bermondsey & Old Southwark

LIB DEM HOLD	PARTY	2010 CANDIDATE	2010 VOTES	2010 % VOTE	PPC FOR 2015
Majority	Lib Dem	Simon Hughes MP	21,590	48.4	Simon Hughes MP
8,530	Labour	Val Shawcross	13,060	29.2	Neil Coyle
Turnout	Conservative	Loanna Morrison	7,638	17.1	
57.52%	Others		2,363	5.3	

Bethnal Green & Bow

LABOUR GAIN FROM RESPECT	PARTY	2010 CANDIDATE	2010 VOTES	2010 % VOTE	PPC FOR 2015
Majority	Labour	Rushanara Ali	21,784	42.9	Rushanara Ali MP
11,574	Lib Dem	Ajmal Masroor	10,210	20.1	
Turnout	Respect	Abjol Miah	8,532	16.8	
62.44%	Others		10,202	20.1	Matthew Smith (Conservative)

Bexleyheath & Crayford

CONSERVATIVE HOLD	PARTY	2010 CANDIDATE	2010 VOTES	2010 % VOTE	PPC FOR 2015
Majority	Conservative	David Evennett MP	21,794	50.5	David Evennett MP
10,344	Labour	Howard Dawber	11,450	26.5	Stefano Borella
Turnout	Lib Dem	Karelia Stewart	5,502	12.7	
66.42%	Others		4,436	10.3	

Brent Central

LIB DEM WIN (NEW SEAT)	PARTY	2010 CANDIDATE	2010 VOTES	2010 % VOTE	PPC FOR 2015
Majority	Lib Dem	Sarah Teather MP	20,026	44.2	Ibrahim Taguri
1,345	Labour	Dawn Butler MP	18,681	41.2	Dawn Butler
Turnout	Conservative	Sachin Rajput	5,067	11.2	
61.21%	Others		1,549	3.4	

Majority 1345 (3%)

A newly created constituency at the 2010 general election, the inaugural battle for Brent Central was won by Liberal Democrat Sarah Teather who had previously represented much of the area in the old Brent East constituency she famously won on an anti-Iraq war ticket at a 2003 by-election. The seat contains some of north London's poorest areas, including Kensal Rise, Harlsden and Stonebridge which are home to large black populations and the Irish bastion of Willesden. Overall, the non-white population here makes up more than 50 per cent of voters – one of the very few constituencies in which this is the case. Roughly one in five electors is Muslim, with the Hindu population standing at around 10 per cent. The Labour candidate will be former minister Dawn Butler, the Labour MP for Brent South from 2005 to 2010, while the Liberal Democrats are fielding Ibrahim Taguri. The Liberal Democrats were decimated here in the 2014 local elections, winning only one seat across the whole of the London Borough of Brent. The gloom for the Liberal Democrats will be compounded by a June 2014 poll from Lord Ashcroft that showed Labour ahead of them by a 54 per cent to 19 per cent margin.

Brent North

LABOUR HOLD	PARTY	2010 CANDIDATE	2010 VOTES	2010 % VOTE	PPC FOR 2015
Majority	Labour	Barry Gardiner MP	24,514	46.9	Barry Gardiner MP
8,028	Conservative	Harshadbhai Patel	16,486	31.5	
Turnout	Lib Dem	James Allie	8,879	17.0	
62.34%	Others		2,419	4.6	

Brentford & Isleworth

CONSERVATIVE GAIN FROM LABOUR	PARTY	2010 CANDIDATE	2010 VOTES	2010 % VOTE	PPC FOR 2015
Majority	Conservative	Mary Macleod	20,022	37.2	Mary Macleod MP
1,958	Labour	Ann Keen MP	18,064	33.6	Ruth Cadbury
Turnout	Lib Dem	Andrew Dakers	12,718	23.7	
64.35%	Others		2,961	5.5	

Majority 1958 (3.6%)

Based alongside the main arterial road out of west London towards Heathrow Airport and the M25, Brentford & Isleworth has been held by Scots-born Conservative Mary Macleod since the 2010 general election. Home to prosperous Chiswick and Osterley which remained loyal to the Conservatives throughout their mid-1990s nadir, Labour needs to secure overwhelming support in Brentford, Hounslow and Gunnersbury to deliver them a majority here. Almost a third of the constituency's residents were born outside of the United Kingdom, leading to sizeable Hindu, Muslim and Sikh communities that tend to side with the Labour Party. Labour outpolled the Conservatives here in the 2014 local elections, taking marginal wards in Hounslow South and Osterley and Spring Grove. The Labour candidate will be Hounslow councillor Ruth Cadbury.

Bromley & Chislehurst

CONSERVATIVE HOLD	PARTY	2010 CANDIDATE	2010 VOTES	2010 % VOTE	PPC FOR 2015
Majority	Conservative	Bob Neill MP	23,569	53.5	Bob Neill MP
13,900	Lib Dem	Sam Webber	9,669	22.0	
Turnout	Labour	Chris Kirby	7,295	16.6	John Courtneid
67.31%	Others		3,504	8.0	

Camberwell & Peckham

LABOUR HOLD	PARTY	2010 CANDIDATE	2010 VOTES	2010 % VOTE	PPC FOR 2015
Majority	Labour	Harriet Harman MP	27,619	59.2	Harriet Harman MP
17,187	Lib Dem	Columba Blango	10,432	22.4	
Turnout	Conservative	Andy Stranack	6,080	13.0	Naomi Newstead
59.34%	Others		2,528	5.4	

Carshalton & Wallington

LIB DEM HOLD	PARTY	2010 CANDIDATE	2010 VOTES	2010 % VOTE	PPC FOR 2015
Majority	Lib Dem	Tom Brake MP	22,180	48.3	Tom Brake MP
5,260	Conservative	Ken Andrew	16,920	36.8	Matthew Maxwell Scott
Turnout	Labour	Shafiqul Khan	4,015	8.7	Siobhan Tate
69.02%	Others		2,803	6.1	

Chelsea & Fulham

CONSERVATIVE WIN (NEW SEAT)	PARTY	2010 CANDIDATE	2010 VOTES	2010 % VOTE	PPC FOR 2015
Majority	Conservative	Greg Hands MP	24,093	60.5	Greg Hands MP
16,722	Labour	Alex Hilton	7,371	18.5	
Turnout	Lib Dem	Dirk Hazell	6,473	16.2	
60.15%	Others		1,919	4.8	

Chingford & Woodford Green

CONSERVATIVE HOLD	PARTY	2010 CANDIDATE	2010 VOTES	2010 % VOTE	PPC FOR 2015
Majority	Conservative	Iain Duncan Smith MP	22,743	52.8	Iain Duncan Smith MP
12,963	Labour	Catharine Arakelian	9,780	22.7	Bilal Mahmood
Turnout	Lib Dem	Geoffrey Sneef	7,242	16.8	
66.49%	Others		3,341	7.8	

Chipping Barnet

CONSERVATIVE HOLD	PARTY	2010 CANDIDATE	2010 VOTES	2010 % VOTE	PPC FOR 2015
Majority	Conservative	Theresa Villiers MP	24,700	48.8	Theresa Villiers MP
11,927	Labour	Damien Welfare	12,773	25.2	Amy Trevethan
Turnout	Lib Dem	Stephen Barber	10,202	20.2	
67.37%	Others		2,933	5.8	

Cities of London & Westminster

CONSERVATIVE HOLD	PARTY	2010 CANDIDATE	2010 VOTES	2010 % VOTE	PPC FOR 2015
Majority	Conservative	Mark Field MP	19,264	52.2	Mark Field MP
11,076	Labour	Dave Rowntree	8,188	22.2	Nick Slingsby
Turnout	Lib Dem	Naomi Smith	7,574	20.5	
55.25%	Others		1,905	5.2	

Croydon Central

CONSERVATIVE HOLD	PARTY	2010 CANDIDATE	2010 VOTES	2010 % VOTE	PPC FOR 2015
Majority	Conservative	Gavin Barwell	19,567	39.4	Gavin Barwell MP
2,879	Labour	Gerry Ryan	16,688	33.6	Sarah Jones
Turnout	Lib Dem	Peter Lambell	6,553	13.2	James Fearnley
65.05%	Others		6,859	13.8	

Majority 2879 (5.8%)

A relatively humdrum slice of suburbia, Croydon Central was won in 2010 by Conservative Gavin Barwell. The seat includes within its boundaries Croydon's thriving shopping areas, wealthy communities on the London and Surrey border and the socially deprived New Addington council estate, which has elected BNP councillors in the past. One in ten voters is black, many of whom live in the Addiscombe and Woodside wards in the north of the constituency. The result of the 2014 local elections was extremely close, with Labour leading the Conservatives by a 39 per cent to 38.2 per cent margin. Sarah Jones will contest the seat for Labour.

Croydon North

LABOUR HOLD	PARTY	2010 CANDIDATE	2010 VOTES	2010 % VOTE
Majority	Labour	Malcolm Wicks MP	28,947	56.0
16,481	Conservative	Jason Hadden	12,466	24.1
Turnout	Lib Dem	Gerry Jerome	7,226	14.0
60.64%	Others		3,037	5.9

Croydon North (2012 by-election)

LABOUR HOLD	PARTY	2012 CANDIDATE	2012 VOTES	2012 % VOTE	PPC FOR 2015
Majority	Labour	Steve Reed	15,892	64.7	Steve Reed MP
11,755	Conservative	Andrew Stranack	4,137	16.8	Vidhi Mohan
Turnout	UKIP	Winston McKenzie	1,400	5.7	
28.82%	Others		3,133	12.8	

Croydon South

CONSERVATIVE HOLD	PARTY	2010 CANDIDATE	2010 VOTES	2010 % VOTE	PPC FOR 2015
Majority	Conservative	Richard Ottaway MP	28,684	50.9	Chris Philp
15,818	Lib Dem	Simon Rix	12,866	22.8	
Turnout	Labour	Jane Avis	11,287	20.0	Emily Benn
69.27%	Others		3,485	6.2	

Dagenham & Rainham

LABOUR WIN (NEW SEAT)	PARTY	2010 CANDIDATE	2010 VOTES	2010 % VOTE	PPC FOR 2015
Majority	Labour	Jon Cruddas MP	17,813	40.3	Jon Cruddas MP
2,630	Conservative	Simon Jones	15,183	34.3	
Turnout	BNP	Michael Barnbrook	4,952	11.2	
63.40%	Others		6,284	14.2	

Dulwich & West Norwood

LABOUR HOLD	PARTY	2010 CANDIDATE	2010 VOTES	2010 % VOTE	PPC FOR 2015
Majority	Labour	Tessa Jowell MP	22,461	46.6	Helen Hayes
9,365	Lib Dem	Jonathan Mitchell	13,096	27.2	James Barber
Turnout	Conservative	Kemi Adegoke	10,684	22.2	
66.21%	Others		1,973	4.1	

Ealing Central & Acton

CONSERVATIVE WIN (NEW SEAT)	PARTY	2010 CANDIDATE	2010 VOTES	2010 % VOTE	PPC FOR 2015
Majority	Conservative	Angie Bray	17,944	38.0	Angie Bray
3,716	Labour	Bassam Mahfouz	14,228	30.1	Rupa Huq
Turnout	Lib Dem	Jon Ball	13,041	27.6	Jon Ball
67.19%	Others		1,987	4.2	

Majority 3716 (7.9%)

A newly created seat at the 2010 general election, the seat was won for the Conservatives by former London Assembly member Angie Bray. The constituency is based around Ealing town centre and is predominantly middle-class and residential in nature, with excellent transport links to Central London. The Conservatives are strongest in the leafy Ealing portions of the seat while Labour run up commanding margins in multi-ethnic Acton, close to the deprived Shepherd's Bush and White City areas of Hammersmith. Labour were the narrow victors here at the 2014 local elections, taking 33 per cent of the vote to the Conservative Party's 31 per cent. The Labour candidate will be Rupa Huq.

Ealing North

LABOUR HOLD	PARTY	2010 CANDIDATE	2010 VOTES	2010 % VOTE	PPC FOR 2015
Majority	Labour	Stephen Pound MP	24,023	50.4	Stephen Pound MP
9,301	Conservative	Ian Gibb	14,722	30.9	
Turnout	Lib Dem	Chris Lucas	6,283	13.2	
65.22%	Others		2,650	5.6	

Ealing, Southall

LABOUR HOLD	PARTY	2010 CANDIDATE	2010 VOTES	2010 % VOTE	PPC FOR 2015
Majority	Labour	Virendra Sharma MP	22,024	51.5	Virenda Sharma MP
9,291	Conservative	Gurcharan Singh	12,733	29.8	James Symes
Turnout	Lib Dem	Nigel Bakhai	6,383	14.9	
63.84%	Others		1,616	3.8	

East Ham

LABOUR HOLD	PARTY	2010 CANDIDATE	2010 VOTES	2010 % VOTE	PPC FOR 2015
Majority	Labour	Stephen Timms MP	35,471	70.4	Stephen Timms MP
27,826	Conservative	Paul Shea	7,645	15.2	
Turnout	Lib Dem	Chris Brice	5,849	11.6	
55.55%	Others		1,408	2.8	

Edmonton

LABOUR HOLD	PARTY	2010 CANDIDATE	2010 VOTES	2010 % VOTE	PPC FOR 2015
Majority	Labour	Andy Love MP	21,665	53.7	Andy Love MP
9,613	Conservative	Andrew Charalambous	12,052	29.8	
Turnout	Lib Dem	Iarla Kilbane-Dawe	4,252	10.5	
63.18%	Others		2,408	6.0	

Eltham

LABOUR HOLD	PARTY	2010 CANDIDATE	2010 VOTES	2010 % VOTE	PPC FOR 2015
Majority	Labour	Clive Efford MP	17,416	41.5	Clive Efford MP
1,663	Conservative	David Gold	15,753	37.5	Spencer Drury
Turnout	Lib Dem	Stephen Toole	5,299	12.6	Alex Cunliffe
67.05%	Others		3,496	8.3	

Majority 1663 (4%)

Held by former London taxi driver Clive Efford since the 1997 general election, the Conservatives are keen to reclaim this south-east London constituency. Located within the boundaries of the London Borough of Greenwich this socially diverse constituency takes in the Ferrier Estate, described by many town planners as the country's worst social housing project, Kidbrooke and the more middle-class New Eltham and Oxleas Wood areas. A third of the housing in the constituency is council or housing association owned. As a rule, the north west of the constituency favours Labour while the south-east areas closest to Bexley and Bromley are more Conservative-inclined. Conservative prospects here are boosted by the sizeable number of affluent commuters who, attracted by the area's excellent transport links, opt to make their homes here. The Conservative will be Greenwich councillor Spencer Drury.

Enfield North

CONSERVATIVE GAIN FROM LABOUR	PARTY	2010 CANDIDATE	2010 VOTES	2010 % VOTE	PPC FOR 2015
Majority	Conservative	Nick de Bois	18,804	42.3	Nick de Bois MP
1,692	Labour	Joan Ryan MP	17,112	38.5	Joan Ryan
Turnout	Lib Dem	Paul Smith	5,403	12.2	
67.09%	Others		3,134	7.1	

Majority 1692 (3.8%)

Gained at the 2010 general election by Conservative candidate Nick de Bois, Enfield North is one of the London's foremost political battlegrounds. Located at the northern tip of the capital city, the constituency is a mixture of gritty urban areas such as Enfield Lock that have much in common with inner-city London and wealthy, semi-rural commuter suburbs. The constituency has a large ethnic minority population with almost a quarter of residents being non-white, and social housing levels well above average for a Conservative-held seat. Labour were the clear winners here at the 2014 local elections, outpacing the Conservatives by a 37.4 per cent to 26.4 per cent margin. 2015 will see a rematch between De Bois and the area's former Labour MP Joan Ryan – the fourth occasion the two have faced off against each other.

Enfield, Southgate

CONSERVATIVE HOLD	PARTY	2010 CANDIDATE	2010 VOTES	2010 % VOTE	PPC FOR 2015
Majority	Conservative	David Burrowes MP	21,928	49.4	David Burrowes MP
7,626	Labour	Bambos Charalambous	14,302	32.2	Bambos Charalambous
Turnout	Lib Dem	Johar Khan	6,124	13.8	
69.15%	Others		1,998	4.5	

Majority 7626 (17.2%)

Made famous for the defeat of then Defence Secretary Michael Portillo on election 1997, Enfield Southgate returned to its Conservative roots in 2005 when it elected local solicitor David Burrowes as its Member of Parliament. The constituency is staunchly middle-class in composition, with owner-occupation rates standing at almost 80 per cent and has a distinctly suburban feel. The Southgate portion of the constituency is particularly favourable towards the Conservatives, while the Bowes Park area in the south of the constituency is solidly Labour. In common with most other north London constituencies, there is a diverse ethnic and religious mix present with a large Greek Cypriot, Hindu and Jewish population. Labour were the narrow victors here at the 2014 local elections, outpolling the Conservatives by a 42.2 per cent to 41.2 per cent margin. The Labour candidate will be Bambos Charalambous.

Erith & Thamesmead

LABOUR HOLD	PARTY	2010 CANDIDATE	2010 VOTES	2010 % VOTE	PPC FOR 2015
Majority	Labour	Teresa Pearce	19,068	44.9	Teresa Pearce MP
5,703	Conservative	Colin Bloom	13,365	31.5	
Turnout	Lib Dem	Alex Cunliffe	5,116	12.0	Samson Iriajen
60.77%	Others		4,927	11.6	

Feltham & Heston

LABOUR HOLD	PARTY	2010 CANDIDATE	2010 VOTES	2010 % VOTE
Majority	Labour	Alan Keen MP	21,174	43.6
4,658	Conservative	Mark Bowen	16,516	34.0
Turnout	Lib Dem	Munira Wilson	6,679	13.8
59.88%	Others		4,167	8.6

Feltham & Heston (2011 by-election)

LABOUR HOLD	PARTY	2011 CANDIDATE	2011 VOTES	2011 % VOTE	PPC FOR 2015
Majority	Labour	Seema Malhotra	12,639	54.2	Seema Malhotra MP
6,203	Conservative	Mark Bowen	6,436	27.6	
Turnout	Lib Dem	Roger Crouch	1,364	5.9	
28.74%	Others		2,860	12.3	

Finchley & Golders Green

CONSERVATIVE GAIN FROM LABOUR	PARTY	2010 CANDIDATE	2010 VOTES	2010 % VOTE	PPC FOR 2015
Majority	Conservative	Mike Freer	21,688	46.0	Mike Freer MP
5,809	Labour	Alison Moore	15,879	33.7	Sarah Sackman
Turnout	Lib Dem	Laura Edge	8,036	17.0	
66.68%	Others		1,554	3.3	

Majority 5809 (12.3%)

Formed out of the majority of the territory represented by Margaret Thatcher for thirty-three years, this north London constituency is one of the country's most closely fought marginals. Despite unfavourable demographic trends for the Conservatives this seat is broadly middle class in nature, encompassing Finchley, Golders Green and well-healed Hampstead Garden Suburb. The Conservatives dominate in Golders Green, Garden Suburb and Church End while Labour posts solid leads in the Finchley and Woodhouse portions of the seat. At almost 20 per cent, the constituency has the largest Jewish community of any British constituency and is also home to a sizeable number of Muslim (6 per cent) and Hindu (6.8 per cent) residents. The Conservatives continue to narrowly hold the upper hand here, outpacing Labour by a 39 per cent to 36 per cent margin at the 2014 local elections. The Labour candidate will be lawyer Sarah Sackman.

Greenwich & Woolwich

LABOUR HOLD	PARTY	2010 CANDIDATE	2010 VOTES	2010 % VOTE	PPC FOR 2015
Majority	Labour	Nick Raynsford MP	20,262	49.2	Matthew Pennycook
10,153	Conservative	Spencer Drury	10,109	24.5	Matt Hartley
Turnout	Lib Dem	Joseph Lee	7,498	18.2	
62.89%	Others		3,319	8.1	

Hackney North & Stoke Newington

LABOUR HOLD	PARTY	2010 CANDIDATE	2010 VOTES	2010 % VOTE	PPC FOR 2015
Majority	Labour	Diane Abbott MP	25,553	55.0	Diane Abbott
14,461	Lib Dem	Keith Angus	11,092	23.9	
Turnout	Conservative	Darren Caplan	6,759	14.5	Amy Gray
62.86%	Others		3,057	6.6	

Hackney South & Shoreditch

LABOUR HOLD	PARTY	2010 CANDIDATE	2010 VOTES	2010 % VOTE	PPC FOR 2015
Majority	Labour	Meg Hillier MP	23,888	55.7	Meg Hillier MP
14,288	Lib Dem	Dave Raval	9,600	22.4	
Turnout	Conservative	Simon Nayyar	5,800	13.5	Jack Tinley
58.84%	Others		3,570	8.3	

Hammersmith

LABOUR WIN (NEW SEAT)	PARTY	2010 CANDIDATE	2010 VOTES	2010 % VOTE	PPC FOR 2015
Majority	Labour	Andrew Slaughter MP	20,810	43.9	Andrew Slaughter MP
3,549	Conservative	Shaun Bailey	17,261	36.4	Charlie Dewhirst
Turnout	Lib Dem	Merlene Emerson	7,567	15.9	
65.59%	Others		1,814	3.8	

Hampstead & Kilburn

LABOUR WIN (NEW SEAT)	PARTY	2010 CANDIDATE	2010 VOTES	2010 % VOTE	PPC FOR 2015
Majority	Labour	Glenda Jackson MP	17,332	32.8	Tulip Siddiq
42	Conservative	Chris Philp	17,290	32.7	Simon Marcus
Turnout	Lib Dem	Ed Fordham	16,491	31.2	Maajid Nawaz
65.72%	Others		1,709	3.2	

Majority 42 (0.1%)

Won by Labour's Glenda Jackson by just forty-two votes at the 2010 general election, Hampstead & Kilburn is the Conservative Party's number one target seat nationally. A socially divided seat, the Hampstead portion of the seat is rapidly gentrifying as young professionals flock to the area to take advantage of its tree-lined avenues and excellent transport links to central London while Kilburn is home to a less well-heeled and more ethnically diverse group of residents. The Liberal Democrats, who had high hopes of winning the constituency at the last general election, were decimated in the 2014 local elections - winning only one council seat in Camden. A June 2014 poll from Lord Ashcroft had Labour ahead of the Conservatives by a 41 per cent to 30 per cent margin with the Liberal Democrats on 19 per cent. With Jackson opting for retirement, the Labour candidate will be Tulip Siddiq while the Conservatives are fielding Simon Marcus.

Harrow East

CONSERVATIVE GAIN FROM LABOUR	PARTY	2010 CANDIDATE	2010 VOTES	2010 % VOTE	PPC FOR 2015
Majority	Conservative	Bob Blackman	21,435	44.7	Bob Blackman MP
3,403	Labour	Tony McNulty MP	18,032	37.6	Uma Kumaran
Turnout	Lib Dem	Nahid Boethe	6,850	14.3	
68.08%	Others		1,689	3.5	

Majority 3403 (7.1%)

Harrow East is a prosperous constituency characterised by long driveways and cedar-lined avenues located on London's northern fringe and contains the communities of Edgware, Kenton, Wealdstone and Stanmore. The constituency is one of the most ethnically diverse seats in the country with large numbers of Hindu (23.9 per cent), Jewish (10.3 per cent) and Muslim (7.1 per cent) residents. Despite poor local election results across most of London in 2014, the Conservatives narrowly outpolled Labour by a margin of 44.6 per cent to 39.7 per cent. Represented since 2010 by Conservative MP Bob Blackman, the Labour candidate will be Uma Kumaran.

Harrow West

LABOUR HOLD	PARTY	2010 CANDIDATE	2010 VOTES	2010 % VOTE	PPC FOR 2015
Majority	Labour	Gareth Thomas MP	20,111	43.6	Gareth Thomas MP
3,143	Conservative	Rachel Joyce	16,968	36.8	Hannah David
Turnout	Lib Dem	Christopher Noyce	7,458	16.2	
67.27%	Others		1,579	3.4	

Hayes & Harlington

LABOUR HOLD	PARTY	2010 CANDIDATE	2010 VOTES	2010 % VOTE	PPC FOR 2015
Majority	Labour	John McDonnell MP	23,377	54.8	John McDonnell MP
10,824	Conservative	Scott Seaman-Digby	12,553	29.4	
Turnout	Lib Dem	Satnam Kaur Khalsa	3,726	8.7	
60.71%	Others		2,981	7.0	

Hendon

CONSERVATIVE GAIN FROM LABOUR	PARTY	2010 CANDIDATE	2010 VOTES	2010 % VOTE	PPC FOR 2015
Majority	Conservative	Matthew Offord	19,635	42.3	Matthew Offord MP
106	Labour	Andrew Dismore MP	19,529	42.1	Andrew Dismore
Turnout	Lib Dem	Matthew Harris	5,734	12.4	
63.58%	Others		1,476	3.2	

Majority 106 (0.2%)

Most famous for its large police training college, Hendon is a predominantly middle-class and ethnically mixed constituency located in north-west London. Between 1992 and 2001 the seat recorded a 19.1 per cent swing to Labour, indicating the scale of the party's progress in this traditionally Conservative area. As with nearby Finchley and Golders Green, one in five of the seat's residents is Jewish (17.3 per cent) while almost one in ten is Hindu (8.7 per cent) or Muslim (7.9 per cent). Labour support is strongest in the south of the constituency with the wards of Burnt Oak and Colindale home to the large Grahame Park and Watling housing estates. Conversely, the Conservatives have traditionally been strongest in the constituency's northern wards with Edgware in particular delivering the party overwhelming support. With a majority of only 106 votes, the sitting Conservative MP Matthew Offord will have a real fight on his hands to hold off the challenge from former Labour MP and sitting London Assembly member Andrew Dismore.

Holborn & St Pancras

LABOUR HOLD	PARTY	2010 CANDIDATE	2010 VOTES	2010 % VOTE	PPC FOR 2015
Majority	Labour	Frank Dobson MP	25,198	46.1	n/s
9,942	Lib Dem	Jo Shaw	15,256	27.9	
Turnout	Conservative	George Lee	11,134	20.4	Will Blair
63.13%	Others		3,061	5.6	

Hornchurch & Upminster

CONSERVATIVE WIN (NEW SEAT)	PARTY	2010 CANDIDATE	2010 VOTES	2010 % VOTE	PPC FOR 2015
Majority	Conservative	Angela Watkinson MP	27,469	51.4	Angela Watkinson MP
16,371	Labour	Kath McGuirk	11,098	20.8	Paul McGreary
Turnout	Lib Dem	Karen Chilvers	7,426	13.9	
67.97%	Others		7,397	13.9	

Hornsey & Wood Green

LIB DEM HOLD	PARTY	2010 CANDIDATE	2010 VOTES	2010 % VOTE	PPC FOR 2015
Majority	Lib Dem	Lynne Featherstone MP	25,595	46.5	Lynne Featherstone MP
6,875	Labour	Karen Jennings	18,720	34.0	Catherine West
Turnout	Conservative	Richard Merrin	9,174	16.7	
69.90%	Others		1,553	2.8	

Majority 6875 (12.5%)

Won in 1997 by Labour's Barbara Roche by more than 2,000 votes, Liberal.Democrat Lynne Featherstone's talented approach to local campaigning saw her party win a 6,875 majority just thirteen years later. The constituency is comprised of the western – and wealthier – half of the London Borough of Haringey, with areas like Muswell Hill and Fortis Green becoming an increasingly attractive base for young professionals priced-out of other fashionable areas of north London. The Liberal Democrats lost considerable ground here at the 2014 local elections, losing fourteen councillors and falling behind Labour by a 42 per cent to 29 per cent margin in the popular vote. The Labour candidate will be Catherine West, the former leader of Islington Council.

Ilford North

CONSERVATIVE HOLD	PARTY	2010 CANDIDATE	2010 VOTES	2010 % VOTE	PPC FOR 2015
Majority	Conservative	Lee Scott MP	21,506	45.8	Lee Scott MP
5,404	Labour	Sonia Klein	16,102	34.3	Wes Streeting
Turnout	Lib Dem	Alex Berhanu	5,924	12.6	
64.91%	Others		3,444	7.3	

Majority 5404 (11.5%)

Located in north-east London – although most of its residents consider it to be in Essex – Ilford North has been represented since 2005 by Conservative Lee Scott. The seat stretches from semi-rural areas in the north that continue on into the Essex countryside to densely populated urban areas such as Hainault to the south. An ethnically diverse constituency, almost half the population is non-white with a third of the population being of Asian heritage. The seat has one of the highest proportions of Jewish residents of any UK constituency. The 2014 local elections put the Conservatives narrowly ahead of Labour by a 41.2 per cent to 38.9 per cent event. The Labour candidate will be Wes Streeting, the deputy leader of Redbridge Council.

Ilford South

LABOUR HOLD	PARTY	2010 CANDIDATE	2010 VOTES	2010 % VOTE	PPC FOR 2015
Majority	Labour	Mike Gapes MP	25,311	49.4	Mike Gapes MP
11,297	Conservative	Toby Boutle	14,014	27.4	
Turnout	Lib Dem	Anood Al-Samerai	8,679	17.0	
59.38%	Others		3,197	6.2	

Islington North

LABOUR HOLD	PARTY	2010 CANDIDATE	2010 VOTES	2010 % VOTE	PPC FOR 2015
Majority	Labour	Jeremy Corbyn MP	24,276	54.5	Jeremy Corbyn MP
12,401	Lib Dem	Rhodri Jamieson-Ball	11,875	26.7	Julian Gregory
Turnout	Conservative	Adrian Berrill-Cox	6,339	14.2	
65.41%	Others		2,064	4.6	

Islington South & Finsbury

LABOUR HOLD	PARTY	2010 CANDIDATE	2010 VOTES	2010 % VOTE	PPC FOR 2015
Majority	Labour	Emily Thornberry MP	18,407	42.3	Emily Thornberry MP
3,569	Lib Dem	Bridget Fox	14,838	34.1	Terry Stacy
Turnout	Conservative	Antonia Cox	8,449	19.4	
64.38%	Others		1,861	4.3	

Kensington

CONSERVATIVE WIN (NEW SEAT)	PARTY	2010 CANDIDATE	2010 VOTES	2010 % VOTE	PPC FOR 2015
Majority	Conservative	Malcolm Rifkind MP	17,595	50.1	Malcolm Rifkind MP
8,616	Labour	Sam Gurney	8,979	25.5	Rod Abouharb
Turnout	Lib Dem	Robin Meltzer	6,872	19.6	
53.28%	Others		1,704	4.8	

Kingston & Surbiton

LIB DEM HOLD	PARTY	2010 CANDIDATE	2010 VOTES	2010 % VOTE	PPC FOR 2015
Majority	Lib Dem	Ed Davey MP	28,428	49.8	Ed Davey MP
7,560	Conservative	Helen Whately	20,868	36.5	James Berry
Turnout	Labour	Max Freedman	5,337	9.3	Lee Godfrey
70.41%	Others		2,478	4.3	

Lewisham, Deptford

LABOUR HOLD	PARTY	2010 CANDIDATE	2010 VOTES	2010 % VOTE	PPC FOR 2015
Majority	Labour	Joan Ruddock MP	22,132	53.7	Vicky Foxcraft
12,499	Lib Dem	Tam Langley	9,633	23.4	Michael Bukola
Turnout	Conservative	Gemma Townsend	5,551	13.5	Bim Afolami
61.47%	Others		3,904	9.5	

Lewisham East

LABOUR HOLD	PARTY	2010 CANDIDATE	2010 VOTES	2010 % VOTE	PPC FOR 2015
Majority	Labour	Heidi Alexander	17,966	43.1	Heidi Alexander MP
6,216	Lib Dem	Pete Pattisson	11,750	28.2	Julia Fletcher
Turnout	Conservative	Jonathan Clamp	9,850	23.6	Peter Fortune
63.28%	Others		2,153	5.2	

Lewisham West & Penge

LABOUR HOLD	PARTY	2010 CANDIDATE	2010 VOTES	2010 % VOTE	PPC FOR 2015
Majority	Labour	Jim Dowd MP	18,501	41.1	Jim Dowd MP
5,828	Lib Dem	Alex Feakes	12,673	28.1	
Turnout	Conservative	Chris Phillips	11,489	25.5	
65.24%	Others		2,365	5.3	

Leyton & Wanstead

LABOUR HOLD	PARTY	2010 CANDIDATE	2010 VOTES	2010 % VOTE	PPC FOR 2015
Majority	Labour	John Cryer	17,511	43.6	John Cryer MP
6,416	Lib Dem	Farooq Qureshi	11,095	27.6	
Turnout	Conservative	Edwin Northover	8,928	22.2	Matthew Scott
63.20%	Others		2,625	6.5	

Mitcham & Morden

LABOUR HOLD	PARTY	2010 CANDIDATE	2010 VOTES	2010 % VOTE	PPC FOR 2015
Majority	Labour	Siobhain McDonagh MP	24,722	56.4	Siobhan McDonagh MP
13,666	Conservative	Melanie Hampton	11,056	25.2	Paul Holmes
Turnout	Lib Dem	Diana Coman	5,202	11.9	
66.42%	Others		2,817	6.4	

Old Bexley & Sidcup

CONSERVATIVE RE-GAIN FROM INDEPENDENT	PARTY	2010 CANDIDATE	2010 VOTES	2010 % VOTE	PPC FOR 2015
Majority	Conservative	James Brokenshire MP	24,625	54.1	James Brokenshire MP
15,857	Labour	Rick Everitt	8,768	19.3	Ibby Mehmet
Turnout	Lib Dem	Duncan Borrowman	6,996	15.4	
69.24%	Others		5,103	11.2	

Orpington

CONSERVATIVE HOLD	PARTY	2010 CANDIDATE	2010 VOTES	2010 % VOTE	PPC FOR 2015
Majority	Conservative	Jo Johnson	29,200	59.7	Jo Johnson MP
17,200	Lib Dem	David McBride	12,000	24.5	
Turnout	Labour	Stephen Morgan	4,400	9.0	Nigel de Gruchy
72.21%	Others		3,311	6.8	

Poplar & Limehouse

LABOUR WIN (NEW SEAT)	PARTY	2010 CANDIDATE	2010 VOTES	2010 % VOTE	PPC FOR 2015
Majority	Labour	Jim Fitzpatrick MP	18,679	40.0	Jim Fitzpatrick MP
6,030	Conservative	Tim Archer	12,649	27.1	
Turnout	Respect	George Galloway	8,460	18.1	
62.30%	Others		6,912	14.8	

Putney

CONSERVATIVE HOLD	PARTY	2010 CANDIDATE	2010 VOTES	2010 % VOTE	PPC FOR 2015
Majority	Conservative	Justine Greening MP	21,223	52.0	Justine Greening MP
10,053	Labour	Stuart King	11,170	27.4	Sheila Boswell
Turnout	Lib Dem	James Sandbach	6,907	16.9	
64.36%	Others		1,485	3.6	

Richmond Park

CONSERVATIVE GAIN FROM LIB DEM	PARTY	2010 CANDIDATE	2010 VOTES	2010 % VOTE	PPC FOR 2015
Majority	Conservative	Zac Goldsmith	29,461	49.7	Zac Goldsmith MP
4,091	Lib Dem	Susan Kramer MP	25,370	42.8	Robin Meltzer
Turnout	Labour	Eleanor Tunnicliffe	2,979	5.0	Sachin Patel
76.23%	Others		1,458	2.5	

Romford

CONSERVATIVE HOLD	PARTY	2010 CANDIDATE	2010 VOTES	2010 % VOTE	PPC FOR 2015
Majority	Conservative	Andrew Rosindell MP	26,031	56.0	Andrew Rosindell MP
16,954	Labour	Rachel Voller	9,077	19.5	Sam Gould
Turnout	Lib Dem	Helen Duffett	5,572	12.0	
65.19%	Others		5,801	12.5	

Ruislip, Northwood & Pinner

CONSERVATIVE WIN (NEW SEAT)	PARTY	2010 CANDIDATE	2010 VOTES	2010 % VOTE	PPC FOR 2015
Majority	Conservative	Nick Hurd MP	28,866	57.5	Nick Hurd MP
19,060	Labour	Anita McDonald	9,806	19.5	Michael Borio
Turnout	Lib Dem	Thomas Papworth	8,345	16.6	
70.84%	Others		3,188	6.3	

Streatham

LABOUR HOLD	PARTY	2010 CANDIDATE	2010 VOTES	2010 % VOTE	PPC FOR 2015
Majority	Labour	Chuka Umunna	20,037	42.8	Chuka Umanna MP
3,259	Lib Dem	Chris Nicholson	16,778	35.8	Amna Ahmed
Turnout	Conservative	Rahoul Bhansali	8,578	18.3	
62.84%	Others		1,444	3.1	

Sutton & Cheam

LIB DEM HOLD	PARTY	2010 CANDIDATE	2010 VOTES	2010 % VOTE	PPC FOR 2015
Majority	Lib Dem	Paul Burstow MP	22,156	45.7	Paul Burstow MP
1,608	Conservative	Phillipa Stroud	20,548	42.4	Paul Scully
Turnout	Labour	Kathy Allen	3,376	7.0	Emily Brothers
72.77%	Others		2,428	5.0	

Majority 1608 (3.3%)

Captured for the first time by the party in a 1972 by-election, Sutton & Cheam returned to the Liberal Democrat fold in 1997 and has remained there ever since. This south-west London seat is comfortably middle-class in nature with four in five homes owner-occupied and extremely low rates of unemployment. Cheam, with its open parks and leafy lanes, provides the bedrock of Conservative support locally while urban Sutton is more strongly inclined towards the Liberal Democrats. The Liberal Democrats have controlled Sutton Borough Council with healthy majorities since 1990, scoring another easy victory in the 2014 local elections – gaining two seats from the Tories. A June 2014 poll by Lord Ashcroft found the Liberal Democrats to be leading the Conservatives by a 42 per cent to 29 per cent margin. The Conservative candidate to face incumbent MP Paul Burstow will be businessman and former Sutton councillor Paul Scully.

Tooting

LABOUR HOLD	PARTY	2010 CANDIDATE	2010 VOTES	2010 % VOTE	PPC FOR 2015
Majority	Labour	Sadiq Khan MP	22,038	43.5	Sadiq Khan MP
2,524	Conservative	Mark Clarke	19,514	38.5	Dan Watkins
Turnout	Lib Dem	Nasser Butt	7,509	14.8	
68.60%	Others		1,594	3.1	

Tottenham

LABOUR HOLD	PARTY	2010 CANDIDATE	2010 VOTES	2010 % VOTE	PPC FOR 2015
Majority	Labour	David Lammy MP	24,128	59.3	David Lammy MP
16,931	Lib Dem	David Schmitz	7,197	17.7	Turhan Ozen
Turnout	Conservative	Sean Sullivan	6,064	14.9	
59.11%	Others		3,298	8.1	

Twickenham

LIB DEM HOLD	PARTY	2010 CANDIDATE	2010 VOTES	2010 % VOTE	PPC FOR 2015
Majority	Lib Dem	Vince Cable MP	32,483	54.4	Vince Cable MP
12,140	Conservative	Deborah Thomas	20,343	34.1	Tania Mathias
Turnout	Labour	Brian Tomlinson	4,583	7.7	Nick Grant
74.12%	Others		2,312	3.9	

Uxbridge & South Ruislip

CONSERVATIVE HOLD	PARTY	2010 CANDIDATE	2010 VOTES	2010 % VOTE	PPC FOR 2015
Majority	Conservative	John Randall MP	21,758	48.3	n/s
11,216	Labour	Sidharath Garg	10,542	23.4	Chris Summers
Turnout	Lib Dem	Mike Cox	8,995	20.0	
63.34%	Others		3,781	8.4	

Vauxhall

LABOUR HOLD	PARTY	2010 CANDIDATE	2010 VOTES	2010 % VOTE	PPC FOR 2015
Majority	Labour	Kate Hoey MP	21,498	49.8	Kate Hoey MP
10,651	Lib Dem	Caroline Pidgeon	10,847	25.1	
Turnout	Conservative	Glyn Chambers	9,301	21.5	
57.73%	Others		1,545	3.6	

Walthamstow

LABOUR HOLD	PARTY	2010 CANDIDATE	2010 VOTES	2010 % VOTE	PPC FOR 2015
Majority	Labour	Stella Creasy	21,252	51.8	Stella Creasy MP
9,478	Lib Dem	Farid Ahmed	11,774	28.7	
Turnout	Conservative	Andy Hemsted	5,734	14.0	
63.43%	Others		2,234	5.4	

West Ham

LABOUR HOLD	PARTY	2010 CANDIDATE	2010 VOTES	2010 % VOTE	PPC FOR 2015
Majority	Labour	Lyn Brown MP	29,422	62.7	Lyn Brown MP
22,534	Conservative	Virginia Morris	6,888	14.7	
Turnout	Lib Dem	Martin Pierce	5,392	11.5	
55.03%	Others		5,249	11.2	

Westminster North

LABOUR WIN (NEW SEAT)	PARTY	2010 CANDIDATE	2010 VOTES	2010 % VOTE	PPC FOR 2015
Majority	Labour	Karen Buck MP	17,377	43.9	Karen Buck MP
2,126	Conservative	Joanne Cash	15,251	38.5	Lindsey Hall
Turnout	Lib Dem	Mark Blackburn	5,513	13.9	
59.33%	Others		1,457	3.7	

Wimbledon

CONSERVATIVE HOLD	PARTY	2010 CANDIDATE	2010 VOTES	2010 % VOTE	PPC FOR 2015
Majority	Conservative	Stephen Hammond MP	23,257	49.1	Stephen Hammond MP
11,408	Lib Dem	Shas Sheehan	11,849	25.0	Shas Sheehan
Turnout	Labour	Andrew Judge	10,550	22.3	Andrew Judge
72.11%	Others		1,739	3.7	

East of England

Eastern England is topographically flat, with few dramatic hilly or mountainous elevations, and at first sight the electoral pattern appears similar. The Conservatives hold fifty-two of the fifty-eight Westminster parliamentary constituencies – but also seem unlikely to make any further gains in their pursuit of an overall majority in the 2015 election.

Labour's two remaining seats are both in Luton, and while their majorities look vulnerable on the surface – less than 2.5 per cent in Luton South – neither are very likely to fall. Luton North was on the Tory target list last time, but most unusually for 2010 there was actually a swing in Labour's favour, and their popular 73-year-old MP, Kelvin Hopkins (named a *Daily Telegraph* 'saint' for low second home claims at the time of the 2009 expenses scandal) is likely to be standing again. Both Luton seats have very ethnically mixed populations, South even more so, with nearly 30 per cent of residents being of Asian background and also ranking fourth in the 'born in Poland' national list of constituencies.

To complete the dearth of chances of Tory gains, they are not going to take any of the four Liberal Democrat seats either. The long-serving Sir Bob Russell (Colchester) and Minister of State for Care and Support Norman Lamb (North Norfolk) are both safe, while if anyone is challenging in the other two it is Labour. Julian Huppert, sometimes called the only genuine professional scientist in the Commons, does seem well suited to his Cambridge constituency, but it has been widely predicted that Simon Wright will be a one-term MP for Norwich South. This argument suggests he only ousted Labour's former

Education Secretary Charles Clarke in 2010 due to discontent among students – for example, from the University of East Anglia in the constituency – whereas Nick Clegg's apparent reneging on promises about student fees will reverse that trend in 2015. It might however be noted that there are not as many students in Norwich South as some think: it ranks only forty-fifth on the list of 'full-time student' seats, and not all of these will vote in the constituency.

Yet despite the un-dramatic surface of the electoral map in this region, there are hidden fault lines that may well help to determine the nature of the future government. Changes of hands in the East of England, if they do come, are actually more likely in two other types of seat. Firstly, Labour must hope to regain some of the eight constituencies they lost to the Conservatives in this region in 2010 (and also perhaps Norwich North, lost to Chloe Smith in the 2009 by-election). They must succeed in over half of these targets to become the largest party, and in pretty much all of them if they aim to secure an overall majority in 2015. For various reasons, however, such a Labour achievement is unlikely in this region. The party did not do well in the East of England in the 2014 European elections, with enough votes to be awarded only one of the seven MEPs.

This is linked to their second problem – it was UKIP that made advances in 2014, securing three MEPs and clearly being the main challengers to the Conservatives. This has a considerable impact on Labour's challenges in their target marginals. For example, their top target – and second on their national list – is Thurrock, but constituency polling sponsored in July 2014 by Lord Ashcroft has suggested that UKIP, not Labour were in the lead there. Clearly if Labour cannot regain Thurrock their chances of making much progress overall in 2015 are in jeopardy. A similar problem may be suggested in Great Yarmouth (a seat needed for an overall majority) by an earlier Ashcroft poll, placing UKIP in second place, and this was before their full surge. Waveney (based in Lowestoft), twelfth on the national target list, did look more promising for Labour, but both there and in the other targets, Ipswich, Bedford, Stevenage, Harlow, South Basildon & East Thurrock and Watford, the Conservatives will now have the advantage of incumbent MPs with five years' worth of service and publicity.

A word about Watford, a rare genuine three-way marginal. It must also be classed as a Liberal Democrat hope too, because they actually finished second in 2010 when Labour fell from first to third. What is more, the Lib Dems have easily held the directly elected mayoralty of Watford borough on all four occasions it has been contested between 2002 and 2014. On the other hand, this has also never yet been translated into winning the parliamentary seat, and a significant element of their vote must be personally for Dorothy Thornhill, the mayor throughout this period.

Finally, UKIP do deserve treatment in their own right in this region. With 34.5 per cent of the vote in the May 2014 European elections, they easily finished first, 6 per cent ahead of the Conservatives. Anti-EU sentiment does seem stronger nearer the coast and nearer the Continent. If UKIP are to win any seats at Westminster, or come close to doing so, eastern England must offer some of the best chances. Some of UKIP's strongest performances in local council elections in 2014 also reinforce this point: as well as Great Yarmouth mentioned above, they took more seats than any other party in Basildon and made five gains in Thurrock, for example. Although many Conservatives feel that UKIP is a threat to their party's chances in the next general election, in the East of England it is Labour who may be denied absolutely vital gains by the increase in the UKIP share of the vote. If Labour do not make significant gains here, as elsewhere, they cannot expect to force a change in the party – or parties – of government.

* * *

On 28 August 2014, the Conservative MP for Clacton, Douglas Carswell, announced not only his defection to UKIP but that he would stand in a parliamentary by-election under his new allegiance. The result will not be at hand before going to press, but it seems clear that this is a high 'risk-and-reward' strategy. If Mr Carswell loses, then UKIP's chances of winning any seats at all in 2015 will be slim. If he wins, the anti-European party will hold much more initiative entering the general election. Clacton on the Essex coast is the seat with the second highest proportion of voters over the age of sixty-five (35 per cent) in the whole of Britain. Douglas Carswell has a personal vote as sitting MP. UKIP won the most votes here in the Euro-elections of May 2014. The circumstances could hardly be more favourable for a first by-election win for UKIP. Of course it is also possible that he might win the by-election, then lose in the general election when the government of the nation is actually at stake. Either way, Douglas Carswell's decision has indeed 'set the cat amongst the pigeons'.

Basildon & Billericay

CONSERVATIVE WIN (NEW SEAT)	PARTY	2010 CANDIDATE	2010 VOTES	2010 % VOTE	PPC FOR 2015
Majority	Conservative	John Baron MP	21,982	52.8	John Baron MP
12,398	Labour	Allan Davies	9,584	23.0	Gavin Callaghan
Turnout	Lib Dem	Mike Hibbs	6,538	15.7	
63.54%	Others		3,525	8.5	

South Basildon & East Thurrock

CONSERVATIVE WIN (NEW SEAT)	PARTY	2010 CANDIDATE	2010 VOTES	2010 % VOTE	PPC FOR 2015
Majority	Conservative	Stephen Metcalfe	19,624	43.9	Stephen Metcalfe MP
5,772	Labour	Angela Smith MP	13,852	31.0	Mike Le Surf
Turnout	Lib Dem	Geoff Williams	5,977	13.4	
62.24%	Others		5,282	11.8	

Majority 5772 (12.9%)

An awkwardly named seat, South Basildon & East Thurrock is essentially comprised of the southern portion of Basildon town, tracts of rural marshland stretching along the banks of the River Thames and the tough dock town of East Tilbury. Both Labour and the Conservatives can call on substantial reserves of support here; the Conservatives holding wide leads in Orsett and Pitsea and Labour dominating in Tilbury. The inaugural contest for this newly formed seat was won in 2010 by Conservative Stephen Metcalfe. UKIP, who were the easy victors here at the 2014 European elections, are expected to play an active role here in the 2015 election. The Labour candidate will be local councillor Mike Le Surf.

Bedford

CONSERVATIVE GAIN FROM LABOUR	PARTY	2010 CANDIDATE	2010 VOTES	2010 % VOTE	PPC FOR 2015
Majority	Conservative	Richard Fuller	17,546	38.9	Richard Fuller MP
1,353	Labour	Patrick Hall MP	16,193	35.9	Patrick Hall
Turnout	Lib Dem	Henry Vann	8,957	19.9	
65.81%	Others		2,406	5.3	

Majority 1353 (3%)

Located some 60 miles north of London, Bedford is home to one the country's most ethnically diverse populations outside of a major city with a sizeable black and Asian community. An educated town, more than 100 languages are spoken locally and the majority of residents are employed in the service sector. The Conservatives are strongest in Kempston, a pleasant commuter town for Bedford and Milton Keynes. Politically divided at a local level, the directly elected mayoralty is held by Liberal Democrat Dave Hodgson while the Conservatives, Labour and Lib Dems each have twelve councillors apiece. Won from Labour's Patrick Hall by Conservative Richard Fuller at the 2010 general election, the two men will face off again in 2015

Mid Bedfordshire

CONSERVATIVE HOLD	PARTY	2010 CANDIDATE	2010 VOTES	2010 % VOTE	PPC FOR 2015
Majority	Conservative	Nadine Dorries MP	28,815	52.5	Nadine Dorries MP
15,152	Lib Dem	Linda Jack	13,663	24.9	
Turnout	Labour	David Reeves	8,108	14.8	Charlynne Pullen
71.94%	Others		4,311	7.9	

North East Bedfordshire

CONSERVATIVE HOLD	PARTY	2010 CANDIDATE	2010 VOTES	2010 % VOTE	PPC FOR 2015
Majority	Conservative	Alistair Burt MP	30,989	55.8	Alistair Burt MP
18,942	Lib Dem	Mike Pitt	12,047	21.7	
Turnout	Labour	Ed Brown	8,957	16.1	Saqhib Ali
71.17%	Others		3,559	6.4	

South West Bedfordshire

CONSERVATIVE HOLD	PARTY	2010 CANDIDATE	2010 VOTES	2010 % VOTE	PPC FOR 2015
Majority	Conservative	Andrew Selous MP	26,815	52.8	Andrew Selous MP
16,649	Lib Dem	Rod Cantrill	10,166	20.0	
Turnout	Labour	Jenny Bone	9,948	19.6	Daniel Scott
66.32%	Others		3,845	7.6	

Braintree

CONSERVATIVE HOLD	PARTY	2010 CANDIDATE	2010 VOTES	2010 % VOTE	PPC FOR 2015
Majority	Conservative	Brooks Newmark MP	25,901	52.6	Brooks Newmark MP
16,121	Labour	Bill Edwards	9,780	19.9	Malcolm Fincken
Turnout	Lib Dem	Steve Jarvis	9,247	18.8	
69.14%	Others		4,275	8.7	

Brentwood & Ongar

CONSERVATIVE HOLD	PARTY	2010 CANDIDATE	2010 VOTES	2010 % VOTE	PPC FOR 2015
Majority	Conservative	Eric Pickles MP	28,792	56.9	Eric Pickles MP
16,920	Lib Dem	David Kendall	11,872	23.5	
Turnout	Labour	Heidi Benzing	4,992	9.9	Liam Preston
72.99%	Others		4,935	9.8	

Broadland

CONSERVATIVE WIN (NEW SEAT)	PARTY	2010 CANDIDATE	2010 VOTES	2010 % VOTE	PPC FOR 2015
Majority	Conservative	Keith Simpson MP	24,338	46.2	Keith Simpson MP
7,292	Lib Dem	Daniel Roper	17,046	32.4	
Turnout	Labour	Allyson Barron	7,287	13.8	Chris Jones
72.71%	Others		4,005	7.6	

Broxbourne

CONSERVATIVE HOLD	PARTY	2010 CANDIDATE	2010 VOTES	2010 % VOTE	PPC FOR 2015
Majority	Conservative	Charles Walker MP	26,844	58.8	Charles Walker MP
18,804	Labour	Michael Watson	8,040	17.6	
Turnout	Lib Dem	Allan Witherick	6,107	13.4	
63.95%	Others		4,667	10.2	

Bury St Edmunds

CONSERVATIVE HOLD	PARTY	2010 CANDIDATE	2010 VOTES	2010 % VOTE	PPC FOR 2015
Majority	Conservative	David Ruffley MP	27,899	47.5	n/s
12,380	Lib Dem	David Chappell	15,519	26.4	
Turnout	Labour	Kevin Hind	9,776	16.6	William Edwards
69.31%	Others		5,524	9.4	

Cambridge

LIB DEM HOLD	PARTY	2010 CANDIDATE	2010 VOTES	2010 % VOTE	PPC FOR 2015
Majority	Lib Dem	Julian Huppert	19,621	39.1	Julian Huppert MP
6,792	Conservative	Nick Hillman	12,829	25.6	Chamali Fernando
Turnout	Labour	Daniel Zeichner	12,174	24.3	Daniel Zeichner
67.11%	Others		5,506	11.0	

Majority 6792 (14.9%)

Located in the heart of Cambridgeshire, this is a vibrant and affluent part of the world. While the constituency will always be best known for its world-leading university, the area is also an important retail centre for the whole of Cambridgeshire and the base of many high-paying jobs in the technology and life sciences sector. Held by the Conservatives for much of its existence, the constituency was gained by the Labour Party in 1992 before being captured by the Liberal Democrats in 2005 after many years of domination. Represented since 2010 by Julian Huppert, the Liberal Democrats have lost significant ground here to Labour on a local government level, losing seven seats at the 2014 local elections. The Conservatives are fielding Chandila Fernando while the Labour candidate will be Daniel Zeichner. UKIP Member of the European Parliament Patrick O'Flynn will also contest the seat.

North East Cambridgeshire

CONSERVATIVE HOLD	PARTY	2010 CANDIDATE	2010 VOTES	2010 % VOTE	PPC FOR 2015
Majority	Conservative	Steve Barclay	26,862	51.6	Steve Barclay MP
16,425	Lib Dem	Lorna Spenceley	10,437	20.0	
Turnout	Labour	Peter Roberts	9,274	17.8	Ken Rustidge
71.10%	Others		5,491	10.5	

North West Cambridgeshire

CONSERVATIVE HOLD	PARTY	2010 CANDIDATE	2010 VOTES	2010 % VOTE	PPC FOR 2015
Majority	Conservative	Shailesh Vara MP	29,425	50.5	Shailesh Vara MP
16,677	Lib Dem	Kevin Wilkins	12,748	21.9	Chris Gudgin
Turnout	Labour	Chris York	9,877	16.9	
65.60%	Others		6,233	10.7	

South Cambridgeshire

CONSERVATIVE HOLD	PARTY	2010 CANDIDATE	2010 VOTES	2010 % VOTE	PPC FOR 2015
Majority	Conservative	Andrew Lansley MP	27,995	47.4	Andrew Lansley MP
7,838	Lib Dem	Sebastian Kindersley	20,157	34.1	Sebastian Kindersley
Turnout	Labour	Tariq Sadiq	6,024	10.2	Sue Birtles
74.76%	Others		4,880	8.3	

South East Cambridgeshire

CONSERVATIVE HOLD	PARTY	2010 CANDIDATE	2010 VOTES	2010 % VOTE	PPC FOR 2015
Majority	Conservative	Jim Paice MP	27,629	48.0	Lucy Frazer
5,946	Lib Dem	Jonathan Chatfield	21,683	37.6	Jonathan Chatfield
Turnout	Labour	John Cowan	4,380	7.6	Huw Jones
69.34%	Others		3,910	6.8	

Castle Point

CONSERVATIVE GAIN FROM INDEPENDENT	PARTY	2010 CANDIDATE	2010 VOTES	2010 % VOTE	PPC FOR 2015
Majority	Conservative	Rebecca Harris	19,806	44.0	Rebecca Harris MP
7,632	Independent	Bob Spink MP	12,174	27.0	n/a
Turnout	Labour	Julian Ware-Lane	6,609	14.7	Joe Cooke
66.92%	Others		6,437	14.3	

Chelmsford

CONSERVATIVE WIN (NEW SEAT)	PARTY	2010 CANDIDATE	2010 VOTES	2010 % VOTE	PPC FOR 2015
Majority	Conservative	Simon Burns MP	25,207	46.2	Simon Burns MP
5,110	Lib Dem	Stephen Robinson	20,097	36.8	
Turnout	Labour	Peter Dixon	5,980	11.0	Chris Vince
70.42%	Others		3,309	6.1	

Clacton

CONSERVATIVE WIN (NEW SEAT)	PARTY	2010 CANDIDATE	2010 VOTES	2010 % VOTE	PPC FOR 2015
Majority	Conservative	Douglas Carswell MP	22,867	53.0	
12,068	Labour	Ivan Henderson	10,799	25.0	Tim Young
Turnout	Lib Dem	Michael Green	5,577	12.9	
64.18%	Others		3,880	9.0	

Colchester

LIB DEM HOLD	PARTY	2010 CANDIDATE	2010 VOTES	2010 % VOTE	PPC FOR 2015
Majority	Lib Dem	Bob Russell MP	22,151	48.0	Bob Russell MP
6,982	Conservative	William Quince	15,169	32.9	William Quince
Turnout	Labour	Jordan Newell	5,680	12.3	Jordan Newell
62.30%	Others		3,139	6.8	

Epping Forest

CONSERVATIVE HOLD	PARTY	2010 CANDIDATE	2010 VOTES	2010 % VOTE	PPC FOR 2015
Majority	Conservative	Eleanor Laing MP	25,148	54.0	Eleanor Laing MP
15,131	Lib Dem	Ann Haigh	10,017	21.5	
Turnout	Labour	Katie Curtis	6,641	14.3	
64.53%	Others		4,778	10.3	

Great Yarmouth

CONSERVATIVE GAIN FROM LABOUR	PARTY	2010 CANDIDATE	2010 VOTES	2010 % VOTE	PPC FOR 2015
Majority	Conservative	Brandon Lewis	18,571	43.1	Brandon Lewis MP
4,276	Labour	Tony Wright MP	14,295	33.2	Lara Norris
Turnout	Lib Dem	Simon Partridge	6,188	14.4	
61.23%	Others		4,003	9.3	

Majority 4276 (9.9%)

Located 20 miles east of Norwich on the Norfolk coast, Great Yarmouth has a long history as a tourist destination and fishing port. Yarmouth's tourist sector, much like the town's once thriving fishing industry, has now seen better days yet still provides a considerable number of jobs locally. The decline of the town's traditional industries and highly seasonal nature of many jobs has resulted in one of the country's highest unemployment rates outside of northern England. Social problems are particularly acute in Yarmouth town particularly in the Nelson, Central and Northgate areas which rank amongst the poorest wards in England. Labour performs strongest in Yarmouth itself while the Conservatives lead by wide margins in the rural Norfolk countryside west of the town. Gained in 2010 by Conservative Brandon Lewis, who now serves as a Minister of State in the Department for Communities and Local Government, the Labour candidate will be Lara Norris. The UK Independence Party, who easily won the seat at the 2014 European elections, have stated their intention to target the constituency.

Harlow

CONSERVATIVE GAIN FROM LABOUR	PARTY	2010 CANDIDATE	2010 VOTES	2010 % VOTE	PPC FOR 2015
Majority	Conservative	Robert Halfon	19,691	44.9	Robert Halfon MP
4,925	Labour	Bill Rammell MP	14,766	33.7	Suzy Stride
Turnout	Lib Dem	Richard Bull	5,990	13.7	
64.92%	Others		3,431	7.8	

Majority 4925 (11.2%)

An Essex marginal captured by Jerry Hayes at the height of the 1983 Tory landslide and lost to Labour in 1997, Conservative Robert Halfon took the seat back for the Conservatives with a majority of close to 5,000 at the 2010 general election. A new town with high-speed rail links to London which grew rapidly in the post-war years, Harlow Town would not win any prizes for its aesthetic beauty. Despite a third of local residents living in local authority housing, Conservative support in the town and its surrounding villages is strong. The Conservatives underperformed here at the 2014 European elections with only 28 per cent of the vote as compared to 34 per cent and 33 per cent for UKIP and Labour respectively. The Conservative incumbent Halfon will be challenged by Labour's Suzy Stride.

Harwich & North Essex

CONSERVATIVE WIN (NEW SEAT)	PARTY	2010 CANDIDATE	2010 VOTES	2010 % VOTE	PPC FOR 2015
Majority	Conservative	Bernard Jenkin MP	23,001	46.9	Bernard Jenkin MP
11,447	Lib Dem	James Raven	11,554	23.6	
Turnout	Labour	Darren Barrenger	9,774	19.9	Edward Carlsson Brown
69.26%	Others		4,671	9.5	

Hemel Hempstead

CONSERVATIVE HOLD	PARTY	2010 CANDIDATE	2010 VOTES	2010 % VOTE	PPC FOR 2015
Majority	Conservative	Michael Penning MP	24,721	50.0	Michael Penning MP
13,406	Lib Dem	Richard Grayson	11,315	22.9	
Turnout	Labour	Ayfer Orhan	10,295	20.8	Tony Breslin
68.00%	Others		3,140	6.3	

Hertford & Stortford

CONSERVATIVE HOLD	PARTY	2010 CANDIDATE	2010 VOTES	2010 % VOTE	PPC FOR 2015
Majority	Conservative	Mark Prisk MP	29,810	53.8	Mark Prisk MP
15,437	Lib Dem	Andrew Lewin	14,373	26.0	
Turnout	Labour	Steve Terry	7,620	13.8	Katherine Chibah
70.58%	Others		3,574	6.5	

North East Hertfordshire

CONSERVATIVE HOLD	PARTY	2010 CANDIDATE	2010 VOTES	2010 % VOTE	PPC FOR 2015
Majority	Conservative	Oliver Heald MP	26,995	53.5	Oliver Heald MP
15,194	Lib Dem	Hugh Annand	11,801	23.4	
Turnout	Labour	David Kirkman	8,291	16.4	
69.84%	Others		3,338	6.6	

South West Hertfordshire

CONSERVATIVE HOLD	PARTY	2010 CANDIDATE	2010 VOTES	2010 % VOTE	PPC FOR 2015
Majority	Conservative	David Gauke MP	30,773	54.2	David Gauke MP
14,920	Lib Dem	Christopher Townsend	15,853	27.9	
Turnout	Labour	Harry Mann	6,526	11.5	Simon Diggins
72.53%	Others		3,598	6.3	Mark Anderson (UKIP)

Hertsmere

CONSERVATIVE HOLD	PARTY	2010 CANDIDATE	2010 VOTES	2010 % VOTE	PPC FOR 2015
Majority	Conservative	James Clappison MP	26,476	56.0	n/s
17,605	Labour	Sam Russell	8,871	18.8	Richard Butler
Turnout	Lib Dem	Anthony Rowlands	8,210	17.4	
64.70%	Others		3,713	7.9	

Hitchin & Harpenden

CONSERVATIVE HOLD	PARTY	2010 CANDIDATE	2010 VOTES	2010 % VOTE	PPC FOR 2015
Majority	Conservative	Peter Lilley MP	29,869	54.6	Peter Lilley MP
15,271	Lib Dem	Nigel Quinton	14,598	26.7	
Turnout	Labour	Oliver de Botton	7,413	13.6	Rachel Burgin
74.08%	Others		2,827	5.2	

Huntingdon

CONSERVATIVE HOLD	PARTY	2010 CANDIDATE	2010 VOTES	2010 % VOTE	PPC FOR 2015
Majority	Conservative	Jonathan Djanogly MP	26,516	48.9	Jonathan Djanogly MP
10,819	Lib Dem	Martin Land	15,697	28.9	
Turnout	Labour	Anthea Cox	5,982	11.0	Nik Johnson
64.94%	Others		6,071	11.2	

Ipswich

CONSERVATIVE GAIN FROM LABOUR	PARTY	2010 CANDIDATE	2010 VOTES	2010 % VOTE	PPC FOR 2015
Majority	Conservative	Ben Gummer	18,371	39.1	Ben Gummer MP
2,079	Labour	Chris Mole MP	16,292	34.7	David Ellesmere
Turnout	Lib Dem	Mark Dyson	8,556	18.2	
61.95%	Others		3,722	7.9	

Majority 2079 (4.4%)

With more than 120,000 residents, Ipswich is easily the largest town in Suffolk. Traditionally a Labour seat but for short spells in 1970 and 1987, Ipswich is home to a working port and strong industrial sector. In common with much of the rest of eastern England, Labour's support here collapsed in 2010 with Conservative Ben Gummer seizing the seat on an 8.1 per cent swing. Labour's support is concentrated on around the tough Gainsborough and Priory Heath areas in the south of the city, both of which contain the bulk of the constituency's substantial social housing stock. While the majority of the town's upscale residential areas are found in the neighbouring Suffolk Central and Ipswich North constituency, the Bixley ward provides the party with near slavish loyalty. Labour outpaced the Conservatives in the 2014 local elections by a 38 per cent to 27 per cent margin — a positive sign for Labour's candidate, Ipswich council leader David Ellesmere.

Luton North

LABOUR HOLD	PARTY	2010 CANDIDATE	2010 VOTES	2010 % VOTE	PPC FOR 2015
Majority	Labour	Kelvin Hopkins MP	21,192	49.3	Kelvin Hopkins MP
7,520	Conservative	Jeremy Brier	13,672	31.8	
Turnout	Lib Dem	Rabi Martins	4,784	11.1	
65.53%	Others		3,370	7.8	

Luton South

LABOUR HOLD	PARTY	2010 CANDIDATE	2010 VOTES	2010 % VOTE	PPC FOR 2015
Majority	Labour	Gavin Shuker	14,725	34.9	Gavin Shuker MP
2,329	Conservative	Nigel Huddleston	12,396	29.4	
Turnout	Lib Dem	Qurban Hussain	9,567	22.7	
64.73%	Others		5,528	13.1	

Maldon

CONSERVATIVE WIN (NEW SEAT)	PARTY	2010 CANDIDATE	2010 VOTES	2010 % VOTE	PPC FOR 2015
Majority	Conservative	John Whittingdale MP	28,661	59.8	John Whittingdale MP
19,407	Lib Dem	Elfreda Tealby-Watson	9,254	19.3	
Turnout	Labour	Swatantra Nandanwar	6,070	12.7	
69.64%	Others		3,910	8.2	

Mid Norfolk

CONSERVATIVE HOLD	PARTY	2010 CANDIDATE	2010 VOTES	2010 % VOTE	PPC FOR 2015
Majority	Conservative	George Freeman	25,123	49.5	George Freeman MP
13,856	Lib Dem	David Newman	11,267	22.2	
Turnout	Labour	Elizabeth Hughes	8,857	17.4	Harry Clarke
68.36%	Others		5,518	10.9	

North Norfolk

LIB DEM HOLD	PARTY	2010 CANDIDATE	2010 VOTES	2010 % VOTE	PPC FOR 2015
Majority	Lib Dem	Norman Lamb MP	27,554	55.5	Norman Lamb MP
11,626	Conservative	Trevor Ivory	15,928	32.1	Ann Steward
Turnout	Labour	Phil Harris	2,896	5.8	Denise Burke
73.19%	Others		3,283	6.6	

North West Norfolk

CONSERVATIVE HOLD	PARTY	2010 CANDIDATE	2010 VOTES	2010 % VOTE	PPC FOR 2015
Majority	Conservative	Henry Bellingham MP	25,916	54.2	Henry Bellingham MP
14,810	Lib Dem	William Summers	11,106	23.2	
Turnout	Labour	Manish Sood	6,353	13.3	Joanne Rust
65.39%	Others		4,425	9.3	

South Norfolk

CONSERVATIVE HOLD	PARTY	2010 CANDIDATE	2010 VOTES	2010 % VOTE	PPC FOR 2015
Majority	Conservative	Richard Bacon MP	27,133	49.3	Richard Bacon MP
10,940	Lib Dem	Jacky Howe	16,193	29.4	Jacky Howe
Turnout	Labour	Michael Castle	7,252	13.2	Deborah Sacks
72.19%	Others		4,415	8.0	

South West Norfolk

CONSERVATIVE HOLD	PARTY	2010 CANDIDATE	2010 VOTES	2010 % VOTE	PPC FOR 2015
Majority	Conservative	Liz Truss	23,753	48.3	Liz Truss MP
13,140	Lib Dem	Stephen Gordon	10,613	21.6	
Turnout	Labour	Peter Smith	9,119	18.6	Peter Smith
66.64%	Others		5,665	11.5	

Norwich North

CONSERVATIVE HOLD	PARTY	2010 CANDIDATE	2010 VOTES	2010 % VOTE	PPC FOR 2015
Majority	Conservative	Chloe Smith MP	17,280	40.6	Chloe Smith MP
3,901	Labour	John Cook	13,379	31.4	Jessica Asato
Turnout	Lib Dem	David Stephen	7,783	18.3	James Wright
65.68%	Others		4,131	9.7	

Majority 3901 (9.2%)

While the name of the seat would suggest that it contains the north of the city of Norwich itself, the Norwich North constituency is largely suburban and rural in nature. An interesting mix of wealthy suburbs, council estates and Norfolk farmland, no party is safe here. Support for the Labour Party is strongest in south of the constituency towards Norwich while the Conservatives perform robustly in the pleasant suburbs of Hellesdon and Sprowston, both located in the Broadland District Council area. Unlike neighbouring Norwich South where almost a quarter of residents are full-time students, the student community here is tiny. Held by former Treasury and Cabinet Office Minister Chloe Smith since a 2009 by-election, the Labour candidate will be former Tessa Jowell special advisor Jessica Asato.

Norwich South

LIB DEM GAIN FROM LABOUR	PARTY	2010 CANDIDATE	2010 VOTES	2010 % VOTE	PPC FOR 2015
Majority	Lib Dem	Simon Wright	13,960	29.4	Simon Wright MP
310	Labour	Charles Clarke MP	13,650	28.7	Clive Lewis
Turnout	Conservative	Antony Little	10,902	22.9	
64.56%	Others		9,039	19.0	

Majority 310 (0.7%)

Comprised of the bulk of urban Norwich, Liberal Democrat Simon Wright took this seat from former Labour Home Secretary Charles Clarke at the 2010 general election. Formerly the safest Labour seat in Norfolk, much of the seat's economic activity revolves around the University of East Anglia, whose student population flocked to the Lib Dems in 2005 and 2010 following the introduction of top-up fees and the war in Iraq. Apart from the student population, there are real pockets of deprivation here with large, Labour-supporting council estates at Lakenham and West Earlham. Following years of success at a local government level, the Liberal Democrats appear to have lost their centre-left cache to the Green Party who hold fifteen seats on Norwich City Council to their three and Labour's twenty-one. Polling conducted by Lord Ashcroft in June 2014 found the Liberal Democrats to be in an extremely vulnerable position with the party polling only 12 per cent of the vote as compared to Labour on 33 per cent, the Greens on 20 per cent and Conservatives on 18 per cent. This is the Green Party's top national target seat. Labour's candidate will be Clive Lewis.

Peterborough

CONSERVATIVE HOLD	PARTY	2010 CANDIDATE	2010 VOTES	2010 % VOTE	PPC FOR 2015
Majority	Conservative	Stewart Jackson MP	18,133	40.4	Stewart Jackson MP
4,861	Labour	Ed Murphy	13,272	29.5	Lisa Forbes
Turnout	Lib Dem	Nick Sandford	8,816	19.6	
63.93%	Others		4,706	10.5	

Majority 4861 (10.8%)

Located just forty-five minutes by train from central London, Peterborough's status as a commuter hub has increased markedly in recent years with new housing estates rapidly springing up around the town. Unusually for a constituency in the East of England, Peterborough has a large ethnic minority population of 16.4 per cent. The Conservatives lost control of the local council in May 2014, yet continue to hold the upper hand locally, holding twenty-eight seats to Labour's twelve. UKIP topped the poll here at the 2014 European elections, gaining a number of council seats at the same time. Conservative Stewart Jackson gained this seat from controversial former Labour MP Helen Brinton in 2005. He will face opposition from Labour's Lisa Forbes in 2015.

Rayleigh & Wickford

CONSERVATIVE HOLD	PARTY	2010 CANDIDATE	2010 VOTES	2010 % VOTE	PPC FOR 2015
Majority	Conservative	Mark Francois MP	30,257	57.8	Mark Francois MP
22,338	Lib Dem	Susan Gaszczak	7,919	15.1	
Turnout	Labour	Mike Le-Surf	7,577	14.5	
69.18%	Others		6,590	12.6	

Rochford & Southend East

CONSERVATIVE HOLD	PARTY	2010 CANDIDATE	2010 VOTES	2010 % VOTE	PPC FOR 2015
Majority	Conservative	James Duddridge MP	19,509	46.9	James Duddridge MP
11,050	Labour	Kevin Bonavia	8,459	20.3	Ian Gilbert
Turnout	Lib Dem	Graham Longley	8,084	19.4	
58.25%	Others		5,579	13.4	

Saffron Walden

CONSERVATIVE HOLD	PARTY	2010 CANDIDATE	2010 VOTES	2010 % VOTE	PPC FOR 2015
Majority	Conservative	Alan Haselhurst MP	30,155	55.5	Alan Haselhurst MP
15,242	Lib Dem	Peter Wilcock	14,913	27.4	Mike Hibbs
Turnout	Labour	Barbara Light	5,288	9.7	Jane Berney
71.51%	Others		4,013	7.4	

Southend West

CONSERVATIVE HOLD	PARTY	2010 CANDIDATE	2010 VOTES	2010 % VOTE	PPC FOR 2015
Majority	Conservative	David Amess MP	20,086	46.1	David Amess MP
7,270	Lib Dem	Peter Welch	12,816	29.4	
Turnout	Labour	Thomas Flynn	5,850	13.4	
65.16%	Others		4,854	11.1	

St Albans

CONSERVATIVE HOLD	PARTY	2010 CANDIDATE	2010 VOTES	2010 % VOTE	PPC FOR 2015
Majority	Conservative	Anne Main MP	21,533	40.8	Anne Main MP
2,305	Lib Dem	Sandy Walkington	19,228	36.4	Sandy Walkington
Turnout	Labour	Roma Mills	9,288	17.6	Kerry Pollard
75.42%	Others		2,786	5.3	

Majority 2305 (4%)

Located just north of London, St Albans is solidly middle-class commuter territory. Held by Labour from 1997 to 2005, the seat has transformed into a closely fought battleground between the Conservatives and Liberal Democrats, who were 2,305 votes short of victory in 2010. Aside from being a base for commuters, St Albans itself is a bustling business centre with significant local employment found in the financial services and legal sectors. The Conservatives led comfortably here in the 2014 local elections, outpacing the Liberal Democrats by a 36.5 per cent to 23.6 per cent margin with Labour not far behind on 19.6 per cent. While the Liberal Democrats remain strongly competitive here on a local government level, they have lost considerable ground in recent election cycles. The sitting Conservative MP Anne Main will face a challenge from Liberal Democrat Sandy Walkington, who first fought the seat for his party back in 1983.

Stevenage

CONSERVATIVE GAIN FROM LABOUR	PARTY	2010 CANDIDATE	2010 VOTES	2010 % VOTE	PPC FOR 2015
Majority	Conservative	Stephen MacPartland	18,491	41.4	Stephen MacPartland MP
3,578	Labour	Sharon Taylor	14,913	33.4	Sharon Taylor
Turnout	Lib Dem	Julia Davies	7,432	16.6	
64.77%	Others		3,815	8.5	

Majority 3578 (8%)

The first place to be officially designated a 'new town' following the Second World War, Stevenage handed Labour an almost 12,000 vote majority at the 1997 general election before returning Conservative Stephen McPartland in 2010. Home to around 80,000 residents, the town of Stevenage is the largest constituent part of this seat. With almost a third of residents living in social housing, the constituency suffers from considerable social problems with one of the highest teenage pregnancy and family breakdown rates in Europe. While Labour holds a tight grip on Stevenage town, the Conservatives enjoy a similarly dominant position in the rural east Hertfordshire portions of the seat. The Conservatives continued their historically poor local government performances here in 2014, with Labour now holding thirty-three councillors to three apiece for the Conservatives and Liberal Democrats. McPartland's Labour challenger will be Stevenage council leader Sharon Taylor.

Central Suffolk & North Ipswich

CONSERVATIVE HOLD	PARTY	2010 CANDIDATE	2010 VOTES	2010 % VOTE	PPC FOR 2015
Majority	Conservative	Daniel Poulter	27,125	50.8	Daniel Poulter MP
13,786	Lib Dem	Andrew Aalders-Dunthorne	13,339	25.0	
Turnout	Labour	Bhavna Joshi	8,636	16.2	Jack Abbott
70.49%	Others		4,320	8.1	

Suffolk Coastal

CONSERVATIVE HOLD	PARTY	2010 CANDIDATE	2010 VOTES	2010 % VOTE	PPC FOR 2015
Majority	Conservative	Therese Coffey	25,475	46.4	Therese Coffey MP
9,128	Lib Dem	Daisy Cooper	16,347	29.8	James Sandbach
Turnout	Labour	Adam Leeder	8,812	16.1	Russell Whiting
71.69%	Others		4,259	7.8	

South Suffolk

CONSERVATIVE HOLD	PARTY	2010 CANDIDATE	2010 VOTES	2010 % VOTE	PPC FOR 2015
Majority	Conservative	Tim Yeo MP	24,550	47.7	James Cartlidge
8,689	Lib Dem	Nigel Bennett	15,861	30.8	Grace Weaver
Turnout	Labour	Emma Bishton	7,368	14.3	Jane Basham
70.92%	Others		3,637	7.1	

West Suffolk

CONSERVATIVE HOLD	PARTY	2010 CANDIDATE	2010 VOTES	2010 % VOTE	PPC FOR 2015
Majority	Conservative	Matthew Hancock	24,312	50.6	Matthew Hancock MP
13,050	Lib Dem	Belinda Brooks-Gordon	11,262	23.4	
Turnout	Labour	Abul Monsur Ohid Ahmed	7,089	14.7	Michael Jeffreys
64.66%	Others		5,426	11.3	

Thurrock

CONSERVATIVE GAIN FROM LABOUR	PARTY	2010 CANDIDATE	2010 VOTES	2010 % VOTE	PPC FOR 2015
Majority	Conservative	Jackie Doyle-Price	16,869	36.8	Jackie Doyle-Price MP
92	Labour	Carl Morris	16,777	36.6	Polly Billington
Turnout	Lib Dem	Carys Davis	4,901	10.7	
58.93%	Others		7,274	15.9	Tim Aker MEP (UKIP)

Majority 92 (0.2%)

A bastion of the white working class, the Thames Gateway town of Thurrock abandoned its Labour roots at the 2010 election and handed Conservative Jackie Doyle-Price a narrow majority of only ninety-two votes. Traditionally speaking, the majority of the pebble-dashed towns of Thurrock and nearby Grays are loyal to Labour with the Conservatives strongest in Ockendon, Aveley and Uplands. Local politics has, however, been rather upended by the growth of the UK Independence Party. UKIP have proved to be a plague on both Conservative and Labour houses, topping the poll at the 2014 European election and seizing equal numbers of council seats from both parties that year. Polling conducted by Lord Ashcroft in June 2014 showed UKIP leading the field locally with a 36 per cent voting intention with Labour and the Conservatives back in 30 per cent and 28 per cent respectively. The UKIP candidate will be Tim Aker, a newly elected Member of the European Parliament while Labour will field former Ed Miliband advisor Polly Billington.

Watford

CONSERVATIVE GAIN FROM LABOUR	PARTY	2010 CANDIDATE	2010 VOTES	2010 % VOTE	PPC FOR 2015
Majority	Conservative	Richard Harrington	19,291	34.9	Richard Harrington MP
1,425	Lib Dem	Sal Brinton	17,866	32.4	
Turnout	Labour	Claire Ward MP	14,750	26.7	Matthew Turmaine
68.33%	Others		3,301	6.0	

Majority 1425 (3%)

One of the very few genuine three-way marginals in the United Kingdom, Conservative incumbent Richard Harrington surprised many by coming from third place to take this seat from Labour at the 2010 general election. In total, only 1,425 votes separated Harrington and the third-placed Lib Dem candidate. Located on the Hertfordshire border just north of London, Watford is home to many commuters who make the fifteen-minute train journey to Euston station each day. As a result of its excellent transport links, the town has come into its own in recent years as an important base for the service and distribution sector. The 2014 European election results put Labour ahead with 26 per cent of the vote to UKIP's 24 per cent and the Conservative Party's 21 per cent while, at the same time, directly elected Liberal Democrat Mayor Dorothy Thornhill was re-elected with 46 per cent of first-preference votes. A voting intention poll carried out by Lord Ashcroft in June 2010 showed the Conservatives narrowly ahead with 29 per cent of the vote to 25 per cent for Labour and 24 per cent for the Lib Dems. Given the schizophrenic state of local politics, only one thing is for sure: 2015 will be another close contest.

Waveney

CONSERVATIVE GAIN FROM LABOUR	PARTY	2010 CANDIDATE	2010 VOTES	2010 % VOTE	PPC FOR 2015
Majority	Conservative	Peter Aldous	20,571	40.2	Peter Aldous MP
769	Labour	Bob Blizzard MP	19,802	38.7	Bob Blizzard
Turnout	Lib Dem	Alan Dean	6,811	13.3	
65.12%	Others		3,957	7.7	Simon Tobin (UKIP)

Majority 769 (1.5%)

Best known as the home to the seaside town of Lowesoft, the Waveney constituency has been held by Conservative surveyor Peter Aldous since the 2010 general election. Located in north Suffolk on the edge of the Broads National Park, Lowesoft has seen better days. Its once bustling tourist trade has all but disappeared and the area has been plagued by job losses since Shell's decision to cease its local oil and gas operations in 2003. Predictably, Lowesoft provides the base of Labour support locally, delivering the party landslide margins in the town's Harbour and Normanston wards while the Conservatives are strongest in the villages of Carlton and Worlingham. Aldous will face a re-run of the 2010 contest, with former Labour MP Bob Blizzard hoping for a return to office.

Welwyn Hatfield

CONSERVATIVE HOLD	PARTY	2010 CANDIDATE	2010 VOTES	2010 % VOTE	PPC FOR 2015
Majority	Conservative	Grant Shapps MP	27,894	57.0	Grant Shapps MP
17,423	Labour	Mike Hobday	10,471	21.4	Anawar Miah
Turnout	Lib Dem	Paul Zukowskyj	8,010	16.4	
67.96%	Others		2,597	5.3	

Witham

CONSERVATIVE WIN (NEW SEAT)	PARTY	2010 CANDIDATE	2010 VOTES	2010 % VOTE	PPC FOR 2015
Majority	Conservative	Priti Patel	24,448	52.2	Priti Patel MP
15,196	Lib Dem	Margaret Phelps	9,252	19.8	
Turnout	Labour	John Spademan	8,656	18.5	
69.94%	Others		4,479	9.6	

East Midlands

Although one of the smaller regions – it only has five members of the European Parliament, for example – the East Midlands of England is a critical marginal battleground to decide the leading party in the Westminster Parliament. In 2010, it was a disaster area for Labour, as they lost a dozen seats, which swung the representation round to a Conservative lead of thirty-one MPs to fifteen in the region. As this may imply, there are now many constituencies on Labour's target list that they have to regain in 2015 in order to win the general election, though the Conservatives have a shorter but equally vital selection of targets that would go a long way to ensuring that this time they will have an overall majority.

National opinion polling evidence and local elections in 2014 suggested that Labour have a decent chance in a number of the constituencies they lost last time. They have already taken one seat back, in the Corby by-election in November 2012 caused by the departure of Louise Mensch to spend more time with her family in New York. Phil Sawford, son of the former Labour MP for Kettering, won with a healthy majority of nearly 8,000 and must be the favourite to hold on, having had the benefits of incumbency.

Labour's easiest target mathematically is Sherwood in Nottinghamshire (Tory majority only 214 in 2010), but it may not actually be the easiest to regain. There have been long-term social changes here. When this division was first created in 1983, it was regarded as a mining seat, based on the Dukeries coalfield sunk in the 1920s beneath the remnants of Robin Hood's forest, and its pits saw some of the fiercest battles between striking and non-striking miners in the coal dispute shortly afterwards. However, the closure of the last of the mines, Thoresby Colliery near Edwinstowe, was announced in 2014. Apart from 1997, Sherwood has never looked like a safe Labour seat, and it would not be astonishing if first-term Conservative MP Andrew Spencer won again in 2015, as Andrew Stewart did in 1983 and 1987.

Council elections suggest that Labour may have a better chance of gains in several other seats they lost in 2010. In Broxtowe (Nottingham's western suburbs), there is an interesting re-match between the much respected former Labour MP Nick Palmer and the first-term incumbent Anna Soubry, who has also made a strong impression as both ministerial material and independent-minded (an unusual mixture). Labour has also been making local gains in Derbyshire, where Amber Valley and to some extent Erewash in the south east of the county seem plausible targets, and to a lesser extent High Peak in its north-west corner and South Derbyshire, once represented by Edwina Currie.

Three other East Midlands counties witnessed Labour losses at the last general election. In the bellwether constituency of Lincoln, Labour won nine of the eleven wards of the city council in the May 2014 elections. In Northamptonshire, Labour must hope that Sally Keeble can regain Northampton North to add to the Corby by-election victory; this seat has a similar majority to Corby, but swings are almost always lower in general elections. Finally, there were two losses in Leicestershire. One, the Leicestershire NW seat, was gained by the Tories by such a large majority that it now lies beyond Labour's national list of the 100 closest targets. This was largely because of the strength of David Taylor, who had died in December 2009, leaving the seat vacant until the general election, and with his Conservative successor Andrew Bridgen also notably active, the seat would now appear out of Labour's reach. However, there will be a fascinating battle in Loughborough, where, only four years after her election, Nicky Morgan has risen to be Secretary of State for Education but still must protect a majority of only 3,744. In this case, Labour is not fielding their former MP but rather Matthew O'Callaghan, a noted promoter of regional foods such as Stilton cheese and Melton Mowbray pork pies.

The Conservatives have four realistic targets in their sights in the East Midlands, and if they hold all of their present seats and win most of these they should be on course for an overall majority. However none will be easy. First up is Derby North, where the former city council leader Chris Williamson held on by only 631 votes last time, but the picture is clouded here by it being a three-way marginal, with a large advance by the Liberal Democrats in 2010 bringing them within a couple of thousand of the other two parties. Their support may fall away in 2015, as in so many other parts of the country, but to whose benefit is a moot point. Second on the list is Gedling (if Broxtowe was Nottingham's western suburban fringe, Gedling fulfils the same role to the east; they are like a pair of ear muffs in shape) – but Labour's Vernon Coaker is regarded as a very strong candidate. Then comes Nottingham South, needing a swing of just over 2 per cent, but with the second highest proportion of students in the country. An interesting fourth and final target in the region is North East Derbyshire, which has been held easily by Labour since 1935, but where there has been long-term social change with the extirpation of coal mining and the growth of commuter suburbs to Sheffield, such as Dronfield's Gosforth valley private housing developments.

For a long time the East Midlands has been a major party battle, and with the Liberal Democrats having lost their solitary seat of Chesterfield in 2010 (it had been gained from Labour on Tony Benn's final retirement from Parliament in 2001) they do not look likely to be represented in the region in 2015. UKIP did easily top the poll in this region (as in so many others in England) in 2014, with 32 per cent of the vote compared with 25 per cent for the Conservatives and 24 per cent for Labour, but when they were presented with a chance to elect their first Westminster MP at the Newark by-election caused by Patrick Mercer's resignation the very next month, their lead Euro-candidate Roger Helmer lost by 7,400 to the Conservatives, which suggests they are unlikely to translate their success into victory – at least in the East Midlands. However, as mentioned above, both the destination of dissipating Lib Dem votes and the impact of a rising UKIP presence will significantly impact the many key Labour–Conservative marginals, and this region will once again be one to watch closely in May 2015.

Amber Valley

CONSERVATIVE GAIN FROM LABOUR	PARTY	2010 CANDIDATE	2010 VOTES	2010 % VOTE	PPC FOR 2015
Majority	Conservative	Nigel Mills	17,746	38.6	Nigel Mills MP
536	Labour	Judy Mallaber MP	17,210	37.4	Kevin Gillott
Turnout	Lib Dem	Tom Snowdon	6,636	14.4	Kate Smith
65.49%	Others		4,366	9.5	

Majority 536 (1.2%)

An ornately named constituency, Amber Valley is named after the River Amber, which runs through the centre of the constituency, taking in the former mining towns of Ripley, Heanor and Alfreton. The seat is somewhat polarised between its urban areas, which favour Labour, and vast rural tracts, whose agricultural nature and attractiveness for commuters to nearby Derby makes for a lean strongly towards the Conservatives. The constituency was gained by Conservative Nigel Mills in 2010. He will face opposition from Kevin Gillott. A poll conducted by Lord Ashcroft in June 2014 showed Labour ahead of the Conservatives by a 37 per cent to 33 per cent margin - figures that closely mirror the local election result that saw Labour take control of Amber Valley District Council with twenty-four seats to the Conservative Party's twenty-one.

Ashfield

LABOUR HOLD	PARTY	2010 CANDIDATE	2010 VOTES	2010 % VOTE	PPC FOR 2015
Majority	Labour	Gloria De Piero	16,239	33.7	Gloria De Piero MP
192	Lib Dem	Jason Zadrozny	16,047	33.3	Jason Zadrozny
Turnout	Conservative	Garry Hickton	10,698	22.2	
62.29%	Others		5,212	10.8	

Majority 192 (0%)

Located in the heart of the Nottinghamshire coalfield, Ashfield came close to causing a political earthquake at the 2010 general election when the Liberal Democrats came within 192 votes of defeating Labour's Gloria de Piero. The Ashfield constituency is located north-west of Nottingham, and the largest towns, Sutton-in-Ashfield and Kirby-in-Ashfield, were previously dominated by the coal mining sector but are now home to a number of textile and light manufacturing operations. Labour were ahead of the Liberal Democrats by a 38 per cent to 30 per cent margin at the 2013 local elections, yet were forced into second place by UKIP – who have said they will target the seat in 2015 – at the European elections. 2015 will see a re-run of the 2010 contest, with De Piero against facing Lib Dem Jason Zadrozny.

Bassetlaw

LABOUR HOLD	PARTY	2010 CANDIDATE	2010 VOTES	2010 % VOTE	PPC FOR 2015
Majority	Labour	John Mann MP	25,018	50.5	John Mann MP
8,215	Conservative	Keith Girling	16,803	33.9	
Turnout	Lib Dem	David Dobble	5,570	11.2	
64.80%	Others		2,186	4.4	

Bolsover

LABOUR HOLD	PARTY	2010 CANDIDATE	2010 VOTES	2010 % VOTE	PPC FOR 2015
Majority	Labour	Dennis Skinner MP	21,994	50.0	Dennis Skinner MP
11,182	Conservative	Lee Rowley	10,812	24.6	
Turnout	Lib Dem	Denise Hawksworth	6,821	15.5	
60.45%	Others		4,361	9.9	

Boston & Skegness

CONSERVATIVE HOLD	PARTY	2010 CANDIDATE	2010 VOTES	2010 % VOTE	PPC FOR 2015
Majority	Conservative	Mark Simmonds MP	21,325	49.4	n/s
12,426	Labour	Paul Kenny	8,899	20.6	
Turnout	Lib Dem	Philip Smith	6,371	14.8	
64.19%	Others		6,530	15.1	

Bosworth

CONSERVATIVE HOLD	PARTY	2010 CANDIDATE	2010 VOTES	2010 % VOTE	PPC FOR 2015
Majority	Conservative	David Tredinnick MP	23,132	42.6	David Tredinnick MP
5,032	Lib Dem	Michael Mullaney	18,100	33.3	Michael Mullaney
Turnout	Labour	Rory Palmer	8,674	16.0	Chris Kealey
70.22%	Others		4,368	8.0	

Broxtowe

CONSERVATIVE GAIN FROM LABOUR	PARTY	2010 CANDIDATE	2010 VOTES	2010 % VOTE	PPC FOR 2015
Majority	Conservative	Anna Soubry	20,585	39.0	Anna Soubry MP
389	Labour	Nick Palmer MP	20,196	38.3	Nick Palmer
Turnout	Lib Dem	David Watts	8,907	16.9	
73.19%	Others		3,039	5.8	

Majority 389 (0.7%)

Located in Nottingham's western suburbs close to the border with Derbyshire, the Broxtowe constituency was narrowly won by now-Defence Minister Anna Soubry at the 2010 general election. With around 20,000 residents apiece, the two largest towns here are Beeston and Stapleford — both of which are largely populated by professional and managerial workers. The constituency is generally suburban in nature, although patches of Conservative-inclined rural territory are found towards the north of the constituency. Aside from commuters to nearby Nottingham, a large number of local jobs are provided by the high-tech IT software industry. More than three quarters of homes in the constituency are owner-occupied, with only one in ten residents living in social housing stock. Anna Soubry will be challenged by former Labour MP Dr Nick Palmer, who served three terms here from 1997 to 2010.

Charnwood

CONSERVATIVE HOLD	PARTY	2010 CANDIDATE	2010 VOTES	2010 % VOTE	PPC FOR 2015
Majority	Conservative	Stephen Dorrell MP	26,560	49.6	Stephen Dorrell MP
15,029	Lib Dem	Robin Webber-Jones	11,531	21.5	Eric Neal Goodyer
Turnout	Labour	Eric Goodyer	10,536	19.7	Sean Kelly-Walsh
71.89%	Others		4,915	9.2	

Chesterfield

LABOUR GAIN FROM LIB DEM	PARTY	2010 CANDIDATE	2010 VOTES	2010 % VOTE	PPC FOR 2015
Majority	Labour	Toby Perkins	17,891	39.0	Toby Perkins MP
549	Lib Dem	Paul Holmes MP	17,342	37.8	Julia Cambridge
Turnout	Conservative	Carolyn Abbott	7,214	15.7	
63.77%	Others		3,392	7.4	

Majority 549 (1%)
Located in North East Derbyshire, Chesterfield is best known as the former constituency of Labour firebrand Tony Benn. Largely urban in nature, Chesterfield is steeped in the area's coal-mining and industrial history – a factor which has given rise to the area's Labour tendencies. Following Benn's retirement in 2001, left-leaning Liberal Democrat Paul Holmes was able to capitalise on years of local government gains for his party. He was defeated by Labour's Toby Perkins in 2010. The 2014 European elections were very disappointing for the Liberal Democrats, who slumped to fourth place locally with only 9 per cent of the vote – roughly a quarter of Labour's 36.9 per cent showing. Labour won the 2014 European elections here with 37 per cent of the vote, with their former challengers the Liberal Democrats polling less than 10 per cent of the vote across the seat. The Lib Dem candidate will be Julia Cambridge.

Corby

CONSERVATIVE GAIN FROM LABOUR	PARTY	2010 CANDIDATE	2010 VOTES	2010 % VOTE
Majority	Conservative	Louise Bagshaw	22,886	42.2
1,951	Labour	Phil Hope MP	20,935	38.6
Turnout	Lib Dem	Portia Wilson	7,834	14.5
69.44%	Others		2,525	4.7

Majority 1895 (3.5%)
One of the most politically polarised seats in the United Kingdom, the Corby constituency is split down the middle between working-class Corby town and rural East Northamptonshire. Corby, a heavily industrial town whose economy was decimated by the closure of its steelworks in the 1980s, is tribally loyal to the Labour Party. Labour has controlled the Corby Borough Council outright since 1979. It is on Corby's rural fringes that the Conservatives are all-conquering, running up huge margins of victory in the East Northamptonshire market towns of Oundle, Raunds and Irthlingborough. The constituency was won for the Conservatives by author Louise Mensch (née Bagshawe), yet comfortably gained by Labour's Andy Sawford following her resignation in 2012. Her replacement as Conservative candidate will be Wellingborough Councillor Thomas Pursglove.

Corby (2012 by-election)

LABOUR RE-GAIN FROM CONSERVATIVE	PARTY	2012 CANDIDATE	2012 VOTES	2012 % VOTE	PPC FOR 2015
Majority	Labour	Andy Sawford	17,267	48.4	Andy Sawford MP
7,791	Conservative	Christine Emmett	9,476	26.6	Tom Pursglove
Turnout	UKIP	Margot Parker	5,108	14.3	
45.71%	Others		3,814	10.7	

Daventry

CONSERVATIVE HOLD	PARTY	2010 CANDIDATE	2010 VOTES	2010 % VOTE	PPC FOR 2015
Majority	Conservative	Chris Heaton-Harris	29,252	56.5	Chris Heaton-Harris MP
19,188	Lib Dem	Christopher McGlynn	10,064	19.4	
Turnout	Labour	Paul Corazzo	8,168	15.8	Abigail Campbell
72.46%	Others		4,290	8.3	

Derby North

LABOUR HOLD	PARTY	2010 CANDIDATE	2010 VOTES	2010 % VOTE	PPC FOR 2015
Majority	Labour	Chris Williamson	14,896	33.0	Chris Williamson MP
613	Conservative	Stephen Mold	14,283	31.7	Amanda Solloway
Turnout	Lib Dem	Lucy Care	12,638	28.0	Lucy Care
63.07%	Others		3,263	7.2	

Majority 613 (1.4%)

The more politically competitive of the two Derby constituencies, Labour won Derby North by just 613 votes in 2010. Labour chances of retaining the seat were boosted considerably then by boundary changes which transferred many of the constituency's safest Tory wards – namely Allestree, Oakwood and Spondon – to the rural Mid Derbyshire constituency. A socially polarised constituency, Labour's support is at its strongest in deprived inner-city areas such Mackworth and Littleover, while the Conservatives dominate in the suburban areas stretching out into the Derbyshire countryside. The manufacturing sector remains a significant employer locally with the constituency being home to Toyota, Bombardier and Rolls Royce facilities. The Liberal Democrats have traditionally had a strong base in this constituency, yet they have lost ground in recent years. Represented since 2010 by Labour MP Chris Williamson, he will face a challenge from Conservative Amanda Solloway.

Derby South

LABOUR HOLD	PARTY	2010 CANDIDATE	2010 VOTES	2010 % VOTE	PPC FOR 2015
Majority	Labour	Margaret Beckett MP	17,851	43.3	Margaret Beckett MP
6,122	Conservative	Jack Perschke	11,729	28.5	
Turnout	Lib Dem	David Batey	8,430	20.5	Joe Naitta
58.01%	Others		3,178	7.7	

Derbyshire Dales

CONSERVATIVE HOLD	PARTY	2010 CANDIDATE	2010 VOTES	2010 % VOTE	PPC FOR 2015
Majority	Conservative	Patrick McLoughlin MP	24,378	52.1	Patrick McLoughlin MP
13,866	Lib Dem	Joe Naitta	10,512	22.5	Ben Fearn
Turnout	Labour	Colin Swindell	9,061	19.4	Andy Botham
73.81%	Others		2,829	6.0	

Mid Derbyshire

CONSERVATIVE WIN (NEW SEAT)	PARTY	2010 CANDIDATE	2010 VOTES	2010 % VOTE	PPC FOR 2015
Majority	Conservative	Pauline Latham	22,877	48.3	Pauline Latham MP
11,292	Labour	Hardyal Dhindsa	11,585	24.5	Nicola Heaton
Turnout	Lib Dem	Sally McIntosh	9,711	20.5	Hilary Jones
71.65%	Others		3,169	6.7	

North East Derbyshire

LABOUR HOLD	PARTY	2010 CANDIDATE	2010 VOTES	2010 % VOTE	PPC FOR 2015
Majority	Labour	Natascha Engel MP	17,948	38.2	Natascha Engel MP
2,445	Conservative	Huw Merriman	15,503	33.0	Lee Rowley
Turnout	Lib Dem	Richard Bull	10,947	23.3	
65.88%	Others		2,636	5.6	

South Derbyshire

CONSERVATIVE GAIN FROM LABOUR	PARTY	2010 CANDIDATE	2010 VOTES	2010 % VOTE	PPC FOR 2015
Majority	Conservative	Heather Wheeler	22,935	45.5	Heather Wheeler MP
7,128	Labour	Michael Edwards	15,807	31.4	Cheryl Pidgeon
Turnout	Lib Dem	Alexis Diouf	8,012	15.9	
71.41%	Others		3,665	7.3	Alan Graves (UKIP)

Majority 7128 (14.1%)

Held for thirteen years by controversial former minister Edwina Currie, South Derbyshire was regained for the Conservatives by the altogether less bumptious Heather Wheeler in 2010. While a large portion of the constituency is rural and Conservative-inclined, the once thriving industrial town of Swadlincote and former coal-mining area of Woodville are strongly inclined towards the Labour Party. In keeping with its status as a key marginal seat, the Conservatives were ahead of Labour by a margin of 8,237 to 8,032 votes at the 2013 county council elections. The Labour candidate will be Cheryl Pidgeon.

Erewash

CONSERVATIVE GAIN FROM LABOUR	PARTY	2010 CANDIDATE	2010 VOTES	2010 % VOTE	PPC FOR 2015
Majority	Conservative	Jessica Lee	18,805	39.5	Maggie Throup
2,501	Labour	Cheryl Pidgeon	16,304	34.2	Caroline Atkinson
Turnout	Lib Dem	Martin Garnett	8,343	17.5	Steve Gee
68.40%	Others		4,190	8.8	

Majority 2501 (5.3%)

Nestled between Derby and Nottingham, Erewash is a strange name for a constituency that would be better referred to as South East Derbyshire. The seat is largely based around the towns of Ilkeston and Long Eaton which share dramatically different party political loyalties. Ilkeston, formerly the home to the Stanton Ironworks which closed for the last time in May 2007, is a Labour bastion while Long Eaton and the rural areas surrounding the two towns are considerably more Tory-friendly. The seat was gained in 2010 by Conservative barrister Jessica Lee who will be standing down after one term. The Conservatives have selected businesswoman Maggie Throup while the Labour candidate will be Catherine Atkinson.

Gainsborough

CONSERVATIVE HOLD	PARTY	2010 CANDIDATE	2010 VOTES	2010 % VOTE	PPC FOR 2015
Majority	Conservative	Edward Leigh MP	24,266	49.3	Edward Leigh MP
10,559	Lib Dem	Pat O'Connor	13,707	27.8	
Turnout	Labour	Jamie McMahon	7,701	15.6	
67.52%	Others		3,577	7.3	

Gedling

LABOUR HOLD	PARTY	2010 CANDIDATE	2010 VOTES	2010 % VOTE	PPC FOR 2015
Majority	Labour	Vernon Coaker MP	19,821	41.1	Vernon Coaker MP
1,859	Conservative	Bruce Laughton	17,962	37.3	Carolyn Abbott
Turnout	Lib Dem	Julia Bateman	7,350	15.3	
68.00%	Others		3,057	6.3	

Majority 1859 (3.9%)

Located just to the east of Nottingham, the previously safe Conservative seat of Gedling was gained from Andrew Mitchell at the 1997 general election. The constituency is generally middle-class and suburban in nature, taking in the towns of Gedling, Arnold and Carlton and substantial rural areas. The Conservatives are strongest in the semi-rural Woodthorpe and Ravenshead while Labour's strength is built around the industrial Netherfield and Colwick area. Labour's chances of holding this seat were slightly improved in 2010 by the transfer of the Conservative ward of Lambley to neighbouring Sherwood – which the Conservatives, in turn, gained. Sitting MP and shadow Defence Secretary Vernon Coaker will face a challenge from Conservative Carolyn Abbott.

Grantham & Stamford

CONSERVATIVE RE-GAIN FROM LABOUR	PARTY	2010 CANDIDATE	2010 VOTES	2010 % VOTE	PPC FOR 2015
Majority	Conservative	Nick Boles	26,552	50.3	Nick Boles MP
14,826	Lib Dem	Harrish Bisnauthsing	11,726	22.2	
Turnout	Labour	Mark Bartlett	9,503	18.0	
67.68%	Others		5,018	9.5	

Harborough

CONSERVATIVE HOLD	PARTY	2010 CANDIDATE	2010 VOTES	2010 % VOTE	PPC FOR 2015
Majority	Conservative	Edward Garnier MP	26,894	49.0	Edward Garnier MP
9,877	Lib Dem	Zuffar Haq	17,017	31.0	Zuffar Haq
Turnout	Labour	Kevin McKeever	6,981	12.7	Sundip Meghani
70.41%	Others		3,973	7.2	

High Peak

CONSERVATIVE GAIN FROM LABOUR	PARTY	2010 CANDIDATE	2010 VOTES	2010 % VOTE	PPC FOR 2015
Majority	Conservative	Andrew Bingham	20,587	40.9	Andrew Bingham MP
4,677	Labour	Caitlin Bisknell	15,910	31.6	Caitlin Bisknell
Turnout	Lib Dem	Alistair Stevens	10,993	21.8	
70.44%	Others		2,847	5.7	

Majority 4677 (9.3%)

A curiously named constituency, the High Peak constituency is formed of the bulk of the Peak District National Park. As one might expect, the seat is predominantly rural and characterised by dramatic open landscapes yet several small towns are also found within its boundaries. Labour support is generally drawn from the small towns of Buxton, New Mills, Hadfield and Glossop while the Conservatives are strongest in the Manchester commuter villages on the seat's north-west edge. While many seats close to large cities have witnessed rapid housing growth in recent years, High Peak's status as a national park will likely preserve its rural feel for decades to come. Sitting Conservative Andrew Bingham will be opposed by Labour's Caitlin Bisknell, the leader of High Peak District Council.

Kettering

CONSERVATIVE HOLD	PARTY	2010 CANDIDATE	2010 VOTES	2010 % VOTE	PPC FOR 2015
Majority	Conservative	Philip Hollobone MP	23,247	49.1	Philip Hollobone MP
9,094	Labour	Phil Sawford	14,153	29.9	Rhea Keehn
Turnout	Lib Dem	Chris Nelson	7,498	15.8	
68.77%	Others		2,430	5.1	

Leicester East

LABOUR HOLD	PARTY	2010 CANDIDATE	2010 VOTES	2010 % VOTE	PPC FOR 2015
Majority	Labour	Keith Vaz MP	25,804	53.8	Keith Vaz MP
14,082	Conservative	Jane Hunt	11,722	24.4	Kishan Devani
Turnout	Lib Dem	Ali Asghar	6,817	14.2	
65.76%	Others		3,652	7.6	

Leicester South

LABOUR HOLD	PARTY	2010 CANDIDATE	2010 VOTES	2010 % VOTE
Majority	Labour	Peter Soulsby MP	21,479	45.6
8,808	Lib Dem	Parmjit Singh Gill	12,671	26.9
Turnout	Conservative	Ross Grant	10,066	21.4
61.06%	Others		2,908	6.2

Leicester South (2011 by-election)

LABOUR HOLD	PARTY	2011 CANDIDATE	2011 VOTES	2011 % VOTE	PPC FOR 2015
Majority	Labour	Jon Ashworth	19,771	57.8	Jon Ashworth MP
12,078	Lib Dem	Zuffar Haq	7,693	22.5	
Turnout	Conservative	Jane Hunt	5,169	15.1	Leon Hadjjinikolaou
44.29%	Others		1,547	4.5	

Leicester West

LABOUR HOLD	PARTY	2010 CANDIDATE	2010 VOTES	2010 % VOTE	PPC FOR 2015
Majority	Labour	Liz Kendall	13,745	38.4	Liz Kendall MP
4,017	Conservative	Celia Harvey	9,728	27.2	Paul Bessant
Turnout	Lib Dem	Peter Coley	8,107	22.6	
55.19%	Others		4,239	11.8	

North West Leicestershire

CONSERVATIVE GAIN FROM LABOUR	PARTY	2010 CANDIDATE	2010 VOTES	2010 % VOTE	PPC FOR 2015
Majority	Conservative	Andrew Bridgen	23,147	44.6	Andrew Bridgen MP
7,511	Labour	Ross Wilmott	15,636	30.1	Jamie McMahon
Turnout	Lib Dem	Paul Reynolds	8,639	16.6	
72.95%	Others		4,530	8.7	

Majority 7511 (14.5%)

Won by local Conservative businessman Andrew Bridgen at the 2010 general election, the Leicestershire North West constituency is largely formed out of the small towns Coalville and Ashby-de-la-Zouch and the surrounding rural areas. The constituency has a rich industrial heritage, having at one time been home to an active coal-mining industry as well as substantial amounts of gravel and brick clay extraction. While many of the seat's traditional industries have long since vanished, the manufacturing sector remains vibrant and provides a considerable amount of local employment. The fast-growing East Midlands Airport is located inside the boundaries of the constituency. The Labour candidate will be Jamie McMahon.

South Leicestershire

CONSERVATIVE WIN (NEW SEAT)	PARTY	2010 CANDIDATE	2010 VOTES	2010 % VOTE	PPC FOR 2015
Majority	Conservative	Andrew Robathan MP	27,000	49.5	Andrew Robathan MP
15,524	Lib Dem	Aladdin Ayesh	11,476	21.0	
Turnout	Labour	Sally Gimson	11,392	20.9	Amanda Hack
71.22%	Others		4,709	8.6	

Lincoln

CONSERVATIVE GAIN FROM LABOUR	PARTY	2010 CANDIDATE	2010 VOTES	2010 % VOTE	PPC FOR 2015
Majority	Conservative	Karl McCartney	17,163	37.5	Karl McCartney MP
1,058	Labour	Gillian Merron MP	16,105	35.2	Lucy Rigby
Turnout	Lib Dem	Reginald Shore	9,256	20.2	David Harding-Price
62.17%	Others		3,197	7.0	

Majority 1058 (2.3%)

Situated in the centre of Lincolnshire and with a population of approaching 100,000, Conservative Karl McCartney seized Lincoln from Labour at the 2010 general election. Dominated by its enormous cathedral, the historic city is home to a mix of light industries, professional services and a growing university. Around two-thirds of the homes here are owner occupied with around a fifth of residents living in social housing. Despite the town's pleasant architecture, one should not assume this is a wealthy area: many jobs pay low wages and unemployment is above the national average. Locally, Labour's support is strongest in the Park and Boultham areas in the centre of the town while the Conservatives dominate the areas to the north, east and south of the constituency. Labour are the dominant force on Lincoln City Council, holding twenty-seven seats to the Conservative Party's six.

Loughborough

CONSERVATIVE GAIN FROM LABOUR	PARTY	2010 CANDIDATE	2010 VOTES	2010 % VOTE	PPC FOR 2015
Majority	Conservative	Nicky Morgan	21,971	41.6	Nicky Morgan MP
3,744	Labour	Andy Reed MP	18,227	34.5	Matthew O'Callaghan
Turnout	Lib Dem	Mike Willis	9,675	18.3	
68.17%	Others		2,965	5.6	

Majority 3744 (7.1%)

Located mid-way between Leicester and Nottingham in the heart of the East Midlands, Loughborough is a vibrant engineering town with significant pharmaceutical and scientific research facilities. With a university located here and 15.6 per cent of residents engaged in full-time studies, education is also a significant local employer. Loughborough town is generally loyal to the Labour Party with Garendon, Hastings and Lemyington providing the party with the basis of its support while the Conservatives dominate in the town's suburbs and rural Sileby, Quorn and Mountsorrel Castle wards. With the 2010 victor Nicky Morgan having risen quickly through the ministerial ranks to become Education Secretary, this will be one of the most closely watched contests in the country. Morgan's Labour challenger will be Matthew O'Callaghan.

Louth & Horncastle

CONSERVATIVE HOLD	PARTY	2010 CANDIDATE	2010 VOTES	2010 % VOTE	PPC FOR 2015
Majority	Conservative	Peter Tapsell MP	25,065	49.6	Victoria Atkins
13,871	Lib Dem	Fiona Martin	11,194	22.2	
Turnout	Labour	Patrick Mountain	8,760	17.3	Matthew Brown
65.03%	Others		5,475	10.8	

Mansfield

LABOUR HOLD	PARTY	2010 CANDIDATE	2010 VOTES	2010 % VOTE	PPC FOR 2015
Majority	Labour	Alan Meale MP	18,753	38.7	Alan Meale MP
6,012	Conservative	Tracy Critchlow	12,741	26.3	
Turnout	Lib Dem	Michael Wyatt	7,469	15.4	
60.44%	Others		9,432	19.5	

Newark

CONSERVATIVE HOLD	PARTY	2010 CANDIDATE	2010 VOTES	2010 % VOTE	
Majority	Conservative	Patrick Mercer MP	27,590	53.9	
16,152	Labour	Ian Campbell	11,438	22.3	
Turnout	Lib Dem	Pauline Jenkins	10,246	20.0	
71.39%	Others		1,954	3.8	

Newark (2014 by-election)

CONSERVATIVE HOLD	PARTY	2014 CANDIDATE	2014 VOTES	2014 % VOTE	PPC FOR 2015
Majority	Conservative	Robert Jenrick	17,431	45.0	Robert Jenrick MP
7,403	UKIP	Roger Helmer	10,028	25.9	
Turnout	Labour	Michael Payne	6,842	17.7	Michael Payne
53.94%	Others		4,406	11.4	

Northampton North

CONSERVATIVE GAIN FROM LABOUR	PARTY	2010 CANDIDATE	2010 VOTES	2010 % VOTE	PPC FOR 2015
Majority	Conservative	Michael Ellis	13,735	34.1	Michael Ellis MP
1,936	Labour	Sally Keeble MP	11,799	29.3	Sally Keeble
Turnout	Lib Dem	Andrew Simpson	11,250	27.9	
65.11%	Others		3,487	8.7	

Majority 1936 (4.8%)

Won by Conservative Michael Ellis in 2010, the Northampton North constituency has alternated between the two major parties for nearly the past half-century. While the local job sector has shifted towards white-collar professions in recent decades, the constituency remains home to a good amount of industry including Britain's largest shoe factory. Both of the main parties find pockets of considerable support here: Labour in the Dallington and Links areas and the Conservatives in the suburban areas to the north of the seat. Former Labour MP and former Transport Minister Sally Keeble will seek to reclaim the seat she lost in 2010.

Northampton South

CONSERVATIVE HOLD	PARTY	2010 CANDIDATE	2010 VOTES	2010 % VOTE	PPC FOR 2015
Majority	Conservative	Brian Binley MP	15,917	40.8	David Mackintosh
6,004	Labour	Clyde Loakes	9,913	25.4	Kevin McKeever
Turnout	Lib Dem	Paul Varnsverry	7,579	19.4	
61.77%	Others		5,569	14.3	

Majority 6004 (15.4%)

A socially mixed seat, the Northampton South constituency stretches from socially depressed wards such as Castle and St Crispin in the centre of the former manufacturing town to Conservative bastions such as Weston. Owner occupation levels in the constituency are below the regional average and a fifth of residents live in social housing. With the sitting MP Brian Binley opting for retirement, he will be replaced as Conservative candidate by Northampton council leader David Mackintosh. The Labour candidate will be public affairs consultant Kevin McKeever.

South Northamptonshire

CONSERVATIVE WIN (NEW SEAT)	PARTY	2010 CANDIDATE	2010 VOTES	2010 % VOTE	PPC FOR 2015
Majority	Conservative	Andrea Leadsom	33,081	55.2	Andrea Leadsom MP
20,478	Lib Dem	Scott Collins	12,603	21.0	Scott Collins
Turnout	Labour	Matthew May	10,380	17.3	Lucy Mills
73.01%	Others		3,826	6.4	

Nottingham East

LABOUR HOLD	PARTY	2010 CANDIDATE	2010 VOTES	2010 % VOTE	PPC FOR 2015
Majority	Labour	Chris Leslie	15,022	45.4	Chris Leslie MP
6,969	Lib Dem	Sam Boote	8,053	24.3	
Turnout	Conservative	Ewan Lamont	7,846	23.7	
56.40%	Others		2,191	6.6	

Nottingham North

LABOUR HOLD	PARTY	2010 CANDIDATE	2010 VOTES	2010 % VOTE	PPC FOR 2015
Majority	Labour	Graham Allen MP	16,646	48.6	Graham Allen MP
8,138	Conservative	Martin Curtis	8,508	24.8	
Turnout	Lib Dem	Tim Ball	5,849	17.1	
54.21%	Others		3,282	9.6	

Nottingham South

LABOUR HOLD	PARTY	2010 CANDIDATE	2010 VOTES	2010 % VOTE	PPC FOR 2015
Majority	Labour	Lilian Greenwood	15,209	37.3	Lilian Greenwood MP
1,772	Conservative	Rowena Holland	13,437	32.9	Jane Hunt
Turnout	Lib Dem	Tony Sutton	9,406	23.1	
60.48%	Others		2,737	6.7	

Rushcliffe

CONSERVATIVE HOLD	PARTY	2010 CANDIDATE	2010 VOTES	2010 % VOTE	PPC FOR 2015
Majority	Conservative	Kenneth Clarke MP	27,470	51.2	Kenneth Clarke MP
15,811	Lib Dem	Karrar Khan	11,659	21.7	
Turnout	Labour	Andrew Clayworth	11,128	20.7	David Mellen
73.59%	Others		3,430	6.4	

Rutland & Melton

CONSERVATIVE HOLD	PARTY	2010 CANDIDATE	2010 VOTES	2010 % VOTE	PPC FOR 2015
Majority	Conservative	Alan Duncan MP	28,228	51.1	Alan Duncan MP
14,000	Lib Dem	Grahame Hudson	14,228	25.8	
Turnout	Labour	John Morgan	7,893	14.3	
71.54%	Others		4,871	8.8	

Sherwood

CONSERVATIVE GAIN FROM LABOUR	PARTY	2010 CANDIDATE	2010 VOTES	2010 % VOTE	PPC FOR 2015
Majority	Conservative	Mark Spencer	19,211	39.2	Mark Spencer MP
214	Labour	Emilie Oldknow	18,997	38.8	Leonie Mathers
Turnout	Lib Dem	Kevin Moore	7,283	14.9	
68.52%	Others		3,463	7.1	

Majority 214 (0.4%)

Located at the heart of the Nottinghamshire coalfield and taking in parts of the Newark & Sherwood, Ashfield & Gedling council areas, the Sherwood constituency was gained by Conservative candidate and local farmer Mark Spencer at the 2010 general election. His victory ended an eighteen-year run for Labour. With almost 30,000 residents, the town of Hucknall is the largest population centre in the constituency. Located 7 miles north-west of Nottingham on the city's tramline, the town has moved away from its coal-mining past and is now regarded as a relatively quiet slice of suburbia. While the speed of suburban house-building in the area may prove a boon for the Conservatives' long-term chances locally, Labour performed well at the 2013 county council elections. The Labour candidate will be Leonie Mathers, an advisor to shadow Home Secretary Yvette Cooper.

Sleaford & North Hykeham

CONSERVATIVE HOLD	PARTY	2010 CANDIDATE	2010 VOTES	2010 % VOTE	PPC FOR 2015
Majority	Conservative	Stephen Phillips	30,719	51.6	Stephen Phillips MP
19,905	Lib Dem	David Harding-Price	10,814	18.2	
Turnout	Labour	James Normington	10,051	16.9	
70.20%	Others		7,946	13.3	

South Holland & The Deepings

CONSERVATIVE HOLD	PARTY	2010 CANDIDATE	2010 VOTES	2010 % VOTE	PPC FOR 2015
Majority	Conservative	John Hayes MP	29,639	59.1	John Hayes MP
21,880	Lib Dem	Jennifer Conroy	7,759	15.5	
Turnout	Labour	Gareth Gould	7,024	14.0	
65.83%	Others		5,766	11.5	

Wellingborough

CONSERVATIVE HOLD	PARTY	2010 CANDIDATE	2010 VOTES	2010 % VOTE	PPC FOR 2015
Majority	Conservative	Peter Bone MP	24,918	48.2	Peter Bone MP
11,787	Labour	Jayne Buckland	13,131	25.4	Richard Garvie
Turnout	Lib Dem	Kevin Barron	8,848	17.1	
67.23%	Others		4,764	9.2	

West Midlands

When the Labour Party was voted out of government in 2010, the West Midlands played a very significant role. There was an above average negative swing, and Labour were reduced to holding a minority of the region's seats. It is clear looking down the list of the twenty-four they did win (out of a regional total of fifty-nine) that they are now almost entirely confined to very urban constituencies in the cities and metropolitan conurbation. There are eight in Birmingham, three in each of Coventry and Stoke-on-Trent, two in each of Walsall, West Bromwich and Wolverhampton. None has a significant rural or small-town element.

Labour will therefore have to reverse most of the fourteen losses they suffered last time, and this means they will have to regain the appeal outside the urban centres that enabled Tony Blair to become Prime Minister three times between 1997 and 2005. This task is epitomised in two of their most promising opportunities. In both North Warwickshire (majority in 2010 just fifty-four votes) and Cannock Chase (swing required 4 per cent) Labour will not be facing a sitting Conservative MP, as both Dan Byles and Aidan Burley have announced their retirement after one term – the latter under something of a cloud after attending a stag party at which Nazi uniforms and salutes were spotted. Both these seats can be categorised as composed of small towns and ex-mining areas. Other essential gains include Worcester, Nuneaton and Warwick & Leamington, again seats outside the main conurbation.

In order to win the 2015 general election Labour will also have to take back some seats they lost within the former West Midlands metropolitan county as well: Enoch Powell's old constituency of Wolverhampton SW, which had also been seized by 'New Labour' in 1997 (swing needed from Paul Uppal: 1 per cent); Halesowen & Rowley Regis (2.5 per cent) and even Dudley South, where the swing required is over 5 per cent, and Stourbridge (nearly 6 per cent). This reveals that the Conservatives actually took several seats by rather large margins in 2010, so Labour faces a hefty task to regain them.

For example, the Tory lead in Stafford (where David Cameron first tried to enter the Commons, unsuccessfully, in 1997) is 5,400, and in Redditch, where Jacqui Smith was one of the most high-profile casualties in 2010, it is nearly 6,000. It gets worse for Labour: Rugby, Burton and Tamworth all have majorities of over 6,000. What all these divisions have in common is that they are outside the big cities, in the heartlands of Worcestershire or Staffordshire or Warwickshire. What is more, apart from the first two mentioned above, they all have Tory MPs with five years of incumbency to build a personal vote.

Nor can Labour hope to gain many seats from the junior coalition partners. Like the North East of England region, this is not good territory for the Liberal Democrats and they only won two seats in 2010. Also like the North East, both are considered vulnerable next time, one to each of the biggest parties. Labour's chance lies in Birmingham Yardley, where John Hemming's majority is 3,002. However, this will not be a foregone conclusion by any means, for besides Mr Hemming's personal vote as an independently minded representative, the Lib Dems are very well entrenched in the wards making up the constituency, such as Acocks Green, Sheldon and South Yardley – all of which they retained in the May 2014 Birmingham city council contests.

A numerical ordering of the Conservative Party's targets in the West Midlands also starts with a Liberal Democrat seat. In this case it is Solihull, where Lorely Burt has now won twice, with majorities of just 279 then 175. Solihull seems an unlikely place for the Tories not to win. It is one of the ten most heavily owner-occupied seats in the

United Kingdom, with over 82 per cent of the housing stock in this sector. Along with the very safe Sutton Coldfield, it has the most residents in managerial jobs in the Greater Birmingham area. The Liberal Democrats did not do as well in Solihull council elections in 2014 as in the same wards in 2010. Yet it would be foolish to write off so resilient a candidate as Lorely Burt, as she has proven more than once before.

For the Tories to take an overall majority nationally they also need to gain from Labour, and there are several good chances in the West Midlands. Dudley North would take a swing of just 1 per cent, and Telford, Walsall North, Birmingham Edgbaston and Newcastle under Lyme would need less than 2 per cent. However among these are some doughty defenders. David Winnick has been reselected to fight Walsall North; he first entered the Commons for Croydon South in 1966 and turned eighty in June 2013. German-born Gisela Stuart of leafy and academic Edgbaston has defied national swings consistently.

It may be thought that the West Midlands is thoroughly multicultural and it does indeed include some of the most mixed-population constituencies in Britain. In this region is found the constituency with the highest proportion of Muslims: Birmingham Hodge Hill, with 52.1 per cent, which makes it the only Muslim majority seat in Britain at the time of the 2011 census. Some of the largest communities of Sikhs are to be found in Wolverhampton, Warley and Birmingham Perry Barr. Four Birmingham divisions have a minority of white residents. This cosmopolitan ambience does make for some very safe Labour seats, and some complex local politics, with some success for both Respect and Justice for Kashmir parties in council elections some years ago. However there are also areas, including white working-class wards, where UKIP has enjoyed recent breakthroughs and overall across the region the anti-EU party did well enough to elect three MEPs in May 2014.

In fact, the West Midlands as a whole was one of UKIP's strongest regions, and we now confront the curious situation that despite topping that poll with over 31 per cent of the vote, compared with Labour's

26 per cent and the Tories' 24 per cent, UKIP are not likely to win a single Westminster constituency in 2015. This is partly because their strength is at its greatest in European contests, but also because their vote is the most evenly spread of the parties – the problem that has for many decades led to the under-representation of the centre ground of politics. The Conservatives, on the other hand, will probably rise from the low point of that third place in 2014 to take the most MPs again in the region.

Aldridge-Brownhills

CONSERVATIVE HOLD	PARTY	2010 CANDIDATE	2010 VOTES	2010 % VOTE	PPC FOR 2015
Majority	Conservative	Richard Shepherd MP	22,913	59.3	Richard Shepherd MP
15,266	Labour	Ashiq Hussain	7,647	19.8	John Fisher
Turnout	Lib Dem	Ian Jenkins	6,833	17.7	
65.58%	Others		1,241	3.2	

Birmingham, Edgbaston

LABOUR HOLD	PARTY	2010 CANDIDATE	2010 VOTES	2010 % VOTE	PPC FOR 2015
Majority	Labour	Gisela Stuart MP	16,894	40.6	Gisela Stuart MP
1,274	Conservative	Deirdre Alden	15,620	37.6	Luke Evans
Turnout	Lib Dem	Roger Harmer	6,387	15.4	
60.62%	Others		2,670	6.4	

Majority 1274 (3.1%)

Located in the Birmingham's south-western suburbs, German-born and accented Gisela Stuart succeeded Tory grandee Dame Jill Knight at the 1997 general election. Home to the University of Birmingham, the area is largely middle-class in nature. Historically one of the safest Conservative constituencies in the West Midlands, this was the most marginal Labour seat the party failed to win in 2010. Edgbaston's long-term demographics are not on the Conservative Party's side. With almost a third of the constituency's residents living in social housing and many of the area's elegant town-houses being converted into flats, Labour's natural support base here is growing. The Conservatives remain the largest party here on a local government level, outpacing Labour by 9,610 votes to 8,299 at the 2014 local elections. The Conservative candidate will be local GP Dr Luke Evans.

Birmingham, Erdington

LABOUR HOLD	PARTY	2010 CANDIDATE	2010 VOTES	2010 % VOTE	PPC FOR 2015
Majority	Labour	Jack Dromey	14,869	41.8	Jack Dromey MP
3,277	Conservative	Robert Alden	11,592	32.6	Robert Alden
Turnout	Lib Dem	Ann Holtom	5,742	16.2	
53.53%	Others		3,343	9.4	

Birmingham, Hall Green

LABOUR HOLD	PARTY	2010 CANDIDATE	2010 VOTES	2010 % VOTE	PPC FOR 2015
Majority	Labour	Roger Godsiff MP	16,039	32.9	Roger Godsiff MP
3,799	Respect	Salma Yaqoob	12,240	25.1	
Turnout	Lib Dem	Jerry Evans	11,988	24.6	Jerry Evans
63.63%	Others		8,460	17.4	

Birmingham, Hodge Hill

LABOUR HOLD	PARTY	2010 CANDIDATE	2010 VOTES	2010 % VOTE	PPC FOR 2015
Majority	Labour	Liam Byrne MP	22,077	52.0	Liam Byrne MP
10,302	Lib Dem	Tariq Khan	11,775	27.7	
Turnout	Conservative	Shailesh Parekh	4,936	11.6	
56.60%	Others		3,684	8.7	

Birmingham, Ladywood

LABOUR HOLD	PARTY	2010 CANDIDATE	2010 VOTES	2010 % VOTE	PPC FOR 2015
Majority	Labour	Shabana Mahmood	19,950	55.7	Shabana Mahmood MP
10,105	Lib Dem	Ayoub Khan	9,845	27.5	
Turnout	Conservative	Nusrat Ghani	4,277	11.9	
48.66%	Others		1,761	4.9	

Birmingham, Northfield

LABOUR HOLD	PARTY	2010 CANDIDATE	2010 VOTES	2010 % VOTE	PPC FOR 2015
Majority	Labour	Richard Burden MP	16,841	40.3	Richard Burden MP
2,782	Conservative	Keely Huxtable	14,059	33.6	Rachel Maclean
Turnout	Lib Dem	Mike Dixon	6,550	15.7	Steve Haynes
58.61%	Others		4,364	10.4	

Birmingham, Perry Barr

LABOUR HOLD	PARTY	2010 CANDIDATE	2010 VOTES	2010 % VOTE	PPC FOR 2015
Majority	Labour	Khalid Mahmood MP	21,142	50.3	Khalid Mahmood MP
11,908	Lib Dem	Karen Hamilton	9,234	22.0	
Turnout	Conservative	William Norton	8,960	21.3	
58.97%	Others		2,709	6.4	

Birmingham, Selly Oak

LABOUR HOLD	PARTY	2010 CANDIDATE	2010 VOTES	2010 % VOTE	PPC FOR 2015
Majority	Labour	Steve McCabe MP	17,950	38.5	Steve McCabe MP
3,482	Conservative	Nigel Dawkins	14,468	31.1	Alex Avern
Turnout	Lib Dem	David Radcliffe	10,371	22.3	Colin Green
62.25%	Others		3,774	8.1	

Birmingham, Yardley

LIB DEM HOLD	PARTY	2010 CANDIDATE	2010 VOTES	2010 % VOTE	PPC FOR 2015
Majority	Lib Dem	John Hemming MP	16,162	39.6	John Hemming MP
3,002	Labour	Lynette Kelly	13,160	32.2	Jess Phillips
Turnout	Conservative	Meirion Jenkins	7,836	19.2	
56.48%	Others		3,692	9.0	

Majority 3002 (7.3%)

Located in the eastern part of Birmingham, Yardley has long been the site of close battles between Labour and the Liberal Democrats. This is a classic case of hard work at a local government level over a long period of time translating into a Lib Dem victory on a parliamentary level, with Hemmimg having fought the seat on three occasions before winning in 2005. The seat is compromised of the largely residential Yardley, Acocks Green, Sheldon and Stechford areas of the city. Unlike many Birmingham constituencies, the ethnic minority population is relatively low at roughly a third and almost two-thirds of homes are owner-occupied. Despite their slippage on a local government level elsewhere in Birmingham, the Liberal Democrats remain a potent force in Yardley, beating Labour in the 2014 poll by a 46 per cent to 29 per cent margin. Hemming's Labour challenger will be Jess Phillips, a Birmingham city councillor.

Bromsgrove

CONSERVATIVE HOLD	PARTY	2010 CANDIDATE	2010 VOTES	2010 % VOTE	PPC FOR 2015
Majority	Conservative	Sajid Javid	22,558	43.7	Sajid Javid MP
11,308	Labour	Sam Burden	11,250	21.8	Tom Ebbutt
Turnout	Lib Dem	Philip Ling	10,124	19.6	
70.69%	Others		7,698	14.9	

Burton

CONSERVATIVE GAIN FROM LABOUR	PARTY	2010 CANDIDATE	2010 VOTES	2010 % VOTE	PPC FOR 2015
Majority	Conservative	Andrew Griffiths	22,188	44.5	Andrew Griffiths MP
6,304	Labour	Ruth Smeeth	15,884	31.9	Jon Wheale
Turnout	Lib Dem	Michael Rogers	7,891	15.8	
66.54%	Others		3,860	7.7	

Majority 6304 (12.7%)

Held by Labour from 1997 to 2010, Burton was gained by Conservative Andrew Griffiths at the 2010 general election. The seat is largely centred on Burton-upon-Trent, the centre of the country's beer-brewing industry and the market town of Uttoxeter. A politically divided seat, Labour's support is greatest in the Horninglow and Stapenhill areas of Burton which are dominated by social housing, while the strength of the Conservative vote in rural East Staffordshire ensures that this will always be a closely fought marginal. Indeed, the results of the 2013 county council election showed the Conservatives leading Labour by a tight 40 per cent to 35 per cent margin. The Labour candidate will be former army officer Jon Wheale.

Cannock Chase

CONSERVATIVE GAIN FROM LABOUR	PARTY	2010 CANDIDATE	2010 VOTES	2010 % VOTE	PPC FOR 2015
Majority	Conservative	Aidan Burley	18,271	40.1	Amanda Milling
3,195	Labour	Susan Woodward	15,076	33.1	Janos Toth
Turnout	Lib Dem	Jon Hunt	7,732	17.0	
61.15%	Others		4,480	9.8	

Majority 3195 (7%)

Traditionally Labour territory, this constituency was seized by Conservative Aidan Burley on a dramatic 14 per cent swing – the highest pro-Conservative swing in the country. Located in the south of Staffordshire, the Labour-dominated town of Cannock grew rapidly in the post-war years on the back of rapid industrial expansion. North of the town the rugged Cannock Chase heathland, which mixes upmarket

Tory-inclined villages with Labour-dominated former coal-mining areas, has been designated an Area of Outstanding Natural Beauty. Following Burley's retirement after just one term, the Conservatives are fielding businesswoman Amanda Milling while the Labour candidate will be Janos Toth, a long-serving Cannock Chase councillor.

Coventry North East

LABOUR HOLD	PARTY	2010 CANDIDATE	2010 VOTES	2010 % VOTE	PPC FOR 2015
Majority	Labour	Bob Ainsworth MP	21,384	49.3	Colleen Fletcher
11,775	Conservative	Hazel Noonan	9,609	22.1	
Turnout	Lib Dem	Russell Field	7,210	16.6	
59.40%	Others		5,180	11.9	

Coventry North West

LABOUR HOLD	PARTY	2010 CANDIDATE	2010 VOTES	2010 % VOTE	PPC FOR 2015
Majority	Labour	Geoffrey Robinson MP	19,936	42.8	Geoffrey Robinson MP
6,288	Conservative	Gary Ridley	13,648	29.3	
Turnout	Lib Dem	Vincent McKee	8,344	17.9	
63.89%	Others		4,632	9.9	

Coventry South

LABOUR HOLD	PARTY	2010 CANDIDATE	2010 VOTES	2010 % VOTE	PPC FOR 2015
Majority	Labour	Jim Cunningham MP	19,197	41.8	Jim Cunningham MP
3,845	Conservative	Kevin Foster	15,352	33.4	
Turnout	Lib Dem	Brian Patton	8,278	18.0	
62.35%	Others		3,097	6.7	

Dudley North

LABOUR HOLD	PARTY	2010 CANDIDATE	2010 VOTES	2010 % VOTE	PPC FOR 2015
Majority	Labour	Ian Austin MP	14,923	38.7	Ian Austin MP
649	Conservative	Graeme Brown	14,274	37.0	Afzal Amin
Turnout	Lib Dem	Mike Beckett	4,066	10.5	
63.45%	Others		5,339	13.8	

Majority 649 (1.7%)

The safer for Labour of the town's two constituencies, sitting MP Ian Austin narrowly avoided defeat at the hands of the Conservatives in 2010. Both the Conservatives and Labour have significant support here; Labour leading in the urban Gornal, Castle and Priory areas while the Tories are ahead by strong margins in the commuter suburb of Sedgley. At 64.1 per cent, levels of home ownership are considerably lower here than in the south of the town. The 2014 council elections were disastrous for the Conservatives, with UKIP topping the poll with 8,086 to Labour's 7,439 with the party trailing in a distant third place with 4,925 votes. The Conservative candidate will be Afzal Amin, while UKIP are fielding Bill Etheridge MEP.

Dudley South

CONSERVATIVE GAIN FROM LABOUR	PARTY	2010 CANDIDATE	2010 VOTES	2010 % VOTE	PPC FOR 2015
Majority	Conservative	Chris Kelly	16,450	43.1	Chris Kelly MP
3,856	Labour	Rachel Harris	12,594	33.0	Natasha Milward
Turnout	Lib Dem	Jonathan Bramall	5,989	15.7	
63.01%	Others		3,132	8.2	

Majority 3856 (10.1%)

Situated just west of Birmingham and on the edge of the Black Country, the Dudley South constituency was wrestled from Labour by Conservative Chris D. Kelly at the 2010 general election. Labour is strongest here in the Brierley Hill area, a former steel and glass manufacturing town which is plagued by high unemployment. Even in a bad year, the Conservatives are strongly competitive in the Birmingham commuter town of Kingswinford – an area which is expected to expand rapidly in the coming decades. The UK Independence Party, who recorded a creditable 8 per cent of the vote at the 2010 general election, topped the poll here at the 2014 local government and European elections and have declared their intention to target the constituency. Natasha Millward will stand for Labour.

Halesowen & Rowley Regis

CONSERVATIVE GAIN FROM LABOUR	PARTY	2010 CANDIDATE	2010 VOTES	2010 % VOTE	PPC FOR 2015
Majority	Conservative	James Morris	18,115	41.2	James Morris MP
2,023	Labour	Sue Hayman	16,092	36.6	Stephanie Peacock
Turnout	Lib Dem	Philip Tibbetts	6,515	14.8	
69.05%	Others		3,257	7.4	

Majority 2023 (4.6%)

Located in the heart of the Black Country and gained by Labour at the 1997 general election, this constituency is comprised of parts of the Sandwell and Dudley boroughs. This is a socially divided constituency; the middle-class town of Halesowen being largely comprised of detached homes for Birmingham commuters while Rowley Regis and Cradley Heath are dominated by council housing. A political divide is apparent here too: Halesowen supporting the Tories and Rowley Regis backing Labour. The 2014 local elections were similarly divided, with Labour outpacing the Conservatives by 8,927 votes to 7,415. At 70.8 per cent, levels of owner occupation are high in the constituency yet almost a quarter of residents live in social housing. Gained in 2010 by Conservative think tank boss James Morris, he will be opposed by Labour's Stephanie Peacock.

Hereford & South Herefordshire

CONSERVATIVE GAIN FROM LIB DEM	PARTY	2010 CANDIDATE	2010 VOTES	2010 % VOTE	PPC FOR 2015
Majority	Conservative	Jesse Norman	22,366	46.2	Jesse Norman MP
2,481	Lib Dem	Sarah Carr	19,885	41.1	Lucy Hurds
Turnout	Labour	Philippa Roberts	3,506	7.2	
67.18%	Others		2,624	5.4	

North Herefordshire

CONSERVATIVE WIN (NEW SEAT)	PARTY	2010 CANDIDATE	2010 VOTES	2010 % VOTE	PPC FOR 2015
Majority	Conservative	Bill Wiggin MP	24,631	51.8	Bill Wiggin MP
9,887	Lib Dem	Lucy Hurds	14,744	31.0	
Turnout	Labour	Neil Sabharwal	3,373	7.1	
71.05%	Others		4,820	10.1	

Kenilworth & Southam

CONSERVATIVE WIN (NEW SEAT)	PARTY	2010 CANDIDATE	2010 VOTES	2010 % VOTE	PPC FOR 2015
Majority	Conservative	Jeremy Wright MP	25,945	53.6	Jeremy Wright MP
12,552	Lib Dem	Nigel Rock	13,393	27.7	
Turnout	Labour	Nicholas Milton	6,949	14.3	Bally Singh
75.25%	Others		2,144	4.4	

Lichfield

CONSERVATIVE HOLD	PARTY	2010 CANDIDATE	2010 VOTES	2010 % VOTE	PPC FOR 2015
Majority	Conservative	Michael Fabricant MP	28,048	54.4	Michael Fabricant MP
17,683	Lib Dem	Ian Jackson	10,365	20.1	
Turnout	Labour	Steve Hyden	10,230	19.8	Chris Worsey
71.04%	Others		2,920	5.7	

Ludlow

CONSERVATIVE HOLD	PARTY	2010 CANDIDATE	2010 VOTES	2010 % VOTE	PPC FOR 2015
Majority	Conservative	Philip Dunne MP	25,720	52.8	Philip Dunne MP
9,749	Lib Dem	Heather Kidd	15,971	32.8	
Turnout	Labour	Tony Hunt	3,272	6.7	Simon Slater
73.14%	Others		3,769	7.7	

Meriden

CONSERVATIVE HOLD	PARTY	2010 CANDIDATE	2010 VOTES	2010 % VOTE	PPC FOR 2015
Majority	Conservative	Caroline Spelman MP	26,956	51.7	Caroline Spelman MP
16,253	Labour	Ed Williams	10,703	20.5	Tom McNeil
Turnout	Lib Dem	Simon Slater	9,278	17.8	
63.44%	Others		5,225	10.0	

Newcastle under Lyme

LABOUR HOLD	PARTY	2010 CANDIDATE	2010 VOTES	2010 % VOTE	PPC FOR 2015
Majority	Labour	Paul Farrelly MP	16,393	38.0	Paul Farrelly MP
1,552	Conservative	Robert Jenrick	14,841	34.4	Tony Cox
Turnout	Lib Dem	Nigel Jones	8,466	19.6	
62.21%	Others		3,491	8.1	

Majority 1552 (3.6%)

Located in Staffordshire's north-eastern corner Newcastle under Lyme is a socially mixed constituency which has, throughout its electoral history, been steadfastly loyal to the Labour Party. Parts of this constituency fall within the former Staffordshire coalfield, notably Silverdale whose colliery closed for the last time in 1998. This is not a wealthy area, less than half of all homes being owner-occupied and unemployment being some way above the national average. Despite the area's natural inclination towards Labour, the seat is not entirely hostile to the Conservatives with the rural western portion of the seat heavily favouring the party. Labour MP Paul Farrelly will be challenged by Conservative Tony Cox, an engineer.

Nuneaton

CONSERVATIVE GAIN FROM LABOUR	PARTY	2010 CANDIDATE	2010 VOTES	2010 % VOTE	PPC FOR 2015
Majority	Conservative	Marcus Jones	18,536	41.5	Marcus Jones MP
2,069	Labour	Jayne Innes	16,467	36.9	Vicky Fowler
Turnout	Lib Dem	Christina Jebb	6,846	15.3	
65.81%	Others		2,797	6.3	

Majority 2069 (4.6%)

The largest town in Warwickshire, Nuneaton was gained by Conservative Marcus Jones at the 2010 general election. Once an important manufacturing and textiles town, these industries have now largely disappeared and the constituency is now mostly home to commuters to nearby Birmingham and Coventry. Labour have traditionally performed best in the Nuneaton town wards, especially around the former National Coal Board housing estate of Camp Hill while the Conservatives are convincingly ahead in the affluent suburb of Whitestone. Labour dominated Nuneaton and Bedworth council at the 2014 council elections, winning twenty-eight seats to the Conservative Party's three – a particularly poor result for the Tories in a council they controlled as recently as 2010. The Labour candidate will be Vicky Fowler, a former Nuneaton councillor.

Redditch

CONSERVATIVE GAIN FROM LABOUR	PARTY	2010 CANDIDATE	2010 VOTES	2010 % VOTE	PPC FOR 2015
Majority	Conservative	Karen Lumley	19,138	43.5	Karen Lumley MP
5,821	Labour	Jacqui Smith MP	13,317	30.3	Rebecca Blake
Turnout	Lib Dem	Nicholas Lane	7,750	17.6	
66.12%	Others		3,813	8.7	

Majority 5821 (13.2%)

Gained by Conservative Karen Lumley on her third attempt at the 2010 general election, Redditch is a key seat Labour needs to take in order to form a majority. Located 15 miles south of Birmingham, the Redditch constituency is neither particularly wealthy nor poor in terms of its composition. A classic new town, Redditch's population grew substantially during the '60s as demand for housing close to Birmingham accelerated while more upscale housing developments on the town's fringes have sprung up in recent years. A fifth of residents live in social housing, yet owner-occupation levels remain above average for a Midlands constituency. This remains strongly competitive territory for the Conservatives and Labour, with the two parties being essentially tied at the 2013 local elections on the back of a strong UKIP performance. The Labour candidate will be Rebecca Blake.

Rugby

CONSERVATIVE WIN (NEW SEAT)	PARTY	2010 CANDIDATE	2010 VOTES	2010 % VOTE	PPC FOR 2015
Majority	Conservative	Mark Pawsey	20,901	44.0	Mark Pawsey MP
6,000	Labour	Andy King MP	14,901	31.4	Claire Edwards
Turnout	Lib Dem	Jerry Roodhouse	9,434	19.9	
68.88%	Others		2,232	4.7	

Majority 6000 (12.6%)

Won by Conservative Mark Pawsey at the 2010 general election, the town of Rugby has long been a closely fought marginal seat. As is the case with many West Midlands constituencies, the urban core of the town is dominated by densely populated terraced housing and a strong industrial base that is favourable to the Labour Party. It is in the suburbs and in the Warwickshire countryside surrounding the town that the Conservatives score the majority of their support. Despite a modest swing to Labour in recent years, the Conservatives retained control of Rugby Borough Council at the 2014 local elections. The Labour candidate will be Claire Edwards.

Shrewsbury & Atcham

CONSERVATIVE HOLD	PARTY	2010 CANDIDATE	2010 VOTES	2010 % VOTE	PPC FOR 2015
Majority	Conservative	Daniel Kawczynski MP	23,313	43.9	Daniel Kawczynski MP
7,944	Lib Dem	Charles West	15,369	29.0	Christine Tinker
Turnout	Labour	Jon Tandy	10,915	20.6	John Turnbull
70.31%	Others		3,448	6.5	

North Shropshire

CONSERVATIVE HOLD	PARTY	2010 CANDIDATE	2010 VOTES	2010 % VOTE	PPC FOR 2015
Majority	Conservative	Owen Paterson MP	26,692	51.5	Owen Paterson MP
15,828	Lib Dem	Ian Croll	10,864	20.9	
Turnout	Labour	Ian McLaughlan	9,406	18.1	Graeme Currie
65.72%	Others		4,907	9.5	

Solihull

LIB DEM HOLD	PARTY	2010 CANDIDATE	2010 VOTES	2010 % VOTE	PPC FOR 2015
Majority	Lib Dem	Lorely Burt MP	23,635	42.9	Lorely Burt MP
175	Conservative	Maggie Throup	23,460	42.6	Julian Knight
Turnout	Labour	Sarah Merrill	4,891	8.9	Nigel Knowles
72.26%	Others		3,143	5.7	

Majority 175 (0.3%)

An overwhelmingly white, middle-class and residential constituency, Solihull is located just to the south of the Birmingham conurbation in easy reach of the city centre, the city's international airport and open countryside. While the bulk of residents work in white-collar professions, the seat is also home to a significant number of jobs in the automotive sector at Jaguar Land Rover. The Liberal Democrats incumbent Lorely Burt surprised many by dramatically taking the seat from the Conservatives in 2005 and retaining it in 2010. A Lord Ashcroft poll published in June 2014 showed the Conservatives ahead of the Liberal Democrats by a 37 per cent to 28 per cent margin. These numbers were similar to the 2014 local elections where the Conservatives posted a 38 per cent to 23 per cent advantage over the Liberal Democrats. The Conservative candidate will be Julian Knight, Money and Property Editor for the *Independent on Sunday*.

Stafford

CONSERVATIVE GAIN FROM LABOUR	PARTY	2010 CANDIDATE	2010 VOTES	2010 % VOTE	PPC FOR 2015
Majority	Conservative	Jeremy Lefroy	22,047	43.9	Jeremy Lefroy MP
5,460	Labour	David Kidney MP	16,587	33.0	Kate Godfrey
Turnout	Lib Dem	Barry Stamp	8,211	16.3	
71.09%	Others		3,394	6.8	

Majority 5460 (10.9%)

The county town of Staffordshire, Stafford was gained by Conservative Jeremy Lefroy at the 2010 general election. A largely middle-class town, many local people find employment in the electrical engineering and light industrial sector. Labour has traditionally dominated in Stafford town, holding wide leads over the Conservatives in the Highfields, Western Downs and Manor districts while the Conservatives are strongest in the town's suburbs and outlying villages. Kate Godfrey will seek to take the seat back for Labour.

Staffordshire Moorlands

CONSERVATIVE GAIN FROM LABOUR	PARTY	2010 CANDIDATE	2010 VOTES	2010 % VOTE	PPC FOR 2015
Majority	Conservative	Karen Bradley	19,793	45.2	Karen Bradley MP
6,689	Labour	Charlotte Atkins MP	13,104	29.9	Trudie McGuinness
Turnout	Lib Dem	Henry Jebb	7,338	16.7	
70.51%	Others		3,580	8.2	

Majority 6689 (15.3%)

Located just east of Stoke-on-Trent, Staffordshire Moorlands was won for the Conservatives by the Home Office Minister Karen Bradley in 2010. The seat is a slightly uneasy mixture of market towns such as Leek, the former mining and industrial bastion of Biddulph and scores of tourism-reliant villages located inside the Peak District National Park. Demographically speaking, the constituency is mostly white and relatively affluent with below average rates of unemployment – both factors which aid the Conservatives. The UK Independence Party were the convincing winners of the 2014 European elections and have declared their intention to target the seat in 2015. The Labour candidate will be higher education lecturer Trudie McGuinness.

South Staffordshire

CONSERVATIVE HOLD	PARTY	2010 CANDIDATE	2010 VOTES	2010 % VOTE	PPC FOR 2015
Majority	Conservative	Gavin Williamson	26,834	53.2	Gavin Williamson MP
16,590	Labour	Kevin McElduff	10,244	20.3	Kevin McElduff
Turnout	Lib Dem	Sarah Fellows	8,427	16.7	
68.30%	Others		4,935	9.8	

Stoke-on-Trent Central

LABOUR HOLD	PARTY	2010 CANDIDATE	2010 VOTES	2010 % VOTE	PPC FOR 2015
Majority	Labour	Tristram Hunt	12,605	38.8	Tristram Hunt MP
5,566	Lib Dem	John Redfern	7,039	21.7	
Turnout	Conservative	Norsheen Bhatti	6,833	21.0	
53.23%	Others		5,993	18.5	

Stoke-on-Trent North

LABOUR HOLD	PARTY	2010 CANDIDATE	2010 VOTES	2010 % VOTE	PPC FOR 2015
Majority	Labour	Joan Walley MP	17,815	44.3	Ruth Smeeth
8,235	Conservative	Andy Large	9,580	23.8	
Turnout	Lib Dem	John Fisher	7,120	17.7	
55.79%	Others		5,681	14.1	

Stoke-on-Trent South

LABOUR HOLD	PARTY	2010 CANDIDATE	2010 VOTES	2010 % VOTE	PPC FOR 2015
Majority	Labour	Robert Flello MP	15,446	38.8	Robert Flello MP
4,130	Conservative	James Rushton	11,316	28.4	
Turnout	Lib Dem	Zulfiqar Ali	6,323	15.9	
58.58%	Others		6,767	17.0	

Stone

CONSERVATIVE HOLD	PARTY	2010 CANDIDATE	2010 VOTES	2010 % VOTE	PPC FOR 2015
Majority	Conservative	Bill Cash MP	23,890	50.6	Bill Cash MP
13,292	Lib Dem	Christine Tinker	10,598	22.4	
Turnout	Labour	Joanne Lewis	9,770	20.7	Sam Hale
70.43%	Others		2,971	6.3	

Stourbridge

CONSERVATIVE GAIN FROM LABOUR	PARTY	2010 CANDIDATE	2010 VOTES	2010 % VOTE	PPC FOR 2015
Majority	Conservative	Margot James	20,153	42.7	Margot James MP
5,164	Labour	Lynda Waltho MP	14,989	31.7	Peter Lowe
Turnout	Lib Dem		7,733	16.4	
67.83%	Others		4,359	9.2	

Majority 5164 (10.9%)

An increasingly aspirational seat, the Stourbridge constituency typifies the mix of wealthy commuter suburbs, social housing and light industry increasingly common to many seats on the fringes of the West Midlands conurbation. Labour's long-term prospects here are not helped by the near frenetic construction of private housing estates which have tended to favour the Conservatives. Surrounded by pleasant countryside, three-quarters of homes in this middle-class constituency are owner-occupied. Conservative support is strongest in Amblecote and Pedmore while Labour dominates in Stourbridge town and Dudley Wood. Support for the Conservatives at the 2014 local elections remained fairly robust with the party outpacing Labour by 8,330 votes to 7,695 with UKIP close behind on 7,004. Sitting Conservative MP Margot James, who gained the seat in 2010, will be challenged by Labour's Pete Lowe and UK Independence Party MEP Jim Carver.

Stratford-on-Avon

CONSERVATIVE HOLD	PARTY	2010 CANDIDATE	2010 VOTES	2010 % VOTE	PPC FOR 2015
Majority	Conservative	Nadhim Zahawi	26,052	51.5	Nadhim Zahawi MP
11,346	Lib Dem	Martin Turner	14,706	29.1	Elizabeth Adams
Turnout	Labour	Robert Johnston	4,809	9.5	Jeff Kenner
72.70%	Others		4,975	9.8	

Sutton Coldfield

CONSERVATIVE HOLD	PARTY	2010 CANDIDATE	2010 VOTES	2010 % VOTE	PPC FOR 2015
Majority	Conservative	Andrew Mitchell MP	27,303	54.0	Andrew Mitchell MP
17,005	Labour	Robert Pocock	10,298	20.4	Robert Pocock
Turnout	Lib Dem	Richard Brighton	9,117	18.0	
67.91%	Others		3,871	7.7	

Tamworth

CONSERVATIVE GAIN FROM LABOUR	PARTY	2010 CANDIDATE	2010 VOTES	2010 % VOTE	PPC FOR 2015
Majority	Conservative	Christopher Pincher	21,238	45.8	Christopher Pincher MP
6,090	Labour	Brian Jenkins MP	15,148	32.7	Carol Dean
Turnout	Lib Dem	Jenny Pinkett	7,516	16.2	
64.46%	Others		2,488	5.4	

Majority 6090 (13.1%)

Gained from Labour by Conservative Chris Pincher at the 2010 general election, Tamworth is a perfect example of the type of West Midlands marginal the Conservatives need to win in order to stand any chance of forming a majority in the House of Commons. The constituency is a mix of an elegant town centre, wealthy Birmingham commuter villages and pockets of real deprivation in Tamworth's Bolehill, Castle and Glascote areas. In keeping with its politically divided nature, the 2014 local elections provided to be a close-run contest with the Conservatives leading Labour by a 43 per cent to 38 per cent margin with UKIP taking 17 per cent of the vote. The Labour candidate will be Carol Dean.

Telford

LABOUR HOLD	PARTY	2010 CANDIDATE	2010 VOTES	2010 % VOTE	PPC FOR 2015
Majority	Labour	David Wright MP	15,977	38.7	David Wright MP
981	Conservative	Tom Biggins	14,996	36.3	Lucy Allan
Turnout	Lib Dem	Philip Bennion	6,399	15.5	
63.50%	Others		3,941	9.5	

Majority 978 (2.4%)

A relatively safe Labour seat for most of its existence, Telford supported the Conservatives for Margaret Thatcher's first two parliaments before being recaptured by future Lords Chief Whip Bruce Grocott in 1987. Located around 30 miles east of Birmingham, Telford has carved itself a niche as a centre for the high-tech and IT sector. The town's population is projected to grow from 104,000 in 1980 to 200,000 within the next twenty years. Despite recent investment, high unemployment has been a long-term problem for Telford with only one in ten residents holding university degrees (12.1 per cent) and more than a third (34.1 per cent) having no qualifications. Sitting MP David Wright will stand again for Labour while former Wandsworth councillor Lucy Allen will represent the Conservatives.

Walsall North

LABOUR HOLD	PARTY	2010 CANDIDATE	2010 VOTES	2010 % VOTE	PPC FOR 2015
Majority	Labour	David Winnick MP	13,385	37.0	David Winnick MP
990	Conservative	Helyn Clack	12,395	34.3	Douglas Hansen-Luke
Turnout	Lib Dem	Nadia Fazal	4,754	13.1	
56.51%	Others		5,653	15.6	

Majority 990 (2.7%)

Held since 1983 by veteran Labour MP David Winnick, he had the closest call of his career in 2010 when the Conservatives came within 1,000 votes of defeating him. The largest employer locally is the manufacturing sector, with the town of Walsall and neighbouring Willenhall home to numerous factories. At 43 per cent, the constituency has a higher than average level of public sector housing, while unemployment is also higher than in most other West Midlands seats. Unlike neighbouring Walsall South, the constituency's non-white population is negligible – a factor which has helped the Conservatives. A poll conducted by Lord Ashcroft in June 2014 made grim reading for Conservatives, placing Labour ahead on 37 per cent, UKIP on 30 per cent and the Tories way back on 21 per cent. Winnick will once again seek re-election at the age of eighty-one while the Conservative candidate will be Douglas Hansen-Luke.

Walsall South

LABOUR HOLD	PARTY	2010 CANDIDATE	2010 VOTES	2010 % VOTE	PPC FOR 2015
Majority	Labour	Valerie Vaz	16,211	39.7	Valerie Vaz MP
1,755	Conservative	Richard Hunt	14,456	35.4	
Turnout	Lib Dem	Murli Sinha	5,880	14.4	
63.49%	Others		4,335	10.6	

Warley

LABOUR HOLD	PARTY	2010 CANDIDATE	2010 VOTES	2010 % VOTE	PPC FOR 2015
Majority	Labour	John Spellar MP	20,240	52.9	John Spellar MP
10,756	Conservative	Jas Parmer	9,484	24.8	
Turnout	Lib Dem	Edward Keating	5,929	15.5	
60.99%	Others		2,617	6.8	

Warwick & Leamington

CONSERVATIVE GAIN FROM LABOUR	PARTY	2010 CANDIDATE	2010 VOTES	2010 % VOTE	PPC FOR 2015
Majority	Conservative	Chris White	20,876	42.6	Chris White MP
3,513	Labour	James Plaskitt MP	17,363	35.4	Lynette Kelly
Turnout	Lib Dem	Alan Beddow	8,977	18.3	
72.32%	Others		1,816	3.7	

Majority 3513 (7.2%)

Gained from Labour by Conservative Chris White at the 2010 general election, Warwick & Leamington is an attractive and relatively affluent constituency in easy commuting distance of both Birmingham and Coventry. Warwick itself derives considerable local employment from the tourism sector while Leamington is a logistical hub with a vibrant manufacturing and engineering sector. Despite a considerable amount of residual Conservative support, both Warwick and Leamington include pockets of real poverty in the Clarendon and Willes areas which boost Labour. The 2013 local elections were a score-draw here, with Labour and the Conservatives both polling 29 per cent of the vote. The Labour candidate here will be Lynnette Kelly.

North Warwickshire

CONSERVATIVE GAIN FROM LABOUR	PARTY	2010 CANDIDATE	2010 VOTES	2010 % VOTE	PPC FOR 2015
Majority	Conservative	Dan Byles	18,993	40.2	n/a
54	Labour	Mike O'Brien MP	18,939	40.1	Mike O'Brien
Turnout	Lib Dem	Stephen Martin	5,481	11.6	
67.39%	Others		3,852	8.1	

Majority 54 (0.1%) HS2

Gained by Conservative Dan Byles by the very slimmest of margins at the 2010 general election, North Warwickshire is Labour's top national target in 2015. The constituency is set in the heart of the former Warwickshire coalfield, taking in the towns of Bedworth and Atherstone, Coleshill. While the coal-mining industry has long since vanished, the area retains a strong link with light manufacturing and industry. As a rule, urban areas in this constituency tend to favour Labour while the many rural areas which house commuters to Birmingham and Coventry are more inclined towards the Tories. Dan Byles will be retiring after one rebellious term with former MP and government minister Mike O'Brien who held this seat from 1992 to 2010 hoping to take back the seat for Labour.

West Bromwich East

LABOUR HOLD	PARTY	2010 CANDIDATE	2010 VOTES	2010 % VOTE	PPC FOR 2015
Majority	Labour	Tom Watson MP	17,657	46.5	Tom Watson MP
6,696	Conservative	Alistair Thompson	10,961	28.9	
Turnout	Lib Dem	Ian Garrett	4,993	13.2	
60.56%	Others		4,339	11.4	

West Bromwich West

LABOUR HOLD	PARTY	2010 CANDIDATE	2010 VOTES	2010 % VOTE	PPC FOR 2015
Majority	Labour	Adrian Bailey MP	16,263	45.0	Adrian Bailey MP
5,651	Conservative	Andrew Hardie	10,612	29.3	
Turnout	Lib Dem	Sadie Smith	4,336	12.0	
55.77%	Others		4,960	13.7	

Wolverhampton North East

LABOUR HOLD	PARTY	2010 CANDIDATE	2010 VOTES	2010 % VOTE	PPC FOR 2015
Majority	Labour	Emma Reynolds	14,448	41.4	Emma Reynolds MP
2,484	Conservative	Julie Rook	11,964	34.3	
Turnout	Lib Dem	Colin Ross	4,711	13.5	
59.21%	Others		3,771	10.8	

Wolverhampton South East

LABOUR HOLD	PARTY	2010 CANDIDATE	2010 VOTES	2010 % VOTE	PPC FOR 2015
Majority	Labour	Pat McFadden MP	16,505	47.7	Pat McFadden MP
6,593	Conservative	Ken Wood	9,912	28.6	
Turnout	Lib Dem	Richard Whitehouse	5,207	15.0	
57.84%	Others		3,013	8.7	

Wolverhampton South West

CONSERVATIVE GAIN FROM LABOUR	PARTY	2010 CANDIDATE	2010 VOTES	2010 % VOTE	PPC FOR 2015
Majority	Conservative	Paul Uppal	16,344	40.7	Paul Uppal MP
691	Labour	Rob Marris MP	15,653	39.0	Rob Marris
Turnout	Lib Dem	Robin Lawrence	6,430	16.0	
68.25%	Others		1,733	4.3	

Majority 691 (1.7%)

A socially polarised West Midlands marginal, Wolverhampton South West will be forever known as Enoch Powell's former constituency. Labour support here is strongest in the densely populated St Peter's ward, a city centre area with an unemployment rate of nearly four times the national average. The Conservatives could not possibly be more dominant in Tettenhall, a pleasant suburb whose detached houses, tree-lined avenues and ornate village green are faintly reminiscent of the Surrey commuter belt. Wolverhampton South West is an ethnically diverse constituency with one of the highest Sikh populations in the country (8.2 per cent) as well as a substantial amount of Hindu (4.4 per cent), black (4.4 per cent) and Muslim (3.6 per cent) residents. It is a mark of how far things have come since Mr Powell's time as MP here that the Conservative incumbent is Paul Uppal – a Sikh businessman. He will face a challenge from former Labour MP Rob Marris who held the seat from 2001 to 2010.

Worcester

CONSERVATIVE GAIN FROM LABOUR	PARTY	2010 CANDIDATE	2010 VOTES	2010 % VOTE	PPC FOR 2015
Majority	Conservative	Robin Walker	19,358	39.5	Robin Walker MP
2,982	Labour	Michael Foster MP	16,376	33.4	Joy Squires
Turnout	Lib Dem	Jackie Alderson	9,525	19.4	
67.24%	Others		3,715	7.6	

Majority 2982 (6.1%)

From 'pebble dash man' to 'Holby city woman', every election has a stereotypical type of voter political parties declare key to their election-winning efforts. In 1997 it was the turn of 'Worcester woman' – a middle-income West Midlands woman. The Worcester constituency, which broke decisively for Labour in 1997 before returning to the Conservatives in 2010, is a diverse mix of manufacturing and professional industries, inner-city terraces and pleasant commuter suburbia. Labour are strongest in the urban Worcester wards, scoring big leads in the Gorse Hill and Nunnery areas while the Conservatives perform best in Warndon Parish and Bedwardine just outside the city. The Conservatives were the narrow winners of the 2014 local elections, outpacing Labour by a 33 per cent to 29 per cent margin. The incumbent Conservative MP Robin Walker will be challenged by Labour's Joy Squires, a Worcester city councillor.

Mid Worcestershire

CONSERVATIVE HOLD	PARTY	2010 CANDIDATE	2010 VOTES	2010 % VOTE	PPC FOR 2015
Majority	Conservative	Peter Luff MP	27,770	54.5	Nigel Huddleston
15,864	Lib Dem	Margaret Rowley	11,906	23.4	Margaret Rowley
Turnout	Labour	Robin Lunn	7,613	14.9	
70.60%	Others		3,642	7.2	

West Worcestershire

CONSERVATIVE HOLD	PARTY	2010 CANDIDATE	2010 VOTES	2010 % VOTE	PPC FOR 2015
Majority	Conservative	Harriett Baldwin	27,213	50.3	Harriett Baldwin MP
6,754	Lib Dem	Richard Burt	20,459	37.8	
Turnout	Labour	Penelope Barber	3,661	6.8	Daniel Walton
74.30%	Others		2,760	5.1	

The Wrekin

CONSERVATIVE HOLD	PARTY	2010 CANDIDATE	2010 VOTES	2010 % VOTE	PPC FOR 2015
Majority	Conservative	Mark Pritchard MP	21,922	47.7	Mark Pritchard MP
9,450	Labour	Paul Kalinauckas	12,472	27.1	Katrina Gilman
Turnout	Lib Dem	Alyson Cameron-Daw	8,019	17.4	
70.13%	Others		3,555	7.7	

Wyre Forest

CONSERVATIVE GAIN FROM INDEPENDENT KHHC	PARTY	2010 CANDIDATE	2010 VOTES	2010 % VOTE	PPC FOR 2015
Majority	Conservative	Mark Garnier	18,793	36.9	Mark Garnier MP
2,643	Independent KHHC	Richard Taylor MP	16,150	31.7	
Turnout	Labour	Nigel Knowles	7,298	14.3	Matthew Lamb
66.35%	Others		8,658	17.0	

North West England

The European Parliament region covering the North West of England is huge, and varied. It consists not only of the former metropolitan areas of Greater Manchester and Merseyside, and the administrative county of Lancashire, but stretches down to take in Cheshire and up to include Cumbria, reaching the Scottish border (indeed the one constituency which has 'The Border' in its name, linked with Penrith, provides a safe Conservative haven for the adventurous Rory Stewart MP).

Returning eight MEPs and no fewer than seventy-six to Westminster, the North West not surprisingly has a claim to have more key battlegrounds than any other region. Well over twenty seats can be classed as critical marginals, and these include almost every type of main party contest.

To start with the Conservative targets presently held by Labour, although the Tories made a dozen gains in this region in 2010, they still only hold twenty-two of the seventy-six seats and need to take more if they are to win an overall majority on their own in 2015. On the face of it, this should be far from impossible, with eight targets requiring a swing of 4 per cent or less. The 'easiest' is Bolton West, where Julie Hilling's majority is a mere ninety-two votes. However, this may prove a tougher nut to crack than a nominal swing of 0.1 per cent would imply. The Conservatives were disappointed not to win any of the Bolton constituencies in 2010, and made hardly any progress against a sitting MP, David Crausby, in the North East. Julie Hilling was a new candidate, and will have five years' incumbency to give an added boost. Meanwhile, Wirral South is also vulnerable to a tiny movement of votes of less than 1 per cent. The Wirral peninsula has a reputation as a leafy suburbia compared with the grittier parts of Merseyside, and this is the sort of seat that would undoubtedly not be Labour if it were in a sub-region other than Merseyside, which has been moving in a notably anti-Tory direction since the 1960s. Again, to make a gain here would be a considerable achievement – the pro-Conservative swing in 2010 was distinctly lower than the national average.

The next two seats on the Conservative hit list are in Lancashire. Chorley should be a possibility, as it was won by Den Dover throughout the previous period of Tory government from 1979 to 1997. Blackpool South however, though also needing a 3 per cent swing, is a constituency that has suffered increasing hardship in recent years, with structural as well as seasonal unemployment. Now ranking among the twenty seats with fewest voters in high-ranking occupations, it is hard to believe that Blackpool South was one of two very safe Tory seats in the town as recently as the 1980s. Oldham East & Saddleworth technically needs a 3 per cent swing too, but its recent electoral history has been complicated: the Tories were actually third behind a knife-edge Lab–LD battle in 2010, then this outcome was declared void and there had to be a by-election (January 2011) in which Labour beat the Liberal Democrats by a relatively comfortable 3,000 margin, and the Conservatives were squeezed down to a vote share of only 13 per cent – so it shouldn't really be on their target list at all.

Swings of 4 per cent would enter comfortable overall majority territory for the Tories, but would entail winning seats such as Stalybridge & Hyde in Tameside, which they last did in a by-election in 1937; Bury South; and Sefton Central. The last named seat was chosen as the regional 'one to watch' in the 2010 *Total Politics* guide, and it certainly is a remarkable seat. Sefton Central ranks number one of any seat in England as far as the proportion of its housing that is owner-occupied (87.0 per cent), yet the area (which includes Formby, Maghull and parts of Crosby) has dealt several blows to the Conservatives in recent decades, including Shirley Williams's by-election gain for the SDP in 1981 and a 22 per cent swing to Labour in 1997. Its history is truly more evidence of the 'Merseyside factor', and its swing was only 2 per cent away from Labour in 2010. It seems unlikely to register double that in 2015.

Labour will seek to regain many losses which did occur last time. These range widely from north to south – the north being the border city of Carlisle with its bloody history, where expansion of the boundaries helped the Tories to a narrow win, their first since 1959. Also needing a swing of around 1 per cent is Weaver Vale in Cheshire at the other end of the region, plus two in north Lancashire: Lancaster & Fleetwood and Morecambe & Lunesdale, two seats that pair rather depressed seaside towns with somewhat more affluent inland territory. Next in line is the south division of Warrington, a town traditionally in Lancashire but administratively part of Cheshire from 1974 to 1998 – and since then a proud unitary authority. Other seats lost in 2010 but open to regain on swings of 2–4 per cent are Bury North, Blackpool North & Cleveleys, the City of Chester and the fast-rising Esther McVey's Wirral West (the only seat the Conservatives have won in Merseyside in any election since 1992). The list of possibles goes on and on: Pendle and Rossendale & Darwen in richly accented east Lancashire, South Ribble near Preston, where the first-term MP Lorraine Fullbrook is not standing for re-election. The chances probably run out at Crewe & Nantwich, which needs a swing of 6 per cent, a solid Labour seat before Gwyneth Dunwoody's death in 2008, but looking safe for Edward Timpson ever since.

Still, if Labour can gain twelve from the Tories in the North West region they are on track for forming the next government, and they also have chances against the Liberal Democrats too. It will be very hard for John Leech to hold the heavily student and academic Manchester Withington, following his party leader's statement that he regretted making a pledge on university fees. In Burnley, it is possible that Gordon Birtwistle won in 2010 because of disarray among local

Labour groups, and council results in the town since then suggest he can only win a second time on a largely personal vote.

The Conservatives will also try to gain from the Lib Dems in Cheadle and possibly Hazel Grove, where Andrew Stunell is retiring after eighteen years – but election results in these parts of Stockport are very stable and, as with most of their fifty-seven existing seats, they have a good chance of retention whatever the national polling, European elections, or most council results indicate. On the other hand, it is unlikely the junior coalition party will make many gains. In this region, their two best chances both look unlikely prospects. As mentioned above, they could not gain Oldham East & Saddleworth in a by-election (their speciality) even when the previous Labour MP had effectively been disqualified for malpractice, while in Rochdale, Simon Danczuk has been one of the most voluble and publicised new Labour MPs.

UKIP achieved a strong second place with 27.5 per cent in the 2014 Euro elections in the North West region, which was enough for three MEPs, the same as Labour, but no Westminster constituencies spring to mind where they are likely to challenge. Meanwhile Nick Griffin of the BNP lost his European seat in 2014 when his party polled a wretched 1.9 per cent; two months later he stepped down as leader.

In order to win the next general election outright, the Conservatives must make some progress in this critical region, showing they have an appeal in the northern half of England as well as the south. To achieve the same outcome, Labour have a larger task – they must regain at least ten seats here, as well as regaining their former strength elsewhere in England. As in other regions, there is a strong possibility that neither of these things will happen, and there might therefore again be no overall majority in the House of Commons.

Altrincham & Sale West

CONSERVATIVE HOLD	PARTY	2010 CANDIDATE	2010 VOTES	2010 % VOTE	PPC FOR 2015
Majority	Conservative	Graham Brady MP	24,176	48.9	Graham Brady MP
11,595	Lib Dem	Jane Brophy	12,581	25.5	Jane Broph
Turnout	Labour	Tom Ross	11,073	22.4	James Wright
68.40%	Others		1,563	3.2	

Ashton-under-Lyne

LABOUR HOLD	PARTY	2010 CANDIDATE	2010 VOTES	2010 % VOTE	PPC FOR 2015
Majority	Labour	David Heyes MP	18,604	48.4	n/s
9,094	Conservative	Seema Kennedy	9,510	24.7	
Turnout	Lib Dem	Paul Larkin	5,703	14.8	
56.76%	Others		4,615	12.0	

Barrow & Furness

LABOUR HOLD	PARTY	2010 CANDIDATE	2010 VOTES	2010 % VOTE	PPC FOR 2015
Majority	Labour	John Woodcock	21,226	48.1	John Woodcock MP
5,208	Conservative	John Gough	16,018	36.3	
Turnout	Lib Dem	Barry Rabone	4,424	10.0	
64.00%	Others		2,456	5.6	

Birkenhead

LABOUR HOLD	PARTY	2010 CANDIDATE	2010 VOTES	2010 % VOTE	PPC FOR 2015
Majority	Labour	Frank Field MP	22,082	62.5	Frank Field MP
15,395	Conservative	Andrew Gilbert	6,687	18.9	
Turnout	Lib Dem	Stuart Kelly	6,554	18.6	
56.27%	Others		0	0.0	

Blackburn

LABOUR HOLD	PARTY	2010 CANDIDATE	2010 VOTES	2010 % VOTE	PPC FOR 2015
Majority	Labour	Jack Straw MP	21,751	47.8	Kate Hollern
9,856	Conservative	Michael Law-Riding	11,895	26.1	
Turnout	Lib Dem	Paul English	6,918	15.2	
62.90%	Others		4,935	10.8	

Blackley & Broughton

LABOUR WIN (NEW SEAT)	PARTY	2010 CANDIDATE	2010 VOTES	2010 % VOTE	PPC FOR 2015
Majority	Labour	Graham Stringer MP	18,563	54.3	Graham Stringer MP
12,303	Conservative	James Edsberg	6,260	18.3	
Turnout	Lib Dem	William Hobhouse	4,861	14.2	
49.22%	Others		4,520	13.2	

Blackpool North & Cleveleys

CONSERVATIVE WIN (NEW SEAT)	PARTY	2010 CANDIDATE	2010 VOTES	2010 % VOTE	PPC FOR 2015
Majority	Conservative	Paul Maynard	16,964	41.8	Paul Maynard MP
2,150	Labour	Penny Martin	14,814	36.5	Sam Rushworth
Turnout	Lib Dem	Bill Greene	5,400	13.3	
61.49%	Others		3,413	8.4	

Majority 2150 (5.3%)

A newly created seat at the 2010 election, the inaugural battle for the constituency was won by Conservative Paul Maynard. Conservative strength grows precipitously the further north one travels in the constituency with the densely populated Blackpool town centre wards providing the base of Labour's support. As with neighbouring Blackpool South, the tourist trade is important here which can lead to significant seasonal unemployment. Despite being a low-wage constituency, fewer than one in ten residents live in social housing, although private housing is often in a poor state of repair. Sam Rushworth, a University of East Anglia researcher, will contest the seat for Labour.

Blackpool South

LABOUR HOLD	PARTY	2010 CANDIDATE	2010 VOTES	2010 % VOTE	PPC FOR 2015
Majority	Labour	Gordon Marsden MP	14,449	41.1	Gordon Marsden MP
1,852	Conservative	Ron Bell	12,597	35.8	Peter Anthony
Turnout	Lib Dem	Doreen Holt	5,082	14.4	
55.84%	Others		3,064	8.7	

Bolton North East

LABOUR HOLD	PARTY	2010 CANDIDATE	2010 VOTES	2010 % VOTE	PPC FOR 2015
Majority	Labour	David Crausby MP	19,870	45.9	David Crausby MP
4,084	Conservative	Deborah Dunleavy	15,786	36.5	
Turnout	Lib Dem	Paul Ankers	5,624	13.0	
64.74%	Others		1,997	4.6	

Bolton South East

LABOUR HOLD	PARTY	2010 CANDIDATE	2010 VOTES	2010 % VOTE	PPC FOR 2015
Majority	Labour	Yasmin Qureshi	18,782	47.4	Yasmin Qureshi MP
8,634	Conservative	Andy Morgan	10,148	25.6	
Turnout	Lib Dem	Donal O'Hanlon	6,289	15.9	
56.98%	Others		4,385	11.1	

Bolton West

LABOUR HOLD	PARTY	2010 CANDIDATE	2010 VOTES	2010 % VOTE	PPC FOR 2015
Majority	Labour	Julie Hilling	18,327	38.5	Julie Hilling MP
92	Conservative	Susan Williams	18,235	38.3	Chris Green
Turnout	Lib Dem	Jackie Pearcy	8,177	17.2	
66.74%	Others		2,837	6.0	

Majority 92 (0.2%)

Won by Labour in 2010 by the very narrowest of margins, this Greater Manchester seat is a mix of wealthy commuter-belt villages, such as Heaton, and working-class enclaves of the city of Bolton. Boundary changes prior to the 2010 general election saw Labour's national majority rise from 2000 to 4000 following the addition of Atherton ward from the Leigh constituency and loss of parts of the Tory-inclined Hulton to Bolton South East, slightly shifting the seat's political balance. Unlike other parts of the city, Bolton West is almost entirely white (97 per cent) and more than three-quarters of homes (76.6 per cent) are owner occupied. Labour incumbent Julie Hilling will face a challenge from Conservative candidate Chris Green.

Bootle

LABOUR HOLD	PARTY	2010 CANDIDATE	2010 VOTES	2010 % VOTE	PPC FOR 2015
Majority	Labour	Joe Benton MP	27,426	66.4	n/s
21,181	Lib Dem	James Murray	6,245	15.1	
Turnout	Conservative	Sohail Qureshi	3,678	8.9	
57.79%	Others		3,928	9.5	

Burnley

LIB DEM GAIN FROM LABOUR	PARTY	2010 CANDIDATE	2010 VOTES	2010 % VOTE	PPC FOR 2015
Majority	Lib Dem	Gordon Birtwhistle	14,932	35.7	Gordon Birtwhistle MP
1,818	Labour	Julie Cooper	13,114	31.3	Julie Cooper
Turnout	Conservative	Richard Ali	6,950	16.6	
62.82%	Others		6,849	16.4	

Majority 1818 (4.3%)

Previously a safe Labour constituency, former Burnley council leader Gordon Birtwistle gained this seat in 2010 on his fourth attempt. The constituency is based around the former coal-mining and industrial towns of Burnley and Padiham, both of which have struggled following the decline of the textiles sector and closure of many local manufacturing plants. There are some small pockets of Conservative support here, notably in Worsthorne which is a commuter village for nearby Manchester. Just over one in ten residents are Asian and owner occupation rates are some way below the national average. Unemployment, however, remains fairly low for this part of Lancashire. The Liberal Democrats scored a disastrous performance here in the 2013 election when, having previously held every seat in the constituency, they were reduced to just two seats. The Labour candidate will be Julie Cooper.

Bury North

CONSERVATIVE GAIN FROM LABOUR	PARTY	2010 CANDIDATE	2010 VOTES	2010 % VOTE	PPC FOR 2015
Majority	Conservative	David Nuttall	18,070	40.2	David Nuttall MP
2,243	Labour	Maryam Khan	15,827	35.2	James Frith
Turnout	Lib Dem	Richard Baum	7,645	17.0	
67.35%	Others		3,419	7.6	

Majority 2243 (5%)

Located at the northern edge of the Greater Manchester conurbation, Bury North was gained by Eurosceptic Conservative David Nuttall at the 2010 general election. As a whole, the constituency is broadly middle-class in nature, taking in Bury town centre in the south before gradually moving northwards to the villages of Tottington and Ramsbottom in the shadow of the Rossendale Valley and West Pennine moors. Labour is strongest in the east of Bury town while the Conservatives run up huge leads in the constituency's commuter-populated rural areas. More than three-quarters of homes here are owner occupied. The 2014 local election results were a close-run contest with Labour outpacing the Conservatives by a narrow 39 per cent to 36 per cent margin. The Labour candidate will be Bury councillor James Frith.

Bury South

LABOUR HOLD	PARTY	2010 CANDIDATE	2010 VOTES	2010 % VOTE	PPC FOR 2015
Majority	Labour	Ivan Lewis MP	19,508	40.4	Ivan Lewis MP
3,292	Conservative	Michelle Wiseman	16,216	33.6	
Turnout	Lib Dem	Victor D'Albert	8,796	18.2	
65.63%	Others		3,747	7.8	

Carlisle

CONSERVATIVE GAIN FROM LABOUR	PARTY	2010 CANDIDATE	2010 VOTES	2010 % VOTE	PPC FOR 2015
Majority	Conservative	John Stevenson	16,589	39.3	John Stevenson MP
853	Labour	Michael Boden	15,736	37.3	Lee Sherriff
Turnout	Lib Dem	Neil Hughes	6,567	15.6	
64.66%	Others		3,308	7.8	

Majority 853 (2%)

The most northerly Labour constituency in England, Carlisle is an isolated town located in the rural wilderness just south of the Scottish border. A working-class town with a 99 per cent white population in which the manufacturing sector still provides much employment, Labour repelled Tory challenges by less than 1000 votes at the 1983 and 1987 elections before narrowly electing Conservative solicitor John Stevenson in 2010. While Labour is likely to continue their dominance in urban Carlisle, the Conservatives are particularly strong in the rural wards to the north of the city. The Labour candidate will be Carlisle city councillor Lee Sherriff.

Cheadle

LIB DEM HOLD	PARTY	2010 CANDIDATE	2010 VOTES	2010 % VOTE	PPC FOR 2015
Majority	Lib Dem	Mark Hunter MP	24,717	47.1	Mark Hunter MP
3,272	Conservative	Ben Jeffreys	21,445	40.8	Mary Robinson
Turnout	Labour	Martin Miller	4,920	9.4	Martin Miller
73.30%	Others		1,430	2.7	

City of Chester

CONSERVATIVE GAIN FROM LABOUR	PARTY	2010 CANDIDATE	2010 VOTES	2010 % VOTE	PPC FOR 2015
Majority	Conservative	Stephen Mosley	18,995	40.6	Stephen Mosley MP
2,583	Labour	Christine Russell MP	16,412	35.1	Chris Matheson
Turnout	Lib Dem	Lizzie Jewkes	8,930	19.1	Robert Thompson
66.72%	Others		2,453	5.2	

Majority 2583 (5.5%)

Formerly held by television presenter and well-known raconteur Gyles Brandreth, this constituency takes in the historic city of Chester and a slew of attractive villages just outside the city's walls. While Chester is considerably more middle-class than the majority of nearby Merseyside, the constituency is not without pockets of deprivation, particularly in the social housing-dominated wards of Lache Park, Blacon Lodge and Blacon Hall which heavily favour the Labour Party. The Conservatives, whose candidate Stephen Mosley took this seat from Labour in 2010, are strongest in the city's suburbs, amassing large leads in the Curzon, Westminster and Saughall areas. The Labour candidate will be trade union organiser Chris Matheson.

Chorley

LABOUR HOLD	PARTY	2010 CANDIDATE	2010 VOTES	2010 % VOTE	PPC FOR 2015
Majority	Labour	Lindsay Hoyle MP	21,515	43.2	Linsay Hoyle MP
2,593	Conservative	Alan Cullens	18,922	38.0	Rob Loughenbury
Turnout	Lib Dem	Stephen Fenn	6,957	14.0	
70.13%	Others		2,380	4.8	

Congleton

CONSERVATIVE HOLD	PARTY	2010 CANDIDATE	2010 VOTES	2010 % VOTE	PPC FOR 2015
Majority	Conservative	Fiona Bruce	23,250	45.8	Fiona Bruce MP
7,063	Lib Dem	Peter Hirst	16,187	31.9	
Turnout	Labour	David Bryant	8,747	17.2	Darren Price
70.25%	Others		2,596	5.1	

Copeland

LABOUR HOLD	PARTY	2010 CANDIDATE	2010 VOTES	2010 % VOTE	PPC FOR 2015
Majority	Labour	Jamie Reed MP	19,699	46.0	Jamie Reed MP
3,833	Conservative	Chris Whiteside	15,866	37.1	
Turnout	Lib Dem	Frank Hollowell	4,365	10.2	
67.76%	Others		2,857	6.7	

Crewe & Nantwich

CONSERVATIVE HOLD	PARTY	2010 CANDIDATE	2010 VOTES	2010 % VOTE	PPC FOR 2015
Majority	Conservative	Edward Timpson MP	23,420	45.8	Edward Timpson MP
6,046	Labour	David Williams	17,374	34.0	Adrian Heald
Turnout	Lib Dem	Roy Wood	7,656	15.0	Roy Wood
64.07%	Others		2,634	5.2	

Majority 6046 (11.8%)

The Conservatives were delighted when, in May 2008, Edward Timpson became the first Conservative to gain a by-election from Labour since the Mitcham & Morden by-election in 1982 following the death of maverick MP Gwyneth Dunwoody. Timpson's by-election victory was more than just a flash in the pan, with the Conservatives securing a 6,046 at the 2010 election. Located on the direct train line from London, Crewe is a surprisingly leafy town comprised of a mix of traditionally Labour-supporting terraces and immaculate new housing estates which, along with the attractive market town of Nantwich, strongly favour the Conservatives. Labour's continued strength in Crewe town means the party will always be strong here, although the pace of the construction of new housing estates on the edge of the town is shifting this seat in the Conservatives' direction. The Labour candidate will be Dr Adrian Heald, a local doctor.

Denton & Reddish

LABOUR HOLD	PARTY	2010 CANDIDATE	2010 VOTES	2010 % VOTE	PPC FOR 2015
Majority	Labour	Andrew Gwynne MP	19,191	51.0	Andrew Gwynne MP
9,831	Conservative	Julie Searle	9,360	24.9	
Turnout	Lib Dem	Stephen Broadhurst	6,727	17.9	
56.74%	Others		2,357	6.3	

Eddisbury

CONSERVATIVE HOLD	PARTY	2010 CANDIDATE	2010 VOTES	2010 % VOTE	PPC FOR 2015
Majority	Conservative	Stephen O'Brien MP	23,472	51.7	Stephen O'Brien MP
13,255	Lib Dem	Bob Thompson	10,217	22.5	
Turnout	Labour	Pat Merrick	9,794	21.6	
62.99%	Others		1,931	4.3	

Ellesmere Port & Neston

LABOUR HOLD	PARTY	2010 CANDIDATE	2010 VOTES	2010 % VOTE	PPC FOR 2015
Majority	Labour	Andrew Miller MP	19,750	44.6	Justin Madders
4,331	Conservative	Stuart Penketh	15,419	34.9	
Turnout	Lib Dem	Denise Aspinall	6,663	15.1	
66.51%	Others		2,401	5.4	

Fylde

CONSERVATIVE HOLD	PARTY	2010 CANDIDATE	2010 VOTES	2010 % VOTE	PPC FOR 2015
Majority	Conservative	Mark Menzies	22,826	52.2	Mark Menzies MP
13,185	Lib Dem	Bill Winlow	9,641	22.1	
Turnout	Labour	Liam Robinson	8,624	19.7	Jed Sullivan
66.27%	Others		2,599	5.9	

Garston & Halewood

LABOUR WIN (NEW SEAT)	PARTY	2010 CANDIDATE	2010 VOTES	2010 % VOTE	PPC FOR 2015
Majority	Labour	Maria Eagle MP	25,493	59.5	Maria Eagle MP
16,877	Lib Dem	Paula Keaveney	8,616	20.1	
Turnout	Conservative	Richard Downey	6,908	16.1	
60.05%	Others		1,808	4.2	

Halton

LABOUR HOLD	PARTY	2010 CANDIDATE	2010 VOTES	2010 % VOTE	PPC FOR 2015
Majority	Labour	Derek Twigg MP	23,843	57.7	Derek Twigg MP
15,504	Conservative	Ben Jones	8,339	20.2	
Turnout	Lib Dem	Frank Harasiwka	5,718	13.8	
60.04%	Others		3,438	8.3	

Hazel Grove

LIB DEM HOLD	PARTY	2010 CANDIDATE	2010 VOTES	2010 % VOTE	PPC FOR 2015
Majority	Lib Dem	Andrew Stunell MP	20,485	48.8	Lisa Smart
6,371	Conservative	Annesley Abercorn	14,114	33.6	William Wragg
Turnout	Labour	Richard Scorer	5,234	12.5	Laura Booth
67.39%	Others		2,148	5.1	

Heywood & Middleton

LABOUR HOLD	PARTY	2010 CANDIDATE	2010 VOTES	2010 % VOTE	PPC FOR 2015
Majority	Labour	Jim Dobbin MP	18,499	40.1	Jim Dobbin MP
5,971	Conservative	Mike Holly	12,528	27.2	
Turnout	Lib Dem	Wera Hobhouse	10,474	22.7	
57.53%	Others		4,624	10.0	

Hyndburn

LABOUR HOLD	PARTY	2010 CANDIDATE	2010 VOTES	2010 % VOTE	PPC FOR 2015
Majority	Labour	Graham Jones	17,531	41.1	Graham Jones MP
3,090	Conservative	Karen Buckley	14,441	33.8	
Turnout	Lib Dem	Andrew Rankine	5,033	11.8	
63.48%	Others		5,667	13.3	

Knowsley

LABOUR WIN (NEW SEAT)	PARTY	2010 CANDIDATE	2010 VOTES	2010 % VOTE	PPC FOR 2015
Majority	Labour	George Howarth MP	31,650	70.9	George Howarth MP
25,686	Lib Dem	Flo Clucas	5,964	13.4	Carl Cashman
Turnout	Conservative	David Dunne	4,004	9.0	
56.13%	Others		3,040	6.8	

West Lancashire

LABOUR HOLD	PARTY	2010 CANDIDATE	2010 VOTES	2010 % VOTE	PPC FOR 2015
Majority	Labour	Rosie Cooper MP	21,883	45.1	Rosie Cooper MP
4,343	Conservative	Adrian Owens	17,540	36.2	-
Turnout	Lib Dem	John Gibson	6,573	13.6	
65.65%	Others		2,477	5.1	

Lancaster & Fleetwood

CONSERVATIVE WIN (NEW SEAT)	PARTY	2010 CANDIDATE	2010 VOTES	2010 % VOTE	PPC FOR 2015
Majority	Conservative	Eric Ollerenshaw	15,404	36.1	Eric Ollerenshaw MP
333	Labour	Clive Grunshaw	15,071	35.3	Cat Smith
Turnout	Lib Dem	Stuart Langhorn	8,167	19.1	
63.37%	Others		4,059	9.5	

A newly created constituency at the 2010 general election, Lancaster & Fleetwood is one of the UK's most strangely shaped seats with the two towns physically divided from one another by the Wyre River estuary. Fleetwood, at the end of the Blackpool tramline, has suffered considerably from the near collapse of its traditional fishing industry – three of its five wards being ranked in the top 5 per cent most deprived areas in the UK. Lancaster, a pleasant, stone-clad Lancashire city, is home to a large university whose student and academic population have not traditionally favoured the Tories. The Green Party, fuelled by local opposition to fracking exploration off the Lancashire coastline, are particularly strong in the Lancaster portion of the seat and may save their deposit. The inaugural battle for the seat was won in 2010 by Conservative Eric Ollerenshaw who faces a challenge from Labour's Cat Smith, a local social worker.

Leigh

LABOUR HOLD	PARTY	2010 CANDIDATE	2010 VOTES	2010 % VOTE	PPC FOR 2015
Majority	Labour	Andy Burnham MP	21,295	48.0	Andy Burnham MP
12,011	Conservative	Shazia Awan	9,284	20.9	
Turnout	Lib Dem	Chris Blackburn	8,049	18.2	
58.41%	Others		5,704	12.9	

Liverpool, Riverside

LABOUR HOLD	PARTY	2010 CANDIDATE	2010 VOTES	2010 % VOTE	PPC FOR 2015
Majority	Labour	Louise Ellman MP	22,998	59.3	Louise Ellman MP
14,173	Lib Dem	Richard Marbrow	8,825	22.7	
Turnout	Conservative	Kegang Wu	4,243	10.9	
52.05%	Others		2,735	7.0	

Liverpool, Walton

LABOUR HOLD	PARTY	2010 CANDIDATE	2010 VOTES	2010 % VOTE	PPC FOR 2015
Majority	Labour	Steve Rotheram	24,709	72.0	Steve Rotheram MP
19,818	Lib Dem	Patrick Moloney	4,891	14.2	
Turnout	Conservative	Adam Marsden	2,241	6.5	
54.84%	Others		2,494	7.3	

Liverpool, Wavertree

LABOUR HOLD	PARTY	2010 CANDIDATE	2010 VOTES	2010 % VOTE	PPC FOR 2015
Majority	Labour	Luciana Berger	20,132	53.1	Luciana Berger MP
7,167	Lib Dem	Colin Eldridge	12,965	34.2	
Turnout	Conservative	Andrew Garnett	2,830	7.5	
60.64%	Others		1,987	5.2	

Liverpool, West Derby

LABOUR HOLD/REGAIN FROM INDEPENDENT	PARTY	2010 CANDIDATE	2010 VOTES	2010 % VOTE	PPC FOR 2015
Majority	Labour	Stephen Twigg	18,547	51.8	Stephen Twigg MP
13,874	Lib Dem	Paul Twigger	4,673	13.1	
Turnout	Liberal	Steve Radford	4,304	12.0	
56.73%	Others		3,108	8.7	

Macclesfield

CONSERVATIVE HOLD	PARTY	2010 CANDIDATE	2010 VOTES	2010 % VOTE	PPC FOR 2015
Majority	Conservative	David Rutley	23,503	47.0	David Rutley MP
11,959	Lib Dem	Roger Barlow	11,544	23.1	
Turnout	Labour	Adrian Heald	10,164	20.3	Tim Roca
66.42%	Others		4,848	9.7	

Makerfield

LABOUR HOLD	PARTY	2010 CANDIDATE	2010 VOTES	2010 % VOTE	PPC FOR 2015
Majority	Labour	Yvonne Fovargue	20,700	47.3	Yvonne Fogarvue MP
12,490	Conservative	Itrat Ali	8,210	18.8	
Turnout	Lib Dem	Dave Crowther	7,082	16.2	
59.30%	Others		7,779	17.8	

Manchester Central

LABOUR HOLD	PARTY	2010 CANDIDATE	2010 VOTES	2010 % VOTE	
Majority	Labour	Tony Lloyd MP	21,059	52.7	
10,439	Lib Dem	Marc Ramsbottom	10,620	26.6	
Turnout	Conservative	Suhail Rahuja	4,704	11.8	
44.31%	Others		3,544	8.9	

Manchester Central (2012 by-election)

LABOUR HOLD	PARTY	2012 CANDIDATE	2012 VOTES	2012 % VOTE	PPC FOR 2015
Majority	Labour	Lucy Powell	11,507	69.1	Lucy Powell MP
9,936	Lib Dem	Marc Ramsbottom	1,571	9.4	
Turnout	Conservative	Matthew Sephton	754	4.5	
18.48%	Others		2,816	16.9	

Manchester, Gorton

LABOUR HOLD	PARTY	2010 CANDIDATE	2010 VOTES	2010 % VOTE	PPC FOR 2015
Majority	Labour	Gerald Kaufman MP	19,211	50.1	Gerald Kaufman MP
6,703	Lib Dem	Qassim Afzal	12,508	32.6	
Turnout	Conservative	Caroline Healy	4,224	11.0	
50.47%	Others		2,382	6.2	

Manchester, Withington

LIB DEM HOLD	PARTY	2010 CANDIDATE	2010 VOTES	2010 % VOTE	PPC FOR 2015
Majority	Lib Dem	John Leech MP	20,110	44.7	John Leech MP
1,894	Labour	Lucy Powell	18,216	40.5	Jeff Smith
Turnout	Conservative	Chris Green	5,005	11.1	
60.55%	Others		1,700	3.8	

Majority 1894 (4.2%)

A socially and ethnically diverse seat located on the southern fringes of the city of Manchester, the Withington constituency encompasses the fashionable and wealthy Didsbury and Chorlton districts of the city, as well as poorer areas such as Old Moat and Withington itself. Historically, the constituency's regency housing and tree-lined avenues had made this a safe Conservative seat yet the rapidly expanding student population and sub-division of homes into flats led to Labour seizing this constituency at the 1987 election. The Liberal Democrats shocked the political establishment in 2005 by narrowly taking the constituency from Labour on the back of anger at the introduction of student top-up fees and the Iraq war. The 2014 local elections brought electoral oblivion for the Liberal Democrats who lost every seat they had held in the constituency – and in the entire Manchester city council area. A poll from Lord Ashcroft in June 2014 showed the Liberal Democrats trailing Labour by a dramatic 22 per cent to 56 per cent margin.

Morecambe & Lunesdale

CONSERVATIVE GAIN FROM LABOUR	PARTY	2010 CANDIDATE	2010 VOTES	2010 % VOTE	PPC FOR 2015
Majority	Conservative	David Morris	18,035	41.5	David Morris MP
866	Labour	Geraldine Smith MP	17,169	39.5	Amina Lone
Turnout	Lib Dem	Les Jones	5,791	13.3	
62.43%	Others		2,441	5.6	

Majority 866 (2%)

Located in a remote part of north-west Lancashire, Morecambe & Lunesdale has been held by former Stock, Aitken and Waterman songwriter and current Welsh Office PPS David Morris since the 2010 general election. While almost three-quarters of homes are owner-occupied and fewer than one in ten residents live in social housing, this is a low-wage area where many residents struggle to make a living from the area's declining tourist industry. Industry remains comparatively strong here with a functioning port and nuclear power station operating in Heysham. The Conservatives remain strong in the town of Carnforth and the many inland villages scattered to the east of Morecambe Bay while Labour pile up votes in the town of Morecambe itself. The 2013 county council results produced a score-draw between the Conservatives and Labour – a sign of the politically competitive nature of the seat. The Labour candidate will be Manchester city councillor Amina Lone.

Oldham East & Saddleworth

LABOUR HOLD (VOIDED)	PARTY	2010 CANDIDATE	2010 VOTES	2010 % VOTE
Majority	Labour	Phil Woolas MP	14,186	31.9
103	Lib Dem	Elwyn Watkins	14,083	31.6
Turnout	Conservative	Kashif Ali	11,773	26.4
61.36%	Others		4,478	10.1

Majority 103 (0%)

One of the closest fought seats at the 2010 general election, former Labour MP Phil Woolas's 103 majority over the Liberal Democrats was declared invalid several months later following a High Court ruling that found Labour had lied about Lib Dem candidate Elwyn Watkins's views on a range of issues. A by-election was held in January 2011 which saw the now Labour MP Debbie Abrahams score a convincing ten-point victory over the Liberal Democrats. Located to the east of Manchester, the Oldham portion of the seat is staunchly working-class in nature and has a large Muslim population while Saddleworth is an affluent Pennine commuter town. All three main political parties have significant residual support in the seat – with each having held a version of the constituency at some point in the past twenty-five years.

Oldham East & Saddleworth (2011 re-run)

LABOUR HOLD	PARTY	2011 CANDIDATE	2011 VOTES	2011 % VOTE	PPC FOR 2015
Majority	Labour	Debbie Abrahams	14,718	42.1	Debbie Abrahams MP
3,558	Lib Dem	Elwyn Watkins	11,160	31.9	Richard Marbrow
Turnout	Conservative	Kashif Ali	4,481	12.8	
0.00%	Others		4,571	13.1	

Oldham West & Royton

LABOUR HOLD	PARTY	2010 CANDIDATE	2010 VOTES	2010 % VOTE	PPC FOR 2015
Majority	Labour	Michael Meacher MP	19,503	45.5	Michael Meacher MP
9,352	Conservative	Kamran Ghafoor	10,151	23.7	
Turnout	Lib Dem	Mark Alcock	8,193	19.1	
59.30%	Others		5,063	11.8	

Pendle

CONSERVATIVE HOLD	PARTY	2010 CANDIDATE	2010 VOTES	2010 % VOTE	PPC FOR 2015
Majority	Conservative	Andrew Stephenson	17,512	38.9	Andrew Stephenson MP
3,585	Labour	Gordon Prentice MP	13,927	30.9	Azhar Ali
Turnout	Lib Dem	Afzal Anwar	9,095	20.2	
67.82%	Others		4,511	10.0	

Majority 3585 (8%)

Gained by Conservative Andrew Stephenson at the 2010, the Pendle constituency is a pleasant collection of archetypal Lancashire towns set against the background of the picturesque hills. Nelson and Colne are both traditional mill towns whose fortunes have risen and fallen with the decline of the British textile industry, giving rise to significant social problems. The seat's sizable Muslim community (13.4 per cent) and industrial past makes it favourable to Labour yet the Conservatives are strongly dominant in rural areas. While this is a poor area where more than a third of local residents have no qualifications, three-quarters of homes are owner-occupied – well above average for a North West constituency. Labour outpolled the Conservatives here by a 39 per cent to 29 per cent margin at the 2014 elections. The Labour candidate will be former Pendle council leader Azhar Ali.

Penrith & The Border

CONSERVATIVE HOLD	PARTY	2010 CANDIDATE	2010 VOTES	2010 % VOTE	PPC FOR 2015
Majority	Conservative	Rory Stewart	24,071	53.4	Rory Stewart MP
11,241	Lib Dem	Peter Thornton	12,830	28.5	
Turnout	Labour	Barabra Cannon	5,834	12.9	Lee Rushworth
69.92%	Others		2,352	5.2	

Preston

LABOUR HOLD	PARTY	2010 CANDIDATE	2010 VOTES	2010 % VOTE	PPC FOR 2015
Majority	Labour	Mark Henrick MP	15,668	48.2	Mark Henrick MP
7,733	Lib Dem	Mark Jewell	7,935	24.4	
Turnout	Conservative	Nerissa Warner-O'Neill	7,060	21.7	
53.12%	Others		1,842	5.7	

Ribble Valley

CONSERVATIVE HOLD	PARTY	2010 CANDIDATE	2010 VOTES	2010 % VOTE	PPC FOR 2015
Majority	Conservative	Nigel Evans MP	26,298	50.3	Nigel Evans MP
14,769	Labour	Paul Foster	11,529	22.0	
Turnout	Lib Dem	Allan Knox	10,732	20.5	Jackie Pearcey
67.22%	Others		3,728	7.1	

Rochdale

LABOUR GAIN FROM LIB DEM	PARTY	2010 CANDIDATE	2010 VOTES	2010 % VOTE	PPC FOR 2015
Majority	Labour	Simon Danczuk	16,699	36.4	Simon Danczuk MP
889	Lib Dem	Paul Rowen MP	15,810	34.4	Andy Kelly
Turnout	Conservative	Mudasir Dean	8,305	18.1	
58.15%	Others		5,093	11.1	

Majority 889 (2%)

Located to the north of Manchester, Rochdale is a classic swing seat – lost to Labour in 1997, the Liberal Democrats won the seat back in 2005, before it reverted to Labour's Simon Danczuk at the 2010 general election. The seat itself is comprised of the bulk of the former industrial and textile-manufacturing town of Rochdale and the former mill towns of Littleborough and Milnrow, taking in a tranche of attractive Pennine villages. While Labour has always been dominant in Rochdale itself, the Liberal Democrats have long enjoyed strong support in the town's suburbs and rural areas. The seat is home to a large Muslim community who number almost a quarter of local residents. Synonymous for years with its larger-than-life former Liberal Democrat MP Cyril Smith, Rochdale's residents are now seeking to put all memories of the latterly discovered child sex offender behind them. The Cyril Smith revelations have served to compound problems associated with Liberal Democrats' sagging poll numbers nationally, with the 2014 local election seeing Labour win forty-eight seats to their one.

Rossendale & Darwen

CONSERVATIVE GAIN FROM LABOUR	PARTY	2010 CANDIDATE	2010 VOTES	2010 % VOTE	PPC FOR 2015
Majority	Conservative	Jake Berry	19,691	41.8	Jake Berry MP
4,493	Labour	Janet Anderson MP	15,198	32.2	Will Straw
Turnout	Lib Dem	Bob Sheffield	8,541	18.1	
64.36%	Others		3,698	7.8	

Majority 4493 (9.5%)

Gained by Conservative Jake Berry at the 2010 general election, Rossendale & Darwen is a striking rural constituency located to the north of Greater Manchester. Darwen, Rawtenstall and Bacup are the largest towns here, all of them former textile towns which have gradually diversified into light manufacturing industries over the past two decades. While three-quarters of homes are owner-occupied, around a third of residents have no qualifications and youth unemployment is a problem locally. In contrast with other Lancashire mill towns, the Asian population here is extremely low at only 2 per cent at the time of the 2001 census. The Conservatives have lost considerable ground here on a local government level in recent years, holding only ten seats to Labour's twenty four. The Labour candidate will be Will Straw, the son of the former Foreign Secretary Jack Straw.

Salford & Eccles

LABOUR WIN (NEW SEAT)	PARTY	2010 CANDIDATE	2010 VOTES	2010 % VOTE	PPC FOR 2015
Majority	Labour	Hazel Blears MP	16,655	40.1	Rebecca Long-Bailey
5,725	Lib Dem	Norman Owen	10,930	26.3	
Turnout	Conservative	Matthew Sephton	8,497	20.5	
55.02%	Others		5,451	13.1	

Sefton Central

LABOUR HOLD	PARTY	2010 CANDIDATE	2010 VOTES	2010 % VOTE	PPC FOR 2015
Majority	Labour	Bill Esterton	20,307	41.9	Bill Esterton MP
3,862	Conservative	Debi Jones	16,445	33.9	
Turnout	Lib Dem	Richard Clein	9,656	19.9	
71.79%	Others		2,055	4.2	

South Ribble

CONSERVATIVE GAIN FROM LABOUR	PARTY	2010 CANDIDATE	2010 VOTES	2010 % VOTE	PPC FOR 2015
Majority	Conservative	Lorraine Fullbrook	23,396	45.5	Seema Kennedy
5,554	Labour	David Borrow MP	17,842	34.7	Veronica Bennett
Turnout	Lib Dem	Peter Fisher	7,271	14.1	Sue McGuire
67.87%	Others		2,949	5.7	

Majority 5554 (10.8%)

Formed around the town of Leyland and wealthy suburbs north of Preston, Conservative Lorraine Fullbrook took the seat from Labour by 5,554 votes in 2010. Leyland itself is a medium-sized industrial town which has suffered over the past years from substantial job losses in the manufacturing sector. As one moves south of Leyland and into the Lancashire countryside surrounding Preston, Conservative prospects improve dramatically with the party receiving overwhelming support in the towns of Longton and Hutton. Owner occupation rates, at 83.4%, are exceptionally high with only one in ten people living in social housing. With Fulbrook opting to retire in 2015 after just one term, he will be replaced as Conservative candidate by Seema Kennedy. Veronica Bennett, a Sefton councillor, will fight to take the seat for Labour.

Southport

LIB DEM HOLD	PARTY	2010 CANDIDATE	2010 VOTES	2010 % VOTE	PPC FOR 2015
Majority	Lib Dem	John Pugh MP	21,707	49.6	John Pugh MP
6,024	Conservative	Brenda Porter	15,683	35.8	
Turnout	Labour	Jim Conalty	4,116	9.4	
65.11%	Others		2,251	5.1	

St Helens North

LABOUR HOLD	PARTY	2010 CANDIDATE	2010 VOTES	2010 % VOTE	PPC FOR 2015
Majority	Labour	David Watts MP	23,041	51.7	David Watts MP
13,101	Conservative	Paul Greenall	9,940	22.3	
Turnout	Lib Dem	John Beirne	8,992	20.2	
59.42%	Others		2,583	5.8	

St Helens South & Whiston

LABOUR HOLD	PARTY	2010 CANDIDATE	2010 VOTES	2010 % VOTE	PPC FOR 2015
Majority	Labour	Shaun Woodward MP	24,364	52.9	Marie Rimmer
14,122	Lib Dem	Brian Spencer	10,242	22.2	
Turnout	Conservative	Val Allen	8,209	17.8	
59.10%	Others		3,266	7.1	

Stalybridge & Hyde

LABOUR HOLD	PARTY	2010 CANDIDATE	2010 VOTES	2010 % VOTE	PPC FOR 2015
Majority	Labour	Jonathan Reynolds	16,189	39.6	Jonathan Reynolds MP
2,744	Conservative	Rob Adlard	13,445	32.9	
Turnout	Lib Dem	John Potter	6,965	17.0	
59.18%	Others		4,280	10.5	

Stockport

LABOUR HOLD	PARTY	2010 CANDIDATE	2010 VOTES	2010 % VOTE	PPC FOR 2015
Majority	Labour	Ann Coffey MP	16,697	42.7	Ann Coffey MP
6,784	Conservative	Stephen Holland	9,913	25.3	
Turnout	Lib Dem	Stuart Bodsworth	9,778	25.0	Daniel Hawthorne
62.23%	Others		2,740	7.0	

Stretford & Urmston

LABOUR HOLD	PARTY	2010 CANDIDATE	2010 VOTES	2010 % VOTE	PPC FOR 2015
Majority	Labour	Kate Green	21,821	48.6	Kate Green MP
8,935	Conservative	Alex Williams	12,886	28.7	
Turnout	Lib Dem	Stephen Cook	7,601	16.9	
63.26%	Others		2,602	5.8	

Tatton

CONSERVATIVE HOLD	PARTY	2010 CANDIDATE	2010 VOTES	2010 % VOTE	PPC FOR 2015
Majority	Conservative	George Osborne MP	24,687	54.6	George Osborne MP
14,487	Lib Dem	David Lomax	10,200	22.6	
Turnout	Labour	Richard Jackson	7,803	17.3	
67.77%	Others		2,541	5.6	

Wallasey

LABOUR HOLD	PARTY	2010 CANDIDATE	2010 VOTES	2010 % VOTE	PPC FOR 2015
Majority	Labour	Angela Eagle MP	21,578	51.8	Angela Eagle MP
8,507	Conservative	Leah Fraser	13,071	31.4	
Turnout	Lib Dem	Steve Pitt	5,693	13.7	
63.19%	Others		1,312	3.1	

Warrington North

LABOUR HOLD	PARTY	2010 CANDIDATE	2010 VOTES	2010 % VOTE	PPC FOR 2015
Majority	Labour	Helen Jones MP	20,135	45.5	Helen Jones MP
6,771	Conservative	Paul Campbell	13,364	30.2	
Turnout	Lib Dem	Dave Eccles	9,196	20.8	
62.73%	Others		1,516	3.4	

Warrington South

CONSERVATIVE GAIN FROM LABOUR	PARTY	2010 CANDIDATE	2010 VOTES	2010 % VOTE	PPC FOR 2015
Majority	Conservative	David Mowat	19,641	35.8	David Mowat MP
1,553	Labour	Nick Bent	18,088	33.0	Nick Bent
Turnout	Lib Dem	Jo Crotty	15,094	27.5	
69.30%	Others		2,051	3.7	

Majority 1553 (2.8%)

Seized from Labour by Conservative David Mowat at the 2010 general election, the Warrington South constituency is a largely middle-class constituency populated by commuters to nearby Manchester and Liverpool. While lacking in local amenities, this is a largely pleasant residential seat in which more than four in five homes are owner occupied. Conservative support is at its strongest in the semi-rural areas abutting the neighbouring Tatton constituency while the Warrington town wards are safe for Labour. The Labour candidate will be Nick Bent.

Weaver Vale

CONSERVATIVE GAIN FROM LABOUR	PARTY	2010 CANDIDATE	2010 VOTES	2010 % VOTE	PPC FOR 2015
Majority	Conservative	Graham Evans	16,953	38.5	Graham Evans MP
991	Labour	John Stockton	15,962	36.3	Julia Tickridge
Turnout	Lib Dem	Peter Hampson	8,196	18.6	
65.39%	Others		2,879	6.5	

Majority 991 (2.3%)

The name of an area rather than a town, the Weaver Vale constituency is comprised of the western Cheshire towns of Northwich and Frodsham. Held by Conservative Graham Evans since the 2010 general election, this constituency is an uneasy mix of wealthy Cheshire villages and heavy industry. Northwich, the largest town in the seat, is home to a thriving industrial sector with chemical processing providing a major source of jobs in the area. Located between Chester and Warrington, the attractive town of Frodsham is considerably more middle-class, ordinarily offering the Conservatives its steadfast support. The area is nearly exclusively white with owner-occupation levels standing at close to three-quarters. The Labour candidate will be councillor Julia Tickridge.

Westmorland & Lonsdale

LIB DEM HOLD	PARTY	2010 CANDIDATE	2010 VOTES	2010 % VOTE	PPC FOR 2015
Majority	Lib Dem	Tim Farron MP	30,896	60.0	Tim Farron MP
12,264	Conservative	Gareth McKeever	18,632	36.2	Ann Myatt
Turnout	Labour	Jonathan Todd	1,158	2.2	
76.86%	Others		801	1.6	

Wigan

LABOUR HOLD	PARTY	2010 CANDIDATE	2010 VOTES	2010 % VOTE	PPC FOR 2015
Majority	Labour	Lisa Nandy	21,404	48.5	Lisa Nandy MP
10,487	Conservative	Michael Winstanley	10,917	24.7	
Turnout	Lib Dem	Mark Clayton	6,797	15.4	
58.54%	Others		5,022	11.4	

Wirral South

LABOUR HOLD	PARTY	2010 CANDIDATE	2010 VOTES	2010 % VOTE	PPC FOR 2015
Majority	Labour	Alison McGovern	16,276	40.8	Alison McGovern MP
531	Conservative	Jeff Clarke	15,745	39.5	John Bell
Turnout	Lib Dem	Jamie Saddler	6,611	16.6	
71.13%	Others		1,274	3.2	

Majority 531 (1.3%)

Historically a solidly Conservative seat, Wirral South was seized by Labour's Ben Chapman in a famous by-election only weeks before the 1997 general election. Held since 2010 by Labour's Alison McGovern, the constituency stretches from the Dee Estuary across to the middle-class towns of Heswall and Gayton, possessing some stunning views across the Mersey from Port Sunlight. The Conservatives are all-conquering in Heswall in the southern part of the Wirral Peninsula while Labour is strongest in the former dock town of Bromborough. The constituency is in easy reach of both Manchester and Liverpool and is home to many commuters. Labour were the narrow winners of the 2014 council elections, outpacing the Conservatives by a 35 per cent to 30 per cent margin across the constituency with UKIP in third place on 18 per cent. The Conservatives will be fielding John Bell.

Wirral West

CONSERVATIVE GAIN FROM LABOUR	PARTY	2010 CANDIDATE	2010 VOTES	2010 % VOTE	PPC FOR 2015
Majority	Conservative	Esther McVey	16,726	42.5	Esther McVey MP
2,436	Labour	Philip Davies	14,290	36.3	Margaret Greenwood
Turnout	Lib Dem	Peter Reisdorf	6,630	16.8	Peter Reisdorf MP
71.52%	Others		1,726	4.4	

Majority 2436 (6.2%)

Located just south of Liverpool, Wirral West is a predominantly middle-class and residential constituency home to those who commute daily to Liverpool and, to a lesser extent, Manchester. The constituency encompasses the seaside communities of West Kirby and Hoylake that are favourable towards the Conservatives, as well as more challenging areas closer to urban Birkenhead such as Upton and Prenton that provide the bulk of Labour's support. The Conservatives have lost ground here on a local government level in recent years, yet remain strongly competitive across the constituency. The MP here since 2010 has been the Conservative Work and Pensions Minister Esther McVey. She will be challenged by Labour's Margaret Greenwood.

Workington

LABOUR HOLD	PARTY	2010 CANDIDATE	2010 VOTES	2010 % VOTE	PPC FOR 2015
Majority	Labour	Tony Cunningham MP	17,865	45.5	n/s
4,575	Conservative	Judith Pattinson	13,290	33.9	
Turnout	Lib Dem	Stan Collins	5,318	13.5	
65.86%	Others		2,786	7.1	

Worsley & Eccles South

LABOUR WIN (NEW SEAT)	PARTY	2010 CANDIDATE	2010 VOTES	2010 % VOTE	PPC FOR 2015
Majority	Labour	Barbara Keeley MP	17,892	42.9	Barbara Keeley MP
4,337	Conservative	Iain Lindley	13,555	32.5	
Turnout	Lib Dem	Richard Gadsden	6,883	16.5	
57.54%	Others		3,371	8.1	

Wyre & Preston North

CONSERVATIVE WIN (NEW SEAT)	PARTY	2010 CANDIDATE	2010 VOTES	2010 % VOTE	PPC FOR 2015
Majority	Conservative	Ben Wallace MP	26,877	52.4	Ben Wallace MP
15,844	Lib Dem	Danny Gallagher	11,033	21.5	
Turnout	Labour	Cat Smith	10,932	21.3	
73.09%	Others		2,466	4.8	

Wythenshawe & Sale East

LABOUR HOLD	PARTY	2010 CANDIDATE	2010 VOTES	2010 % VOTE
Majority	Labour	Paul Goggins MP	17,987	44.1
7,575	Conservative	Janet Clowes	10,412	25.6
Turnout	Lib Dem	Martin Eakins	9,107	22.3
50.99%	Others		3,245	8.0

Wythenshawe & Sale East (2014 by-election)

LABOUR HOLD	PARTY	2014 CANDIDATE	2014 VOTES	2014 % VOTE	PPC FOR 2015
Majority	Labour	Mike Kane	13,261	32.5	Mike Kane MP
8,960	UKIP	John Bickley	4,301	10.6	
Turnout	Conservative	Daniel Critchlow	3,479	8.5	
50.99%	Others		2,920	7.2	William Jones (Lib Dem)

North East England

The North East of England is the smallest European Parliament region on the island of Britain, returning only three MEPs (though Northern Ireland has a smaller population). It is also the strongest of all for Labour – in May 2014 they were awarded two of the three, even under the list system of proportional representation. Labour's share of the vote increased by 11.5 per cent compared with 2009, to 36 per cent. The party also currently holds twenty-five of the twenty-nine Westminster parliamentary constituencies – an even more emphatic level of dominance. This is not just because of the predominantly working-class nature of traditional employment on the North East – shipbuilding on the River Tyne, coal mining in County Durham – whose cultural and political legacy has outlasted the decline of those industries themselves. It is also generally true that the further away from the prosperous south of England one goes, the weaker the appeal of the Conservative Party becomes.

This Labour hegemony does not mean that there are no marginal seats in North East England. Middlesbrough South & East Cleveland (an unwieldy name) lies at number fourteen on the Conservatives' national list of targets, and to fall it would require a swing of just 2 per cent since 2010. In its previous guise, Langbaurgh – a shorter name but for many unpronounceable and harder to locate – it swung several times with the electoral tide. Another constituency in this category is Darlington, starkly divided between a leafy western side and a gritty working-class 'east end'. It is the forty-sixth most likely Labour loss, which would betoken a comfortable majority for David Cameron, allowing him to govern without a coalition. A swing of 4 per cent would achieve this goal.

On the other hand, Labour would like to halve the Conservative representation in the region by taking Stockton South, now held by the youngest of all Tory MPs, James Wharton, who turned thirty on 16 February 2014 and whose majority is a vulnerable 332. Stockton South has changed hands several times in living memory, having lasted longer as an SDP seat (for Ian Wrigglesworth) than most did back in the 1980s. A Labour gain is no certainty, though, given Mr Wharton's development of the small but valuable personal vote due to an active incumbent, and because there are some solidly Conservative pockets, such as Yarm, which in 2014 voted in a local referendum to express its preference to 'defect' to North Yorkshire.

Each of the biggest parties also have their eyes on one of the two Liberal Democrat seats, which might afford the most interesting contests of all in this region. For a start, the usual and expected Lib Dem strength where they hold the seat already will be severely weakened by the fact that in neither Berwick-upon-Tweed nor Redcar will there be a sitting MP. In previous centuries of conflict Berwick changed hands many times between England and Scotland, but in parliamentary terms it has not done so since Alan Beith gained it in a by-election in 1973. However, now a very senior Liberal Democrat and a knight, he has announced his retirement. This offers real hope for the Conservatives, who reduced his majority from the steady 8,000 it had been in 1997, 2001 and 2005 to just 2,690 in 2010. Charged with defending this most northerly of all English constituencies is Julie Porksen, one of only a small number of women in winnable seats for her party; but recent local elections are against her, while history suggests a close battle. In Redcar, a much younger and less experienced MP is retiring. Ian Swales took this long-term Labour stronghold by over 5,000 from Vera Baird in 2010, one year after the closure of the local steelworks. It will be even harder to repeat this triumph with a new candidate.

Although it is certain that the vast majority of parliamentary divisions in the North East will remain in Labour hands, we should not close without mentioning the other party that secured an MEP in 2014.

This was not the Conservatives, whose share dropped by two points to less than 18 per cent, which meant the defeat of Martin Callanan, the leader of the Conservative and Reformist group in the European Parliament. Nor was it the Liberal Democrats, whose vote collapsed from 17 per cent to 6 per cent. It was UKIP, who polled an impressive 29 per cent, above their national average. Analysis of this success shows that they did best in working-class Labour strongholds. This gives the lie to the idea that UKIP are right-wing Tories in disguise. However, it probably also means that while they may finish second in a number of Labour seats at the next general election, they are unlikely to win any of them. The first-past-the-post system reinforced by the rejection of any change in the 2011 AV referendum means that Labour may win 90 per cent of the constituencies in this region in 2015, even with under half the total vote.

Berwick-upon-Tweed

LIB DEM HOLD	PARTY	2010 CANDIDATE	2010 VOTES	2010 % VOTE	PPC FOR 2015
Majority	Lib Dem	Alan Beith MP	16,806	43.7	Julie Pörkson
2,690	Conservative	Anne-Marie Trevelyan	14,116	36.7	Anne-Marie Trevelyan
Turnout	Labour	Alan Strickland	5,061	13.2	Scott Dickinson
67.94%	Others		2,456	6.4	

Bishop Auckland

LABOUR HOLD	PARTY	2010 CANDIDATE	2010 VOTES	2010 % VOTE	PPC FOR 2015
Majority	Labour	Helen Goodman MP	16,023	39.0	Helen Goodman MP
5,218	Conservative	Barbara Harrison	10,805	26.3	
Turnout	Lib Dem	Mark Wilkes	9,189	22.3	
60.17%	Others		5,119	12.4	

Blaydon

LABOUR HOLD	PARTY	2010 CANDIDATE	2010 VOTES	2010 % VOTE	PPC FOR 2015
Majority	Labour	David Anderson MP	22,297	49.6	David Anderson MP
9,117	Lib Dem	Neil Bradbury	13,180	29.3	
Turnout	Conservative	Glenn Hall	7,159	15.9	
66.24%	Others		2,277	5.1	

Blyth Valley

LABOUR HOLD	PARTY	2010 CANDIDATE	2010 VOTES	2010 % VOTE	PPC FOR 2015
Majority	Labour	Ronnie Campbell MP	17,156	44.5	Ronnie Campbell MP
6,668	Lib Dem	Jeffrey Reid	10,488	27.2	
Turnout	Conservative	Barry Flux	6,412	16.6	
61.31%	Others		4,510	11.7	

Darlington

LABOUR HOLD	PARTY	2010 CANDIDATE	2010 VOTES	2010 % VOTE	PPC FOR 2015
Majority	Labour	Jenny Chapman	16,891	39.4	Jenny Chapman MP
3,388	Conservative	Edward Legard	13,503	31.5	
Turnout	Lib Dem	Mike Barker	10,046	23.4	
62.93%	Others		2,456	5.7	

North Durham

LABOUR HOLD	PARTY	2010 CANDIDATE	2010 VOTES	2010 % VOTE	PPC FOR 2015
Majority	Labour	Kevan Jones MP	20,698	50.5	Kevan Jones MP
12,076	Conservative	David Skelton	8,622	21.0	Laetitia Glossop
Turnout	Lib Dem	Ian Lindley	8,617	21.0	
60.65%	Others		3,030	7.4	

North West Durham

LABOUR HOLD	PARTY	2010 CANDIDATE	2010 VOTES	2010 % VOTE	PPC FOR 2015
Majority	Labour	Pat Glass	18,539	42.3	Pat Glass MP
7,612	Lib Dem	Owen Temple	10,927	24.9	
Turnout	Conservative	Michelle Tempest	8,766	20.0	Charlotte Haitham-Taylor
62.28%	Others		5,583	12.7	

City of Durham

LABOUR HOLD	PARTY	2010 CANDIDATE	2010 VOTES	2010 % VOTE	PPC FOR 2015
Majority	Labour	Roberta Blackman-Woods MP	20,496	44.3	Roberta Blackman-Woods MP
3,067	Lib Dem	Carol Woods	17,429	37.7	Craig Martin
Turnout	Conservative	Nick Varley	6,146	13.3	Rebecca Coulson
67.20%	Others		2,181	4.7	

Easington

LABOUR HOLD	PARTY	2010 CANDIDATE	2010 VOTES	2010 % VOTE	PPC FOR 2015
Majority	Labour	Grahame Morris	20,579	58.9	Grahame Morris MP
14,982	Lib Dem	Tara Saville	5,597	16.0	
Turnout	Conservative	Richard Harrison	4,790	13.7	Chris Hampsheir
54.66%	Others		3,948	11.3	

Gateshead

LABOUR WIN (NEW SEAT)	PARTY	2010 CANDIDATE	2010 VOTES	2010 % VOTE	PPC FOR 2015
Majority	Labour	Ian Mearns	20,712	54.1	Ian Mearns MP
12,549	Lib Dem	Frank Hindle	8,163	21.3	
Turnout	Conservative	Hazel Anderson	5,716	14.9	
57.54%	Others		3,666	9.6	

Hartlepool

LABOUR HOLD	PARTY	2010 CANDIDATE	2010 VOTES	2010 % VOTE	PPC FOR 2015
Majority	Labour	Iain Wright MP	16,267	42.5	Iain Wright MP
5,509	Conservative	Alan Wright	10,758	28.1	
Turnout	Lib Dem	Reg Clark	6,533	17.1	
55.48%	Others		4,684	12.2	

Hexham

CONSERVATIVE HOLD	PARTY	2010 CANDIDATE	2010 VOTES	2010 % VOTE	PPC FOR 2015
Majority	Conservative	Guy Opperman	18,795	43.2	Guy Opperman MP
5,788	Lib Dem	Andrew Duffield	13,007	29.9	Jeff Reid
Turnout	Labour	Antoine Tinnion	8,253	19.0	Liam Carr
72.04%	Others		3,428	7.9	

Houghton & Sunderland South

LABOUR HOLD	PARTY	2010 CANDIDATE	2010 VOTES	2010 % VOTE	PPC FOR 2015
Majority	Labour	Bridget Phillipson	19,137	50.3	Bridget Philipson MP
10,990	Conservative	Robert Oliver	8,147	21.4	
Turnout	Lib Dem	Christopher Boyle	5,292	13.9	
55.32%	Others		5,445	14.3	

Jarrow

LABOUR HOLD	PARTY	2010 CANDIDATE	2010 VOTES	2010 % VOTE	PPC FOR 2015
Majority	Labour	Stephen Hepburn MP	20,910	53.9	Stephen Hepburn MP
12,908	Conservative	Jeff Milburn	8,002	20.6	
Turnout	Lib Dem	Tom Appleby	7,163	18.5	
60.27%	Others		2,709	7.0	

Middlesbrough

LABOUR HOLD	PARTY	2010 CANDIDATE	2010 VOTES	2010 % VOTE	
Majority	Labour	Stuart Bell MP	15,351	45.9	
8,689	Lib Dem	Chris Foote-Wood	6,662	19.9	
Turnout	Conservative	John Walsh	6,283	18.8	
51.35%	Others		5,159	15.4	

Middlesbrough (2012 by-election)

LABOUR HOLD	PARTY	2012 CANDIDATE	2012 VOTES	2012 % VOTE	PPC FOR 2015
Majority	Labour	Andy McDonald	10,201	60.5	Andy McDonald MP
8,211	UKIP	Richard Elvin	1,990	11.8	
Turnout	Lib Dem	George Selmer	1,672	9.9	Richard Kilpatrick
25.89%	Others		3,003	17.8	

Middlesbrough South & East Cleveland

LABOUR HOLD	PARTY	2010 CANDIDATE	2010 VOTES	2010 % VOTE	PPC FOR 2015
Majority	Labour	Tom Blenkinsop	18,138	39.2	Tom Blenkinsop MP
1,677	Conservative	Paul Bristow	16,461	35.6	Will Goodhand
Turnout	Lib Dem	Nick Emmerson	7,340	15.9	
63.60%	Others		4,275	9.3	

Majority 1677 (3.6%)

Held by the Conservative Michael Bates until 1997, the cumbersomely named Middlesbrough South and East Cleveland seat is a constituency of contrasts. Both Labour and the Conservatives have a solid core vote here, the poverty of southern Middlesbrough's council estates lying in stark contrast to the opulence of the towns and villages dotted along the North Yorkshire moors and East Cleveland coast. More than a third of local residents have no qualifications, a quarter live in council housing and unemployment is higher than the national average. The sitting MP Tom Blenkinsop will square off against Conservative Will Goodhand.

Newcastle upon Tyne Central

LABOUR HOLD	PARTY	2010 CANDIDATE	2010 VOTES	2010 % VOTE	PPC FOR 2015
Majority	Labour	Chi Onwurah	15,692	45.9	Chi Onwurah MP
7,464	Lib Dem	Gareth Kane	8,228	24.1	
Turnout	Conservative	Nick Holder	6,611	19.4	
56.45%	Others		3,624	10.6	

Newcastle upon Tyne East

LABOUR HOLD	PARTY	2010 CANDIDATE	2010 VOTES	2010 % VOTE	PPC FOR 2015
Majority	Labour	Nick Brown MP	17,043	45.0	Nick Brown MP
4,453	Lib Dem	Wendy Taylor	12,590	33.3	
Turnout	Conservative	Dominic Llewellyn	6,068	16.0	
58.68%	Others		2,139	5.7	

Newcastle upon Tyne North

LABOUR HOLD	PARTY	2010 CANDIDATE	2010 VOTES	2010 % VOTE	PPC FOR 2015
Majority	Labour	Catherine McKinnell	17,950	40.8	Catherine McKinnell MP
3,414	Lib Dem	Ron Beadle	14,536	33.1	
Turnout	Conservative	Stephen Parkinson	7,966	18.1	
65.48%	Others		3,494	8.0	

Redcar

LIB DEM GAIN FROM LABOUR	PARTY	2010 CANDIDATE	2010 VOTES	2010 % VOTE	PPC FOR 2015
Majority	Lib Dem	Ian Swales	18,955	45.2	n/s
5,214	Labour	Vera Baird MP	13,741	32.7	Anna Turley
Turnout	Conservative	Steve Mastin	5,790	13.8	
62.51%	Others		3,477	8.3	

Majority 5214 (12.4%)

One of the biggest surprises of election night 2010 was the Liberal Democrats' victory in Redcar. Following on the back of local anger at the closure of the large Corus steel plant, the Lib Dems were able to pull off a dramatic 22 per cent swing to oust Labour minister Vera Baird. Situated between Middlesborough and Hartlepool on the Teesside coast, Redcar is a highly industrialised town with a rich history of involvement in steel-making, oil importation and chemical production. Labour have traditionally been able to rely upon overwhelming support from the heavily unionised local population and large council estates located on the edge of Redcar town. A June 2014 poll by Lord Ashcroft made for grim reading for the Liberal Democrats, with the party trailing Labour by a dramatic 30 per cent margin – 46 per cent to 16 per cent. Incumbent Liberal Democrat MP Ian Swales will stand down at the 2015 general election. Anna Turley will fight to regain the seat for Labour.

Sedgefield

LABOUR HOLD	PARTY	2010 CANDIDATE	2010 VOTES	2010 % VOTE	PPC FOR 2015
Majority	Labour	Phil Wilson MP	18,141	45.1	Phil Wilson MP
8,696	Conservative	Neil Mahapatra	9,445	23.5	
Turnout	Lib Dem	Alan Thompson	8,033	20.0	
62.14%	Others		4,603	11.4	

South Shields

LABOUR HOLD	PARTY	2010 CANDIDATE	2010 VOTES	2010 % VOTE
Majority	Labour	David Miliband MP	18,995	52.0
11,109	Conservative	Karen Allen	7,886	21.6
Turnout	Lib Dem	Stephen Psallidas	5,189	14.2
56.98%	Others		4,448	12.2

South Shields (2013 by-election)

LABOUR HOLD	PARTY	2013 CANDIDATE	2013 VOTES	2013 % VOTE	PPC FOR 2015
Majority	Labour	Emma Lewell-Buck	12,493	50.4	Emma Lewell-Buck MP
6,505	UKIP	Richard Elvin	5,988	24.2	
Turnout	Conservative	Karen Allen	2,857	11.5	
38.67%	Others		3,442	13.9	

Stockton North

LABOUR HOLD	PARTY	2010 CANDIDATE	2010 VOTES	2010 % VOTE	PPC FOR 2015
Majority	Labour	Alex Cunningham	16,923	42.8	Alex Cunningham MP
6,676	Conservative	Ian Galletley	10,247	25.9	
Turnout	Lib Dem	Gordon Parkin	6,342	16.1	
59.17%	Others		5,986	15.2	

Stockton South

CONSERVATIVE GAIN FROM LABOUR	PARTY	2010 CANDIDATE	2010 VOTES	2010 % VOTE	PPC FOR 2015
Majority	Conservative	James Wharton	19,577	38.9	James Wharton MP
332	Labour	Dari Taylor MP	19,245	38.3	Louise Baldock
Turnout	Lib Dem	Jacquie Bell	7,600	15.1	
68.10%	Others		3,862	7.7	

Majority 332 (0.7%)

Seized by locally honed Conservative James Wharton at the 2010 general election, Stockton South is the one of the most affluent and middle-class constituencies in the North East of England. Despite its rather urban name, the constituency includes only a small portion of the industrial Stockton, taking in the pleasant villages of Eaglescliffe, Hartburn and Yarm which house many commuters to nearby Middlesbrough and Newcastle upon Tyne. Perhaps unsurprisingly, it is in these rural areas that the Conservatives find the bulk of their support. Levels of owner-occupation are high in this constituency (78.1 per cent) and the proportion of university graduates (18.5 per cent) is well above average for a North East seat. One of the few truly competitive constituencies in the North East of England, the Labour candidate will be Liverpool city councillor Louise Baldock.

Sunderland Central

LABOUR WIN (NEW SEAT)	PARTY	2010 CANDIDATE	2010 VOTES	2010 % VOTE	PPC FOR 2015
Majority	Labour	Julie Elliot	19,495	45.9	Julie Elliot MP
6,725	Conservative	Lee Martin	12,770	30.1	
Turnout	Lib Dem	n/a	7,191	16.9	
57.01%	Others		3,007	7.1	

Tynemouth

LABOUR HOLD	PARTY	2010 CANDIDATE	2010 VOTES	2010 % VOTE	PPC FOR 2015
Majority	Labour	Alan Campbell MP	23,860	45.3	Alan Campbell MP
5,739	Conservative	Wendy Morton	18,121	34.4	
Turnout	Lib Dem	John Appleby	7,845	14.9	
69.59%	Others		2,842	5.4	

North Tyneside

LABOUR HOLD	PARTY	2010 CANDIDATE	2010 VOTES	2010 % VOTE	PPC FOR 2015
Majority	Labour	Mary Glindon	23,505	50.7	Mary Glindon MP
12,884	Lib Dem	David Ord	10,621	22.9	
Turnout	Conservative	Gagan Mohindra	8,514	18.3	
59.73%	Others		3,765	8.1	

Wansbeck

LABOUR HOLD	PARTY	2010 CANDIDATE	2010 VOTES	2010 % VOTE	PPC FOR 2015
Majority	Labour	Ian Lavery	17,548	45.8	Ian Lavery MP
7,031	Lib Dem	Simon Reed	10,517	27.5	
Turnout	Conservative	Campbell Storey	6,714	17.5	
61.95%	Others		3,494	9.1	

Washington & Sunderland West

LABOUR WIN (NEW SEAT)	PARTY	2010 CANDIDATE	2010 VOTES	2010 % VOTE	PPC FOR 2015
Majority	Labour	Sharon Hodgson MP	19,615	52.5	Sharon Hodgson MP
11,458	Conservative	Ian Cuthbert	8,157	21.8	
Turnout	Lib Dem	Peter Andras	6,382	17.1	
54.18%	Others		3,180	8.5	

Yorkshire and the Humber

There has long been a myth, propagated and believed by some south-erners, that the north of England is composed entirely of 'satanic' mill towns and grim cities, and thus infertile ground for the Conservative Party. However, the truth belies this notion of a stark 'north–south divide'. There is plenty of beautiful countryside surrounding attractive villages and small towns and desirable residential areas, and this sustains some of the safest Tory constituencies in Britain and also many key marginals that will help to decide the outcome of the next general election.

The large region of Yorkshire and the Humber is very much a case in point. Far from being a monolithically one-party state, the Conservatives won nineteen constituencies here and the Liberal Democrats three, in addition to Labour's thirty-two at the last general election – and all parties have power to add more. If we start with the Tories, they advanced very strongly in 2010, gaining eleven seats. As we know, this was not quite enough to secure an overall majority in the Commons for David Cameron, and he will desperately be hoping in 2015 to take 'those that got away'. This would be especially sweet as one of the first on the list is Morley & Outwood, held by 1,201 votes by Labour's shadow Chancellor and general pain in the neck (for the Conservatives) Ed Balls. Also requiring a swing of under 2 per cent are the cathedral city of Wakefield, which has substantial Tory support in its southern wards, and Halifax at the foot of Calderdale. Doubling the pro-Conservative swing to 4 per cent would bring two more targets within reach: Penistone & Stocksbridge on the north-western fringes of Sheffield; and Scunthorpe in Humberside, like Stocksbridge a town based on the steel industry. Despite its gritty reputation (few know that it, rather than Newcastle upon Tyne, was the original setting for the British gangster story *Get Carter*) Scunthorpe was won by the Tories in the 1980s.

The top seat statistically on the Conservative target list is clouded with doubt due to 'third-party' intervention, but in this case that party is UKIP. This seat is Great Grimsby, where the veteran Austin Mitchell has announced his retirement after over thirty-five years as a distinctive and colourful MP. This would normally favour the main challengers, but recent local and European voting, and the demographics of the constituency, all suggest it is one of UKIP's best hopes for a strong showing – again, it is not clear at whose greater expense. UKIP have a better chance of coming close to victory themselves in a hitherto safe Labour seat like Rotherham in South Yorkshire, where they topped the poll in the May 2014 council elections and which has since been rocked by child abuse scandals.

Finally, the Conservatives may entertain hopes in Batley & Spen in West Yorkshire. This is a classic marginal, held by Elizabeth Peacock in the Thatcher years, but the swing against Labour was very low in 2010, unlike in its near neighbour Dewsbury. This may well be because of the popularity of the independently minded Labour MP for Batley & Spen, Mike Wood. However he is retiring in 2015, with his successor (Jo Cox) chosen by an all-women-shortlist system not entirely popular with the local party. The Conservatives have selected a British Asian candidate, Imtiaz Ameen, who may appeal to the large population of Pakistani heritage in Batley. This is one to watch.

Labour will, of course, need to regain most of the divisions they lost last time in order to win the general election itself. Top on their list is actually a Liberal Democrat seat, Bradford East. David Ward gained this in 2010, but since then has made a number of controversial remarks concerning the Middle East, including in the summer of 2014 when he tweeted that he would probably fire a rocket if he lived in Gaza. These interventions have not gone down well with his own central party (he has been both reprimanded and suspended), and whether they shore up his appeal among the 37 per cent of his constituents who are Muslim remains to be seen.

Labour have a large number of targets currently held by the Conservatives. A swing of 1.5 per cent would take Dewsbury, a mixed seat similar demographically to Batley & Spen (and location of the TV series *Educating Yorkshire*). Only a little more difficult on paper is Pudsey, wedged between Leeds and Bradford but more traditionally minded than both, for example providing many great Yorkshire and England cricketers. Next in line, needing a swing of 3 per cent, is Keighley, which has an ethnically varied urban core but also the spa town of Ilkley and some very Conservative villages. It will also be interesting to see how UKIP does here. In 2005 Keighley was the seat that the BNP leader Nick Griffin chose to contest, and although UKIP policies are definitely not like those of his party, the demographic profile of voters have more similarities. In the May 2014 council elections, UKIP did win Keighley West and did well in Worth Valley ward, and although they did not do well enough across the seat to suggest they may win it, they could take enough votes from one or other 'major' party to decide the outcome in this key marginal.

For Labour to regain the overall majority in the Commons that they had between 1997 and 2010 they will also need to take Elmet & Rothwell, located east of Leeds, Cleethorpes in South Humberside, and Brigg & Goole, a very divided seat that crosses the ancient – and indeed modern – Lincolnshire/Yorkshire border. Brigg is very Conservative and looks it, while the port of Goole at the confluence of the Don and Ouse looks very much the part of a Labour stronghold. The seat would need a large swing of around 6 per cent, and at about the same mark are to be found the two West Yorkshire valley seats: Colne Valley and Calder Valley, the former in Kirklees borough and the latter in Calderdale. In both cases the electorate mainly live in a chain of small communities along the eponymous rivers as they flow down from the east side of the Pennines watershed, and in both cases Labour will find it difficult to overcome the personal votes of first-term Conservative MPs.

Bradford West also needs to be mentioned, where George Galloway pulled off a spectacular victory for the Respect Party (or perhaps it was a personal triumph) in a by-election gain from Labour in March 2012. Galloway made a strong appeal to the Asian and Muslim majority and won by over 10,000 on a 36 per cent swing. Galloway will have more trouble in a general election, but he has a large cushion to protect any diminution in his support, and the conflicts that he drew attention to, or exploited, have not eased since the by-election.

Looking at figures alone, the Liberal Democrats also have targets that would fall on a very small swing since 2010. They nearly won Sheffield Central from Labour then, missing by just 165 votes. However both national opinion polls and local election results suggest the Lib Dems actually have no real chance – in May 2014 they polled less than 14 per cent in the wards making up Central, and in fact the Greens, with 30 per cent, were much stronger challengers to Labour. This seat is where the majority of students at Sheffield's two universities are to be found – indeed, with 38 per cent it has the highest proportion of those aged 16–24 in full-time education of any constituency in the country. This is not good news for the Liberal Democrats any more. Their dramatic decline since they entered coalition government also means that they will probably fall well back in Hull North too (2010 Labour majority 641), although their council election performance has not collapsed so catastrophically as in some northern cities. Nor are they likely to regain Harrogate & Knaresborough (lost to the Tories in 2010) or progress in the odd York Outer seat, which surrounds the city of York like a doughnut.

Some have questioned the future of the Liberal Democrat leader himself. Nick Clegg sits for Sheffield Hallam, the affluent south-western quadrant of the city, and it has been asserted that he may lose the seat due to the factors discussed with reference to Sheffield Central in the previous paragraph. However, the hard evidence does not suggest that Mr Clegg is in serious danger of losing. In the May 2014 local elections in the wards that constitute Hallam, the Liberal Democrats were still 15 per cent ahead of Labour. Nor are there as many students in this seat as people seem to think; according to the 2011 census, Hallam ranked only 48th in the list of constituencies on that criterion. Nick Clegg's 15,000 majority will probably be reduced, but not overturned. The Lib Dems are likely to hold their other seat in the region with a strong university presence, Leeds North West, as well.

As well as Nick Clegg, Yorkshire and the Humber has several other high-profile MPs, such as Ed Miliband (Doncaster North), the husband-and-wife team of Ed Balls and Yvette Cooper in neighbouring seats (Morley & Outwood and Pontefract & Castleford), David Davis (Haltemprice & Howden) and William Hague (Richmond) – though the Foreign Secretary, formerly Conservative Party leader and even more formerly Tory Party conference sensation, is not standing again after twenty-five years. Richmond (Yorkshire) is an epitome of the point made at the beginning of this piece. Containing much of the Yorkshire Dales national park, it is a richly deserved destination for tourism. It is also the safest Conservative seat in terms of both numerical (23,336) and percentage majority. Right next door is another very Tory North Yorkshire constituency, Thirsk & Malton. Here, however, the picture may be clouded by the fact that the sitting MP Anne McIntosh has been deselected by her local party, and there are rumours she may stand as an independent. However, such is the loyalty of these very 'broad acres' to the Conservative Party that the new official candidate Kevin Hollinrake is likely to win easily. There are very safe seats for all parties in Yorkshire and the Humber as well as all those critical marginals.

Barnsley Central

LABOUR HOLD	PARTY	2010 CANDIDATE	2010 VOTES	2010 % VOTE	
Majority	Labour	Eric Illsley MP	17,487	47.3	
11,093	Lib Dem	Christopher Wiggin	6,394	17.3	
Turnout	Conservative	Piers Tempest	6,388	17.3	
56.45%	Others		6,732	18.2	

Barnsley Central (2011 by-election)

LABOUR HOLD	PARTY	2011 CANDIDATE	2011 VOTES	2011 % VOTE	PPC FOR 2015
Majority	Labour	Dan Jarvis	14,724	60.8	Dan Jarvis MP
11,771	UKIP	Jane Collins	2,953	12.2	
Turnout	Conservative	James Hockney	1,999	8.3	
36.95%	Others		4,543	18.8	

Barnsley East

LABOUR HOLD	PARTY	2010 CANDIDATE	2010 VOTES	2010 % VOTE	PPC FOR 2015
Majority	Labour	Michael Dugher	18,059	47.0	Michael Dugher MP
11,090	Lib Dem	John Brown	6,969	18.2	
Turnout	Conservative	James Hockney	6,329	16.5	
56.09%	Others		7,029	18.3	

Batley & Spen

LABOUR HOLD	PARTY	2010 CANDIDATE	2010 VOTES	2010 % VOTE	PPC FOR 2015
Majority	Labour	Mike Wood MP	21,565	41.5	Jo Cox
4,406	Conservative	Janice Small	17,159	33.0	Imtiaz Ameen
Turnout	Lib Dem	Neil Bentley	8,925	17.2	
67.68%	Others		4,290	8.3	

Beverley & Holderness

CONSERVATIVE HOLD	PARTY	2010 CANDIDATE	2010 VOTES	2010 % VOTE	PPC FOR 2015
Majority	Conservative	Graham Stuart MP	25,063	47.1	Graham Stuart MP
12,987	Lib Dem	Craig Dobson	12,076	22.7	Margeret Pinder
Turnout	Labour	Ian Saunders	11,224	21.1	Margeret Pinder
67.07%	Others		4,836	9.1	

Bradford East

LIB DEM WIN (NEW SEAT)	PARTY	2010 CANDIDATE	2010 VOTES	2010 % VOTE	PPC FOR 2015
Majority	Lib Dem	David Ward	13,637	33.7	David Ward MP
365	Labour	Terry Rooney MP	13,272	32.8	
Turnout	Conservative	Mohammed Riaz	10,860	26.8	
62.13%	Others		2,688	6.6	

Majority 365 (0.9%)

Captured from Labour by long-serving Bradford councillor David Ward in 2010, Bradford East is the Labour Party's top target seat in Yorkshire. The constituency runs from Bradford city centre, where Labour and George Galloway's Respect Party are dominant, out towards the city's eastern suburbs of Idle and Thackley where support for the Conservatives and Liberal Democrats is more divided. An ethnically diverse constituency, Muslims make up close to a quarter of all electors here while social housing stock is well above the national average. The seat is technically a three-way marginal with the first-placed Liberal Democrats winning 33.7 per cent of the vote in 2010 as compared to 26.8 per cent for the third-placed Conservatives. A poll conducted by Lord Ashcroft in June 2014 found the Liberal Democrats trailing Labour by 22 per cent – 45 per cent to 23 per cent.

Bradford South

LABOUR HOLD	PARTY	2010 CANDIDATE	2010 VOTES	2010 % VOTE	PPC FOR 2015
Majority	Labour	Gerry Sutcliffe MP	15,682	41.3	n/s
4,622	Conservative	Matthew Palmer	11,060	29.1	
Turnout	Lib Dem	Alun Griffiths	6,948	18.3	
59.76%	Others		4,305	11.3	

Bradford West

LABOUR HOLD	PARTY	2010 CANDIDATE	2010 VOTES	2010 % VOTE
Majority	Labour	Marsha Singh MP	18,401	45.3
5,763	Conservative	Zahid Iqbal	12,638	31.1
Turnout	Lib Dem	David Hall-Matthews	4,732	11.7
64.90%	Others		4,805	11.8

Bradford West (2012 by-election)

RESPECT GAIN FROM LABOUR	PARTY	2012 CANDIDATE	2012 VOTES	2012 % VOTE	PPC FOR 2015
Majority	Respect	George Galloway	18,341	55.7	George Galloway MP
10,140	Labour	Imran Hussain	8,201	24.9	
Turnout	Conservative	Jackie Whitely	2,746	8.3	
52.63%	Others				

Brigg & Goole

CONSERVATIVE GAIN FROM LABOUR	PARTY	2010 CANDIDATE	2010 VOTES	2010 % VOTE	PPC FOR 2015
Majority	Conservative	Andrew Percy	19,680	44.9	Andrew Percy MP
5,147	Labour	Ian Cawsey MP	14,533	33.1	Jacky Crawford
Turnout	Lib Dem	Richard Nixon	6,414	14.6	
65.15%	Others		3,247	7.4	

Majority 5147 (11.7%)

Taking in Lincolnshire's bleak north-eastern corner and the southern portion of the East Riding of Yorkshire, this seat was gained by outspoken Conservative Andrew Percy at the 2010 general election. The seat is politically polarised with Labour support unassailable in Goole, a town whose skyline is dominated by the cranes that service its active container port, while the Conservatives are strongest in the Isle of Axholme and the market town of Brigg. There is a diverse range of employment here, including light manufacturing, chemical production and farming. Eurosceptic sentiment is strong here, with UKIP easily topping the poll at the 2014 European elections. The Labour candidate will be Jacky Crawford, a nurse and social worker.

Calder Valley

CONSERVATIVE GAIN FROM LABOUR	PARTY	2010 CANDIDATE	2010 VOTES	2010 % VOTE	PPC FOR 2015
Majority	Conservative	Craig Whittaker	20,397	39.4	Craig Whittaker MP
6,431	Labour	Steph Booth	13,966	27.0	Josh Fenton Glynn
Turnout	Lib Dem	Hilary Myers	13,037	25.2	Alisdair Calder McGregor
67.33%	Others		4,380	8.5	

Majority 6431 (12.4%)

An attractive constituency located on the westerly border between Yorkshire and Lancashire, Calder Valley has been represented by Conservative Craig Whittaker since the 2010 general election. The constituency is largely rural in nature, taking in the small Pennine towns of Brighouse and Todmorden. Once sustained by thriving textiles industries, the area is now popular with commuters to Manchester, Bradford and Leeds. Both major parties are fairly evenly divided in both the rural and urban portions of this seat, although both have pockets of firm support. Unlike the majority of West Yorkshire constituencies, there is an almost total absence of ethnic minority residents here. The Conservatives posted a narrow lead here in the 2014 local elections, leading Labour by a 32 per cent to 28 per cent margin. The Labour candidate will be Josh Fenton-Glynn.

Cleethorpes

CONSERVATIVE GAIN FROM LABOUR	PARTY	2010 CANDIDATE	2010 VOTES	2010 % VOTE	PPC FOR 2015
Majority	Conservative	Martin Vickers	18,939	42.1	Martin Vickers MP
4,298	Labour	Shona McIsaac MP	14,641	32.6	Peter Keith
Turnout	Lib Dem	Doug Pickett	8,192	18.2	
64.04%	Others		3,194	7.1	

Majority 4298 (9.6%)

Located just south of Grimsby, the Cleethorpes constituency was seized from Labour by Conservative Martin Vickers at the 2010 general election. Cleethorpes itself is a small, middle-class town located alongside the Humber Estuary which borders neighbouring Grimsby. The constituency also includes the country's largest deep-water port in the country at Immingham and the Lindsey oil refinery. Support for the two main parties has traditionally been fairly evenly divided locally with Labour strongest in the Crosby and Park areas of Cleethorpes and the Conservatives dominating in the constituency's rather humdrum rural areas. UKIP have, however, performed strongly in the constituency in recent times, topping the poll at the 2014 European elections. Vickers will face a challenge from Peter Keith, the husband of the area's last Labour MP Shona McIsaac.

Colne Valley

CONSERVATIVE GAIN FROM LABOUR	PARTY	2010 CANDIDATE	2010 VOTES	2010 % VOTE	PPC FOR 2015
Majority	Conservative	Jason McCartney	20,440	37.0	Jason McCartney MP
4,837	Lib Dem	Nicola Turner	15,603	28.2	
Turnout	Labour	Debbie Abrahams	14,589	26.4	Jane East
69.07%	Others		4,664	8.4	

Majority 4837 (10.6%)

Politically speaking, this picturesque rural constituency is somewhat of a political oddity having been represented by each of the three major parties in the last thirty years. With no particularly large towns here, the seat is comprised of scores of villages along the Colne and Holme valleys. With the area's industrial sector long since having disappeared, many local residents commute to work in nearby Huddersfield. Levels of owner-occupation are extremely high at 77.5 per cent yet much of the stone-clad housing here is of poor quality – a fifth of homes having no central heating. The Liberal Democrats, whose predecessor party held this seat until 1987, remain strong here on a local government level. Indeed, the 2014 local council elections put Labour (7,573), the Conservatives (7,102) and Liberal Democrats (7,087) within 400 votes of each other. Jason McCartney, the Conservative MP here since 2010, will be challenged by Labour's Jane East and Liberal Democrat Nicola Turner.

Dewsbury

CONSERVATIVE GAIN FROM LABOUR	PARTY	2010 CANDIDATE	2010 VOTES	2010 % VOTE	PPC FOR 2015
Majority	Conservative	Simon Reevell	18,898	35.0	Simon Reevell MP
1,526	Labour	Shahid Malik MP	17,372	32.2	Paula Sheriff
Turnout	Lib Dem	Andrew Hutchinson	9,150	16.9	
68.44%	Others		8,588	15.9	

Majority 1526 (2.8%)

Situated in the heart of West Yorkshire, Dewsbury is a former textile town in easy reach of both Leeds and Bradford. At 12.1 per cent, the constituency has one of the largest Muslim populations in the country which has led to significant local tensions with the predominantly white population in the town's eastern suburbs. At 18.5 per cent the proportion of residents living in social housing is around average for a Yorkshire constituency. Much of the privately owned terraced housing in Dewsbury town is of poor quality with almost a quarter of residents having no central heating systems. Much of Labour's support is derived from the town of Dewsbury itself and the large Pakistani and Indian communities locally, while the Conservatives are dominant in surrounding rural areas such as Skelmanthorpe and Kirkburton. Labour were comfortably ahead of the Conservatives here at the 2014 local elections, outpolling them by 13,126 votes to 10,681. Held by the Conservative barrister Simon Reevell at the 2010 general election, the Labour candidate will be Paula Sherriff.

Don Valley

LABOUR HOLD	PARTY	2010 CANDIDATE	2010 VOTES	2010 % VOTE	PPC FOR 2015
Majority	Labour	Caroline Flint MP	16,472	37.9	Caroline Flint MP
3,595	Conservative	Matt Stephens	12,877	29.7	
Turnout	Lib Dem	Edwin Simpson	7,422	17.1	
59.81%	Others		6,649	15.3	

Doncaster Central

LABOUR HOLD	PARTY	2010 CANDIDATE	2010 VOTES	2010 % VOTE	PPC FOR 2015
Majority	Labour	Rosie Winterton MP	16,569	39.7	Rosie Winterton MP
6,229	Conservative	Gareth Davies	10,340	24.8	
Turnout	Lib Dem	Patrick Wilson	8,795	21.1	
57.20%	Others		6,041	14.5	

Doncaster North

LABOUR HOLD	PARTY	2010 CANDIDATE	2010 VOTES	2010 % VOTE	PPC FOR 2015
Majority	Labour	Ed Miliband MP	19,637	47.3	Ed Miliband MP
10,909	Conservative	Sophie Brodie	8,728	21.0	
Turnout	Lib Dem	Ed Sanderson	6,174	14.9	
57.87%	Others		6,944	16.7	

Elmet & Rothwell

CONSERVATIVE WIN (NEW SEAT)	PARTY	2010 CANDIDATE	2010 VOTES	2010 % VOTE	PPC FOR 2015
Majority	Conservative	Alec Shelbrooke	23,778	42.6	Alex Shelbrooke MP
4,521	Labour	James Lewis	19,257	34.5	Veronica King
Turnout	Lib Dem	Stewart Golton	9,109	16.3	
71.78%	Others		3,645	6.5	

Majority 4521 (8.1%)

A newly created seat at the 2010 general election, the constituency was won by Conservative Alec Shelbrooke. This is a politically mixed constituency with the Conservatives dominating in the market town of Wetherby while Labour lead in Rothwell, only a short distance from deprived city centre Leeds. Located in the north-eastern corner of West Yorkshire, the constituency lies on the outermost boundaries of the city of Leeds. As one might expect in a relatively affluent commuter constituency, almost four out of five homes are owner-occupied and unemployment is below the national average. The 2014 local election results locally were exceptionally close with the Conservatives leading Labour by a 34.3 per cent to 33.8 per cent margin. The Labour candidate will be charity worker Veronica King.

Great Grimsby

LABOUR HOLD	PARTY	2010 CANDIDATE	2010 VOTES	2010 % VOTE	PPC FOR 2015
Majority	Labour	Austin Mitchell MP	10,777	32.7	Melanie Onn
714	Conservative	Victoria Ayling	10,063	30.5	
Turnout	Lib Dem	Andrew de Freitas	7,388	22.4	
53.82%	Others		4,726	14.3	

Majority 714 (2.2%)

Located at the mouth of the Humber estuary, the town of Grimsby has long been a bastion of Labour support. It was a surprise, therefore, when long-serving MP Austin Mitchell scraped home with a majority of only 714 votes and 33 per cent of the vote at the 2010 election. The town of Grimsby is dominated by its large container ports and chemical, fishing and food processing industries – factors which ensure the survival of a robust blue-collar workforce here. UKIP were victorious across north-east Lincolnshire at the 2014 European elections, scoring 6,104 votes in Grimsby to Labour's 4,716 and the Conservative Party's 2,963. This will be one of UKIP's top national targets. Replacing the retiring Austin Mitchell as Labour candidate will be trade union official Melanie Onn. The UKIP candiate will be Victoria Ayling.

Halifax

LABOUR HOLD	PARTY	2010 CANDIDATE	2010 VOTES	2010 % VOTE	PPC FOR 2015
Majority	Labour	Linda Riordan MP	16,278	37.4	Linda Riordan MP
1,472	Conservative	Philip Allott	14,806	34.0	Philip Allott
Turnout	Lib Dem	Elisabeth Wilson	8,335	19.1	Mohammed Ilyas
61.89%	Others		4,136	9.5	

Haltemprice & Howden

CONSERVATIVE HOLD	PARTY	2010 CANDIDATE	2010 VOTES	2010 % VOTE	PPC FOR 2015
Majority	Conservative	David Davis MP	24,486	50.2	David Davis MP
11,602	Lib Dem	Jon Neal	12,884	26.4	
Turnout	Labour	Daniel Marten	7,630	15.7	
69.37%	Others		3,737	7.7	

Harrogate & Knaresborough

CONSERVATIVE GAIN FROM LIB DEM	PARTY	2010 CANDIDATE	2010 VOTES	2010 % VOTE	PPC FOR 2015
Majority	Conservative	Andrew Jones	24,305	45.7	Andrew Jones MP
1,039	Lib Dem	Claire Kelley	23,266	43.8	Helen Flynn
Turnout	Labour	Kevin McNerney	3,413	6.4	
71.07%	Others		2,150	4.0	

Majority 1039 (2%)

Previously a safe Conservative seat, Harrogate & Knaresborough abandoned the Conservatives for the Liberal Democrats in 1997 before being regained by local councillor Andrew Jones on a dramatic swing in 2010. The home of the famous Betty's Tearoom, elegant stone-clad terraces and beautifully manicured gardens, the spa town of Harrogate is a major tourist and conference destination. The nearby town of Knaresborough is similarly ornate with stunning views of the Yorkshire Dales. On a local government level, the Conservatives continue to dominate while June 2014 polling showed the party leading the Liberal Democrats by a 41 per cent to 24 per cent margin with UKIP way back on 16 per cent. With owner occupation rates of almost 80 per cent, Labour support is almost non-existent. The Liberal Democrats have selected Helen Flynn.

Hemsworth

LABOUR HOLD	PARTY	2010 CANDIDATE	2010 VOTES	2010 % VOTE	PPC FOR 2015
Majority	Labour	Jon Trickett MP	20,506	46.8	Jon Trickett MP
9,844	Conservative	Ann Myatt	10,662	24.3	
Turnout	Lib Dem	Alan Belmore	5,667	12.9	
58.03%	Others		7,005	16.0	

Huddersfield

LABOUR HOLD	PARTY	2010 CANDIDATE	2010 VOTES	2010 % VOTE	PPC FOR 2015
Majority	Labour	Barry Sheerman MP	15,725	38.8	Barry Sheerman MP
4,472	Conservative	Karen Tweed	11,253	27.8	
Turnout	Lib Dem	James Blanchard	10,023	24.7	
61.11%	Others		3,523	8.7	

Kingston-upon-Hull East

LABOUR HOLD	PARTY	2010 CANDIDATE	2010 VOTES	2010 % VOTE	PPC FOR 2015
Majority	Labour	Karl Turner	16,387	47.9	Karl Turner MP
8,597	Lib Dem	Jeremy Wilcock	7,790	22.8	
Turnout	Conservative	Christine Mackay	5,667	16.6	Emma Ideson
50.62%	Others		4,340	12.7	

Kingston-upon-Hull North

LABOUR HOLD	PARTY	2010 CANDIDATE	2010 VOTES	2010 % VOTE	PPC FOR 2015
Majority	Labour	Diana Johnson MP	13,044	39.2	Diana Johnson MP
641	Lib Dem	Denis Healy	12,403	37.3	Mike Ross
Turnout	Conservative	Victoria Aitken	4,365	13.1	Dahenna Davison
51.95%	Others		3,479	10.5	

Majority 641 (2%)

Comprised of the northern part of the city of Kingston-upon-Hull (more commonly-known as simply 'Hull'), the Liberal Democrats were just 641 off taking this seat in 2010. Hull North is slightly more middle-class in nature than other parts of the city, taking in the affluent, Conservative-voting suburb of Bricknell as well as the leafy University of Hull campus. One of the chief reasons for Liberal Democrat competitiveness locally is the large numbers of students living in the constituency – a demographic that had been a happy hunting ground for the party at the 2001, 2005 and 2010 general elections. Conservative and Lib Dem-friendly areas are, however, counterbalanced by several large and staunchly Labour council estates. The Liberal Democrats, who controlled Hull City Council as recently as 2011, now hold only fifteen seats on the council to Labour's thirty-nine. The sitting Labour MP Diana Johnson will be challenged by Mike Ross.

Kingston-upon-Hull West & Hessle

LABOUR HOLD	PARTY	2010 CANDIDATE	2010 VOTES	2010 % VOTE	PPC FOR 2015
Majority	Labour	Alan Johnson MP	13,378	42.5	Alan Johnson MP
5,742	Lib Dem	Mike Ross	7,636	24.2	Claire Thomas
Turnout	Conservative	Gary Shores	6,361	20.2	Mike Whitehead
55.02%	Others		4,130	13.1	

Keighley

CONSERVATIVE GAIN FROM LABOUR	PARTY	2010 CANDIDATE	2010 VOTES	2010 % VOTE	PPC FOR 2015
Majority	Conservative	Kris Hopkins	20,003	41.9	Kris Hopkins MP
2,940	Labour	Jane Thomas	17,063	35.8	John Grogan
Turnout	Lib Dem	Nader Fekri	7,059	14.8	
72.38%	Others		3,567	7.5	

Majority 2940 (6.2%)

Located around 10 miles north of the city of Bradford, the Keighley constituency is a mix of former textile towns and pleasant countryside set against the backdrop of the South Pennines. On a political level, Keighley town is a safe bet for Labour while the Conservatives dominate in the tourist town of Ilkley and in the rural Worth Valley. As with many West Yorkshire constituencies, the area has sadly suffered from significant racial tensions between the majority white and 9.4 per cent Asian community. Labour were the victors here in the 2014 local elections, leading the Conservatives by a 36 per cent to 30 per cent margin. Held since 2010 by Conservative Local Government Minister Kris Hopkins, the former Selby MP John Grogan will fight the seat for Labour.

Leeds Central

LABOUR HOLD	PARTY	2010 CANDIDATE	2010 VOTES	2010 % VOTE	PPC FOR 2015
Majority	Labour	Hilary Benn MP	18,434	49.3	Hilary Benn MP
10,645	Lib Dem	Michael Taylor	7,789	20.8	
Turnout	Conservative	Alan Lamb	7,541	20.2	
46.01%	Others		3,630	9.7	

Leeds East

LABOUR HOLD	PARTY	2010 CANDIDATE	2010 VOTES	2010 % VOTE	PPC FOR 2015
Majority	Labour	George Mudie MP	19,056	50.4	Richard Burgon
10,293	Conservative	Barry Anderson	8,763	23.2	
Turnout	Lib Dem	Andrew Tear	6,618	17.5	
58.45%	Others		3,376	8.9	

Leeds North East

LABOUR HOLD	PARTY	2010 CANDIDATE	2010 VOTES	2010 % VOTE	PPC FOR 2015
Majority	Labour	Fabian Hamilton MP	20,287	42.7	Fabian Hamilton MP
4,545	Conservative	Matthew Lobley	15,742	33.1	
Turnout	Lib Dem	Aqila Choudhry	9,310	19.6	Aqila Choudhry
70.01%	Others		2,196	4.6	

Leeds North West

LIB DEM HOLD	PARTY	2010 CANDIDATE	2010 VOTES	2010 % VOTE	PPC FOR 2015
Majority	Lib Dem	Greg Mulholland MP	20,653	47.5	Greg Mulholland MP
9,103	Conservative	Julia Mulligan	11,550	26.6	
Turnout	Labour	Judith Blake	9,132	21.0	Alex Sobal
66.49%	Others		2,148	4.9	

Leeds West

LABOUR HOLD	PARTY	2010 CANDIDATE	2010 VOTES	2010 % VOTE	PPC FOR 2015
Majority	Labour	Rachel Reeves	16,389	42.3	Rachel Reeves MP
7,016	Lib Dem	Ruth Coleman	9,373	24.2	
Turnout	Conservative	Joe Marjoram	7,641	19.7	
57.45%	Others		5,349	13.8	

Morley & Outwood

LABOUR WIN (NEW SEAT)	PARTY	2010 CANDIDATE	2010 VOTES	2010 % VOTE	PPC FOR 2015
Majority	Labour	Ed Balls MP	18,365	37.6	Ed Balls MP
1,101	Conservative	Antony Calvert	17,264	35.3	Andrea Jenkyns
Turnout	Lib Dem	James Monaghan	8,186	16.8	
65.24%	Others		5,041	10.3	

Majority 1101 (2.3%)

Heading into election night 2010, many Conservatives were hopeful that Morley & Outwood – the constituency of then Education Secretary and present shadow Chancellor Ed Balls – would deliver them their 'Portillo moment'. It was not to be and Balls held off a concerted Conservative challenge by 1,101 votes. Located just between Leeds and Wakefield, Morley & Outwood are both former industrial
towns with a heritage of close ties with West Yorkshire's coal-mining industry that are slowly transforming into bases for middle-class
commuters. Demographically, the area remains overwhelmingly white while the proportion of social housing is slightly above the national
average. The Conservatives continue to be competitive here on a local level, yet have suffered losses to Labour in recent years. Balls will
face a challenge from Conservative Andrea Jenkyns.

Normanton, Pontefract & Castleford

LABOUR HOLD	PARTY	2010 CANDIDATE	2010 VOTES	2010 % VOTE	PPC FOR 2015
Majority	Labour	Yvette Cooper MP	22,293	48.2	Yvette Cooper MP
10,979	Conservative	Nick Pickles	11,314	24.5	
Turnout	Lib Dem	Chris Rush	7,585	16.4	
56.16%	Others		5,047	10.9	

Penistone & Stocksbridge

LABOUR WIN (NEW SEAT)	PARTY	2010 CANDIDATE	2010 VOTES	2010 % VOTE	PPC FOR 2015
Majority	Labour	Angela Smith MP	17,565	37.8	Angela Smith MP
3,049	Conservative	Spencer Pitfield	14,516	31.2	
Turnout	Lib Dem	Ian Cuthbertson	9,800	21.1	
67.93%	Others		4,635	10.0	

Pudsey

CONSERVATIVE GAIN FROM LABOUR	PARTY	2010 CANDIDATE	2010 VOTES	2010 % VOTE	PPC FOR 2015
Majority	Conservative	Stuart Andrew	18,874	38.5	Stuart Andrew MP
1,659	Labour	Jamie Hanley	17,215	35.1	Jamie Hanley
Turnout	Lib Dem	Jamie Matthews	10,224	20.8	
70.87%	Others		2,770	5.6	

Majority 1659 (3.4%)

Seized by Conservative charity fundraiser Stuart Andrew at the 2010 general election, Pudsey is located mid-way between Leeds and Bradford in the heart of West Yorkshire. The constituency itself is largely residential in nature, with many of its inhabitants commuting to work in large cities nearby. The seat is a diverse mixture of stone-clad Pennine terraces and more newly built detached homes that skirt the affluent Leeds suburbs of Guiseley, Horsforth and Calverley. The Conservatives narrowly led Labour at the 2014 local elections, scoring 32 per cent of the vote to their 30 per cent. The Labour candidate will be Jamie Hanley.

Richmond (Yorks)

CONSERVATIVE HOLD	PARTY	2010 CANDIDATE	2010 VOTES	2010 % VOTE	PPC FOR 2015
Majority	Conservative	William Hague MP	33,541	62.8	n/s
23,336	Lib Dem	Lawrence Meredith	10,205	19.1	Chris Foote-Wood
Turnout	Labour	Eileen Driver	8,150	15.3	
66.30%	Others		1,516	2.8	

Rother Valley

LABOUR HOLD	PARTY	2010 CANDIDATE	2010 VOTES	2010 % VOTE	PPC FOR 2015
Majority	Labour	Kevin Barron MP	19,147	40.9	Kevin Barron MP
5,866	Conservative	Lynda Donaldson	13,281	28.4	
Turnout	Lib Dem	Wesley Paxton	8,111	17.3	
64.19%	Others		6,219	13.3	

Rotherham

LABOUR HOLD	PARTY	2010 CANDIDATE	2010 VOTES	2010 % VOTE	
Majority	Labour	Denis MacShane MP	16,741	44.6	
10,462	Conservative	Jackie Whiteley	6,279	16.7	
Turnout	Lib Dem	Rebecca Taylor	5,994	16.0	
59.01%	Others		8,492	22.6	

Rotherham (2012 by-election)

LABOUR HOLD	PARTY	2012 CANDIDATE	2012 VOTES	2012 % VOTE	PPC FOR 2015
Majority	Labour	Sarah Champion	9,966	46.7	Sarah Champion MP
5,318	UKIP	Jane Collins	4,648	21.8	
Turnout	BNP	Marlene Guest	1,804	8.5	
33.56%	Others		4,912	23.0	

Scarborough & Whitby

CONSERVATIVE HOLD	PARTY	2010 CANDIDATE	2010 VOTES	2010 % VOTE	PPC FOR 2015
Majority	Conservative	Robert Goodwill MP	21,108	42.8	Robert Goodwill MP
8,130	Labour	Annajoy David	12,978	26.3	
Turnout	Lib Dem	Tani Exley-Moore	11,093	22.5	
65.30%	Others		4,103	8.3	

Majority 8130 (16.5%)

Located on the North Yorkshire coastline, Scarborough and Whitby has been held by Conservative MP and Transport Minister Robert Goodwill since 2005. Both Scarborough and Whitby are tourist resorts that have suffered from significant social problems associated with the decline in popularity of British coastal holidays. There is, however, still a fair amount of industry locally with the port of Scarborough continuing to provide a large number of jobs in the logistics and fishing sector. In addition to the two towns the seat is named after, the constituency contains large swathes of the picturesque Esk Valley and North Yorkshire Moors National Park. The Labour candidate will be Colin Challen, a Scarborough borough councillor and former Labour MP for Morley & Rothwell.

Scunthorpe

LABOUR HOLD	PARTY	2010 CANDIDATE	2010 VOTES	2010 % VOTE	PPC FOR 2015
Majority	Labour	Nic Dakin	14,640	39.5	Nic Dakin MP
2,549	Conservative	Caroline Johnson	12,091	32.6	
Turnout	Lib Dem	Neil Poole	6,774	18.3	
58.70%	Others		3,529	9.5	

Selby & Ainsty

CONSERVATIVE WIN (NEW SEAT)	PARTY	2010 CANDIDATE	2010 VOTES	2010 % VOTE	PPC FOR 2015
Majority	Conservative	Nigel Adams	25,562	49.4	Nigel Adams MP
12,265	Labour	Jan Marshall	13,297	25.7	Mark Hayes
Turnout	Lib Dem	Tom Holvey	9,180	17.7	
71.05%	Others		3,689	7.1	

Sheffield, Brightside & Hillsborough

LABOUR HOLD	PARTY	2010 CANDIDATE	2010 VOTES	2010 % VOTE	PPC FOR 2015
Majority	Labour	David Blunkett MP	21,400	55.0	n/s
13,632	Lib Dem	Jonathon Harston	7,768	20.0	Jonathon Harston
Turnout	Conservative	John Sharp	4,468	11.5	
57.45%	Others		5,278	13.6	

Sheffield Central

LABOUR HOLD	PARTY	2010 CANDIDATE	2010 VOTES	2010 % VOTE	PPC FOR 2015
Majority	Labour	Paul Blomfield	17,138	41.3	Paul Blomfield MP
165	Lib Dem	Paul Scriven	16,973	40.9	
Turnout	Conservative	Andrew Lee	4,206	10.1	
61.38%	Others		3,151	7.6	

Majority 165 (0%)

Located at the heart of the South Yorkshire industrial city of Sheffield, this is a closely fought marginal seat between Labour and the Liberal Democrats. In 2010, the current Labour MP Paul Blomfield repelled a challenge from Lib Dem Sheffield City Council leader Paul Scriven by just 165 votes. Aside from including the city's main commercial districts, the constituency is dominated by the University of Sheffield and Sheffield Hallam University – a factor which fuelled considerable Liberal Democrat support at the 2005 and 2010 general elections. Aside from the student population, the seat also includes the tough Manor and Walkley districts which lean strongly towards Labour. Labour led at the 2014 local elections with close to 40 per cent of the vote with the Greens in second place with 30 per cent. Labour's former challengers, the Liberal Democrats, polled just 12 per cent of the vote.

Sheffield, Hallam

LIB DEM HOLD	PARTY	2010 CANDIDATE	2010 VOTES	2010 % VOTE	PPC FOR 2015
Majority	Lib Dem	Nick Clegg MP	27,324	53.4	Nick Clegg MP
15,284	Conservative	Nicola Bates	12,040	23.5	
Turnout	Labour	Jack Scott	8,228	16.1	Oliver Coppard
74.33%	Others		3,543	6.9	

Sheffield, Heeley

LABOUR HOLD	PARTY	2010 CANDIDATE	2010 VOTES	2010 % VOTE	PPC FOR 2015
Majority	Labour	Meg Munn MP	17,409	42.6	Louise Haigh
5,807	Lib Dem	Simon Clement-Jones	11,602	28.4	Simon Clement-Jones
Turnout	Conservative	Anne Crampton	7,081	17.3	
62.33%	Others		4,779	11.7	

Sheffield South East

LABOUR HOLD	PARTY	2010 CANDIDATE	2010 VOTES	2010 % VOTE	PPC FOR 2015
Majority	Labour	Clive Betts MP	20,169	48.7	Clive Betts MP
10,505	Lib Dem	Gail Smith	9,664	23.3	
Turnout	Conservative	Nigel Bonson	7,202	17.4	
61.74%	Others		4,373	10.6	

Shipley

CONSERVATIVE HOLD	PARTY	2010 CANDIDATE	2010 VOTES	2010 % VOTE	PPC FOR 2015
Majority	Conservative	Phillip Davies MP	24,002	48.6	Philip Davies MP
9,944	Labour	Susan Hinchcliffe	14,058	28.4	
Turnout	Lib Dem	John Harris	9,890	20.0	
73.02%	Others		1,477	3.0	

Skipton & Ripon

CONSERVATIVE HOLD	PARTY	2010 CANDIDATE	2010 VOTES	2010 % VOTE	PPC FOR 2015
Majority	Conservative	Julian Smith	27,685	50.6	Julian Smith MP
9,950	Lib Dem	Helen Flynn	17,735	32.4	
Turnout	Labour	Claire Hazlegrove	5,498	10.0	
70.72%	Others		3,806	7.0	

Thirsk & Malton

CONSERVATIVE WIN (NEW SEAT)	PARTY	2010 CANDIDATE	2010 VOTES	2010 % VOTE	PPC FOR 2015
Majority	Conservative	Anne McIntosh MP	20,167	52.9	Kevin Hollinrake
11,281	Lib Dem	Howard Keal	8,886	23.3	
Turnout	Labour	Jonathan Roberts	5,169	13.6	
49.91%	Others		3,920	10.3	

Wakefield

LABOUR HOLD	PARTY	2010 CANDIDATE	2010 VOTES	2010 % VOTE	PPC FOR 2015
Majority	Labour	Mary Creagh MP	17,454	39.3	Mary Creagh MP
1,613	Conservative	Alex Story	15,841	35.6	
Turnout	Lib Dem	David Smith	7,256	16.3	David Smith
62.76%	Others		3,893	8.8	

Majority 1613 (3.6%)

Situated in the southern portion of West Yorkshire and held by Labour's Mary Creagh, the shadow Environment Secretary, Wakefield was a once thriving industrial town which has successfully capitalised upon its excellent transport links to reinvent itself in recent years as an important retail and commuter centre. The town's 75,000 residents are predominantly employed in the service sector although wages are below the national average, and the city centre juxtaposes an ornate and imposing cathedral with a plethora of rather more low-rent bars and clubs. Politically speaking, Wakefield town is a Labour bastion, delivering the party overwhelming support, while the surrounding rural areas of Horbury and Ossett are considerably more inclined towards the Tories. Three-fifths of homes in the constituency are owner-occupied, while council properties house a third of residents.

Wentworth & Dearne

LABOUR HOLD	PARTY	2010 CANDIDATE	2010 VOTES	2010 % VOTE	PPC FOR 2015
Majority	Labour	John Healey MP	21,316	50.6	John Healey MP
13,920	Conservative	Michelle Donelan	7,396	17.6	
Turnout	Lib Dem	Nick Love	6,787	16.1	
58.01%	Others		6,607	15.7	

York Central

LABOUR HOLD	PARTY	2010 CANDIDATE	2010 VOTES	2010 % VOTE	PPC FOR 2015
Majority	Labour	Hugh Bayley MP	18,573	40.0	Hugh Bayley MP
6,451	Conservative	Susan Wade-Weeks	12,122	26.1	
Turnout	Lib Dem	Christian Vassie	11,694	25.2	
60.81%	Others		4,094	8.8	

York Outer

CONSERVATIVE WIN (NEW SEAT)	PARTY	2010 CANDIDATE	2010 VOTES	2010 % VOTE	PPC FOR 2015
Majority	Conservative	Julian Sturdy	22,912	43.0	Julian Sturdy MP
3,688	Lib Dem	Madeleine Kirk	19,224	36.1	
Turnout	Labour	James Alexander	9,108	17.1	Joe Riches
70.19%	Others		2,056	3.9	

Yorkshire East

CONSERVATIVE HOLD	PARTY	2010 CANDIDATE	2010 VOTES	2010 % VOTE	PPC FOR 2015
Majority	Conservative	Greg Knight MP	24,328	47.5	Greg Knight MP
13,486	Lib Dem	Robert Adamson	10,842	21.2	James Blanchard
Turnout	Labour	Paul Rounding	10,401	20.3	
63.98%	Others		5,683	11.1	

Wales

In the 2010 general election in Wales the overall shares were: Labour 36 per cent, Conservative 26 per cent, Liberal Democrat 20 per cent and Plaid Cymru (Welsh Nationalist) 11 per cent. If we average the specific opinion polls taken in Wales during 2014, we find Labour up seven percentage points at 43 per cent, the Tories down three with 23 per cent, Plaid at 13 per cent – and the Lib Dems more than halved, to not much over 7 per cent. This would actually reduce them to the fifth party in popularity in the principality, for UKIP – though this is one of their weakest regions in Britain – were favoured by nearly 10 per cent of respondents.

What would this all mean as far as the outcome in constituencies is concerned, in the (unlikely) event that these preferences are maintained until May 2015? On a uniform swing, itself far from inevitable, Labour would gain three seats from the Conservatives and one from the Liberal Democrats. Of the potential three Tory losses, two – Cardiff North and the Vale of Glamorgan – were actually gained by Labour in the most recent National Assembly for Wales elections in 2011. Cardiff North is most likely actually to fall – Jonathan Evans squeaked home with a majority of just 194 in 2010, and there won't even be a 'first-term' incumbency effect as he is not standing again, so Labour's Mari Williams is a strong favourite. The Vale of Glamorgan will be a tougher task, as Labour needs a general election swing of 4.5 per cent against a sitting MP. Similarly difficult will be Carmarthen West & South Pembrokeshire, which the Tories managed to hold in the 2011 Assembly elections. Aberconwy in north-west Wales and

Preseli Pembrokeshire in the south-west are even more difficult, needing swings of 6 per cent, even beyond the suggestion of the opinion polls. Therefore the Conservatives are likely to hold most of their eight current constituencies.

Given the parlous state of the Liberal Democrats in these polls, the Tories should be able to win Montgomeryshire again, even though the seat has an extremely long record of Liberalism – it was one of the six they managed to win in each of the 1955, 1959 and 1970 elections, for example, the low points for the party in the twentieth century. In 2010, Lembit Opik was ousted by Glyn Davies, who has announced that he is contesting again although now just into his seventies; and to show that it wasn't just a reaction against Mr Opik's eccentricities, the Tories won the coterminous Assembly seat as well, by 10 per cent in 2011. There has been much suggestion that applying a uniform swing from the opinion polls means that the Tories could well take Brecon & Radnorshire from the Lib Dems in 2015. However this would be to ignore both the fact that the Liberal Democrats fairly easily won here in 2011, when their popularity nationally had already fallen following the formation of the national coalition, and the personal vote built up by Roger Williams since 2001. Incumbency matters in such seats as Brecon & Radnor – it is the largest constituency in Wales geographically, which means that it is composed of isolated hill farms and hamlets, villages and small towns, including Llanwrtyd Wells, which claims to be the smallest town in Britain.

The Liberal Democrat seat that is most vulnerable is threatened by Labour. Jenny Willott gained Cardiff Central in 2005 and increased her majority to over 4,500 in 2010. However, Labour took the assembly seat in 2011 by the hair's breadth of thirty-eight votes. Central is a very mixed constituency, with the third highest percentage of students and the fifth highest proportion of privately rented housing anywhere in Britain (these figures tend to be correlated), and the most multi-ethnic population in Wales. This all leads to a rapid turnover of voters in the heart of the principality's capital, and hence it is subject to large electoral swings. It is defi-nitely 'one to watch' in 2015.

Should the opinion polls register a decline in Labour support as the general election nears – which they may well do, given the evidence of an economic revival – we do need to consider whether they may face any potential losses. However, in this region, a reduction in their dominance is unlikely. Labour won twenty-six seats out of the forty in Wales in 2015. Their closest shaves came where the Liberal Demo-crats were the main challengers. As in many other regions, the Lib Dem surge following the party leader debates in which Nick Clegg made such a strong initial impression that they appeared genuine con-tenders in hitherto safe Labour seats. They fell just 504 votes short in Swansea West, and cut the Labour lead to under 2,000 in Newport East and under 3,000 even in Pontypridd, in that historic heartland of the Labour Party for over 100 years, the South Wales valleys. But, as elsewhere, such seats are likely to witness a Lib Dem collapse in 2015. Even by the 2011 Assembly elections, they had dropped from second to third place in Swansea West and Newport East, and there was a 9 per cent swing to Labour in Pontypridd.

The Conservatives do not look likely to gain from Labour either. There are four seats where they reduced the Labour lead in 2010 to between 2,00 and 3,000, but they are all places where the Tories have won only at the height of Thatcherite success in the general elections of the 1980s: Bridgend in 1983 and Delyn in 1983 and 1987. Alyn & Dee-side did not fall even then, and Vale of Clwyd did not exist. Labour will thus continue to win around three-quarters of the constituencies in Wales, which is particularly fortunate for them as this region is the most over-represented in the whole of the United Kingdom.

What we mean by this is that the seats are, on average, the smallest of any region, with an average electorate of 57,000 in 2010, compared with 66,000 in each of Scotland and Northern Ireland and 72,000 in England. On a strictly proportionate basis, Wales should have many fewer constituencies. It would have been reduced from forty to thirty (out of 600 rather than 650) in the so-called 'zombie review' – officially the Sixth Periodic Review – of parliamentary boundaries, which was postponed till beyond 2015 after the Liberal Democrats withdrew their support and the Lords voted it down in January 2013. Clearly, Labour would also have suffered from the equalisation of electorates, and nowhere is this clearer than in Wales.

Finally, we should not leave the principality without discussing Plaid Cymru, who currently have three MPs. One of these, Arfon, is on the Labour target list, with a majority when it was first contested in 2010 of just 1,508. On the other hand, the Welsh Nationalists did win two constituencies in the Assembly in 2011 that they had not in the previous year – Ynys Mon (Anglesey), a Labour seat in the Commons, and Ceredigion (Cardiganshire) which is Liberal Democrat. However, these may not be the realistic chances of Plaid gains they appear. For a start, it is logical that the Nationalists should do better in the devolved assemblies than in Westminster contests, as is the case in Scotland; they are unlikely to form part of a UK-wide government, whereas the Welsh executive is much more likely to be subject to coalition on a regular basis, being elected by proportional representation. Also, more people are likely to vote for 'the party of Wales' in a purely Welsh Assembly election. Moreover, specific circumstances apply: in Ynys Mon, the Plaid Cymru AM elected in 2011 was their party leader, Ieuan Wyn Jones, who had held the seat since the first Assembly elections in 1999. Similarly, Elin Jones has represented Ceredigion since 1999, so has built up a large personal vote that cannot be translated to Westminster elections. However, it might be noted that when Ieuan Wyn Jones left the Assembly in 2013, the subsequent by-election in Ynys Mon was won by Plaid Cymru's Rhun ap Iorwerth by a massive margin – so they cannot be written off when the island next sends someone to the Commons in 2015.

A major Nationalist breakthrough is almost impossible, though, as, unlike the SNP, they are hampered by their vote being very variable, because it is largely confined to Welsh-speaking areas. Unlike in

Scotland and Northern Ireland, the next general election in Wales will be mainly dominated by competition between the three parties vying to run, or be included in, the next national government.

Aberavon

LABOUR HOLD	PARTY	2010 CANDIDATE	2010 VOTES	2010 % VOTE	PPC FOR 2015
Majority	Labour	Hywel Francis MP	16,073	63.0	Stephen Kinnock
11,039	Lib Dem	Keith Davies	5,034	19.7	
Turnout	Conservative	Caroline Jones	4,411	17.3	
60.90%	Others		5,440	21.3	

Aberconwy

CONSERVATIVE GAIN FROM LABOUR	PARTY	2010 CANDIDATE	2010 VOTES	2010 % VOTE	PPC FOR 2015
Majority	Conservative	Guto Bebb	10,734	35.8	Guto Bebb MP
3,398	Labour	Ronnie Hughes	7,336	24.5	Mary Wimbury
Turnout	Lib Dem	Mike Priestley	5,786	19.3	
67.20%	Others		6,110	20.4	

Majority 3398 (11.3%)

Located on Wales's north coast, Aberconwy was gained for the Conservatives by Guto Bebb at the 2010 general election. Stretching along the north Wales coastline, the constituency includes the picturesque (and Labour-leaning) coastal towns of Conwy and Llandudno before curving inland to take in Welsh-speaking villages such as Betws-y-Coed in the Conwy Valley that are a battleground between the Conservatives and Plaid Cymru. Historically, the area included within the constituency has been competitive for the Conservatives, Labour and Plaid Cymru with each having held versions of the Westminster and Welsh Assembly seats in the area in the past decade. The Welsh-speaking incumbent Bebb will be challenged by Labour's Mary Wimbury and Plaid Cymru's Iwan Huws.

Alyn & Deeside

LABOUR HOLD	PARTY	2010 CANDIDATE	2010 VOTES	2010 % VOTE	PPC FOR 2015
Majority	Labour	Mark Tami MP	15,804	39.6	Mark Tami MP
2,919	Conservative	Will Gallagher	12,885	32.3	Laura Knightly
Turnout	Lib Dem	Paul Brighton	7,308	18.3	
65.52%	Others		3,926	9.8	

Arfon

PLAID CYMRU WIN (NEW SEAT)	PARTY	2010 CANDIDATE	2010 VOTES	2010 % VOTE	PPC FOR 2015
Majority	Plaid Cymru	Hywel Williams MP	9,383	36.0	Hywel Williams MP
1,455	Labour	Alun Pugh	7,928	30.4	Alan Pugh
Turnout	Conservative	Robin Millar	4,416	16.9	
63.30%	Others		4,351	16.7	

Majority 1455 (5.6%)

One of the most geographically stunning constituencies in the whole of the United Kingdom, this north-west Wales constituency takes in parts of the Snowdonia National Park, the picturesque town of Caernarfon and the coastal city of Bangor. The constituency contains one of the highest proportions of Welsh speakers in the country, which partly explains Plaid Cymru's traditional strength in the area. The constituency's two main towns are politically divided, with Caernarfon siding with Plaid Cymru while Labour is highly competitive in Bangor. The Conservative Party has historically performed weakly in this constituency. Represented since 2010 by Plaid's Hywel Williams, the Labour candidate will be former Welsh Assembly member Alun Pugh.

Blaenau Gwent

LABOUR GAIN FROM BG PEOPLE'S VOICE	PARTY	2010 CANDIDATE	2010 VOTES	2010 % VOTE	PPC FOR 2015
Majority	Labour	Nick Smith	16,974	52.4	Nick Smith MP
10,516	BG People's Voice	Dai Davies MP	6,458	19.9	
Turnout	Lib Dem	Matt Smith	3,285	10.1	
61.77%	Others		5,678	17.5	

Brecon & Radnorshire

LIB DEM HOLD	PARTY	2010 CANDIDATE	2010 VOTES	2010 % VOTE	PPC FOR 2015
Majority	Lib Dem	Roger Williams MP	17,929	46.2	Roger Williams MP
3,747	Conservative	Suzy Davies	14,182	36.5	Chris Davies
Turnout	Labour	Chris Lloyd	4,096	10.5	Matthew Dorrance
72.49%	Others		2,638	6.8	

Bridgend

LABOUR HOLD	PARTY	2010 CANDIDATE	2010 VOTES	2010 % VOTE	PPC FOR 2015
Majority	Labour	Madeleine Moon MP	13,931	36.3	Madeleine Moon MP
2,263	Conservative	Helen Baker	11,668	30.4	Meirion Jenkins
Turnout	Lib Dem	Wayne Morgan	8,658	22.6	
65.33%	Others		4,090	10.7	

Caerphilly

LABOUR HOLD	PARTY	2010 CANDIDATE	2010 VOTES	2010 % VOTE	PPC FOR 2015
Majority	Labour	Wayne David MP	17,377	44.9	Wayne David MP
10,755	Conservative	Maria Caulfield	6,622	17.1	
Turnout	Plaid Cymru	Lindsay Whittle	6,460	16.7	
62.28%	Others		8,233	21.3	

Cardiff Central

LIB DEM HOLD	PARTY	2010 CANDIDATE	2010 VOTES	2010 % VOTE	PPC FOR 2015
Majority	Lib Dem	Jenny Willott MP	14,976	41.4	Jenny Willott MP
4,576	Labour	Jenny Rathbone	10,400	28.8	Jo Stevens
Turnout	Conservative	Karen Robson	7,799	21.6	
59.10%	Others		2,976	8.2	

Majority 4576 (12.7%)

As the name of the constituency would suggest, Cardiff Central is based upon the urban centre of the city, taking in the University of Wales campus and Millennium Stadium. The seat is severely socially polarised, encompassing the wealthy, suburban Cyncoed area of the city as well as the tough Adamsdown neighbourhood. With a large number of local residents employed at the university and a vast number of students living in the constituency, the Liberal Democrats were able to make considerable political hay out of opposition to student tuition fees and the Iraq war in order to help incumbent MP Jenny Willott take the seat from Labour in 2005. Labour took this seat back from the Liberal Democrats at the 2011 Welsh Assembly elections and has gained a considerable number of councillors since. The Labour candidate will be Jo Stevens, a trade union solicitor.

Cardiff North

CONSERVATIVE GAIN FROM LABOUR	PARTY	2010 CANDIDATE	2010 VOTES	2010 % VOTE	PPC FOR 2015
Majority	Conservative	Jonathan Evans	17,860	37.5	Craig Williams
194	Labour	Julie Morgan MP	17,666	37.1	Mari Williams
Turnout	Lib Dem	John Dixon	8,724	18.3	
72.66%	Others		3,380	7.1	

Majority 194 (0.4%)

Captured by the narrowest of margins by former MEP and Welsh Office Minister Jonathan Evans at the 2010 general election, Cardiff North is the most marginal seat. Cardiff North is to the Welsh capital what Bromley is to London. Easily the most middle-class seat in the principality, 83 per cent of homes are owner-occupied and unemployment is low. The constituency stretches from Labour-inclined urban areas out to the Rhiwbina, Tongwynlais and Whitchurch wards which have long since ceased to be distinct from Cardiff's urban sprawl but retain a pleasant village feel. The Conservatives have lost ground here in recent years, with the former MP Julie Morgan taking the Welsh Assembly seat from the Conservatives in 2011 and Labour making solid gains on a local government level. Evans is retiring after only one term, with his replacement being Cardiff councillor Craig Williams. Labour will field Mari Williams, a former member of her party's national policy forum.

Cardiff South & Penarth

LABOUR HOLD	PARTY	2010 CANDIDATE	2010 VOTES	2010 % VOTE
Majority	Labour	Alun Michael MP	17,262	38.9
4,709	Conservative	Simon Hoare	12,553	28.3
Turnout	Lib Dem	Dominic Hannigan	9,875	22.3
60.20%	Others		4,679	10.5

Cardiff South & Penarth (2012 by-election)

LABOUR HOLD	PARTY	2012 CANDIDATE	2012 VOTES	2012 % VOTE	PPC FOR 2015
Majority	Labour	Stephen Doughty	9,193	47.3	Stephen Doughty MP
5,334	Conservative	Craig Williams	3,859	19.9	
Turnout	Lib Dem	Bablin Molik	2,103	10.8	
26.37%	Others		4,281	22.0	

Cardiff West

LABOUR HOLD	PARTY	2010 CANDIDATE	2010 VOTES	2010 % VOTE	PPC FOR 2015
Majority	Labour	Kevin Brennan MP	16,893	41.2	Kevin Brennan MP
4,750	Conservative	Angela Jones-Evans	12,143	29.6	
Turnout	Lib Dem	Rachel Hitchinson	7,186	17.5	
65.23%	Others		4,735	11.6	

Carmarthen East & Dinefwr

PLAID CYMRU HOLD	PARTY	2010 CANDIDATE	2010 VOTES	2010 % VOTE	PPC FOR 2015
Majority	Plaid Cymru	Jonathan Edwards	13,546	35.6	Jonathan Edwards MP
3,481	Labour	Christine Gwyther	10,065	26.5	Calum Higgins
Turnout	Conservative	Andrew Morgan	8,506	22.4	Matthew Paul
72.56%	Others		5,894	15.5	

Majority 3481 (9.2%)

The Carmarthen East & Dinefwr constituency is a constituency of two halves. The Carmarthen portion of the seat leans strongly towards Labour while rural Dinefwr in the west of the constituency is largely Welsh-speaking and agricultural in nature. Held since 2010 by Plaid Cymru's Jonathan Edwards, the Westminster seat was first gained from Labour in 2001 following their success locally in the inaugural Welsh Assembly elections in 1999. While Plaid Cymru remain the dominant political force locally, Labour have made some inroads on a local government recently and substantially cut Plaid's majority at the 2010 Welsh Assembly poll. The Labour candidate will be Calum Higgins, a member of Carmarthenshire county council.

Carmarthen West & South Pembrokeshire

CONSERVATIVE GAIN FROM LABOUR	PARTY	2010 CANDIDATE	2010 VOTES	2010 % VOTE	PPC FOR 2015
Majority	Conservative	Simon Hart	16,649	41.1	Simon Hart MP
3,423	Labour	Nicholas Ainger MP	13,226	32.7	Delyth Evans
Turnout	Lib Dem	John Gossage	4,890	12.1	
69.71%	Others		5,742	14.2	

Majority 3423 (8.5%)

A wonderfully varied constituency, Carmarthen West & South Pembrokeshire stretches from the west Wales' stunning coast and the port of Pembroke Dock inland to the Welsh-speaking town of Carmarthen. More than a quarter of local residents are of pensionable age with many retirees choosing to make their homes on the Pembrokeshire coast. The Tories and Plaid Cymru are fairly evenly divided in rural areas while Labour's support is chiefly drawn from Pembroke Dock, a working-class town scarred by the decline of the British maritime industry. The seat was comfortably gained by former Countryside Alliance boss and Conservative candidate Simon Hart at the 2010 election. He will be opposed by Delyth Evans, a former Member of the Welsh Assembly for Mid and West Wales.

Ceredigion

LIB DEM HOLD	PARTY	2010 CANDIDATE	2010 VOTES	2010 % VOTE	PPC FOR 2015
Majority	Lib Dem	Mark Williams MP	19,139	50.0	Mark Williams MP
8,324	Plaid Cymru	Penri James	10,815	28.3	
Turnout	Conservative	Luke Evetts	4,421	11.6	
63.89%	Others		3,883	10.1	Huw Thomas (Labour)

Clwyd South

LABOUR HOLD	PARTY	2010 CANDIDATE	2010 VOTES	2010 % VOTE	PPC FOR 2015
Majority	Labour	Susan Jones	13,311	38.4	Susan Elan Jones MP
2,834	Conservative	John Bell	10,477	30.2	
Turnout	Lib Dem	Bruce Roberts	5,965	17.2	
64.53%	Others		4,928	14.2	

Clwyd West

CONSERVATIVE HOLD	PARTY	2010 CANDIDATE	2010 VOTES	2010 % VOTE	PPC FOR 2015
Majority	Conservative	David Jones MP	15,833	41.5	David Jones MP
6,419	Labour	Donna Hutton	9,414	24.7	Gareth Thomas
Turnout	Plaid Cymru	Llyr Huws Gruffydd	5,864	15.4	
65.81%	Others		7,000	18.4	

Majority 6419 (16.8%)

Located on the north Wales coast, Clwyd West has been held since 2005 by former Welsh Secretary David Jones. The majority of the seat's residents live along the coastline in the strip that runs from the Penrhyn Bay and Rhos-on-Sea in the west to Kinmel Bay in the east, before stretching inland to take in a large number of picturesque villages — many of which are Welsh-speaking. Given its stunning coastline and close proximity to the Snowdonia National Park, tourism joins agriculture as the largest employer in the constituency. The Conservatives performed well here at the 2011 Welsh Assembly elections, substantially increasing their majority. The Labour candidate will be Gareth Thomas, the area's MP from 1997 to 2005.

Cynon Valley

LABOUR HOLD	PARTY	2010 CANDIDATE	2010 VOTES	2010 % VOTE	PPC FOR 2015
Majority	Labour	Ann Clwyd MP	15,681	52.5	n/s
9,617	Plaid Cymru	Dafydd Trystan Davies	6,064	20.3	
Turnout	Lib Dem	Lee Thacker	4,120	13.8	
58.99%	Others		4,011	13.4	

Delyn

LABOUR HOLD	PARTY	2010 CANDIDATE	2010 VOTES	2010 % VOTE	PPC FOR 2015
Majority	Labour	David Hanson MP	15,083	40.8	David Hanson MP
2,272	Conservative	Antoinette Sandbach	12,811	34.6	Mark Isherwood
Turnout	Lib Dem	Bill Brereton	5,747	15.5	
69.17%	Others		3,343	9.0	

Dwyfor Meirionnydd

LABOUR HOLD	PARTY	2010 CANDIDATE	2010 VOTES	2010 % VOTE	PPC FOR 2015
Majority	Labour	David Hanson MP	15,083	40.8	David Hanson MP
2,272	Conservative	Antoinette Sandbach	12,811	34.6	Mark Isherwood
Turnout	Lib Dem	Bill Brereton	5,747	15.5	
69.17%	Others		3,343	9.0	

Gower

LABOUR HOLD	PARTY	2010 CANDIDATE	2010 VOTES	2010 % VOTE	PPC FOR 2015
Majority	Labour	Martin Caton MP	16,016	38.4	Liz Evans
2,683	Conservative	Byron Davies	13,333	32.0	Byron Davies
Turnout	Lib Dem	Mike Day	7,947	19.1	
67.54%	Others		4,375	10.5	

Islwyn

LABOUR HOLD	PARTY	2010 CANDIDATE	2010 VOTES	2010 % VOTE	PPC FOR 2015
Majority	Labour	Chris Evans	17,069	49.2	Chris Evans MP
12,215	Conservative	Daniel Thomas	4,854	14.0	
Turnout	Plaid Cymru	Steffan Lewis	4,518	13.0	
63.22%	Others		8,243	23.8	

Llanelli

LABOUR HOLD	PARTY	2010 CANDIDATE	2010 VOTES	2010 % VOTE	PPC FOR 2015
Majority	Labour	Nia Griffith MP	15,916	42.5	Nia Griffith MP
4,701	Plaid Cymru	Myfanwy Davies	11,215	29.9	
Turnout	Conservative	Christopher Salmon	5,381	14.4	Selaine Saxby
67.33%	Others		4,949	13.2	

Merthyr Tydfil & Rhymney

LABOUR HOLD	PARTY	2010 CANDIDATE	2010 VOTES	2010 % VOTE	PPC FOR 2015
Majority	Labour	Dai Havard MP	14,007	43.7	Dai Havard MP
4,056	Lib Dem	Amy Kitcher	9,951	31.0	
Turnout	Conservative	Maria Hill	2,412	7.5	
58.62%	Others		5,706	17.8	

Monmouth

CONSERVATIVE HOLD	PARTY	2010 CANDIDATE	2010 VOTES	2010 % VOTE	PPC FOR 2015
Majority	Conservative	David Davies MP	22,466	48.3	David Davies MP
10,425	Labour	Hamish Sandison	12,041	25.9	Ruth Jones
Turnout	Lib Dem	Martin Blakebrough	9,026	19.4	
72.08%	Others		2,986	6.4	

Montgomeryshire

CONSERVATIVE GAIN FROM LIB DEM	PARTY	2010 CANDIDATE	2010 VOTES	2010 % VOTE	PPC FOR 2015
Majority	Conservative	Glyn Davies	13,976	41.3	Glyn Davies MP
1,184	Lib Dem	Lembit Opik MP	12,792	37.8	Jane Dodds
Turnout	Plaid Cymru	Heledd Fychan	2,802	8.3	
69.39%	Others		4,243	12.5	

Majority 1184 (4%)

Montgomeryshire made national headlines in 2010 when Conservative farmer and former Welsh Assembly member Glyn Davies defeated colourful Liberal Democrat incumbent Lembit Opik. This is a sparsely populated, rural constituency located based in the northern part of the Powys local authority area that, until the Conservative Party's victory in 2010, had been almost uninterruptedly in the hands of the Liberals for more than a century. The constituency includes the small towns of Welshpool and Newton which are home to a diverse range of light industries. Unsurprisingly, the largest local employer is the agricultural sector. Following Davies's victory, the Conservatives have moved to shore up their position locally; also taking the contiguous Welsh Assembly seat at the 2011 elections.

Neath

LABOUR HOLD	PARTY	2010 CANDIDATE	2010 VOTES	2010 % VOTE	PPC FOR 2015
Majority	Labour	Peter Hain MP	17,172	46.3	n/s
9,775	Plaid Cymru	Alun Llwelyn	7,397	19.9	
Turnout	Lib Dem	Frank Little	5,535	14.9	
64.79%	Others		7,018	18.9	

Newport East

LABOUR HOLD	PARTY	2010 CANDIDATE	2010 VOTES	2010 % VOTE	PPC FOR 2015
Majority	Labour	Jessica Morden MP	12,744	37.0	Jessica Morden MP
1,650	Lib Dem	Ed Townsend	11,094	32.2	Paul Halliday
Turnout	Conservative	Dawn Parry	7,918	23.0	
63.28%	Others		2,692	7.8	

Majority 1650 (5%)

Comprised of the eastern part of the south-east Wales town of Newport and its surrounding rural areas, this seat is staunchly industrial territory. The constituency is perhaps best known as the base of the Llanwern steelworks, although local employment has shifted towards the light manufacturing and logistics sector in recent years. Historically a safe Labour seat, the Liberal Democrats finished 1,650 votes off victory here in 2010. The area's sitting MP, Labour's Jessica Morden, will be challenged by Liberal Democrat Paul Halliday.

Newport West

LABOUR HOLD	PARTY	2010 CANDIDATE	2010 VOTES	2010 % VOTE	PPC FOR 2015
Majority	Labour	Paul Flynn MP	16,389	41.3	Paul Flynn MP
3,544	Conservative	Matthew Williams	12,845	32.3	Nick Webb
Turnout	Lib Dem	Veronica German	6,587	16.6	Ed Townsend
63.95%	Others		3,899	9.8	

Ogmore

LABOUR HOLD	PARTY	2010 CANDIDATE	2010 VOTES	2010 % VOTE	PPC FOR 2015
Majority	Labour	Huw Irranca-Davies MP	18,644	53.8	Huw Irranca-Davies MP
13,246	Conservative	Emma Moore	5,398	15.6	
Turnout	Lib Dem	Jackie Radford	5,260	15.2	
62.40%	Others		5,348	15.4	

Pontypridd

LABOUR HOLD	PARTY	2010 CANDIDATE	2010 VOTES	2010 % VOTE	PPC FOR 2015
Majority	Labour	Owen Smith	14,220	38.8	Owen Smith MP
2,785	Lib Dem	Mike Powell	11,435	31.2	Mike Powell
Turnout	Conservative	Lee Gonzalez	5,932	16.2	
63.00%	Others		5,084	13.9	

Preseli Pembrokeshire

CONSERVATIVE HOLD	PARTY	2010 CANDIDATE	2010 VOTES	2010 % VOTE	PPC FOR 2015
Majority	Conservative	Stephen Crabb MP	16,944	42.8	Stephen Crabb MP
4,605	Labour	Mari Rees	12,339	31.2	Paul Miller
Turnout	Lib Dem	Nick Tregoning	5,759	14.5	
68.99%	Others		4,560	11.5	

Majority 4605 (11.6%)

The constituency of the Secretary of State for Wales Stephen Crabb, Preseli Pembrokeshire was won by the Conservatives by a 4,605 margin at the 2010 general election. The largest population centres in the constituency are the ports of Fishguard and Milford Haven and Haverfordwest, a commercial hub for the west of Wales. For most part, however, Preseli Pembrokeshire is a sparsely populated rural seat whose local economy is reliant upon tourists visiting the stunning Pembrokeshire Coast Natural Park. In addition to tourism, a large number of residents work in the oil and gas logistics sector. The northern portion of the constituency is predominantly Welsh-speaking while South Pembrokeshire is home to a large number of retirees from England who are strongly inclined towards the Conservatives.

Rhondda

LABOUR HOLD	PARTY	2010 CANDIDATE	2010 VOTES	2010 % VOTE	PPC FOR 2015
Majority	Labour	Chris Bryant MP	17,183	55.3	Chris Bryant MP
11,553	Plaid Cymru	Geraint Davies	5,630	18.1	
Turnout	Lib Dem	Paul Wasley	3,309	10.6	
60.27%	Others		4,950	15.9	

Swansea East

LABOUR HOLD	PARTY	2010 CANDIDATE	2010 VOTES	2010 % VOTE	PPC FOR 2015
Majority	Labour	Siân James MP	16,819	51.5	n/s
10,838	Lib Dem	Rob Speht	5,981	18.3	
Turnout	Conservative	Christian Holliday	4,823	14.8	
54.62%	Others		5,053	15.5	

Swansea West

LABOUR HOLD	PARTY	2010 CANDIDATE	2010 VOTES	2010 % VOTE	PPC FOR 2015
Majority	Labour	Geraint Davies	12,335	34.7	Geraint Davies MP
504	Lib Dem	Peter May	11,831	33.2	
Turnout	Conservative	Rene Kinzett	7,407	20.8	
58.03%	Others		4,020	11.3	

Majority 504 (1%)

Located in the western part of Wales's second city of Swansea and taking in the town's main commercial centres, Labour's Geraint Davies repelled a Liberal Democrat challenge by just 504 votes in 2010. The constituency is home to the University of Swansea, with many students making their homes here. As with many other student-dominated constituencies, the Liberal Democrats made considerable inroads at the 2005 and 2010 general elections on the back of anger at tuition fee increases and the war in Iraq. Aside from the student population, the seat is arguably best known as the headquarters of the DVLA. Despite the closeness of the 2010 general election, Liberal Democrat support fell markedly at the 2011 Welsh Assembly elections – a trend which has continued on a local government level.

Torfaen

LABOUR HOLD	PARTY	2010 CANDIDATE	2010 VOTES	2010 % VOTE	PPC FOR 2015
Majority	Labour	Paul Murphy MP	16,847	44.8	Paul Murphy MP
9,306	Conservative	Jonathan Burns	7,541	20.0	Graham Smith
Turnout	Lib Dem	David Morgan	6,264	16.6	
61.52%	Others		6,988	18.6	

Vale of Clwyd

LABOUR HOLD	PARTY	2010 CANDIDATE	2010 VOTES	2010 % VOTE	PPC FOR 2015
Majority	Labour	Chris Ruane MP	15,017	42.3	Chris Ruane MP
2,509	Conservative	Matt Wright	12,508	35.2	James Davies
Turnout	Lib Dem	Paul Penlington	4,472	12.6	
63.70%	Others		3,537	10.0	

Vale of Glamorgan

CONSERVATIVE GAIN FROM LABOUR	PARTY	2010 CANDIDATE	2010 VOTES	2010 % VOTE	PPC FOR 2015
Majority	Conservative	Alun Cairns	20,341	41.8	Alun Cairns MP
4,307	Labour	Alana Davies	16,034	32.9	Chris Elmore
Turnout	Lib Dem	Eluned Parrott	7,403	15.2	
69.32%	Others		4,889	10.0	

Majority 4307 (8.9%)

Located at Wales's most southerly point, the Vale of Glamorgan constituency is a mixture of pleasant Cardiff commuter villages and the gritty dock town of Barry. Barry, with its cargo-handling docks and manufacturing industries, provides the basis of Labour's support while the Tories are stronger in rural hinterland to the south of Cardiff. Barry's once thriving tourist industry is now in terminal decline. Cardiff International Airport, whose growth is expected to provide a considerable number more local jobs in the coming years, is also located here. Gained from Labour by the Conservative Welsh Office Minister Alun Cairns at the 2010 general election, he will be challenged by Vale of Glamorgan councillor Chris Elmore.

Wrexham

LABOUR HOLD	PARTY	2010 CANDIDATE	2010 VOTES	2010 % VOTE	PPC FOR 2015
Majority	Labour	Ian Lucas MP	12,161	36.9	Ian Lucas MP
3,658	Lib Dem	Tom Rippeth	8,503	25.8	
Turnout	Conservative	Gareth Hughes	8,375	25.4	Andrew Atkinson
64.82%	Others		3,937	11.9	

Ynys Môn

LABOUR HOLD	PARTY	2010 CANDIDATE	2010 VOTES	2010 % VOTE	PPC FOR 2015
Majority	Labour	Albert Owen MP	11,490	33.4	Albert Owen MP
2,461	Plaid Cymru	Dylan Rees	9,029	26.2	
Turnout	Conservative	Anthony Ridge-Newman	7,744	22.5	Michelle Willis
68.78%	Others		6,181	17.9	

Scotland

Setting the scene in Scotland presents difficulties when going to press before the crucial independence referendum takes place. Should 'Yes' prevail, there will be massive consequences of all kinds, but one set of these will involve the impact on the United Kingdom general election set for May 2015. For example, what would happen to the fifty-nine Scottish constituencies – would there be interim contests here to provide representation until an independent Scotland were established, and would there be another general election if there were? How would the result affect the voting patterns? However, with 'No' ahead in every opinion poll taken to date, we can proceed on the basis that Scotland will probably, if not certainly, be remaining within the UK.

We should start with the Scottish National Party. In the 2011 elections for the Scottish Parliament, the SNP did well enough to gain an overall majority even using the largely proportional Additional Member System. They did not achieve a majority of votes (reaching 44 per cent in the regional element and 45 per cent in constituencies) but this was enough to take no fewer than fifty-three of the seventy-three seats decided on the first-past-the-post part of the hybrid electoral system. They gained thirty-two, mainly from Labour. This might be thought to suggest that the SNP may similarly take many in the next general election (whatever the referendum result).

However, the SNP has never made a breakthrough of anything like this extent in Westminster elections. Their best ever performance so far has been to secure eleven seats in the February 1974 election, and these were mainly gained from the Conservatives. Their highest percentage of the vote in general elections was 22.1 per cent in 1997, which only translated to six seats. They returned the same number of MPs – six – in 2010. In the European elections of May 2014, the SNP did come first, but with only a 29 per cent share – which was considerably less than opinion polls had suggested. There are few polls taken of Scottish voting intentions for Westminster, but the latest two in 2014 both suggested they might be 2 per cent ahead of Labour. However, even if this were to come to pass, it would not mean an avalanche of SNP gains in the House of Commons for this reason: their vote is too evenly spread, across urban and rural areas, and all regions within Scotland. On a uniform swing since 2010, it would need more than a 5 per cent shift for the SNP even to take their number one target from Labour, Ochil & South Perthshire. Then comes Falkirk, where nearly an 8 per cent swing is required for an SNP gain, and Dundee West (10 per cent). Glasgow East, which the SNP had taken in a by-election in 2008, was regained by Labour's Margaret Curran in 2010 with a massive swing of over 19 per cent.

It looks as if the SNP will not make many gains in the Commons despite their great successes at Holyrood. If they do, it may well be at the expense of the Liberal Democrats, for example in Gordon, where Malcolm Bruce is retiring after thirty-two years as MP. The SNP will not be too worried. Westminster is not a priority for them; after all, they do not even think they should be there.

For the Liberal Democrats, on the other hand, the Commons matters very much – not least because they now have the taste of government for the first time since the Second World War, and the more seats they have the stronger their bargaining position in another hung parliament. Yet they have been looking shockingly weak north of the border in recent years. After polling only 8 per cent in constituencies and 5 per cent in regions in the 2011 Holyrood elections, they actually finished sixth in May 2014 for the European Parliament, with 7.1 per cent, lagging behind the Greens and UKIP, whose appeal in pro-EU Scotland is rather minimal. This is compared with 19 per cent for Westminster in 2010 and 23 per cent in 2005. They currently have eleven MPs from Scottish constituencies, and were disappointed not to make gains from Labour in Edinburgh South and North & Leith last time. The Liberal Democrats will be concerned about how many seats they can hold. Besides Gordon, they may lose East Dunbartonshire and Edinburgh West to Labour, and Aberdeenshire West & Kincardine and Berwickshire, Roxburgh & Selkirk in the Borders to the Conservatives; Argyll & Bute could possibly fall to any of the other three parties if the Lib Dem vote collapses as dramatically as it has in other elections.

In some ways, given the importance of the referendum, the general election in Scotland will feel like something of a sideshow. It certainly is for David Cameron and the Conservatives, and has been for some time. It is hard to believe that in 1955 they actually won more than half the constituencies north of the border; the Tories have increasingly been perceived as an 'English party', certainly since the Thatcher government and its early introduction of the poll tax in Scotland. The Conservatives won no seats at all in 1997, 2001 and 2005, and just one in 2010 – Dumfriesshire, Clydesdale & Tweeddale. They cannot make a significant number of gains next time. In fact, although the party is campaigning for a 'No' vote, perhaps from a purely electoral perspective the best thing that could happen from a Conservative point of view would be Scottish independence – followed by the removal of nearly sixty now reliably non-Tory MPs from the Commons.

Aberdeen North

LABOUR HOLD	PARTY	2010 CANDIDATE	2010 VOTES	2010 % VOTE	PPC FOR 2015
Majority	Labour	Frank Doran MP	16,746	44.4	Richard Baker
8,361	SNP	Joanne Strathdee	8,385	22.2	
Turnout	Lib Dem	Kristian Chapman	7,001	18.6	
58.17%	Others		5,569	14.8	

Aberdeen South

LABOUR HOLD	PARTY	2010 CANDIDATE	2010 VOTES	2010 % VOTE	PPC FOR 2015
Majority	Labour	Anne Begg MP	**15,722**	36.5	Anne Begg MP
3,506	Lib Dem	John Sleigh	12,216	28.4	
Turnout	Conservative	Amanda Harvey	8,914	20.7	Ross Thompson
67.21%	Others		6,182	14.4	

West Aberdeenshire & Kincardine

LIB DEM HOLD	PARTY	2010 CANDIDATE	2010 VOTES	2010 % VOTE	PPC FOR 2015
Majority	Lib Dem	Robert Smith MP	17,362	38.4	Robert Smith MP
3,684	Conservative	Alan Johnstone	13,678	30.3	Alexander Burnett
Turnout	SNP	Dennis Robertson	7,086	15.7	
68.36%	Others		7,069	15.6	

Airdrie & Shotts

LABOUR HOLD	PARTY	2010 CANDIDATE	2010 VOTES	2010 % VOTE	PPC FOR 2015
Majority	Labour	Pamela Nash	20,849	58.2	Pamela Nash MP
12,408	SNP	Sophia Coyle	8,441	23.5	
Turnout	Conservative	Ruth Whitfield	3,133	8.7	
57.48%	Others		3,426	9.6	

Angus

SNP HOLD	PARTY	2010 CANDIDATE	2010 VOTES	2010 % VOTE	PPC FOR 2015
Majority	SNP	Michael Weir MP	15,020	39.6	Michael Weir MP
3,282	Conservative	Alberto Costa	11,738	30.9	Derek Wann
Turnout	Labour	Kevin Hutchens	6,535	17.2	
60.39%	Others		4,667	12.3	

Argyll & Bute

LIB DEM HOLD	PARTY	2010 CANDIDATE	2010 VOTES	2010 % VOTE	PPC FOR 2015
Majority	Lib Dem	Alan Reid MP	14,292	31.6	Alan Reid MP
3,431	Conservative	Gary Mulvaney	10,861	24.0	Alastair Redman
Turnout	Labour	David Graham	10,274	22.7	Mary Galbraith
67.31%	Others		9,780	21.6	

Majority 3431 (8.9%)

One of the largest and most remote constituencies in the United Kingdom, the Argyll & Bute constituency takes in almost a third of western Scotland's coastline and scores of sparsely populated islands. There are no particularly large towns in this constituency with even the Glasgow commuter towns of Oban and Helensburgh being home to less than 15,000 residents. While still firmly a minority language, around one in ten residents of this constituency is fluent in the Gaelic language. On a Westminster level, this seat has been held by the Liberal Democrats since 1987, most recently in the form of Alan Reid who has been the MP here since 2001. The seat has the distinction of being the only four-way marginal in the UK, with only 13 per cent dividing the Lib Dems from the fourth-placed Scottish National Party in 2010. The SNP won the broadly contiguous Scottish Parliament seat with 50 per cent of the vote in 2011 – way ahead of the fourth-placed Lib Dems who only received a 12 per cent vote share. At the 2014 European elections, the SNP led the voting with 28 per cent to the Conservatives' and Lib Dems' 19 per cent apiece.

Ayr, Carrick & Cumnock

LABOUR HOLD	PARTY	2010 CANDIDATE	2010 VOTES	2010 % VOTE	PPC FOR 2015
Majority	Labour	Sandra Osborne MP	21,632	47.1	Sandra Osborne MP
9,911	Conservative	William Grant	11,721	25.5	
Turnout	SNP	Chic Brodie	8,276	18.0	
62.59%	Others		4,264	9.3	

Central Ayrshire

LABOUR HOLD	PARTY	2010 CANDIDATE	2010 VOTES	2010 % VOTE	PPC FOR 2015
Majority	Labour	Brian Donohoe MP	20,950	47.7	Brian Donohoe MP
12,007	Conservative	Maurice Golden	8,943	20.4	
Turnout	SNP	John Mullen	8,364	19.0	
64.25%	Others		5,658	12.9	

North Ayrshire & Arran

LABOUR HOLD	PARTY	2010 CANDIDATE	2010 VOTES	2010 % VOTE	PPC FOR 2015
Majority	Labour	Katy Clark MP	21,860	47.4	Katy Clark MP
9,895	SNP	Patricia Gibson	11,965	25.9	
Turnout	Conservative	Philip Lardner	7,212	15.6	
62.13%	Others		5,079	11.0	

Banff & Buchan

SNP HOLD	PARTY	2010 CANDIDATE	2010 VOTES	2010 % VOTE	PPC FOR 2015
Majority	SNP	Eilidh Whiteford	15,868	41.3	Eilidh Whiteford MP
4,027	Conservative	Jimmy Buchan	11,841	30.8	
Turnout	Labour	Glen Reynolds	5,382	14.0	
59.82%	Others		5,375	14.0	

Berwickshire, Roxburgh & Selkirk

LIB DEM HOLD	PARTY	2010 CANDIDATE	2010 VOTES	2010 % VOTE	PPC FOR 2015
Majority	Lib Dem	Michael Moore MP	22,230	45.4	Michael Moore MP
5,675	Conservative	John Lamont	16,555	33.8	John Lamont
Turnout	Labour	n/a	5,003	10.2	
66.39%	Others		5,226	10.7	

Caithness, Sutherland & Easter Ross

LIB DEM HOLD	PARTY	2010 CANDIDATE	2010 VOTES	2010 % VOTE	PPC FOR 2015
Majority	Lib Dem	John Thurso MP	11,907	41.4	John Thurso MP
4,826	Labour	John Mackay	7,081	24.6	John Erskine
Turnout	SNP	Jean Urquhart	5,516	19.2	
60.87%	Others		4,264	14.8	

Majority 4826 (16.8%)

The northernmost constituency in Scotland, Caithness, Sutherland & Easter Ross is comprised of vast tracts of sparsely populated rural territory and spans many hundreds of square miles. The main town in the constituency is Caithness in which the main employer is the fisheries and agricultural sector. As a result of its picture-postcard landscape and vast coastline, tourism plays a big role in the local economy with hundreds of thousands of tourists a year flocking to the northerly tip of John O'Groats. Held for more than thirty years by the Liberal Democrats, the present MP is John Thurso – the only former hereditary peer to have sat in the House of Lords and made the transition to the Commons. The local government picture is complicated by the large number of independents, yet there have been clear gains by both the Scottish National Party and Labour parties in recent years.

Coatbridge, Chryston & Bellshill

LIB DEM HOLD	PARTY	2010 CANDIDATE	2010 VOTES	2010 % VOTE	PPC FOR 2015
Majority	Lib Dem	John Thurso MP	11,907	41.4	John Thurso MP
4,826	Labour	John Mackay	7,081	24.6	John Erskine
Turnout	SNP	Jean Urquhart	5,516	19.2	
60.87%	Others		4,264	14.8	

Cumbernauld, Kilsyth & Kirkintilloch East

LABOUR HOLD	PARTY	2010 CANDIDATE	2010 VOTES	2010 % VOTE	PPC FOR 2015
Majority	Labour	Gregg McClymont	23,549	57.2	Gregg McClymont MP
13,755	SNP	Julie Hepburn	9,794	23.8	
Turnout	Lib Dem	Rod Ackland	3,924	9.5	
64.26%	Others		3,883	9.4	

Dumfries & Galloway

LABOUR HOLD	PARTY	2010 CANDIDATE	2010 VOTES	2010 % VOTE	PPC FOR 2015
Majority	Labour	Russell Brown MP	23,950	45.9	Russell Brown MP
7,449	Conservative	Peter Duncan	16,501	31.6	
Turnout	SNP	Andrew Wood	6,419	12.3	
69.95%	Others		5,303	10.2	

Dumfriesshire, Clydesdale & Tweeddale

CONSERVATIVE HOLD	PARTY	2010 CANDIDATE	2010 VOTES	2010 % VOTE	PPC FOR 2015
Majority	Conservative	David Mundell MP	17,457	38.0	Fin Carson
4,194	Labour	Claudia Beamish	13,263	28.9	Archie Dryburgh
Turnout	Lib Dem	Catriona Bhatia	9,080	19.8	
68.88%	Others		6,092	13.3	

Majority 4194 (9.1%)

Dumfriesshire, Clydesdale & Tweeddale holds the distinction of being the only Conservative-held seat in Scotland. A large, rural constituency with few major settlements, the seat runs from the English border in the south northwards to the Solway Firth. The seat's best known urban centres include Lockerbie, Gretna Green, Sanquhar and Annan, none of which have more than a few thousand residents. Unlike the majority of Scotland, this area remained resistant to the Scottish National Party surge at the 2011 Scottish Parliament elections with Labour retaining the Dumfries seat and the Conservatives holding Galloway and Upper Nithsdale – both of which take in parts of this Westminster constituency. The sitting MP since 2005 is David Mundell, a Minister of State at the Scottish Office. He will be challenged by Labour's Archie Dryburgh, a Dumfries & Galloway councillor.

East Dunbartonshire

LIB DEM HOLD	PARTY	2010 CANDIDATE	2010 VOTES	2010 % VOTE	PPC FOR 2015
Majority	Lib Dem	Jo Swinson MP	18,551	38.7	Jo Swinson MP
2,184	Labour	Mary Galbraith	16,367	34.1	Armanjit Jhund
Turnout	Conservative	Mark Nolan	7,431	15.5	
75.16%	Others		5,599	11.7	

Majority 2184 (4.6%)

Situated just north of Glasgow, East Dunbartonshire is a wealthy and middle-class constituency that is home to many commuters. A previous version of the seat was won by the Conservatives in 1983, yet the party's toxicity north of the border has seen this seat transform into a Labour/Liberal Democrat marginal. In keeping with most suburban constituencies, owner-occupation rates are well above the UK average and the proportion of residents having completed higher education is amongst the highest in Scotland. The Liberal Democrats have performed weakly in this constituency, trailing in fourth place in the area's contiguous Scottish Parliament seats in the 2011 and 2014 European elections. Since 2005, the constituency has been represented by Liberal Democrat Business, Innovation and Skills Minister Jo Swinson. She will be challenged by Labour's Amanjit Jhund.

West Dunbartonshire

LABOUR HOLD	PARTY	2010 CANDIDATE	2010 VOTES	2010 % VOTE	PPC FOR 2015
Majority	Labour	Gemma Doyle	25,905	61.3	Gemma Doyle MP
17,408	SNP	Graeme McCormick	8,497	20.1	
Turnout	Lib Dem	Helen Watt	3,434	8.1	
63.96%	Others		4,430	10.5	

Dundee East

SNP HOLD	PARTY	2010 CANDIDATE	2010 VOTES	2010 % VOTE	PPC FOR 2015
Majority	SNP	Stewart Hosie MP	15,350	37.8	Stewart Hosie MP
1,821	Labour	Katrina Murray	13,529	33.3	Lesley Brennan
Turnout	Conservative	Chris Bustin	6,177	15.2	
61.96%	Others		5,512	13.6	

Majority 1821 (4.5%)

A coastal constituency, Dundee East is home to the docks that service north-east Scotland's booming oil sector as well as a healthy mix of other manufacturing and engineering industries. The constituency stretches from the centre of Dundee itself, up the coast to the famous golf resort of Carnoustie. A long-term Scottish National Party target, the party succeeded in winning the Westminster parliamentary constituency in 2005 and holds significant majorities in the area's Scottish Parliament constituencies. The SNP continue to perform well on a local government level, yet this area remains politically competitive and cannot be considered safe for any one party. Stewart Hosie, the Scottish National Party's finance spokesman and MP here since 2005, will face Labour candidate Lesley Brennan, a Dundee city councillor.

Dundee West

LABOUR HOLD	PARTY	2010 CANDIDATE	2010 VOTES	2010 % VOTE	PPC FOR 2015
Majority	Labour	Jim McGovern MP	17,994	48.5	Jim McGovern MP
7,278	SNP	Jim Barrie	10,716	28.9	
Turnout	Lib Dem	John Barrett	4,233	11.4	
58.92%	Others		4,183	11.3	

Dunfermline & West Fife

LABOUR RE-GAIN FROM SNP	PARTY	2010 CANDIDATE	2010 VOTES	2010 % VOTE	PPC FOR 2015
Majority	Labour	Thomas Docherty	22,639	46.3	Thomas Docherty MP
5,470	Lib Dem	Willie Rennie MP	17,169	35.1	
Turnout	SNP	Joe McCall	5,201	10.6	
66.51%	Others		3,938	8.0	

East Kilbride, Strathaven & Lesmahagow

LABOUR HOLD	PARTY	2010 CANDIDATE	2010 VOTES	2010 % VOTE	PPC FOR 2015
Majority	Labour	Michael McCann	26,241	51.5	Michael McCann MP
14,503	SNP	John McKenna	11,738	23.0	
Turnout	Conservative	Graham Simpson	6,613	13.0	Graham Simpson
66.57%	Others		6,354	12.5	

East Lothian

LABOUR HOLD	PARTY	2010 CANDIDATE	2010 VOTES	2010 % VOTE	PPC FOR 2015
Majority	Labour	Fiona O'Donnell	21,919	44.6	Fiona McDonnell MP
12,258	Conservative	Michael Vietch	9,661	19.7	
Turnout	Lib Dem	Stuart Ritchie	8,288	16.9	
67.02%	Others		9,293	18.9	

Edinburgh East

LABOUR HOLD	PARTY	2010 CANDIDATE	2010 VOTES	2010 % VOTE	PPC FOR 2015
Majority	Labour	Sheila Gilmore	17,314	43.4	Sheila Gilmore MP
9,181	SNP	George Kerevan	8,133	20.4	
Turnout	Lib Dem	Beverley Hope	7,751	19.4	
65.41%	Others		6,667	16.7	

Edinburgh North & Leith

LABOUR HOLD	PARTY	2010 CANDIDATE	2010 VOTES	2010 % VOTE	PPC FOR 2015
Majority	Labour	Mark Lazarowicz MP	17,740	37.5	Mark Lazarowicz MP
1,724	Lib Dem	Kevin Lang	16,016	33.8	
Turnout	Conservative	Iain McGill	7,079	14.9	
68.43%	Others		6,521	13.8	

Majority 1724 (4%)

Comprised of the northern portion of Edinburgh and the historic port of Leith, this constituency has traditionally favoured the Labour Party. As in many city constituencies, there is a diverse social mix of poorly maintained social housing properties, elegant detached homes and trendy 'loft house' conversions which strongly hint at the seat's industrial and maritime past. The Liberal Democrats were only 1,724 votes away from winning the constituency at the 2010 general election, yet saw their vote slashed by two-thirds from 27 per cent to 9 per cent in the broadly contiguous Scottish Parliament constituency one year later amidst a surge for the Scottish National Party. Any further advance for the Liberal Democrats is unlikely.

Edinburgh South

LABOUR HOLD	PARTY	2010 CANDIDATE	2010 VOTES	2010 % VOTE	PPC FOR 2015
Majority	Labour	Alistair Darling MP	19,473	42.8	Alistair Darling MP
8,447	Conservative	Jason Rust	11,026	24.3	Gordon Lindhurst
Turnout	Lib Dem	Tim McKay	8,194	18.0	
68.51%	Others		6,769	14.9	

Majority 316 (1%)

A closely fought marginal constituency, Labour MP Ian Murray won Edinburgh South by a margin of only 316 over the Liberal Democrats in 2010. This is one of the most middle-class and educated constituencies in Scotland, taking in the opulent Morningside and housing many of the University of Edinburgh's staff and students. Despite being the dominant force in local government in the area for many years, Liberal Democrat fortunes have weakened markedly in recent years with the loss of several council seats and the Edinburgh South Scottish Parliament constituency to the Scottish National Party.

Edinburgh South West

LABOUR HOLD	PARTY	2010 CANDIDATE	2010 VOTES	2010 % VOTE	PPC FOR 2015
Majority	Labour	Alistair Darling MP	19,473	42.8	Alistair Darling MP
8,447	Conservative	Jason Rust	11,026	24.3	Gordon Lindhurst
Turnout	Lib Dem	Tim McKay	8,194	18.0	
68.51%	Others		6,769	14.9	

Edinburgh West

LIB DEM HOLD	PARTY	2010 CANDIDATE	2010 VOTES	2010 % VOTE	PPC FOR 2015
Majority	Lib Dem	Mike Crockart	16,684	35.9	Mike Crockart MP
3,803	Labour	Cameron Day	12,881	27.7	Cameron Day
Turnout	Conservative	Stewart Geddes	10,767	23.2	
71.28%	Others		6,115	13.2	

Majority 3803 (8.2%)

Comprised of the western portion of Scotland's capital city of Edinburgh, this constituency is one of the most affluent and middle-class seats north of the border. Since taking the seat in 1997, the Liberal Democrats have dominated political life in the seat; at one point holding nearly every council seat in the area along with the Westminster and Scottish Parliament seats. The coalition has, however, taken its toll on the Lib Dem vote locally with the party losing the broadly contiguous Scottish Parliament seat to the Scottish National Party in 2011 and losing ground in the local election a year later. A long-term Liberal Democrat/Conservative marginal, the seat has been represented by Mike Crockart since the 2010 general election. He would fall to Labour's Cammy Day on a 4.2 per cent swing.

Falkirk

LABOUR HOLD	PARTY	2010 CANDIDATE	2010 VOTES	2010 % VOTE	PPC FOR 2015
Majority	Labour	Eric Joyce MP	23,207	45.7	Karen Whitefield
7,843	SNP	John McNally	15,364	30.3	
Turnout	Conservative	Katie Mackie	5,698	11.2	
62.02%	Others		6,508	12.8	

North East Fife

LIB DEM HOLD	PARTY	2010 CANDIDATE	2010 VOTES	2010 % VOTE	PPC FOR 2015
Majority	Lib Dem	Menzies Campbell MP	17,763	44.3	Tim Brett
9,048	Conservative	Miles Briggs	8,715	21.8	Huw Bell
Turnout	Labour	Mark Hood	6,869	17.1	
63.83%	Others		6,717	16.8	

Glasgow Central

LABOUR HOLD	PARTY	2010 CANDIDATE	2010 VOTES	2010 % VOTE	PPC FOR 2015
Majority	Labour	Anas Sarwar	15,908	52.0	Anas Sarwar MP
10,551	SNP	Osama Saeed	5,357	17.5	
Turnout	Lib Dem	Chris Young	5,010	16.4	
50.88%	Others		4,305	14.1	

Glasgow East

LABOUR RE-GAIN FROM SNP	PARTY	2010 CANDIDATE	2010 VOTES	2010 % VOTE	PPC FOR 2015
Majority	Labour	Margaret Curran	19,797	61.6	Margaret Curran MP
11,840	SNP	John Mason MP	7,957	24.7	
Turnout	Lib Dem	n/a	1,617	5.0	
51.99%	Others		2,793	8.7	

Glasgow North

LABOUR HOLD	PARTY	2010 CANDIDATE	2010 VOTES	2010 % VOTE	PPC FOR 2015
Majority	Labour	Ann McKechin MP	13,181	44.5	Ann McKechin MP
3,898	Lib Dem	Katy Gordon	9,283	31.3	
Turnout	SNP	Patrick Grady	3,530	11.9	
57.51%	Others		3,619	12.2	

Glasgow North East

LABOUR HOLD	PARTY	2010 CANDIDATE	2010 VOTES	2010 % VOTE	PPC FOR 2015
Majority	Labour	Willie Bain MP	20,100	68.3	Willie Bain MP
15,942	SNP	Billy McAllister	4,158	14.1	
Turnout	Lib Dem	Eileen Baxendale	2,262	7.7	
49.13%	Others		2,889	9.8	

Glasgow North West

LABOUR HOLD	PARTY	2010 CANDIDATE	2010 VOTES	2010 % VOTE	PPC FOR 2015
Majority	Labour	John Robertson MP	19,233	54.1	John Robertson MP
13,611	Lib Dem	Natalie McKee	5,622	15.8	
Turnout	SNP	Margaret Park	5,430	15.3	
58.33%	Others		5,297	14.9	

Glasgow South

LABOUR HOLD	PARTY	2010 CANDIDATE	2010 VOTES	2010 % VOTE	PPC FOR 2015
Majority	Labour	Tom Harris MP	20,736	51.7	Tom Harris MP
12,658	SNP	Malcolm Fleming	8,078	20.1	
Turnout	Lib Dem	Shabnum Mustapha	4,739	11.8	
61.62%	Others		6,541	16.3	

Glasgow South West

LABOUR HOLD	PARTY	2010 CANDIDATE	2010 VOTES	2010 % VOTE	PPC FOR 2015
Majority	Labour	Ian Davidson MP	19,863	62.5	Ian Davidson MP
14,671	SNP	Chris Stephens	5,192	16.3	
Turnout	Lib Dem	Isabel Nelson	2,870	9.0	
54.61%	Others		3,856	12.1	

Glenrothes

LABOUR HOLD	PARTY	2010 CANDIDATE	2010 VOTES	2010 % VOTE	PPC FOR 2015
Majority	Labour	Lindsay Roy MP	25,247	62.3	Melanie Ward
16,448	SNP	David Alexander	8,799	21.7	
Turnout	Lib Dem	Harry Wills	3,108	7.7	
59.77%	Others		3,347	8.3	

Gordon

LIB DEM HOLD	PARTY	2010 CANDIDATE	2010 VOTES	2010 % VOTE	PPC FOR 2015
Majority	Lib Dem	Malcolm Bruce MP	17,575	36.0	Christine Jardine
6,748	SNP	Richard Thomson	10,827	22.2	
Turnout	Labour	Barney Crockett	9,811	20.1	
66.43%	Others		10,562	21.7	

Majority 6748 (15.9%)

A sparsely populated rural constituency located in north-east Scotland, Gordon has been represented by Liberal Democrat Malcolm Bruce since 1983. The seat is seen as an affluent commuter territory for those working in nearby Aberdeen. Aside from a vibrant local agriculture sector, the main employer in the constituency is the oil and gas industry which has a significant base in the town of Ellon. With Bruce opting for retirement, his replacement as Liberal Democrat candidate will be Christine Jardine. The Scottish National Party have made considerable inroads in this constituency in recent years, holding each of the area's Scottish Parliament constituencies by significant margins. Opposition to the Liberal Democrats is, however, bitterly divided with the party having won the seat in 2010 with 36 per cent of the vote with the Conservatives, Labour and the SNP on 19 per cent, 20 per cent an 22 per cent respectively.

Inverclyde

LABOUR HOLD	PARTY	2010 CANDIDATE	2010 VOTES	2010 % VOTE
Majority	Labour	David Cairns MP	20,993	56.0
14,416	SNP	Innes Nelson	6,577	17.5
Turnout	Lib Dem	Simon Hutton	5,007	13.3
63.36%	Others		4,935	13.2

Inverclyde (2011 by-election)

LABOUR HOLD	PARTY	2011 CANDIDATE	2011 VOTES	2011 % VOTE	PPC FOR 2015
Majority	Labour	Iain McKenzie	15,118	53.8	Iain McKenzie MP
5,838	SNP	Anne McLaughlin	9,280	33.0	
Turnout	Conservative	David Wilson	2,784	9.9	
47.45%	Others		915	3.3	

Inverness, Nairn, Badenoch & Strathspey

LIB DEM HOLD	PARTY	2010 CANDIDATE	2010 VOTES	2010 % VOTE	PPC FOR 2015
Majority	Lib Dem	Danny Alexander MP	19,172	40.7	Danny Alexander MP
8,765	Labour	Mike Robb	10,407	22.1	Mike Robb
Turnout	SNP	John Finnie	8,803	18.7	
64.92%	Others		8,704	18.5	

Kilmarnock & Loudoun

LABOUR HOLD	PARTY	2010 CANDIDATE	2010 VOTES	2010 % VOTE	PPC FOR 2015
Majority	Labour	Cathy Jamieson	24,460	52.5	Cathy Jamieson MP
12,378	SNP	George Leslie	12,082	26.0	
Turnout	Conservative	Janette McAlpine	6,592	14.2	
62.80%	Others		3,419	7.3	

Kirkcaldy & Cowdenbeath

LABOUR HOLD	PARTY	2010 CANDIDATE	2010 VOTES	2010 % VOTE	PPC FOR 2015
Majority	Labour	Gordon Brown MP	29,559	64.5	Gordon Brown MP
23,009	SNP	Douglas Chapman	6,550	14.3	
Turnout	Lib Dem	John Mainland	4,269	9.3	
62.29%	Others		5,424	11.8	David Dempsey (Conservative)

Lanark & Hamilton East

LABOUR HOLD	PARTY	2010 CANDIDATE	2010 VOTES	2010 % VOTE	PPC FOR 2015
Majority	Labour	Jimmy Hood MP	23,258	50.0	Jimmy Hood MP
13,478	SNP	Clare Adamson	9,780	21.0	
Turnout	Conservative	Colin McGavigan	6,981	15.0	
62.26%	Others		6,535	14.0	

Linlithgow & East Falkirk

LABOUR HOLD	PARTY	2010 CANDIDATE	2010 VOTES	2010 % VOTE	PPC FOR 2015
Majority	Labour	Michael Connarty MP	25,634	49.8	Michael Connarty MP
12,553	SNP	Tam Smith	13,081	25.4	
Turnout	Lib Dem	Stephen Glenn	6,589	12.8	
63.59%	Others		6,146	11.9	

Livingston

LABOUR HOLD	PARTY	2010 CANDIDATE	2010 VOTES	2010 % VOTE	PPC FOR 2015
Majority	Labour	Graeme Morrice	23,215	48.5	Graeme Morrice MP
10,791	SNP	Lis Bardell	12,424	25.9	
Turnout	Lib Dem	Charles Dundas	5,316	11.1	
63.10%	Others		6,952	14.5	

Midlothian

LABOUR HOLD	PARTY	2010 CANDIDATE	2010 VOTES	2010 % VOTE	PPC FOR 2015
Majority	Labour	David Hamilton MP	18,449	47.0	David Hamilton MP
10,349	SNP	Colin Beattie	8,100	20.6	
Turnout	Lib Dem	Ross Laird	6,711	17.1	
63.93%	Others		5,982	15.2	

Moray

SNP HOLD	PARTY	2010 CANDIDATE	2010 VOTES	2010 % VOTE	PPC FOR 2015
Majority	SNP	Angus Robertson MP	16,273	39.7	Angus Robertson MP
5,590	Conservative	Douglas Ross	10,683	26.1	
Turnout	Labour	Keiron Green	7,007	17.1	Sean Morton
62.20%	Others		7,041	17.2	

Motherwell & Wishaw

LABOUR HOLD	PARTY	2010 CANDIDATE	2010 VOTES	2010 % VOTE	PPC FOR 2015
Majority	Labour	Frank Roy MP	23,910	61.1	Frank Roy MP
16,806	SNP	Marion Fellows	7,104	18.2	
Turnout	Lib Dem	Stuart Douglas	3,840	9.8	
58.46%	Others		4,269	10.9	

Na h-Eileanan an Iar (Western Isles)

SNP HOLD	PARTY	2010 CANDIDATE	2010 VOTES	2010 % VOTE	PPC FOR 2015
Majority	SNP	Angus MacNeil MP	6,723	45.7	Angus MacNeil MP
1,885	Labour	Donald John Macsween	4,838	32.9	
Turnout	Independent	Murdo Murray	1,412	9.6	
67.57%	Others		1,744	11.9	

Majority 1885 (12.8%)

More popularly known as the outer Hebrides, Na h-Eileanan an Iar is the Gaelic name for the 'Western Isles', a set of isolated island communities located off the coast of north-west Scotland. The largest town – and only major settlement – in the constituency is Stornoway which provides a vital sea link to the mainland. Aside from a small local agricultural and fisheries sector, many local jobs are derived from the vibrant tourism sector that sees hundreds of thousands of people a year visit the islands of Uist, Barra and Benbecula. Na h-Eileanan an Iar enjoys somewhat of a protected status amongst parliamentary constituencies given its isolated nature and predominantly Gaelic speaking population – factors which allow it to continue to have its own representatives, despite being only a third of the size of a usual UK constituency. This is one of the few constituencies in which the Conservative Party lost its deposit in 2010. Represented by the Scottish National Party's Angus MacNeil since 2005, the area can be judged to be fairly safe for the SNP who took 65 per cent of the vote in the 2011 Scottish Parliament elections.

Ochil & South Perthshire

LABOUR HOLD	PARTY	2010 CANDIDATE	2010 VOTES	2010 % VOTE	PPC FOR 2015
Majority	Labour	Gordon Banks MP	19,131	37.9	Gordon Banks MP
5,187	SNP	Annabelle Ewing	13,944	27.6	
Turnout	Conservative	Gerald Michaluk	10,342	20.5	
67.19%	Others		7,052	14.0	

Orkney & Shetland

LIB DEM HOLD	PARTY	2010 CANDIDATE	2010 VOTES	2010 % VOTE	PPC FOR 2015
Majority	Lib Dem	Alistair Carmichael MP	11,989	62.0	Alistair Carmichael MP
9,928	Labour	Mark Cooper	2,061	10.7	
Turnout	SNP	John Mowat	2,042	10.6	
58.47%	Others		3,254	16.8	

Paisley & Renfrewshire North

LABOUR HOLD	PARTY	2010 CANDIDATE	2010 VOTES	2010 % VOTE	PPC FOR 2015
Majority	Labour	James Sheridan MP	23,613	54.0	Jim Sheridan MP
15,280	SNP	Mags MacLaren	8,333	19.1	
Turnout	Conservative	Alistair Campbell	6,381	14.6	
68.61%	Others		5,380	12.3	

Paisley & Renfrewshire South

LABOUR HOLD	PARTY	2010 CANDIDATE	2010 VOTES	2010 % VOTE	PPC FOR 2015
Majority	Labour	Douglas Alexander MP	23,842	59.6	Douglas Alexander MP
16,614	SNP	Andrew Doig	7,228	18.1	
Turnout	Conservative	Gordon McCaskill	3,979	9.9	
65.36%	Others		4,949	12.4	

Perth & North Perthshire

SNP HOLD	PARTY	2010 CANDIDATE	2010 VOTES	2010 % VOTE	PPC FOR 2015
Majority	SNP	Peter Wishart MP	19,118	39.6	Peter Wishart MP
4,379	Conservative	Peter Lyburn	14,739	30.5	
Turnout	Labour	Jamie Glackin	7,923	16.4	
66.91%	Others		6,488	13.4	

East Renfrewshire

LABOUR HOLD	PARTY	2010 CANDIDATE	2010 VOTES	2010 % VOTE	PPC FOR 2015
Majority	Labour	Jim Murphy MP	25,987	50.8	Jim Murphy MP
10,420	Conservative	Richard Cook	15,567	30.4	
Turnout	Lib Dem	Gordon McDonald	4,720	9.2	
77.26%	Others		4,907	9.6	

Ross, Skye & Lochaber

LIB DEM HOLD	PARTY	2010 CANDIDATE	2010 VOTES	2010 % VOTE	PPC FOR 2015
Majority	Lib Dem	Charles Kennedy MP	18,335	52.6	Charles Kennedy MP
13,070	Labour	John McKendrick	5,265	15.1	
Turnout	SNP	Alisdair Stephen	5,263	15.1	
67.21%	Others		5,975	17.2	

Rutherglen & Hamilton West

LABOUR HOLD	PARTY	2010 CANDIDATE	2010 VOTES	2010 % VOTE	PPC FOR 2015
Majority	Labour	Tom Greatrex	28,566	60.8	Tom Greatrex MP
21,002	SNP	Graeme Horne	7,564	16.1	
Turnout	Lib Dem	Ian Robertson	5,636	12.0	
61.49%	Others		5,215	11.1	

Stirling

LABOUR HOLD	PARTY	2010 CANDIDATE	2010 VOTES	2010 % VOTE	PPC FOR 2015
Majority	Labour	Anne McGuire MP	19,558	41.8	Johanna Boyd
8,354	Conservative	Bob Dalrymple	11,204	23.9	
Turnout	SNP	Alison Lindsay	8,091	17.3	
70.81%	Others		7,938	17.0	

Northern Ireland

General elections in Northern Ireland present a very different pattern of contestation from the rest of the United Kingdom. The main political cleavage is between those who wish to remain constitutionally with Britain (unionists) and those who identify with the rest of Ireland (nationalists and republicans). As a result, there is a set of parties that scarcely overlap with this elsewhere in our regional surveys, although the Conservatives have dipped their toes into Northern Irish politics recently, with conspicuous lack of success.

For several elections now, a significant feature in Northern Ireland has been the strengthening of the more 'extreme' parties on each side of the political and 'community identity' divide. In 2010 Sinn Fein, the party associated with the Provisional IRA, won five seats at Westminster, compared to just three for the nationalist SDLP. The Democratic Unionist Party (DUP), founded and for a long time led by Ian Paisley, cemented its position as the largest in the province by winning eight of the eighteen constituencies, while the Ulster Unionist Party, for so many decades up to and including 2001, completed their dramatic slide by winning none at all.

There was success for two other candidates. The immensely popular Lady Sylvia Hermon won a landslide victory as an independent in North Down, the most affluent of all seats in Northern Ireland (it includes Bangor and Holywood, home town of the world no. 1 golfer Rory McIlroy), achieving more than three times as many votes as the candidate of the grandly named Ulster Conservatives and Unionists – New Force (UCUNF), who proved less than forceful. In Belfast East,

Naomi Long of the liberal and non-sectarian Alliance Party pulled off the surprise of the whole general election by ousting the DUP's leader, Peter Robinson, who had been weakened by revelations earlier in 2010 concerning his wife Iris's financial arrangements and affair with a nineteen-year-old man.

If Lady Sylvia stands again in North Down she is a certain victor, but should she retire at any point the most likely winners are the DUP, who did not stand here in 2010 but won three of the six seats for the same constituency in the Northern Ireland Assembly elections of 2011, which (like all but Westminster elections) are conducted by the PR–STV system. Meanwhile in Belfast East it remains to be seen whether Naomi Long's win was a flash in the pan. Peter Robinson is still DUP leader and First Minister of Northern Ireland, and easily topped the 2011 assembly poll in this constituency. A DUP regain must be a strong possibility.

There is one more seat that has also recently challenged the complexity of party competition in Northern Ireland. In 2010 the closest result of any constituency in the United Kingdom was recorded in Fermanagh and South Tyrone, where Sinn Fein's Michelle Gildernew held on against an independent, Rodney Connor, by just four votes. Connor had the support of the DUP and UCUNF, neither of whom put forward a candidate. Fermanagh & South Tyrone is the most evenly divided of the eighteen Northern Irish divisions in a cultural and hence political sense, with 52 per cent of the population counted in the census identifying themselves as Roman Catholic. The outcome here next time will depend on the pattern of candidature. Anyone who can unite the Unionist vote, as it were, might just manage to win – as long as the SDLP stands as well as Sinn Fein, as they did in 2010. It is also very much a question of 'getting the maximum vote out'.

There are other seats where the political balance is close, though with the entrenched lines drawn in the province, large swings are unlikely. In starkly divided Belfast North, which includes still-troubled neighbourhoods such as the Ardoyne, 45 per cent of the population identify with the 'Catholic tradition', and Sinn Fein finished only 2,000 behind the DUP's Nigel Dodds in 2010, but without major population shifts, this is likely to remain the case for some time to come. Most of the Northern Ireland constituencies are now very safe for either the DUP or Sinn Fein due to residential segregation between the two communities (seen most visibly in the 'peace walls' that still divide Belfast, making it the present-day Berlin) creating clear majorities for one tradition. This was illustrated by the two by-elections that took place during the current parliament, caused by the retirements of the two long-standing SF leaders, Gerry Adams in Belfast West and Martin McGuinness in Mid Ulster. Both were able to hand on without much difficulty – there was virtually no swing (a very unusual feature) in Belfast West, where Sinn Fein achieved over 70 per cent in both 2010 and the 2011 by-election. In 2013 in Mid Ulster, the unionists did unite behind a single independent, Nigel Lutton. However, unlike in its next-door seat Fermanagh & South Tyrone, Sinn Fein won comfortably by nearly 5,000 votes. We can say now that in 2015 Sinn Fein is likely to hold their five seats, the SDLP their three, and the DUP their eight.

There is, though, one seat where the pattern of community majority determining the electoral outcome is broken. This is the atypical Belfast South, where the SDLP's Alasdair McDonnell won in 2010 despite only 41 per cent informing the national census that they were of the Catholic tradition, the tenth highest on that criterion of the eighteen constituencies. It is true that Sinn Fein did not put forward a candidate, while the unionist vote was split. However, Dr McDonnell, a family GP in Belfast for over thirty years, had first won the seat in 2005 when Sinn Fein *did* stand, and he may well be able to win again with something of a personal vote in 2015. This is so unusual in Northern Ireland that it needs further analysis. Belfast South contains a substantial academic and student vote as it includes the campus of Queen's University – 18.4 per cent of its population were full-time students in 2011, by far the highest in Northern Ireland. It also contains some of the most affluent and desirable residential areas in the city, for example along the Malone Road. As well as having the highest educational qualifications of any seat in the province, it has the highest concentration of ethnic minorities, and a notably young age structure.

It might be concluded that all of these characteristics account for Belfast South being the only seat that can effectively be said to have broken the sectarian divide that has dominated Northern Irish politics since, it seems, time immemorial. Even with its age distribution it would, however, be too optimistic to see that seat as a model of the way things might go in the province in the future. Belfast West, so rigidly set in its ways as that 2011 by-election proved, has even fewer pensioners, and considerably more children aged up to fifteen. Overall, Northern Ireland remains the most predictable of all regions in the UK, and that may be somewhat depressing even for those not thrilled by the 'ins and outs' of electoral politics and national governments.

Belfast East

ALLIANCE GAIN FROM DUP	PARTY	2010 CANDIDATE	2010 VOTES	2010 % VOTE	PPC FOR 2015
Majority	Alliance	Naomi Long	12,839	37.2	Naomi Long MP
1,533	DUP	Peter Robinson MP	11,306	32.8	
Turnout	UCU-NF	Trevor Ringland	7,305	21.2	
58.4%	Others		3,038	8.8	

Belfast North

DUP HOLD	PARTY	2010 CANDIDATE	2010 VOTES	2010 % VOTE	PPC FOR 2015
Majority	DUP	Nigel Dodds MP	14,812	40.0	Nigel Dodds MP
2,224	Sinn Féin	Gerry Kelly	12,588	34.0	
Turnout	SDLP	Alban Maginness	4,544	12.3	
56.5%	Others		5,049	13.7	

Belfast South

SDLP HOLD	PARTY	2010 CANDIDATE	2010 VOTES	2010 % VOTE	PPC FOR 2015
Majority	SDLP	Alasdair McDonnell MP	14,026	41.0	Alasdair McDonnell MP
5,926	DUP	Jimmy Spratt	8,100	23.7	
Turnout	UU/UCUNF	Paula Bradshaw	5,910	17.3	
57.4%	Others		6,150	18.0	

Belfast West

SINN FÉIN HOLD	PARTY	2010 CANDIDATE	2010 VOTES	2010 % VOTE
Majority	Sinn Féin	Gerry Adams MP	22,840	71.1
17,579	SDLP	Alex Attwood	5,261	16.4
Turnout	DUP	William Humphrey	2,436	7.6
54.0%	Others		1,596	5.0

Belfast West (2011 by-election)

SINN FÉIN HOLD	PARTY	2011 CANDIDATE	2011 VOTES	2011 % VOTE	PPC FOR 2015
Majority	Sinn Féin	Paul Maskey	16,211	70.6	Paul Maskey MP
13,123	SDLP	Alex Attwood	3,088	13.5	
Turnout	DUP	William Humphrey	1,751	7.6	
37.5%	Others		1,901	8.3	

East Antrim

DUP HOLD	PARTY	2010 CANDIDATE	2010 VOTES	2010 % VOTE	PPC FOR 2015
Majority	DUP	Sammy Wilson MP	13,993	45.9	Sammy Wilson MP
6,770	UU/UCUNF	Rodney McCune	7,223	23.7	
Turnout	Alliance	Gerry Lynch	3,377	11.1	
50.7%	Others		5,909	19.4	

East Londonderry

DUP HOLD	PARTY	2010 CANDIDATE	2010 VOTES	2010 % VOTE	PPC FOR 2015
Majority	DUP	Gregory Campbell MP	12,097	34.6	Gregory Campbell MP
5,355	Sinn Féin	Cathal ó hOisín	6,742	19.3	
Turnout	UU/UCUNF	Lesley Macaulay	6,218	17.8	
55.3%	Others		9,893	28.3	

Fermanagh & South Tyrone

SINN FÉIN HOLD	PARTY	2010 CANDIDATE	2010 VOTES	2010 % VOTE	PPC FOR 2015
Majority	Sinn Féin	Michelle Gildernew MP	21,304	45.5	Michelle Gildernew MP
4	Independent	Rodney Connor	21,300	45.5	
Turnout	SDLP	Fearghal McKinney	3,574	7.6	
68.9%	Others		625	1.3	

Foyle

SDLP	PARTY	2010 CANDIDATE	2010 VOTES	2010 % VOTE	PPC FOR 2015
Majority	SDLP	Mark Durkan MP	16,922	44.7	Mark Durkan MP
4,824	Sinn Féin	Martina Anderson	12,098	31.9	
Turnout	DUP	Maurice Devenney	4,489	11.8	
57.5%	Others		4,380	11.6	

Langan Valley

DUP HOLD	PARTY	2010 CANDIDATE	2010 VOTES	2010 % VOTE	PPC FOR 2015
Majority	DUP	Jeffrey Donaldson MP	18,199	49.8	Jeffrey Donaldson MP
10,486	UU/UCUNF	Daphne Trimble	7,713	21.1	
Turnout	Alliance	Trevor Lunn	4,174	11.4	
56.0%	Others		6,454	17.7	

Mid Ulster

SINN FÉIN HOLD	PARTY	2010 CANDIDATE	2010 VOTES	2010 % VOTE	
Majority	Sinn Féin	Martin McGuinness MP	21,239	52.0	
15,363	DUP	Ian McCrae	5,876	14.4	
Turnout	SDLP	Tony Quinn	5,826	14.3	
63.2%	Others		7,901	19.3	

Mid Ulster (2013 by-election)

SINN FÉIN HOLD	PARTY	2013 CANDIDATE	2013 VOTES	2013 % VOTE	PPC FOR 2015
Majority	Sinn Féin	Francie Molloy	17,462	46.9	Francie Molloy MP
4,681	Independent	Nigel Lutton	12,781	34.4	
Turnout	SDLP	Patsy McGlone	6,478	17.4	
55.7%	Others		487	1.3	

Newry & Armagh

SINN FÉIN HOLD	PARTY	2010 CANDIDATE	2010 VOTES	2010 % VOTE	PPC FOR 2015
Majority	Sinn Féin	Conor Murphy MP	18,857	42.0	Conor Murphy MP
8,331	SDLP	Dominic Bradley	10,526	23.4	
Turnout	UU/UCUNF	Danny Kennedy	8,558	19.1	
60.4%	Others		6,965	15.5	

North Antrim

DUP HOLD	PARTY	2010 CANDIDATE	2010 VOTES	2010 % VOTE	PPC FOR 2015
Majority	DUP	Ian Paisley Jr	19,672	46.4	Ian Paisley Jr MP
12,558	TUV	Jim Allister	7,114	16.8	
Turnout	Sinn Féin	Daithí McKay	5,265	12.4	
57.8%	Others		10,346	24.4	

North Down

INDEPENDENT GAIN FROM UU/UCUNF	PARTY	2010 CANDIDATE	2010 VOTES	2010 % VOTE	PPC FOR 2015
Majority	Independent	Sylvia Hermon MP	21,181	63.3	Sylvia Hermon MP
14,346	UU/UCUNF	Ian Parsely	6,817	20.4	
Turnout	Alliance	Stephen Farry	1,876	5.6	
55.2%	Others		3,607	10.8	

South Antrim

DUP HOLD	PARTY	2010 CANDIDATE	2010 VOTES	2010 % VOTE	PPC FOR 2015
Majority	DUP	William McCrea MP	11,536	33.9	William McCrea MP
1,183	UU/UCUNF	Reg Empey	10,353	30.4	
Turnout	SDLP	Mitchel McLaughlin	4,729	13.9	
53.9%	Others		7,391	21.7	

South Down

SDLP HOLD	PARTY	2010 CANDIDATE	2010 VOTES	2010 % VOTE	PPC FOR 2015
Majority	SDLP	Margaret Ritchie	20,648	48.5	Margaret Ritchie MP
8,412	Sinn Féin	Catriona Ruane	12,236	28.7	
Turnout	DUP	Jim Wells	3,645	8.6	
60.2%	Others		6,060	14.2	

Strangford

DUP HOLD	PARTY	2010 CANDIDATE	2010 VOTES	2010 % VOTE	PPC FOR 2015
Majority	DUP	Jim Shannon	14,926	45.9	Jim Shannon MP
5,876	UU/UCUNF	Mike Nesbitt	9,050	27.8	
Turnout	Alliance	Deborah Girvan	2,828	8.7	
53.7%	Others		6,701	17.5	

Upper Bann

DUP HOLD	PARTY	2010 CANDIDATE	2010 VOTES	2010 % VOTE	PPC FOR 2015
Majority	DUP	David Simpson MP	14,000	33.9	David Simpson MP
3,361	UU/UCUNF	Harry Hamilton	10,639	25.8	
Turnout	Sinn Féin	John O'Dowd	10,237	24.8	
55.4%	Others		6,507	15.8	

West Tyrone

SINN FÉIN HOLD	PARTY	2010 CANDIDATE	2010 VOTES	2010 % VOTE	PPC FOR 2015
Majority	Sinn Féin	Pat Doherty MP	18,050	48.4	Pat Doherty MP
10,685	DUP	Thomas Buchanan	7,365	19.8	
Turnout	UU/UCUNF	Ross Hussey	5,281	14.2	
61.0%	Others		6,579	17.6	

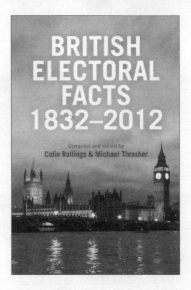